MW01711020

Sharing the Harvest

The Road to Self-Reliance

Report of the National Round Table on Aboriginal Economic Development and Resources

Royal Commission on Aboriginal Peoples

© Minister of Supply and Services Canada 1993

Available in Canada through
your local bookseller
or by mail from
Canada Communication Group – Publishing
Ottawa, Canada K1A 0S9

Canadian Cataloguing in Publication Data
National Round Table on Aboriginal Economic Development and Resources
(1993: Ottawa, Ont.)
Sharing the harvest, the road to self-reliance: report of the
National Round Table on Aboriginal Economic Development and Resources

Cat. no. Z1-1991/1-11-5E
ISBN 0-660-15367-X

1. Native peoples – Canada.
2. Native peoples – Canada – Economic conditions.
3. Native peoples – Canada – Social conditions.
I. Canada. Royal Commission on Aboriginal Peoples.
II. Title. III. Title: Report of the National Round Table on
Aboriginal Economic Development and Resources.

E78.C2N37 1993 971'.00497 C94-98007-4

Issued also in French under the title:
Un partage garant d'autonomie.

Canada	Groupe
Communication	Communication
Group	Canada
Publishing	Édition

Contents

Members of the Royal Commission on Aboriginal Peoples

René Dussault, j.c.a.
Co-Chair

Georges Erasmus
Co-Chair

Paul Chartrand
Commissioner

J. Peter Meekison
Commissioner

Viola Marie Robinson
Commissioner

Mary Sillett
Commissioner

Bertha Wilson
Commissioner

Preface

The Royal Commission on Aboriginal Peoples has undertaken to host a series of National Round Tables on selected themes. The Round Tables bring together academics, practitioners, political leaders and community leaders with knowledge and expertise on the selected themes in order to assist the Commission in the preparation of recommendations for the final report.

The National Round Tables all have a similar format. We invite certain experts or leading-edge thinkers to produce papers on a series of questions that we intend to ask participants to consider. (The questions participants were asked to address are set out in the next section.) In the course of panel presentations, round table discussions and plenary sessions, participants have the opportunity to put forward their views and recommendations as they relate to the questions. A rapporteur is asked to write a report based on the proceedings of the Round Table, setting out what was said, along with any recommendations or consensus that may have been reached by participants.

The published proceedings of the National Round Tables will help to inform the general public about the issues addressed there. It is anticipated that publication of the Round Table proceedings will prompt further consideration of the ideas and debate captured in the reports and encourage Canadians to come forward at the public hearings or to make written submissions with further thoughts and recommendations.

We are deeply indebted to the authors of the discussion papers on issues pertaining to economic development and resources that are part of this proceedings report. They undertook to prepare papers on short notice and in accordance with a tight schedule, so that the papers could be made available to participants in advance of the Round Table. We are grateful to the rapporteur, Dr. Peter Douglas Elias, Associate Professor and Co-ordinator of the BESS Program, Faculty of Management, University of Lethbridge, Alberta, whose report synthesizes the proceedings of the National Round Table on Aboriginal Economic Development and Resources. Finally, we appreciate the advice and contributions of all participants.

This report of the proceedings is intended to stimulate further dialogue and positive changes in policy. Your views and recommendations on this important issue are welcome. We invite you to write to us at the address set out elsewhere in this document and to appear before us when we hold public hearings in your area.

René Dussault, j.c.a.
Co-Chair

Georges Erasmus
Co-Chair

Round Table
Objectives and Issues

The objectives of the National Round Table on Aboriginal Economic Development and Resources were to stimulate discussion of the economic development challenges facing Aboriginal peoples and to elicit suggestions on how these challenges can best be met. The results of the Round Table were to contribute to the formulation of the Royal Commission`s final recommendations.

To bring a broad range of perspectives to the discussion, participants included those knowledgeable in economic development and resources issues and those with expertise in the creation and implementation of economic development initiatives benefitting Aboriginal communities — with a balance in terms of gender, age and Aboriginal identification.

Economic development issues are very broad-ranging. To help focus discussion, five issue groups or themes were selected, and participants were asked to consider particular questions relating to each of the themes. Discussion papers were commissioned on each of the themes, and a series of examples or models of individual and community enterprise in economic development were presented. The themes and questions addressed to participants were as follows:

I The Land and Resource Base

- What are the innovative ideas for making better use of the Aboriginal land and resource base for building the economies of the future?
- What is the potential for expanding the land and resource base of Aboriginal communities in both urban and rural areas?

- What is the particular situation of the Métis in gaining control over their own land and resource base?
- What are the emerging trends in the Canadian and world economies, and what are the implications of these trends for Aboriginal economies?

II Strengthening Traditional Economies and Perspectives

- What are the forces that threaten the continuation of traditional ways of making a living, and what steps need to be taken to support, rather than undermine, the traditional economy, including the role of both Aboriginal men and Aboriginal women?
- What unique perspectives on development emerge from Aboriginal belief systems and practices?
- To what extent can wildlife resources in the North support the numbers of Aboriginal people wishing to live a traditional lifestyle?

III Providing Services Within Communities

- What is the scope for the development of service establishments to be located within or adjacent to Aboriginal communities and owned and controlled by Aboriginal men and women?
- Why is it that only slow progress is being made with respect to increasing the proportion of Aboriginal men and women in the provision of business and professional services, even when it comes to the provision of such services to Aboriginal people?

IV Expanding Employment in the Canadian Economy

- To what extent are portions of the Aboriginal labour force particularly vulnerable to displacement as a result of existing patterns of employment, the development of new labour saving technologies, the impact of competing markets, and so forth?
- What has been the employment experience of the large number of Aboriginal graduates of post-secondary programs over the last two decades?
- How effective have provincial and federal programs directed to countering discrimination and promoting affirmative action and employment equity been for Aboriginal persons in particular?

V Building Institutions and Policies for Long-Term Economic Development

- What is the linkage between political and economic development?
- What kinds of political structures are required to support economic development over the longer term?
- What financial institutions are required to support the economic development of Aboriginal communities and meet the needs of Aboriginal men and women in urban and rural locations?
- How should the education and training system be restructured to contribute more effectively to the objectives of employment and economic development for Aboriginal men and women and different age groups?
- What changes are needed in economic development and related policies to support the growth of Aboriginal businesses?
- What is the current situation regarding tax exemptions and immunity from taxation for Aboriginal communities?

Chairman's Opening Address

*Ron Jamieson**

Elder Noel Knockwood, Co-Chairs Georges Erasmus and René Dussault, Commissioners, moderators, participants and observers, greetings and welcome to the National Round Table on Aboriginal Economic Development and Resources. It is a great pleasure for me to be here today and to have the honour and privilege of serving as Round Table Chairman. I am thankful for the opportunity to contribute in any way I can to the historic work of the Royal Commission, and I look forward to working with all of you. Together we can assist the Commission in completing its important work.

Over the next few days, we will be focusing our undivided attention on a number of important themes relating to the economic development and prosperity of Aboriginal communities and individuals. This national Round Table is the fourth of eight or nine major focus sessions of the Royal Commission. As part of the Commission's public consultation process, we have an opportunity to make real and substantive change in the economic conditions in Aboriginal communities, be they in the North, Métis settlements, villages, reserves, or communities in large urban centres. This is more than an opportunity; it is our obligation as Aboriginal people to preserve and protect future generations of our people.

When I agreed to accept the role of Chairman for the Round Table, and when I further discussed the arrangements in detail with the co-ordinators, I decided to adopt a strict business-like role in conducting this important work. The Royal

---

* Vice-President, Aboriginal Banking, Bank of Montreal, and Chairman of the National Round Table on Aboriginal Economic Development and Resources.

Commission seeks solutions to the problems of poverty, underdevelopment in Aboriginal communities, unemployment at rates often reaching 80% to 90%. The problems are known; what is needed now are solutions. It is not the time to blame and criticize past and present governments and the Canadian society at large. It is time to be imaginative in finding solutions that will give hope for a better future to our youth, that will give pride and peace of mind to our elders and will mobilize the incredible energy of our women and men who are both capable and willing to contribute to building a better society.

The challenge to make this Round Table a success is ours collectively. The organizers worked hard to make our participation as productive as possible, and Commissioners are expecting nothing less than quality. You have been selected because of your talent, so let's work hard, constructively and co-operatively to focus on building a better future for all of us.

I would like now to explain to you how we will work together for the next two and a half days.

We all received some 13 short, precise and excellent discussion papers as a background for our work. We also all received with the program a series of fundamental questions that will form the basis of our discussions. You will permit me to insist on the importance of focusing our dialogue on these specific questions. The Royal Commission has been on the road for more than a year and a half now, heard from more than 1,400 interveners, received hundreds of briefs and started an extensive research program. These fundamental questions have been prepared by the Royal Commission because they need to be answered. We will not agree on all the answers, and the Royal Commission does not expect that we will reach consensus on all these issues. What is really important is for each of us to debate, and explain with our experience, what our solutions are. Permit me to emphasize again that word, solutions.

You have been invited to participate at the Round Table, not just to listen. Two days and a half is very short to cover all the material that we have to cover, and the organizers wanted to make sure that you all will have the opportunity to express your solution. So the time allowed to review the background material has been kept to a minimum. For the discussions and the round tables, moderators will help us keep the focus on the fundamental questions and facilitate the discussions.

Simultaneous translation in French and English is available, so you can use the langauge of your choice. The Royal Commission will prepare a summary at the end of each day for the following morning, and, at the end of the conference, Professor Peter Douglas Elias will present his report. In the months following the Round Table, the Royal Commission will publish a report that will be used in its final report.

I wish you luck, and may the Great Spirit guide your thought process.

Report from the Round Table Rapporteur

*Peter Douglas Elias**

This paper is a summary of what was said at the National Round Table on Aboriginal Economic Development and Resources. When every idea and concept is taken into account, a very complex agenda for economic development emerges, but complexity can be reduced to an inventory of key recommendations. This paper will elaborate the basis of each recommendation briefly set out below.

- Eliminate disparities among Aboriginal populations.
- Eliminate Canadian government hostility to the idea of extending land and resource rights to all Aboriginal people.
- Settle outstanding Aboriginal claims to lands and resources in ways that admit opportunities to change the terms of settlement should a community's need for lands and resources change.
- Provide rigorous environmental protections in order to maintain lands and resources for very long-term, sustainable use.
- Recognize Aboriginal practices as economic activities.
- Recognize Aboriginal capacities and capabilities as inherently capable of change and adaptation.
- Create policies dedicated to advancing education.
- Create opportunities for Aboriginal education institutions to take a lead role in providing education services to Aboriginal people.

* Associate Professor, Co-ordinator, BESS Program, Faculty of Management, University of Lethbridge.

- Create opportunities for Aboriginal educational institutions to form partnerships and joint ventures with universities and colleges.
- Overhaul local school curricula to educate Aboriginal youth better in what is available and possible in their communities and culture; overhaul Canadian school curricula to emphasize Canada's obligations to Aboriginal people.
- Create an Aboriginal, development-oriented research facility.
- Institute self-government with the capacity to match as closely as possible local historical and cultural circumstances and contemporary economic needs.
- Eliminate government policy tying self-government to specific territories.
- Compel Aboriginal governments to respect the political and economic rights of all constituents.
- Position Aboriginal governments as political equals and peers of Canadian government, and not as subordinates.
- Clarify questions of jurisdiction, management and control to reduce uncertainty in the development situation.
- Create a neutral dispute settlement mechanism to deal with persisting uncertainty.
- Create a development-oriented environment.

I acted as Rapporteur for National Round Table on Aboriginal Economic Development and Resources in Ottawa, April 27-29, 1993. My task was to summarize the conclusions at the end of the proceedings, and then provide this written report. Earlier, I received copies of written papers solicited by the Royal Commission, and by the time I left Ottawa, I had accumulated an additional four inches of paper. I kept careful notes during the first day of the Round Table, but when I studied the record kept by Infolink, I paid closer attention to recording my understanding and appreciation of what was said. In writing my report, I was invited to draw on my personal experience and understanding, and I have done so.

The Royal Commission demanded policy, but there were relatively few, formal policy recommendations presented at the Round Table. What the speakers said can be generalized, and policy directions can be inferred. I do not think convoluted interpretation of meaning is necessary. Scholars have developed complex definitions of policy, but most speakers discussed problems encountered in life, and their recommendations centre on how to solve those problems. We mostly heard of successful initiatives. The *Oxford English Dictionary* defines policy as "any course of action adopted as advantageous or expedient". According to the dictionary, this definition is the "chief living use" of the word. Most speakers added their common-sense, solution-oriented approach to their recommendations for change. Many examples then illustrated how speakers overcame the main challenge of policy making – assessing advantage and expedience. Assessment of advantage and expedience is routine in larger regional, national and international affairs, and many speakers told how they balanced the cold blood of business and the hot blood of community. Indeed, so distinctive were some of the case studies, I might conclude that how people assess advantage and expedience distinguishes one culture from another.

Participation in the Round Table showed me that Aboriginal people continue to support a comprehensive or holistic approach to development. Single-dimension strategies for development have little place in such an approach, and since economic development and resources are only parts of the Royal Commission's mandate, the Royal Commission will likely be refining policy recommendations in the larger context of its concerns. Rather than set out an inventory of partial recommendations here, I will attempt to present broad generalizations to help Commissioners link issues in economic development and resources to their larger body of findings.

By the end of the Round Table numerous recommendations had been offered. Some were specific, dealing with particular problems faced by particular individuals or communities. Others were general, implying vast systemic change without identifying a particular course of action. Between were recommendations intended to address classes of issues concerning some, but not all individuals and communities. Together, these recommendations fall into four overarching groups, each containing a principle that might be useful in shaping policy. When stated as broad principles, these overarching recommendations do not appear to contain anything new. Although it is disturbing to realize these same recommendations have been made and ignored many times in the past 25 years of my experience, it is obvious the constituent parts of Aboriginal people's holistic concepts of development have changed over the decades. The 13 commissioned discussion papers and several other written briefs submitted at the time of the Round Table added depth and substance to the discussion of economic development and resources. However, I think the whole is best revealed in the diversity, nuance and subtlety of what people said at the Round Table. Therefore, and in preparing this report, I have relied mostly on Infolink's record of proceedings, supplemented by my notes and the commissioned discussion papers.*

---

* In the following discussion, I refer directly to Infolink's record of proceedings. This record is more accessible than my own written notes, and it should be easy for a reader to determine whether I have understood what was said by individuals. The endnotes in this report contain the references in the following style:

Name 27:6 - a reference to page 6 of Infolink's record for April 27, 1993.

Name 28:12 - a reference to page 12 of Infolink's record for April 28, 1993.

Name 29:2 - a reference to page 2 of Infolink's record for April 29, 1993.

Eliminate Disparities Among Aboriginal Populations

Several speakers discussed problems arising from imposed definitions of Indian, Inuit and Métis, status and non-status, treaty and non-treaty, urban, on-reserve and off-reserve peoples. These definitions reinforce the easy conclusion that Indians, Inuit and Métis cannot and, perhaps, should not attempt to solve common problems through common efforts. Indeed, much of the disagreement evident in the agendas of Indian, Inuit and Métis political organizations can be traced to the differences imposed by Canadian legislators and regulators. The imposed differences and their practical consequences are apparent in several important aspects of development in Aboriginal communities. Perhaps the most obvious and tangible difference between Aboriginal peoples is the extent to which each has access to a land base and natural resources. Several speakers stated that their economic future relied to a great extent on continuing access to lands and resources, either for traditional uses and practices or for industrial exploitation. Del Anaquod, President of Anaquod Traders International, decried fascination with the idea that Aboriginal people's new economy must follow national and international trends into high technology and information. According to Anaquod, land and resources have always been at the base of the Canadian economy, Aboriginal people have always been resource producers, and they will continue in their traditional roles.[1] Even if the new economy settles on some mix of productive sectors, Aboriginal peoples without clearly recognized land and resource rights will be disadvantaged economically and culturally. Clem Chartier of the Métis Society of Saskatchewan compared the situation of the Métis with that of the Inuvialuit of the western Arctic described by Roger Gruben; the Métis cannot match the economic and cultural initiatives of the Inuvialuit who have possession and control of lands and resources.[2]

At present, Canadian governments allow comprehensive claims only if claimants still occupy their traditional lands. In principle, settlement of a claim results in the return of at least some traditional lands to the possession and control of the claimant group. In the case of the Métis (and many non-status and urban people), their lands were expropriated long ago and their comprehensive claims are typically rejected out of hand by Canadian governments. Numerous speakers, including Indians, Métis, non-status, and urban Aboriginal speakers, recommended that Canadian governments eliminate hostility to the idea of extending land and resource rights to all Aboriginal people.[3] They urged governments to adopt a model of settlement that admits opportunities to change the terms of settlement, should a community's need for lands and resources change.[4] Several innovative mechanisms were proposed to accomplish this, including according resource-specific interests that could be used to generate royalty, economic rent, licence, and tax incomes for Aboriginal communities,[5] or by assuring access to resources that could be used as collateral for generating investment capital.[6]

Even if all Aboriginal people acquire rights to lands and resources, these rights will not yield benefits if Aboriginal people are constrained in their ability to address lands and resources as potential economic assets. Speakers urged governments to provide rigorous environmental protections in order to maintain lands and resources for very long-term, sustainable utilization.[7] Speakers were particularly concerned that traditional land and resource use activities be perpetuated as vital components of community life. At present, Canadian governments and institutions view hunting, fishing, trapping and gathering as cultural activities and, therefore, ineligible for explicit economic support and legal protection. To maintain ecologically and culturally appropriate use of the environment, traditional Aboriginal practices of land and resource use must be recognized as economic activities.[8]

Round Table participants heard several descriptions of how prevailing views interfere with Aboriginal interests and aspirations. Very generally, the distinction between cultural and economic activities makes Aboriginal interests vulnerable when decision makers are comparing the benefits of an economic activity and a cultural activity. In Alberta, for example, spurious distinctions helped lead courts to decide that the benefits of forestry are inherently more valuable than those of hunting, and that irrigation agriculture is inherently more valuable than broad-spectrum use of land and water. In particular, Dorothy Grant, President of Feastware, described how on the West Coast monument carvers are threatened by forestry operations that have an enforceable claim on the very large trees needed for canoe and pole carving.[9] The definitions giving resources for economic activities and denying them for cultural activities at once threatens the livelihood of individual carvers and the traditions of monumental carving that can only persist if appropriate working materials are available. Peter George of McMaster University stated that provincial governments do not make funds available to train youth in traditional economic activities, thus allowing these activities to languish in the face of technological change.[10] Some speakers felt Canadian governments failed to protect Aboriginal people's economic interests. For example, Ann Noonan, Dorothy Grant and William Lyall stated that Aboriginal intellectual products are not accorded economic value and are, therefore, exposed to expropriation by non-Aboriginal businesses.[11]

Speakers gave examples of how they are already integrating traditional activities and markets in spite of imposed definitions that virtually preclude recognition of traditional activities as economic activities capable of contributing to development. Rodney Parenteau of Parenteau's Saskatoon Berry Chocolates and Preserves described how his thoroughly business-like enterprise uses the products of traditional harvesting activities to manufacture goods for consumer markets.[12] His enterprise purchases blueberries from northern Cree who harvest wild berries throughout their traditional territories. The Cree have been harvesting and selling berries for several generations now, and the marketing of blueberries cannot be identified as a purely cultural activity. Michael Rice,

Manager of the Caisse populaire of Kahnawake, describes how Mohawk of good standing in the community may act as trustees for a borrower, thus interpreting traditional standards of reputation and trust in the competitive field of financial services. In contrast, Chief George Wapachee of the Nemiska Band described the James Bay Cree Income Security Program, an elaborate and institutionalized redefinition of traditional activities as economic activities. While the program seems to reach the goal of sustaining traditional activities as important components of the regional economy, this was achieved through the James Bay Crees' unique (at that time) constitutional position, set out in the James Bay and Northern Quebec Agreement. The Cree enjoy lands, capital and control not available to many other Aboriginal people and they were able to use these to entrench traditional activities in the regional economy. Terry Fenge of the Canadian Arctic Resources Committee urged similar programs throughout the North,[13] but massive parallel institutional change would be necessary to replicate the Cree achievement elsewhere.

Finally, Aboriginal people are seeking new ways of having their traditional activities contribute to local economies – tourism in particular was identified as an excellent medium for using traditional activities, skills and knowledge to take advantage of opportunities in the larger market economy.[14] These activities must be given support as economic activities. Yves-Jean Assiniwi of the Native Council of Canada summed the whole matter up by insisting that the heart of tradition is not found in technologies and markets, but in the values that guide activities. He pointed out that Inuit carving has only a 40-year history, but in essential respects carving is a thoroughly Inuit activity. Spurious distinctions consign many activities to economic doom, and "deny our right to evolution."[15]

The effects of imposed disparities extend far beyond land and resource matters. Jean Rivard of the Métis National Council asserted that Métis are systematically excluded from access to development funds available under the Canadian Aboriginal Economic Development Strategy.[16] Rivard and Muriel Stanley Venne of the National Film Board of Canada described similar problems in dealings with Pathways to Success.[17] Pat Baxter of EDCAW pointed out that Métis, off-reserve and non-status Aboriginal people do not have access to education funds enjoyed by Indians.[18] Gerald Morin, President of the Métis National Council, and Ruth Williams, Executive Director of the Interior Indian Friendship Society, agreed Métis and urban Indians are excluded from many government programs.[19] The history of inequity has greatly hampered development of some Aboriginal communities in the past, and continuing inequities promise to thwart the ambitions of some Aboriginal people for the future. Speakers suggested Aboriginal people should pool their financial resources to create a critical mass of investment capital.[20] However, formal definitions of Aboriginal people inhibit such an initiative and make it as difficult for Indian individuals and communities to co-operate with Inuit and Métis as it is for them to co-operate with private industry: interests and concerns are defined as immutably different and institutions treat them as different.[21] Other speakers suggested a variety of taxation strategies for promoting development, in addition to those provided in the *Indian Act*. Scott Smith, Vice-President of the Canadian Council on Aboriginal Business, for example, recommended tax-free zones on reserves,[22] Harold Derickson, President of the Intertribal Forestry Association of British Columbia, suggested an immigration tax,[23] and Robin Wortman, Executive Director of the Canadian Association of Native Development Officers, recommended a program of education and training tax credits for companies doing business in Aboriginal communities.[24] Without major parallel changes in the instruments defining 'varieties of Aboriginality', such schemes would likely benefit Indians more than Métis and perhaps more than Inuit. In any event, the recent Supreme Court of Canada decision in *Williams* seems to have dampened prospects for beneficial tax solutions to development problems. I think *Williams* is a prime example of the mean-spirited way in which Canada seizes on every opportunity to diminish opportunities for Aboriginal people.

Aboriginal people are a small minority in Canada and in national and international economies, and speakers recognized these imposed distinctions as major obstacles to the co-operative pursuit of common solutions to common problems. These obstacles and ways of conquering them were discussed by Delia Opekokew some time ago,[25] but there has been little interest in actual effecting the changes needed to eliminate disparities between Aboriginal people. A few days before the Round Table convened, Chiefs of Treaty Bands in the Prairie Provinces met in Calgary to discuss separating from the Assembly of First Nations and forming a Treaty Indian association. On April 19, the federal cabinet refused to put all Aboriginal people in Canada on an equal footing when dealing with the federal government.[26] This decision runs contrary to the Round Table participants who want the creation of a single agency to deal with Aboriginal affairs.[27] Clearly, achieving equity among Aboriginal people will be a major task, but Florence Gaucher, a Métis entrepreneur from Alberta, insisted that leaders must increase their efforts to achieve this objective.[28]

Expand Educational Opportunities

Round Table participants generally agreed that a primary obstacle to economic development was the low levels of education achieved by too many Aboriginal people. Recommendations receiving the greatest support urged the creation of policies dedicated to advancing education.[29] Not too long ago, such a recommendation would have implied opportunities to acquire a Canadian education in Canadian institutions. Today, Aboriginal people's ideas of education and the advantages of education have much wider scope, and advanced education is now seen to have a role in political and cultural development as well as economic development. Speakers said the entire field of education must be reshaped to meet Aboriginal people's demands for all kinds of educational services, from numeracy and literacy skills to management applications of traditional knowledge.

Several speakers insisted education must be controlled by Aboriginal people, either because non-Aboriginal education managers cannot be trusted to create programs most useful to Aboriginal people or, put more positively, because Aboriginal people are in the best position to determine their own educational needs.[30] For example, some speakers discussed innovative programs that would prepare individuals for self-sufficiency in their own lands and communities. Harold Derickson encouraged "capacity building" which involves strategic planning to set in place the skills needed in each community, given local needs and aspirations.[31] Derickson was speaking in particular of supplying the skills needed in the forestry industry, and others spoke from their own local perspectives. Thus, Albert Diamond, George Wapachee, Chesley Andersen and Oscar Kistabish addressed the need for special education to meet the needs of eco-tourism, a rapidly growing sector of their regional economies. Education is also needed to improve performance in the traditional subsistence economy, a living adjunct of eco-tourism.[32]

Control, however, need not be absolute. Many speakers recognized that non-Aboriginal post-secondary educational institutions possess much valuable knowledge, information and skills. These institutions also possess the vast infrastructure needed to deliver the sophisticated education necessary in today's economies. As well, these are the accredited institutions with the capacity to confer professional status demanded by Aboriginal and non-Aboriginal employers and institutions. In the longer term, some Aboriginal people intend to provide equivalent or superior educational services as a function of self-government in the broader context of cultural development. These institutions would offer an appropriate mix of programs based on Aboriginal and non-Aboriginal knowledge. Until then, speakers suggested how education services could be quickly and effectively expanded to help meet urgent educational needs. Participants spoke of an urgent need for training in management,[33] the sciences,[34] and technology.[35] Several tactics were proposed for forming partnerships and joint ventures to give Aboriginal educational institutions access to university or college infrastructure, technical expertise, and credentials.[36] In turn, non-Aboriginal institutions would gain preferential access to a rapidly expanding population of learners, and the opportunity for academic and scholarly participation in an increasingly important and dynamic aspect of Canada's unique culture. Academic institutions also gain access to Aboriginal educators working in local educational institutions. Several speakers stressed the importance of role models of success and ability as an important part of the whole process of development; formal educational settings present ideal opportunities for role models.[37]

My own institution, the University of Lethbridge, offers an example of how this can work. Two programs in our Faculty of Management specialize in management education for people working in fields where Aboriginal interests are dominant. The BESS Program (Business Enterprises and Self-Governing Systems) is an academic unit offering degrees and certificates in management, and CAMET

(Centre for Aboriginal Management) offers practice-oriented short courses tailored to the particular needs of a client group of students. In the past, BESS courses were offered on-campus and CAMET courses were offered in the students' home community or work site, and there was minimal overlap in the two programs. More recently, we have been approached by Aboriginal institutions to create programs offering university credit, practical approaches to problem solving, and courses that stress local history, culture and knowledge. The result combines university credit courses taught by qualified academics, problem-solving courses taught by experienced practitioners, and culture-specific courses taught by knowledgeable community members. The majority of courses offered in these programs carry university credits, including some courses taught by knowledgeable local people; individuals who decide to complete their academic studies can apply these credits toward a degree or certificate at the University of Lethbridge or any other university with which we have a credit transfer agreement. Thus far, successful arrangements have been made with Maskwachees College at Hobbema, the Peigan of southwestern Alberta, the Gwich'in Tribal Council in the Northwest Territories, the Métis Settlements in Alberta, and the Nicola Valley Institute of Technology in British Columbia. Similar partnerships are being discussed with Aboriginal educational institutions in other provinces and territories. Similar arrangements can also be made with industry. Jim Carbery of Syncrude's Public Affairs Department described the extensive educational opportunities offered by his company to Aboriginal people. Control of the arrangement lies with the local communities, since the communities must initiate any joint strategies and tactics. Community members identify their education needs, and Syncrude responds within the limits of their industrial interests and funding capacity. Syncrude is involved in internal and external cultural awareness efforts, business support and training, life skills training, apprenticeships for skilled workers, and bursaries and scholarships for college and university students.[38]

Several speakers addressed the need to overhaul local school curricula better to educate Aboriginal youth in what is available and possible in their communities and culture; they also recommended an overhaul of Canadian school curricula to emphasize Canada's obligations to Aboriginal people.[39] For some speakers, overhauled curricula would take advantage of traditional knowledge which has usually been ignored or slighted in Canadian schools.[40] To achieve this objective, speakers recommended the creation of a research facility to document and preserve traditional knowledge and make that knowledge available in a form that promotes development.[41] In tandem with research that returns traditional knowledge to contemporary communities, there must be a facility to monitor quality of life and the consequences of change at the community level.[42] There must be a facility to assemble and route vital business, financial, and administrative information directly to Aboriginal users.[43]

Then, there must be a facility to communicate information between Aboriginal communities and individuals so people do not continue working in a vacuum, continuously confronting problems that may have been solved elsewhere by other Aboriginal people.[44] Finally, there must be a facility to help communities and regions create long-term strategic plans for development.[45] Lester Lafond, for example, described how his band has been following a 35-year plan for human resource development and now, well into the life of the plan, they see the consequences in terms of the number of well-educated band members.[46] No speaker considered what such facilities would look like or what it would cost, but it is safe to assume that a lot of money would be involved; in effect, such a facility would be a major investment in the future of Aboriginal economies. Some participants suggested using unemployment, other transfer funds, and taxes collected from Aboriginal people to help pay the costs.[47] Clem Chartier approved of the Inuvialuit investing claims settlement funds in education as a way of assuring local people have the knowledge and skills of greatest advantage to the Inuvialuit,[49] but this possibility is not available to Aboriginal people excluded from the claims settlement process.

Entrench Self-Government

Not surprising, there was general agreement that self-government must be fully instituted for all Aboriginal constituencies, including Indians, Inuit, and Métis, status and non-status people, and people living on- and off-reserve. No doubt, the Royal Commission will hear much about self-government by the time its work is done, and participants at the Round Table avoided digressing into the larger issues surrounding this matter. Instead, participants focused their attention on relationships between self-government, economic development, and resources.

Speakers at the Round Table expressed the principle that Aboriginal people are better able to govern and manage local affairs for purposes of development than is any level of non-Aboriginal government. Self-government must go far beyond anything contained in the *Indian Act* or any other administrative instrument favoured by non-Aboriginal governments. In particular, self-government for urban, non-status, and Métis people will remain elusive so long as Canadian governments insist on tying self-government to specific territories.[49] In the end, Aboriginal people must have the capacity to create systems of government to match as closely as possible local historical and cultural circumstances and contemporary economic needs. Aboriginal governments must be created that respect the political and economic rights of all constituents;[50] Harold Derickson suggested instituting regulations to bring local political affairs into line with the *Canadian Charter of Rights and Freedoms*.[51] Mechanisms must be put in place to ensure that decision makers are fully accountable to their constituents for their actions.[52] Finally, self-government must not exceed the actual capacity of people to govern; Sheila Cloutier said skills of governance must be built to ensure that local institutions will remain independent of imposed regulations.[53]

Peter Apikan, President of Apikan Limited, insisted Canadian governments must respect their Aboriginal counterparts as political equals and peers, and not as subordinates.[54] Peer respect would allow Aboriginal people to make alliances with international partners, unencumbered by regulations that serve Canadian interests but harm Aboriginal interests.[55] For example, Chesley Andersen, Vice-President of the Inuit Tapirisat of Canada, said Inuit in the Canadian Arctic want to participate in the creation of a circumpolar economy that includes the Aboriginal peoples of Canada, Alaska, Scandinavia, and the former U.S.S.R.[56] Until Aboriginal people achieve the goal of international competency, Anderson urged clarification of questions of jurisdiction, management and control to reduce uncertainty in the development situation.[57] No doubt, uncertainty will linger until new political accommodations are reached, and to deal with persisting uncertainty Peter Apikan and Ann Noonan urged the creation of a neutral dispute settlement mechanism.[58]

Self-government would allow Aboriginal communities to arrange their own affairs to achieve development.[59] Several speakers addressed the need for Aboriginal financial institutions created and managed to meet the particular needs of enterprise in Aboriginal communities.[60] Even though the experiences of a few speakers suggested such financial institutions do not always provide appropriate services, especially with respect to meeting the needs of women,[61] they are likely to be more responsive than are standard financial institutions. Not all traditional Aboriginal activities are related to lands and resources, but like harvesting activities, these traditions need the recognition as important contributors to local and regional economies, and they need the support of financial services. Métis speakers, for example, pointed out that Métis are traditional entrepreneurs.[62] These activities are often very small-scale cottage industries and micro-enterprises and thus are overlooked in most business support programs. To reinforce these activities as true components of local economies, appropriate support mechanisms must be in place, including lending-circles and domestic support for women who are the primary operators of micro-enterprise.[63] Co-operatives and credit unions were specifically identified as structures that could give Aboriginal people direct access to financial services in a form most appropriate to community needs.[64] Indeed, Inuit communities are so committed to credit unions that on April 30, Arctic Co-operatives took the decision to by-pass established banks and create their own local credit unions.[65] Other participants spoke of co-management as a potential tool for managing entire regions and resources for the mutual benefit of all communities and individuals. Co-management is most potent where Aboriginal and non-Aboriginal interests have equal ability to shape management strategies, and from an Aboriginal manager's perspective this is best achieved under the sanction of self-government.[66] There was general and emphatic insistence that community politics and business be kept as separate as possible.[67] Rather, the role of government should be restricted to encouraging and promoting economic development.[69] This objective is not encouraged under the *Indian Act*, but should be designed as a primary feature of self-government.

Create a Development-Oriented Environment

All speakers made it clear that development of Aboriginal communities will require great change, and not just change of a technical nature. Land claims, self-government and education will not be enough unless they are supported in an environment that fosters beneficial change in the day-to-day operations of enterprise and the daily lives of individuals. Creating such an environment, I suspect, will be a great challenge facing the Royal Commission and Canadians in general; communities, government and industry must all shed their traditional hostilities.

Joint ventures, partnerships, and co-management were discussed as potentially important instruments for promoting development in Aboriginal communities, but for these to work, the economic environment must be clear of illusion, misconception and mistrust. Rather, an environment must be created that is infused with shared confidence, trust and wisdom.[69] Similarly, enterprise and programs cannot flourish if the enterprise and its Aboriginal operator are viewed as the enemy within, rather than as the ally of community interests.[70] All participants in development – Aboriginal government, Canadian government, industry, and community members – must increase and improve what they know about all other participants.[71] Participants suggested a prominent role for Aboriginal agencies to serve as advocates, intermediaries, mentors, and follow-up supporters to guide the construction of fruitful relations between Aboriginal and non-Aboriginal interests and the successful function of those relationships once they are established.[72]

Conclusion

Since World War II, three well-known schools of thought have dominated economic development efforts in remote regions, including most Aboriginal communities in Canada. Huskey and Morehouse have briefly described the "modernization", "dependency", and "interdependence" schools of development:

> "Development" as the overcoming of obstacles is associated with the "modernization" school in the development literature. Emerging in the 1950s, this school saw modernization of Third World countries as "a phased, irreversible, progressive, lengthy process that moves in the direction of the American model" (citing So 1990). Modernity in this model is set against and expected to overcome the obstacles particularly of indigenous traditions.
>
> A contrasting meaning of development came out of the "dependency" school, which arose in the 1960s in part as a reaction to the failures of modernization in theory and practice. This school "conceptualized the linkages between Western and

> Third World countries as a set of externally imposed, exploitative, dependent economic relationships incompatible with development" (*ibid*). In the view of dependency theorists, development controlled by Western capitalists leads inevitably to systematic "underdevelopment" of Third World regions.
>
> The modernization school emphasizes overcoming *internal* obstacles to development. These obstacles are associated with traditionalism and the conditions of remoteness....On the other hand, the dependency school and its relative "world-system" theory focus on *external* forces of capitalism. These forces are viewed as suppressing indigenous peoples, destroying their traditions, and expropriating their property.
>
> A third, less definite perspective arose in the 1970s and 1980s, and it has been labelled the "interdependence" school. This school compensates for the one-sidedness of the modernization and dependency schools by focusing on complex interdependencies of internal and external factors. It also emphasizes the use of countervailing political power to shape economic relationships. Core-capitalist domination of peripheral Third World economies is not taken for granted.
>
> The modernization and dependency schools have been converging, although neither of them has lost its distinctive focus. These schools increasingly share a concern for "historically specific concrete cases" and for "multi-institutional analysis" that focuses on the complex interplay of "family, religion, ethnic groups, classes, the interstate system, and the world economy" in Third World countries (*ibid*). In current research, the question of whether development is considered good or bad for indigenous peoples is left open, with the answer presumably depending more on the outcomes than on the theoretical assumptions of the analysis.[73]

Of the three models discussed here, it seems many Aboriginal people have recently embraced models of development that are variants of the interdependence school. According to Huskey and Lee, this is a general trend in remote regions. Aboriginal people throughout the world are viewing development as a process involving change in both internal and external factors, backed by enough political (and legal) power to secure external change and manage internal change. I think the papers by Newhouse and Brascoupé set out the basic principles of interdependence development and the case studies offered by Rock, Parenteau, Derickson, Lyall, Jones, Poitras-Young, and Rice are good examples of the principles in operation. These and other speakers supported principles in which development is viewed as the successful merging of

Aboriginal interests and ways of doing things and Canadian interests and ways of doing things.[74] Each showed how they balanced their need to succeed in larger regional, national and international affairs and at the same time meet their responsibilities and obligations as Aboriginal people and members of their community. These ideas, however, were not shared with equal enthusiasm.[75]

For those Aboriginal people who strive to achieve a way of life that is as consistent as possible with tradition, merging is a begrudged necessity.[76] In 1991, the Penticton Band advanced a model of development that virtually rejected any notion of merging.[77] More recently, the break-away Mokh-e-saun Blood in Alberta might take a similar position on development. Then, there are the numerous Aboriginal people who do not embrace capitalism, with or without a friendly face. For example, two or three generations of Métis in north central Saskatchewan have had reputations as political radicals and unless they have changed their ways recently, are likely to be reluctant participants in capitalism. Then, some speakers cast a very narrow scope for development.[78] George Bacon, President of Régime des bénéfices autochtones, urged adoption of long-term economic development policies based on individual entrepreneurship and business. He said business can be "despiritualizing", but that Aboriginal people would have to make necessary cultural adjustments. In stark contrast, some Métis spokespersons suggested development must begin with political development; Jane Gottfriedson wanted development to start with community and individual healing,[79] Florence Gaucher wanted development to focus on youth and children,[80] Mary Jamieson suggested business should be conducted in Inuktitut,[81] and Sheila Cloutier wanted an emphasis on languages and development of the traditional spirit.[82] These differences may be more apparent than real since it is quite possible to take a comprehensive approach to development that emphasizes one or another aspect of political, cultural and economic development. For example, in recent public comments, Chief Harley Frank of the Blood in southwestern Alberta virtually rejected economic development in favour of initiatives needed to stabilize his people's cultural environment. Once cultural stability is regained and social pathologies have been eliminated, Chief Frank would lead his community toward political stability, and only then would economic problems be attacked.

Finally, some Aboriginal constituencies were not well represented at the Round Table. Women were not, as was pointed out by Muriel Stanley-Venne. Ms. Venne, Mary Jamieson, Sharon McIvor, Winnie Giesbrecht and others attempted to present women's issues in economic development, but it seemed taxation got more attention. Issues of concern to people from truly remote regions were not well represented; their interests and capacities are not the same as those of urban and rural communities. Chief George Wapachee's description of the James Bay Cree Income Security Program was as close as the discussion got to the role of domestic and subsistence production. The most recent evidence clearly identifies domestic production as an essential part of the economies of northern communities, and several speakers insisted domestic production be viewed as a real economic activity and not as a social activity or worse, as a cultural relic. The implications of this view go far beyond anything I heard at the Round Table. For domestic producers, issues centre on land and environmental management policy, the role of commodity production, and legitimation of local knowledge, and only incidentally on questions of capital accumulation and return on investment. I assume the Royal Commission's northern component and women's component are giving these matters the attention they deserve.

In the end, most speakers expressed a conviction that development must be suited to local history, culture and circumstances, and that development strategies must be tailored for local needs, capacities and capabilities. Nevertheless, there is apparent potential for controversy and even conflict when it comes time to dedicate scarce resources to operationalize a particular development policy unless it is broad and flexible enough to accommodate the spectrum of Aboriginal people's aspirations. There is already public conflict in Aboriginal communities flowing from differing ideas of how to achieve development. For example, on May 13, the blockade stopping logging in northwestern Saskatchewan will celebrate its first anniversary of continuous occupation; the bands to which many of the protesters belong are co-venturers in the industrial forestry operations being blockaded. Considering what is needed to achieve comprehensive or holistic development, I think locating the resources to make a serious commitment to development will be a major challenge in an era of economic restraint.

References

1. Anaquod 29:10
2. Chartier 27:2
3. Swain 27:9, 11; Noonan 27:10; Williams 27:12; Diamond 27:12; Andersen 27:11; Morin 29:7.
4. Diamond 27:12
5. Noonan 27:8; Andersen 27:9; Swain 27:9; Lafond 27:10; Apikan 27:10; Fenge 27:21.
6. Anderson 27:10; Allen 27:10; Forester 27:10; Lafond 27:11.
7. Chartier 27:2; Andersen 27:8; Assiniwi 27:11.
8. Brascoupé 27:15, 16; George 27:19, 22; Fenge 27:21; Roberts 27:21; Ross 29:3; Morin 29:7; Rivard 29:8.
9. Grant 27:19.
10. George 27:20.
11. Noonan 27:23; Grant 27:23; Lyall 27:23.
12. Parenteau 27:2.

13. Fenge 27:21.
14. Diamond 27:9; Ares 27:21; Augustine 27:21; Kistabish 27:22.
15. Assiniwi 27:22.
16. Rivard 28:10.
17. Rivard 28:21; Venne 28:20.
18. Baxter 28:19.
19. Morin 29:7; Ruth Williams 27:12.
20. Chartier 27:4; Smith 28:6.
21. Smith 28:6; Forth 28:6.
22. Smith 28:9.
23. Derickson 27:4.
24. Wortman 29:10.
25. Opekokew 1987.
26. Windspeaker, 26 April 1993, page 2.
27. Derickson 27:4; Green 28:17; Stach 28:18.
28. Gaucher 28:19.
29. Andersen 27:8; Guay 27:9; Miller 27:10; Forester 27:10; Newhouse 27:15; Brascoupé 27:16; Jetté 28:1; Jewell 28:6; George 28:11-12; Ruth Williams 28:16; Ron Williams 28:16; Andersen 28:18.
30. Assiniwi 27:11; Jetté 28:2; Wortman 28:6; Yang 28:16; Andersen 28:28; Anaquod 28:4; Cloutier 29:7.
31. Derickson 27:4.
32. Diamond 27:9, 27; Wapachee 27:17; Kistabish 27:22; Andersen 28:18.
33. Ruth Williams 28:16.
34. Anaquod 28:4.
35. Jetté 28:2; Rothschild 29:8-9.
36. Newhouse 27:15; Brascoupé 27:16; Green 28:20; Robertson 28:22.
37. Gottfriedson 28:9; Andersen 28:18; Gaucher 28:19.
38. Carbery 28:13.
39. Forster 27:10; M. Jamieson 28:8; Cloutier 29:8; McIvor 29:9; Belcourt 29:10.
40. Brascoupé 27:15.
41. Brascoupé 27:16; Arès 27:20; Anaquod 29:4.
42. Anderson 27:8; George 28:12, 13; Rivard 29:8.
43. Diamond 27:2; Brascoupé 27:16; Henderson 28:5; Smith 28:9; Kistabish 28:10; Ross 28:3; Rivard 29:9.
44. Jetté 28:2; Forth 28:6; Wortman 28:6; Andersen 28:18; Rivard 29:9.
45. Jetté 28:1; Bacon 28:10; Reid 28:11; Williams 28:20; Lacasse 29:4.

46. Lafond 27:8-9.
47. Andersen 28:18; Williams 28:19; Anaquod 29:4.
48. Chartier 27:3.
49. Swain 27:12.
50. Newhouse 27:15; Jetté 28:2.
51. Derickson 27:5.
52. Newhouse 27:15; Gottfriedson 28:9.
53. Cloutier 29:10.
54. Apikan 27:7.
55. Anaquod 29:3; Montour 29:7.
56. Andersen 27:8.
57. Andersen 27:10.
58. Apikan 27:10; Noonan 27:10.
59. Montour 29:7.
60. Swain 27:8; Assiniwi 27:11; Rivard 29:9; Ross 29:3.
61. Gottfriedson 28:9; Poitras-Young 28:14.
62. Genaille 27:19.
63. Williams 28:19.
64. Lyall 28:3-4; Smith 28:6; Rice 29:5-6; Bacon 29:9.
65. CBC, 30 April 1993.
66. Brascoupé 27:16; George 27:20.
67. Jones 28:4; Giesbrecht 28:5; Wortman 28:8; Mary Jamieson 28:8; Reid 28:11; Andersen 28:11; Morin 29:7; Montour 29:7.
68. Andersen 28:11.
69. Chartier 27:3; Rock 27:5-6; Forester 27:9; Miller 27:10; Arès 27:20; Jetté 28:1,2; Assiniwi 28:5; Henderson 28:5; Smith 28:7; Mary Jamieson 28:8; Gaucher 28:19; Hawco 28:20; Cloutier 29:7-8; Belcourt 29:10.
70. Mary Jamieson 28:8.
71. Jetté 28:2; Dupuis 28:17; Ruth Williams 28:19; Bacon 29:9.
72. Baxter 28:9; Kistabish 28:10; Carbery 28:13-14; Hawco 28:20; Satsun George 28:20; Robertson 28:22; Montour 29:7; Rivard 29:9.
73. Huskey and Morehouse 1992: 129.
74. Augustine 27:19; George 27:20.
75. Robertson 27:20; Angnaka 27:20; unidentified Métis 27:23.
76. Poitras 1992; Young 1992.
77. Penticton Indian Band 1991.
78. Chartier 27:3; Rivard 27:10; Morin 29:7.

79. Gottfriedson 28:9.

80. Gaucher 28:19.

81. Mary Jamieson 28:7.

82. Cloutier 29:8.

Additional References

Huskey, Lee and Thomas A. Morehouse. "Development in remote regions: What do we know?" *Arctic* 45(2):128-137, 1992.

Opekokew, Delia. "The Political and Legal Inequities Among Aboriginal Peoples in Canada." Institute of Government Relations. Background Paper Number 4. Kingston: Queen's University, 1987.

Penticton Indian Band. Position Paper submitted to Union of British Columbia Indian Chiefs at Special General Assembly. Penticton, 12-14 April 1991.

Poitras, Jane Ash. "The essential spirituality of North American Indian culture." In *Human Ecology: Issues in the North*. Rick Riewe and Jill Oakes, eds. Circumpolar Institute and Faculty of Home Economics, Occasional Publications Series No.30. Edmonton: University of Alberta.

Young, Doris. "Northern Manitoba Hydro Electric projects and their impact on Cree culture." In *People and Land in Northern Manitoba*. George Lithman, Rick R. Riewe, Raymond E. Wiest and Robert E. Wrigley (eds). University of Manitoba, Anthropology Papers 32, Winnipeg: University of Manitoba, Department of Anthropology, 1992.

KEYNOTE ADDRESSES

International Economic Trends and Opportunities

*Dian Cohen**

Thank you for the opportunity to speak to you today. I've known Georges Erasmus for some time, so I'm delighted to have a chance to broaden the discussions we've had over the years.

I'm sure you'll have noticed that despite the failure of the Charlottetown Accord, Canadians are very keen on resolving the outstanding issues with Aboriginal peoples. More and more, Canadians suspect that the traditional ways and knowledge of Aboriginal peoples may contain some of the secrets our culture seems to have lost.

In many dimensions, deep cultural changes are taking place in western society. The women's movement, the environmental movement as well as New Age and the Gaia Movement, to name just a few, have developed into powerful political and economic forces changing western society.

At their root is a common hunger for a new way to relate to the planet and the universe, the search for a partnership rather than a relationship based on what looks like exploitation. There are some goofy aspects to some of these trends. But one important by-product of these movements and the changes they are causing is a new openness and sympathy with Aboriginal cultures around the world.

* President, Dian Cohen Productions.

Southern Canadians are now keen to settle Aboriginal land claims and self-government issues, to work out better resource policies, and to find ways to solve jurisdictional disputes. Looking ahead, then, the question we have to ask ourselves is what happens when we resolve our current problems. In my view, that's when the real work has to start.

You've asked me to speak about international economic trends and opportunities. In looking through the excellent briefing material I was provided, I found quite a number of references to globalization and the emerging knowledge economy. So I suspect that for me to dwell on this in detail would just be repetitious.

The main trends are now widely acknowledged. The world has divided into three interdependent trading blocs – Asia-Pacific, Europe, and North America. Each bloc is loosely defined: where does Eastern Europe fit in relation to the 12? Will Latin American countries use the NAFTA accession clause? Will the countries of Indo-China play an expanding role in Asia-Pacific, and to what extent will common institutions emerge? These are just some of the questions.

And while internal bloc trade seems to be growing more rapidly than trade between blocs, trade between the blocs is growing faster than national economic growth. And growing even faster than trade is international investment.

Foreign direct investment is still thought of as something confined to big companies. If you stick to strict capital flow numbers, that may be true.

But if you widen the notion of investment to include licensing, marketing agreements, and strategic alliances of all kinds, then the pattern changes somewhat to include small and medium-sized suppliers.

Despite concerns about strategic trade policy and new protectionism, the international economy is growing increasingly interdependent. Everybody, whether they export or not, is competing against global competitors.

The other defining trend of our economies is the combination of computers and telecommunications. This change, which some people are calling the second wave of telecommunications, is a complement of internationalization. There are different ways to measure this. One is the fact that employment in what are called knowledge-based businesses is higher and growing more rapidly than employment in traditional sectors.

- Government figures show that the information technology sector has some 11,000 firms, employs 150,000 people and develops and distributes products and services worth more than $17 billion.
- More Canadians are employed in electronics than in pulp and paper.
- More Canadians are now employed in communications and telecommunications than mining and petroleum combined.
- Almost as many people work in the computer industry as in the entire air transport industry. And the list goes on.

Another is the value of sales and shipments. Canada's new industries lag somewhat in this respect. Their productivity is nothing like the productivity of our traditional sectors. But the U.S. numbers show that, for example, computers and office equipment are bigger in terms of sales than chemicals, forest and paper products, industrial and farm equipment or metals and metal products combined.

The point is that the information businesses hardly existed 20 years ago. Now they're among the biggest businesses in the world. What's more, their potential is clearly understood by investors.

Microsoft, the world's most important software producer, has only about 2% of the sales of General Motors ($2 billion vs $124 billion), but the market puts about the same value on their capitalization. Why? Linked computers need software. Like oil in industrial society, software is the oxygen of a computerized economy.

This sectoral shift is interesting. But even more intriguing is the impact of this new technology on the way we do things. Essentially, as *The Economist* magazine reminded us last week, Big Business is vulnerable to small business because of this sectoral shift. Here are some of the shifts this new technology imposes:

The new technology:

- moves control over information downstream into the hands of the consumer;
- changes the role of a consumer to a "pro-sumer"; i.e., an active participant in designing a product for her individual needs;
- ends the distinction between goods and services – so businesses become "manuservices" – and the old control functions that used to be cost centres are now profit centres and potential new businesses.

Example: look at the contest between the airlines reservation services – why Gemini vs Sabre is such an important contest. Airlines make more money from their reservations systems than they do from the machines they fly. American's takeover of Canadian would not only provide more slots in Asia, it would also open up 20 million potential customers to that reservation system – plus add additional Pacific coverage for new reservations for its existing U.S. market.

The new technology also trashes national borders and time zones. The global village is an electronic bazaar. Home shopping, distance learning, banking by telephone: these are no respecters of frontiers. When you call an 800 or 900 number, you and it could be anywhere.

Some repercussions:

- economies and national boundaries no longer coincide;
- jobs are no longer hooked to economic growth or to natural resources;
- big business and large organizations are vulnerable to small, highly focused organizations;

- education and other "batch-processing" is a relic that will either be scrapped or by-passed. Individuals want to learn what they want to know and they want to learn it "on demand" – that is, when and where they happen to be.

The new technologies also change the way we think about economics. Judging from the briefing material, and its references to continuous flow economies, these changes may be particularly interesting to those considering Aboriginal economies.

Markets are still driven by the desire to accumulate. But the new technologies are changing the way economists think about markets and the way business people behave in them.

Economists now think of markets as information processors – with prices as signals of what to do. As markets are seen more as flows of information than of money, economists are becoming more interested in the properties of information. Information to us western economists is weird, because you don't exchange it, you only share it. So now there's a surge of interest in the economics of sharing.

Something similar is happening to managers. Before, they used to focus on beating the competition. The focus is still there. But the way to compete is increasingly seen as by creating kinship structures of companies. Corporate alliances. To be effective, corporate alliances have to be based on mutual respect and must work informally – without lawyers. Trust, confidence, sincerity, mutual obligation – these are increasingly the ingredients of modern business culture.

We have not yet reached the point of Aboriginal circles, where we act on the interdependence of everything. But we're heading in that direction.

Reading through some of the briefing material I was provided, I was also struck by the focus on the land in Aboriginal communities and the search for ways to make that organic connection into something the market will value. The danger here is that you might succeed.

For if the developed world no longer highly values resource-based economies, that means they will be happy to see its stewardship pass into the hands of others. In your own terms, you may be better off. But in economic development terms, the uphill distance will remain the same.

Some economists believe that economies move from stage to stage like snakes shed their skin. Others point out that what changes is not the sectors so much as the way the sectors work. That is, resource-based economies may still be valuable, but only if they become thoroughly informational. This is my position.

Call it Cohen's Law of Economic Dominance: dominant sectors tell us how to do things, not what things to do.

The practical implications of both perspectives are the same. Up means up. The good side of the new technologies is that they pass so much power into the hands of smaller units. New technology grants small businesses and individuals the power to hook up their imaginations to the world and to derive profit from that.

The good side of these new technologies and the globalizing trends is that the combination will allow Aboriginal communities to interact with each other, with other Aboriginal cultures and with western culture in exciting, innovative and economically wealth-producing ways. Compared to what we had before, the new economies are much more inclusive and offer many, many more opportunities to people who didn't have them before.

This, it seems to me, is where the interests of Aboriginal economic development and that of Canada coincide – and where it is most important to raise questions about land-based development strategies.

All the changes I've been talking about, when taken together, mean Canada must totally reconfigure itself. Like the Aboriginal economies, Canada will have to change or remain what some of your commentators have called a "bungee" economy – where the money may flow in, but then bounces back out again.

We have a surplus on our merchandise trade account. But what we make in goods trade, plus a lot more, we return to our investors in debt service payments. Because we don't actually earn enough to cover those payments, we have to borrow more.

Getting that under control means we take a big hit in our standard of living. Or we find a way to turn a $26 billion trade deficit into a $26 billion trade surplus.

The practical upshot of this is that Canada needs all the help it can get in generating innovations, trade and productive investment. Aboriginal enterprise – especially, I think, Aboriginal knowledge products – have a lot to contribute to turning Canada's economy around. In today's new, knowledge-based economies, imagination is the most valuable natural resource. In this kind of economy, the opportunities for Aboriginal people and cultures to participate are larger than ever before.

Tribal Economic Development

*Thomas R. Acevedo**

I am the director of the Enterprise Office for the Salish and Kootenai tribes, and I serve as the CEO for tribally owned businesses. The Salish and Kootenai Tribes live on their 1.2 million acre reservation in western Montana, approximately 75 miles southwest of Glacier National Park. The reservation area is a beautiful mountainous setting with the largest natural fresh water lake west of the Mississippi River. The western Montana region is a prime tourist area given its natural beauty and resting within the travel corridor between Glacier and Yellowstone Park. The reservation home land of Salish and Kootenai has a resident population of approximately 25,000 of which 5,000 are Indians. The Indian unemployment rate is three times that of the state of Montana; 15% and 5% respectively. The tribes in both their combined business and government sectors employ 1,200 people. The Salish and Kootenai tribes have a total annual operating budget of approximately $90 million. Of this amount the tribes self-generate approximately $17 million annually from their businesses and resource usage. The federal funds are administered by the tribes through the *Indian Self-Determination Act*.

The tribes are engaged in hydroelectric production, under a co-licensee arrangement with the Montana Power Company, timber harvesting, electronics manufacturing, a tourist resort hotel, construction company, electric utility management distribution contract, and agricultural leasing. In addition to tribally owned and operated businesses, approximately 125 individual tribal members

* Director of the Enterprise Development Office for the Salish and Kootenai Tribes, Flathead Nation.

are engaged to non-agricultural businesses. In a further effort to diversify their economy, the tribes are seeking to develop a gambling casino but, because of political problems with the state of Montana, this has yet to occur. Gaming enterprises for other tribes in the United States have proved to be the single most successful revenue producer. They have accomplished what federal programs for economic development have failed to do.

The federal programs offered by the United States government have been of some assistance in helping the Salish and Kootenai tribes obtain some measure of their current economic success. These programs include a loan guarantee program administered through the Bureau of Indian Affairs, an agency of the Department of Interior. Under this program the Bureau of Indian Affairs acts as a guarantor for 90% of the loan amount borrowed by an Indian tribe from a private lending institution. The Salish and Kootenai tribes used this program partially to finance their resort hotel call Kwataqnuk Resort. Even with the guarantee program it took the tribes a full year to secure bank financing. Maintenance of the same board of directors and diligence to the project finally convinced the financing bank to commit.

Another federal program used by the tribes was a direct dollar grant program for facilities construction (bricks and mortar) administered by the Economic Development Administration, an agency of the Department of Commerce. The tribes used this program to help partially finance the construction of their electronics manufacturing plant. To access this grant program, Indian tribes had to provide a certain percentage of matching dollars or in-kind contributions. Generally the requirement is a three-to-one match.

The federal government, through the Small Business Administration, an agency of the Department of Commerce, offers a business contract minority set-aside program. Under this program certain goods and services procurement contracts that the United States government would normally let under its competitive bidding policy are set aside exclusively for minority-owned businesses. This program is known as the 8A program. Tribally owned and individually owned businesses are a subset within the overall small disadvantaged minority-owned business category as defined by the Small Business Administration.

The set-aside contracts offered by the federal government under this 8A program are almost exclusively let by the Department of Defense. The benefits of the 8A procurement contract approach is that the tribal business sits down and negotiates a contract directly, rather than having to bid competitively. An 8A certified company can only remain one, as the law stands now, for nine years. The Salish and Kootenai tribes' S&K Electronics Company entered the 8A program two years ago.

Government initiatives would be useless if the S + K tribal government did not change to fit the requirements of the business world. The 10 members of the tribal government council are elected for a four-year term; they can serve as many terms as the electorate returns them to office. The average term served is 12 to 16 years and some councillors have sat for more than 30 years. The 10 members stand for election on staggered terms. This procedure has created stability and continuity with respect to tribal policy. In addition to this important development, the Tribal Council instituted a civil service program. This has served to give job security to tribal employees and thereby to attract highly qualified and motivated people to work for the tribes. The tribes are also supportive of higher education for their members. They provide financial assistance and encourage tribal members to return, once they have their education, to work for the tribes. In fact, the tribes believe so strongly in education that they operate a highly successful community college called SKC.

As part of their continuing evaluation of their governing policies, the tribes have been in the process of separating the management of their businesses from direct governmental control. Historically the tribes, through the 10-member council, had direct involvement in their business enterprises. Although their motives were good, their business goals were misdirected; as elected officials, their commitment was to job creation and not to job or business profitability.

Having had little financial success in their business enterprises under this approach, they began to change course with the establishment of a corporate board of directors and the creation of the Enterprise Development Office.

Under this approach the board of directors is responsible for directing, managing and setting the policy of each of the tribal businesses under the board's umbrella. The director of the Enterprise Development Office serves as the chairman of the board of directors. Under the director's management, the staff of the Enterprise Office provides technical assistance, forecasting, spread sheet analyses for each of the businesses, and plans and develops new businesses. The Office also provides business planning and management assistance to individually owned Indian businesses, as requested.

The businesses the tribes are involved in take into consideration the cultural, environmental and long-term goals of the tribes. For example, the tribes have established a tribally managed wilderness area, shoreline protection laws for Flathead Lake (the lake is 28 miles long and 15 miles wide and reaches a depth of 300 feet), aquatic lands protection laws, and has designated the reservation air shed for no further degradation. The tribes embrace the holistic concept of the reservation as their homeland which must therefore be carefully stewarded. Protection of what we have today and wise uses of the resources for the generations yet to come are the overriding commitment of the tribes.

Sovereignty and Economic Development on American Indian Reservations: Lessons from the United States

*Joseph P. Kalt**

It is a pleasure to be here. Ken Paul asked me to come and address this group. I have to preface my remarks by noting that my background and experiences fall entirely within the context of the United States and what I have to say will deal with the experience in the United States. I hope that some of the things that we are learning there may be of some use up here, but you will have to be the judge of that. I ask you to understand the lack of knowledge that I reveal about the Canadian situation.

Let me begin by giving you a little bit of background on the project that has led to the work that I'll talk about this morning. I, along with Professor Steven Cornell of the University of California and Manley Biguay of the Harvard Graduate School of Education, direct the Harvard Project on American Indian Economic Development. This is a project that began in the mid-1980s to examine the state of economic development on American Indian reservations in the United States. The work began with some straightforward observations that Native Americans are the poorest minority in the United States. By the mid-1980s there was a handful of reservations that seemed to be breaking away from the pack, if you will; that is, there was a handful of reservations that seemed to be launching sustainable economic development, reducing unemployment and raising incomes, and reducing some of the social ills that are often associated with poverty and unemployment.

* Ford Foundation Professor of International Political Economy, Harvard University, and Director, Harvard Project on American Indian Economic Development.

Well, that observation that out of more than 300 reservations, there was a handful beginning to break out in terms of economic development led me and others to begin to ask the question: "What's going on differently at those places where economic development is taking hold, where economic development is being sustained?" And so we stood about, myself an economist, my partners, one a sociologist, one an educator, trying to answer those kinds of questions. We hit the field and began looking at the sources of economic development. In some sense there were too many causes for the lack of economic development on American Indian reservations. We got in rental cars and drove around the rural United States for a month, interviewing people, talking with people, gathering information. One of the things we gathered was long lists of everything that could possibly go wrong, and those bad lists consisted of such things as lack of access to capital, lack of education, lack of training, racism in the majority society, a lack of support from the federal government, a lack of support from the state government and problems of rural isolation. On and on, a long list; and every item had a grain of truth to it. So the question then became, notwithstanding these problems, there was a group of tribes who had started to break out in sustained economic development; what was happening with the relatively successful tribes?

So we launched the Harvard Project on American Indian Economic Development by striking a co-operative relationship with about a dozen American Indian tribes in the United States. These tribes include Flathead Tribes from Montana, White Mountain Apache in Arizona, San Carlos Apache in Arizona, Cochiti Pueblo, Muckleshoot in Washington, Pine Ridge Sioux in South Dakota, Rosebud Sioux in South Dakota, Hualapa in Arizona, Yakima in Washington, Northern Cheyenne in Montana, Crow in Montana, and, in addition to these tribes, we have worked with a number of other tribes. All of our masters students are required to do client projects in order to receive their degrees in public policy. This gives me a pool of free labour, and I have been able to place approximately 60 students on projects for tribes at no cost to the tribes. These projects have ranged from constitutional reformation to the design of personnel systems, to the assessment of forestry plans and so forth. This has allowed us to work with and for tribes in a way that allows us for the first time in the United States to study economic development from a perspective other than Washington, D.C. In the United States, every major economic development analysis and study that has been done in the last 20 to 25 years has been done from Washington, D.C., except for ours. We work by dealing with and for tribes in our attempts to understand what is distinguishing the relatively successful from the relatively unsuccessful tribes.

Now let me give you some of the findings and results that we think we are seeing when we are out in the field and working on this matter. The obstacles to economic development make up a long list. But this is a list that many societies face – lack of access to financial capital, lack of education, lack of effective planning, too much planning, poverty and natural resources, rural market isolation, intense competition from surrounding communities, federal and state bureaucracies that are either counterproductive or discriminatory. Under these conditions, what can tribes do to spur economic development?

Let me give you a bit of background on the legal setting within which tribes operate. American Indian reservations in the United States have quite a high degree of sovereignty over their affairs. Reservation governments in the United States have full rights of taxation on reservations, they have the right to create their own court systems, police systems, constitutions, schools systems, regulatory environments for both environmental and business regulation and in some cases even criminal law. This sovereignty waxes and wanes with the decisions that come out of the United States Supreme Court. Sovereignty rises when the Supreme Court finds, as it did in the *Crow Nation* versus *Montana*, that the Crow Tribe had the right to levy taxes on coal mine operations on the reservation. Sovereignty collapses when the Supreme Court rules, as it did in the case involving the Yakima, that there is shared jurisdiction over a predominantly non-Indian town that sits on the Yakima reservation in Washington. So sovereignty waxes and wanes, but when all is said and done, there is a relatively high degree of sovereignty, there is a right to self-government on American Indian reservations.

We believe that the keys to American Indian economic development on U.S. reservations are the same as those that other sovereign nations face; American Indian reservations are very much like developing countries around the world. Their problems are very similar and their solutions are very similar, although both within American Indian societies and between American Indian societies and other developing countries there are tremendous cultural differences.

When we look around reservations, we find key ingredients to economic development. The first is sovereignty itself. One of the interesting phenomena that we see in the United States is that those tribes who have broken out economically and really begun to sustain economic development are uniformly marked by an assertion of sovereignty that pushes the Bureau of Indian Affairs into a pure advisory role rather than a decision-making role. In some cases, these drives for sovereignty are startling. One of the most successful tribes in the United States right now is the White Mountain Apache Tribe in Central Arizona. White Mountain Apache Tribe operates a major ski resort with three mountains; they operate a $50 million to $60 million sawmill; they operate a major logging operation; they operate an aerospace manufacturing company doing subcontracting work for McDonnell Douglas; they operate movie theatres, grocery stores, car washes and so on; they operate a tribal grazing herd and tribal farm and a tribal feed operation. Their unemployment rate is reported somewhere between 11% and 22%. The White Mountain Apache in Central Arizona appear to have a lower unemployment rate on the reservation than in the surrounding white communities of that part of Arizona. It is a society that has shown very rapid economic growth over the last 15 years with rising incomes and falling unemployment.

Although their story is interesting and illustrative of a pattern that we are seeing throughout tribes, what happened to the White Mountain Apache? In the United States, tribal governments traditionally have been governed by the Bureau of Indian Affairs. Most tribes in the United States operate under a tribal constitution that was drafted for them by the federal government of the United States in the 1930s during the Roosevelt years. These constitutions are known as IRA constitutions – *Indian Reorganization Act* constitutions – drafted by the Department of Interior, sent to tribes, voted on by the tribes in the 1930s. An abstention or a failure to vote was counted as a yes. Well you can imagine what voter turn out must have been in the 1930s by a people as disfranchised as any people could be. Consequently these constitutions that were drafted in Washington, D.C., were almost uniformally adopted without modification. There were some modifications in some cases. The White Mountain Apache, which I have just described running ski resorts, sawmills, aerospace manufacturing and so forth, operates under one of these IRA constitutions. So what have they done under this constitution to allow them to break out and sustain the economic development that they have?

Well, it is interesting. For decades, what in the United States is called the BIA superintendent, the official of the Bureau of Indian Affairs who was the superintendent for that reservation, sat at the right hand of the tribal chairman at tribal council meetings. The tribal council would discuss decisions and when it came time to vote they would all look to the superintendent. The superintendent would tell them how to vote, and then they would vote. This was not sovereignty, this was not self-government.

In the late 1960s, the father of the gentleman who is currently the chairman of the tribe said one day to the Bureau of Indian Affairs superintendent (BIA offices were across the street from tribal headquarters), "You cannot cross the street anymore unless we tell you you can." And they kicked the Bureau of Indian Affairs out of council meetings. This seemed to mark the start of this sustainable economic development for the White Mountain Apache. If you want to see even starker actions, within a few years the White Mountain Apache found themselves in a situation where, as a result of decades-long leases for home sites and a beautiful recreation lake on the tribe's property, the tribe was facing the renewal of those leases. These leases were paying on the order of $70 a year rental for a lease site. The Bureau of Indian Affairs said, well it's time to renew the leases we'll renew them at the same prices. The tribe said no. This precipitated a long set of struggles between the tribe and the federal government of the United States. Eventually the tribe won and won the right to set its own lease rates for these home sites. The tribe also decided to expand its operations in the recreational area which eventually led to the ski resort that I have described and they wanted to build a small lake, an impoundment of water that could be used for recreational and other purposes. The federal government of the United States wanted to stop them and after a wonderful story with lots of drama, the tribe one night decided to go ahead, and they brought in the bulldozers and the dynamite and they brought out the rifles and the shotguns and they held United States marshalls at bay as they built this water impoundment. This lake is now a major income producer for the tribe. It is a major source of fishing revenues for the hunting and fishing operation that the tribe operates.

Why tell this story? Well, this story illustrates a pattern that we see repeated in most of the successful tribes we see in the States. And that is a pattern of tribal assertion of self-decision making, self-government over the key economic development decisions on the reservation. Why would this be a key? Why is the exercise of sovereignty a key? Well, we think in part it's because our Bureau of Indian Affairs in the United States faces a severe conflict of interest. The fate of the Bureau of Indian Affairs rises and falls with the fate of Indian country. You can actually go and see the data. The worst things are in Indian country. The higher the unemployment rate, the worse the poverty, the better off is the Bureau of Indian Affairs, its budget rises, its staff rises, its power rises. The individuals who work for our Bureau of Indian Affairs are in general perfectly fine individuals but they work within a system that creates a tremendous conflict of interest in which it is not in the interest of the Bureau of Indian Affairs to spur economic development and reduce dependence on reservations. And in case after case after case, we find the Bureau of Indian Affairs standing as an impediment to economic development.

Increasingly in these aggressive and successful tribes, however, the Bureau of Indian Affairs starts to perform a much more useful role. As a tribe asserts its sovereignty, begins to make its own decisions, the Bureau of Indian Affairs holds a lot of resources, financial and advisory. The Bureau of Indian Affairs in some of these successful tribes has been pushed, appropriately I believe, into the position of being an adviser to tribes rather than a decision maker for tribes. The first thing that we find out there is that successful tribes are marked by these very aggressive assertions of self-government, self-decision making over economic development affairs on the reservations.

But that is not enough. Let me turn to the second major finding. Sovereignty itself it not enough, self-government itself is not enough on American Indian reservations to spur economic development. Rather sovereignty has to be complemented by capable institutions of self-government. It's one thing to have sovereignty, it's another thing to be able to use it effectively.

And now let me tell a not so good story. We have done a lot of work over the years with the Crow Tribe of Montana. The Crow Tribe of Montana – on paper – may be the wealthiest people in North America. They have more coal on the

Crow Reservation in Montana than any other owner of coal in the world other than the United States federal government and apparently the government of Australia. The reservation is rich in natural resources, rich in agricultural resources. And yet at the Crow Reservation in Montana, unemployment stands – depending on how it is measured – somewhere between 60% and 90%. I have worked closely with this tribe and I have watched campaigns for election between contending parties to be chairman of the tribe in which the incumbent chair of the tribe was so aggressive that he succeeded in getting unemployment down from 87% to 85%. It is a very stark situation. The suicide rates are somewhere on the order of 10 times the national U.S. average at the Crow reservation. It is a place of extreme economic poverty and social desperation. It is also a place that has recently revealed even more upsetting tendencies as factions have come into severe conflict with each other, verging on the breaking out of violence. What's going on at the Crow Reservation in Montana? You may have picked up a few minutes ago that I mentioned a case, the *Crow Tribe of Montana* versus *Montana*. The Crow Tribe of Montana has been an aggressive asserter of its sovereignty. It fights again and again in the courts for the rights to self-government. Yet once it earns those rights of sovereignty, the tribe continues to operate under a system that is unable to sustain economic development. With 85% unemployment, you are watching a society where the only jobs are jobs dealing with those who don't have jobs in some form of social service delivery. In other words, there is no sustainable economic production going on. So the Crow Tribe of Montana, while it has sovereignty, has been unable to exercise the right to self-government effectively. And why is that?

We believe that here the key lies in effective and capable institutions of self-government. The Crow Tribe of Montana operates under a constitution that is known in the United States as a general council form of government. This is a constitution in which every voting-age member of the tribe is a member of the tribal council. It is a pure form of town meeting or Athenian democracy in which every voting-age member of the tribe is a legislator, is a senator, is a representative. Their constitution provides for no separation of powers, no delineation of powers as to what the tribal government should be able to do. The consequence of this is that the tribal government serves as a somewhat organized system of mob rule. The constitution provides that a quorum of the tribal council shall consist of 100 people. This leads to a form of government in which, quite literally, every quarter, every three months, the tribal council meets and then the faction leaders play a game with each other in which they drag the meeting on for days and people don't get to go to sleep. If they start on a Saturday and if by Tuesday night at three in the morning you and 99 of your faction are still awake, you can impeach the current office holders, you can make your own laws and take over this operation of government.

Well this kind of governmental system, needless to say, does not create a very healthy environment for economic development or for life in general. Outside investors are completely deterred. But, in addition, inside investors, tribal members investing in their education, potentially investing in that ranch, potentially investing in small manufacturing or other cottage industries are discouraged from operating under this kind of governmental system. This contains a very interesting lesson. One of the things we find with American Indian reservations is that tribal sovereignty is sufficient to screw things up. That is, there is not perfect sovereignty out there and there are constant battles in the United States over tribal sovereignty versus the federal government and the state governments. But tribal sovereignty is such that if the central government of the tribe cannot set in place an economic and social and cultural environment in which inside and outside economic actors, investors and others feel safe and secure in making investments in tribal development, the tribal government has the ability to destroy those opportunities. In that sense, American Indian reservations are like developing countries around the world. What is the lesson of Eastern Europe, what is the lesson of Asia, what is the lesson of Africa, what is the lesson of Latin America, and what is the lesson of North America? It is interesting that we economists used to go around the world and tell everybody what to do. And what we would usually tell people to do is to get their governmental policies in order and get their markets right. But people would ask us, what causes economic development? Our answer would focus on resources, investment and savings. And, indeed, Paul Samuelson, the Nobel Prize-winning economist, tells the story.

He says that in the late 1950s, he "was getting famous and people are starting to ask all these questions about predictions for the future of the world and they were asking where is the next growth area of the world?" This is in the late 1950s. He said that it was clearly Latin American, South America, not Asia; it was clearly South America. At that time Argentina had the eighth highest standard of living in the world. Rich; the whole continent was rich in natural resources. It did not have the stark problems of over-population as many parts of Asia had. And to Paul Samuelson, Nobel Prize-winning economist, that was clearly where economic development was going to happen. He said: "I was wrong; the key to economic development is not resources. The key to economic development is effective self-government." Every society has labour. And the lesson of much of Asia has been, that if you can get your basic economic environment in place, economic development can take hold. After all, in some sense, these tests of Taiwan versus Mainland China, East Germany versus West Germany, these are classic cases in which the world experiments to see what the sources of economic development are. In the case of Taiwan, there were very few natural resources – essentially a rock immediately following World War II – and yet it became one of the growth areas of Asia in the post-World War II period.

The message so far, then, is two-fold. First, sovereignty seems to be a key to economic development on our American Indian reservations because the Bureau of Indian Affairs simply lacks the incentive and the ability to spur economic development. Second, effective institutions of sovereignty, effective institutions of self-government, have to be in place in order for sovereignty to be effectively used and in order for a healthy economic environment to be put in place.

Let me say just a word now about what the dimensions of effective institutions of self-government are. What does it take? Clearly, in the Crow situation, everybody is a member of the legislative form of government. It isn't working very well. What is working? In the United States, we have three basic kinds of tribal governments. One of these general councils forms a government. We cannot find a single case of the general council form of government in which there is any sustainable economic development going on. Another kind of tribal government that we see is a parliamentary system of government.

Most fundamentally a parliamentary system in these tribal governments is one in which the tribal chair, the president or chairman or chairwoman of the tribe is not directly elected by the citizens of the tribe but is elected as the chair or president of the tribal council. It is the tribal council that is elected by the citizens of the tribe. The third type of government that we have on the United States reservations are what we call directly elected or strong chairman forms of government in which the tribal chair is directly elected by the people. This is a strong tribal chair form of government because that tribal chair then has a separate power block associated with the voters who have supported her or him.

We have done some statistical studies looking across about 75 different reservations with populations over 1,000. And we find that, statistically, the strong tribal chair forms of government are performing relatively better than the parliamentary forms of government. We find that the presence of an independent judicial system on the reservation is also a positive supporter of economic development. And we find that the general council forms of government simply are not able to keep pace with the parliamentary or the strong chair forms of government.

For example, just to give you the flavour, we find that a strong chair form of government, compared to a general council form of government, contributes on the order of a 15 percentage point reduction in unemployment on reservations. So these forms of government matter. None of this is to say that resources don't matter; all else being equal, of course, you would like to have more resources rather than fewer. Of course you would like to have a mountain that can support a ski resort, of course you would like to have a coal resource, of course you would like to have access to fisheries and so forth. But we find case after case in which relatively resource-rich tribes are unable to sustain economic development.

The story of the Crow Tribe of Montana is perhaps one of the most extreme, yet it illustrates how ineffective tribal government, ineffective exercise of sovereignty, can destroy the opportunity for economic development.

What is it that effective governments really do? From what we can tell, they do three primary things. They settle disputes, particularly disputes over capital assets. They operate effective day-to-day bureaucracies. They separate politics from business. Those three things seem to be what effective governments out in the field are doing. On the first point, dispute resolution. Effective government is a key to effective social organization, effective economic development. But how do you keep a government from stepping over the boundary between being the party that sets down the rules of the game for society and enforces those rules, and the party that uses the power of government to take all the resources? Governments around the world have a long history of what we call Marcosian behaviour, after Ferdinand Marcos. By Marcosian behaviour we mean using the power of government not to set in place an environment for safe investment and savings and economic productivity but using the power of government to steal the wealth. Governments that do that destroy economic development. That, in a sense, has been the story of Latin America where the power of government for much of the post-World War II period has been used in constant coups and counter-coups to see who can rule and thereby take control of the wealth of a society. Effective governments around the world, including American Indian governments on reservations in the United States, serve as effective dispute resolution organizations but have their power limited so that those governments do not become Marcosian; that is, they do not become the thieves of the wealth of the reservation. How is this done?

The general council form of government of the Crow Tribe in Montana clearly does not have that ability because there is no delineation of powers, there is no separation of powers within that governmental structure. Every quarter, they get together in the high school gym with all the members of the tribe and see who can stay awake the longest, and you get to have a coup, so to speak, and take control of the tribe. The effective tribal governments operate under a system both traditional in some cases and, if you will, European in other cases. The effective tribal governments find the mechanism for creating what we would call a separation of powers. Let me comment on this. The biggest problem of the Flathead Tribe of Montana, for example, over the late 1980s when the economy was booming was that they did not have enough employees. In the Flathead Tribe of Montana, unemployment was not the problem; there was a labour shortage. This is a society that has unemployment somewhere down around 10%. For the rural United States, that is a very low unemployment rate. The Flathead of Montana have, so far as we can tell, the best developed tribal judicial system anywhere in the United States. They have a separate judiciary with attorneys general and judges and so forth. They have joined an inter-tribal Supreme Court or Appeals Court system whereby tribal court decisions may be appealed to an inter-tribal court that serves as the arbitrator of last resort and solves disputes. This has created a very stable judicial system within the Flathead Tribe. Accordingly, the Flathead reservation is now viewed as a very safe place for investment both by tribal members and non-members. And you have capital flowing into the economy in a way that many states in the United States wish they could. The state of Arkansas, where President Clinton comes from, wishes it could create as safe an environment for investors as the Flathead have. The Flathead represent a case that looks like my high school civics textbook: separation of power, separate judicial system, separate judiciary, separate legislature and so forth.

On the other hand, we have tribes that operate under no written constitutions. The Cochiti Pueblo in New Mexico is a reservation of Pueblo Indians operating under no written constitution. The Cochiti Pueblo has a pure theocracy form of government. Every December 29, the single religious leader of the tribe goes into the tribal plaza, a square in the middle of the little town, or into the high school gym if it is raining, and the tribal theocrat known as the Caseeca appoints the tribal politicians. You will be governor this year, you will be the vice-governor, you will be the treasurer and so on. This form of government would appear to be an enigma to democratic traditions, but it is in keeping with Cochiti traditions. Are the Cochiti doing well? Well, it turns out that the Cochiti Pueblo represents a very interesting case. Some of you may have heard of the Hunt brothers; they used to own the Kansas City football team, they are a major oil industry family. The Hunt brothers own a town on the Cochiti reservation under a 49-year lease. This town was created for the purpose of creating a retirement community where non-Indian retirees could come and build nice homes and live out in the beautiful southwestern desert of New Mexico. They created a booming community, swimming pools, tennis courts and so forth. The Hunt brothers went bankrupt in the 1980s with the collapse in the oil market, and the tribe bought the town out. The Cochiti Pueblo bought back a town, essentially a big real estate factory project, and faced a decision. There was some sentiment within the tribe that said, let's just destroy the incentive of the people who live here; those homes are pretty, we'll put tribal members in them. Another faction within the tribe said no; we can make money from this. We have a golf course, a tennis ranch, beautiful homes; we can make a go of this. The tribe eventually decided to stay in the real estate business and is making a go of it in this town. Unemployment at Cochiti has been collapsing since the tribe took over its economic affairs in the 1980s, especially with the collapse of Hunt brothers. And they are doing this under a completely traditional form of government. Unemployment at Cochiti is well within the teens; they have had one of the highest rates of per capita growth of income in the United States and, by all appearances, they are resource-poor. They just have desert. There is not much else out there.

Now, I tell this story because the lesson is important. When I sit here and use words like separation of powers and judicial system, I don't mean to imply that all tribal governments have to adopt my high school civics textbook version of government. We believe that the story of Cochiti Pueblo illustrates that every tribe, every society, every developing country faces the same kinds of problems in creating environments in which people want to invest their capital and their own education. Every society faces problems of dispute resolution. Every society faces the problem of laying down rules of the game by which we will organize ourselves as people. That was as true 500 years ago as it is today. All successful societies face those kinds of problems, too. The answers that societies come up with may differ. Cochiti may be able to operate effectively under theocracy. Flathead may be able to operate effectively under an almost U.S.-style constitution, except for the judicial system and so forth. The mechanisms by which different societies answer these problems of shutting down Ferdinand Marcos, of laying in place effective institutions of government, may differ, but they all face the same basic problems.

I mentioned that separation of politics from business was a crucial component of successful economic development. This is something that we find again and again in the field. On American Indian reservations, the land base is, in a fundamental sense, owned by the tribe. It's appropriate that the members of that society, the tribal members, exercise control almost as stockholders over the economic direction that the tribe takes. It is appropriate that members of the Yakima reservation decide they don't want a ski resort; they regard that mountain as sacred. It is appropriate that the members of the White Mountain Apache say we want a ski resort. Those are appropriate decisions that each society should make for itself. Those are the strategic decisions about where society is going. On many Indian reservations we encounter a problem where tribal politics, getting tribal members involved in decisions, gets filtered down to the day-to-day decisions of who gets hired, who gets fired, what pension plan will be adopted. Will we buy this piece of equipment or that piece of equipment? In case after case after case, unless those basic day-to-day business decisions are separated from tribal politics, we find the economy or the enterprise being destroyed by those politics.

Many tribes in the United States have set up what they call independent boards, enterprise boards. These are often chartered as corporations separate from the tribal government, for the purposes of running the tribe's enterprises and assets. Many other tribes try to run their enterprises through the tribal council where the tribal council members are also on the board of directors of enterprises. We have sampled up to 80 different enterprises out in Indian country. We find that the odds of having a profitable enterprise in Indian country are five times higher when the tribe organizes itself with an independent management board, separate from the tribal council and tribal government — five times higher than when the tribal council itself takes on those business-management decisions.

Some of you here may be tribal council members yourselves. It sounds like we are asking some tribal councils to give up the power of legitimate elective leaders, but, in some cases, individuals giving up power is the way to find those mechanisms of self-government that allow the people to empower themselves.

This is the key to these successful enterprises.

There is a third and last key that I'll touch on in what we see out in Indian country in terms of success. The first two keys are the strong assertion of sovereignty and effective institutions of self-government. The third key is something in the jargon of our research that we call cultural match. The idea is this. Unless the formal institutions of government, the basic structure – independent judiciary/no independent judiciary, pure theocracy/no theocracy, parliamentary/strong chief executive – unless the formal institutions of government match the underlying cultural norms of legitimacy and propriety, those institutions of government will not be effective, and economic development will not take place. This is an important finding. To illustrate it, let me tell a story of two comparative tribes.

As I have mentioned, we have these IRA constitutions in the United States. We work very closely with two tribes that have, almost verbatim, the same constitution. One is the White Mountain Apache that I have already described. Another tribe we work with is the Oglala Sioux of the Pine Ridge Reservation in South Dakota. The Pine Ridge Sioux operate under virtually the same constitution as the White Mountain Apache. Pine Ridge, South Dakota, is the poorest place in the United States according to the 1990 Census — the poorest place; poorer than our inner cities.

Now you should be saying to yourselves: Wait a minute. This guy just told us these effective institutions of self-government were the answer and now he's saying that he has two side-by-side societies, one doing extremely well and one, operating under the same government, the poorest place in the United States. What is going on? Here, we believe, the issue of cultural match is absolutely crucial. The Apache culture, from as far back as the Apache or anyone else can determine, has had a form of government that centred on single chieftains as the legitimate points of focus and concentration of political power. The Apache traditional form of government was dominated by single strong chieftains to the point that the tribal chieftains had the right to select sub-chieftains and create a tribal council. The tribal council was being created by the chieftains rather than by the people — a very central chief-dominated form of government in an Apache society. In addition, this strong central chieftain had judicial powers. When a major dispute arose, a murder or some other crime, the strong central chief of the Apache tribe would select two other members of the tribe, and the three of them would form a jury and they would hold court. But the judicial authorities centred in the strong central chief in the Apache society. Hold on to that for a moment, and let me turn to the Sioux.

In Sioux society, there was a parliamentary system of government prior to the reservation years. That is, when the tribe was operating in the pre-conquest pre-reservation years, first the people would select a group, a relatively large group, to form a council of elders. That council of elders would then select some administrative officers, known by the white guys who came in as chiefs. They were really just administrative officers, running military affairs, running agricultural affairs and so forth, even when the tribal council of elders – they are often called the big bellies within the Sioux language because they were older and had big bellies – the big bellies would select three executives; they would not select one, they would always disperse the power. There was no strong central chieftain within the Sioux society. They tended to be dominated more by a parliamentary system rather that a strong chief executive form of government. Both White Mountain Apache and Pine Ridge Sioux currently operate under a strong chief executive form of government. The Pine Ridge Sioux have a strong centrally elected chair and a council of a handful of individuals. But the tribal chair is elected directly by the people and thereby has a separate power base.

White Mountain Apache have the same government. At White Mountain Apache, the same individual has been chair of the tribe for 18 of the last 20 years. Of the Messcalaro Apache, by the way, Wendel Chino has been chair now for more than 30 years. At Pine Ridge Sioux, since the 1930s only one individual has succeeded in getting re-elected as chair of the tribe. There is no legitimacy in a central tribal chieftain in Sioux society. Consequently, they are saddled with a government imposed upon them in the 1930s by the federal government of the United States and they keep ripping themselves apart with it. And that central governmental still has power formally. It's where all the money comes through from the federal government. It's where all the business investors have to go for approval of investment. But it lacks fundamental legitimacy in Sioux society. And the Sioux, quite reasonably, are very aggressively confronting the issue of constitutional reform. Sioux societies in general– there are seven major Sioux reservations – operate under this strong chief executive form of government which does not match the indigenous form of government that centred on a council of elders. There is only one Sioux tribe that is doing relatively well. The Lower Bruel is the one Sioux tribe with a parliamentary system of government rather than a strong chief executive form of government. The Lower Bruel have gone to a system of government that avoids the strong central chieftain and moves to a system of parliamentary, council-based government.

The lesson is that a formal institution of government has to match the informal cultural norms of what is legitimate. Every society has cultural norms. And they differ. At Cochiti Pueblo, a theocracy is legitimate. You ask the question: "Why doesn't the theocrat become Ferdinand Marcos? Why doesn't the theocrat declare that the deity has told me I can live in the best house in the Hunt brothers' neighbourhood? Why doesn't that happen?" And the answer is: "We wouldn't let it happen. There is no form of government written down, but the culture says that that's not the right of the theocrat to do that; the theocrat has restricted powers just as Apache chieftains have restricted power." The lesson that we see here and elsewhere in the world is that tribal government has to match the underlying norms of legitimacy in that society. One of the lessons of that is that outsiders cannot design these governments for tribes. Knowing what your culture is, knowing what is legitimate and what isn't is a very hard thing. We can sit around and talk about it but, in general, it is a very hard thing for outsiders even to have a clue about. We think, therefore, that these governments imposed from outside have been relatively ineffective. We have more than 300 reservations with only a handful of them doing any significant economic development. This issue of cultural match appears to be a key around the world.

There is research on Africa right now indicating that the success in Africa, where it has occurred – and success has been rare in Africa – has occurred where the underlying culture supported the form of government that the British and the French and the Portuguese left when they pulled out. Those places in Africa where there is violent conflict now or where the economy and the society are coming apart are those places where the British, French and Portuguese systems did not match the cultural norms of the people. So when the British and the French and the Portuguese pulled out, they had a formal system of government that simply lacked legitimacy. And therefore the government became an instrument of harm rather than an instrument of benefit and successful economic development.

DISCUSSION PAPERS

The Land and the Resource Base

*Roger T. Gruben**

I am pleased to have the opportunity to provide a discussion paper today on the subject of the land and resource base as it relates to building our economies. This is an area that interests me greatly, largely because it poses tough challenges and carries with it tremendous promise for our economic future. It is also an extremely complex area, and I am cautious to avoid simple generalizations and pat answers.

We come here today from many different parts of the country with diverse circumstances and needs. We share at least one common interest: building a stable economic base for our people. I cannot presume to speak to the uniqueness of each circumstance, nor foresee in every instance how my observations will apply to your experience and the world which you know. My intention here is to offer up some observations from my experience that may serve as a point of departure for our discussions today.

The Inuvialuit Settlement Region

My home is the Inuvialuit Settlement Region (ISR), an area in the Western Arctic (that's the top left-hand corner of Canada), where we Inuvialuit retain title to 90,000 square kilometres of land, including 13,000 square kilometres of subsurface oil and gas minerals. This title was formally recognized in 1984 with the signing of the Inuvialuit Final Agreement (IFA) and the passage by the Canadian

* Chairman, Inuvialuit Regional Corporation, Inuvik, Northwest Territories.

Parliament of the *Western Arctic Settlement Act*. The Act is also protected under the Canadian Constitution. Practically, this means that the IFA cannot be changed by Parliament without the approval of the Inuvialuit.

Since our claims settlement was enacted, it has made us the largest landholder in North America. It is important to note that this will soon be assumed by the Inuit of the Eastern Arctic with the passage of the Tungavik Federation of Nunavut claim through Parliament. Our claim has given us complete control over industrial activity on private lands and permits us to continue traditional activities without interference. The IFA also granted us financial compensation and special rights and benefits, such as exclusive opportunities for wildlife harvesting and the mandatory review of development projects. The IFA provides for cash payments of $170 million to the Inuvialuit on a scheduled basis until 1997.

The IFA

The IFA was signed after 10 years of negotiations. The impetus for reaching an agreement was the resource development pressures we were facing on our lands in our Settlement Region.

The Mackenzie Delta and the Beaufort Sea are areas of important oil and gas potential. In the mid-1960s many large oil companies conducted exploration programs. These programs were undertaken with very little regard for protection of the environment, wildlife and our traditional hunting, trapping and fishing lifestyle. The oil companies generally provided no compensation for the disruption that they caused. It was very evident that the oil industry did not recognize our ownership of land and resources. However, we had never signed a treaty or an agreement surrendering ownership of our lands to Canada.

In 1974 we entered negotiations to address and resolve this matter. The world we Inuvialuit live in today has been dramatically shaped by those 10 years of negotiations.

IFA Institutions

In order to manage the IFA, various functional institutions and corporate structures were created. These mechanisms enable Inuvialuit to capitalize on preserving our heritage moneys while creating employment, training and business opportunities for our people.

We have established a Land Corporation to hold title to our lands; an Investment Corporation conservatively to manage the majority of the claims capital; a Development Corporation and a Petroleum Corporation to develop aggressively and expand Inuvialuit business operations; and the Inuvialuit Social Development Program generally to improve the health, housing, education and standard of living of Inuvialuit.

All of these corporations are subsidiaries of and report to the Inuvialuit Regional Corporation (IRC). The IRC is directly controlled by the Inuvialuit beneficiaries through democratically held elections.

IFA Objectives

In negotiating our claim, we borrowed from the experiences of other Aboriginal groups. Based on our examination of Alaskan and Quebec claims and our own cultural values and aspirations, we have guided our efforts and implementation of the IFA according to several key objectives:

- protection of our wildlife, environment and traditional hunting lifestyle;
- complete control over the lands we own;
- creation of institutions and corporate structures that are self-sustaining and independent of government;
- investment of Inuvialuit capital in profitable corporations.

With these objectives we are pursuing a development path that is sustainable, one that balances and maintains the integrity between development and our environment; one that is outward looking and global in orientation, while maintaining a "laser-like focus on *our* economy", as President Clinton put it, through initiatives to diversify and stabilize our regional economic base, and provide new and enhanced employment, training and small business opportunities for Inuvialuit.

We are implementing our land claims settlement with a view to passing on the social and economic benefits that return from our development initiatives, wherever they occur, to our beneficiaries, the vast majority of whom wish to live and work and raise their families in the Inuvialuit Settlement Region.

The IFA and Beyond

As I have said, it took us 10 years to negotiate our land claim agreement. Next year, we will have had 10 years of experience in implementing it. The certainty that the IFA has brought to our region has allowed us, in no small part, to focus on our social and economic development. Although the work of implementing the IFA has carried its own unique and often frustrating challenges – and I will refer to some of them later – it has allowed us to define and build new public and private sector relationships.

For example the IFA has redefined our relationship with government and industry in many areas from co-operation and participation agreements to wildlife co-management bodies and environmental review processes. It has been an important vehicle for responsible economic development in our region, and a means for the Inuvialuit, industry and government to work toward a better economic future for Inuvialuit, as well as other northerners and Canadians.

At the same time, and I emphasize, the IFA is not the only vehicle available to us, nor the only one that we have used. We have used it as a basis from which to work, a point of departure, but have travelled far beyond its own provisions. Both the IFA and the Inuvialuit Settlement Region are not adequate in and of themselves to guarantee our future economic well-being and healthy wildlife populations for our people. We have reached out to new opportunities, partnerships and resources that are far from home and our land claim agreement.

Private Sector Initiatives

Our private sector initiatives provide a good demonstration of our approach. I turn briefly to some of the institutions established pursuant to the IFA and where their activities have taken us.

The Inuvialuit Investment Corporation

Consider, for example, the Inuvialuit Investment Corporation (IIC). One of our initial fundamental decisions was that the majority of our capital should be placed in secure investments. Using the services of professional managers such as Wood Gundy and Nesbitt Thompson, the IIC has established a diverse and secure portfolio in the domestic market. We currently hold investments in very stable and conservative short- and long-term securities such as treasury bills and bonds. We have also invested a very small percentage of our total capital in the equity markets.

However, to ensure that our investments and investment portfolios always provide the best returns and are protected from regional and national economic downturns, IIC has globally diversified our investments in the United States, Japan, Europe and the Asian "Tiger" markets of Hong Kong, Singapore, South Korea and Taiwan. We recently completed a major share purchase in a substantial Asian investment and finance corporation and are now one of the largest shareholders of that corporation. This investment has placed us more securely in the Asian market.

The Inuvialuit Petroleum Corporation

The Inuvialuit Petroleum Corporation (IPC) provides another example of our effort to build on but reach out beyond regional resource development opportunities.

The massive oil and gas potential of the Mackenzie Delta and the Beaufort Sea will ultimately result in the creation of a large oil and gas industry in our region. In order for the Inuvialuit to participate in these projects and take the greatest advantage of the opportunities associated with the development of our own resources, we believed that it was important for us to establish our own oil company.

With a few modest investments in the early 1980s, the Inuvialuit Petroleum Corporation began its operations. Developing and expanding our operations throughout the 1980s, we recently achieved the first major objective set forth for IPC – the creation of a 100% Inuvialuit-owned, fully functional oil and gas company. Currently producing 3,300 barrels of oil and gas per day, and actively drilling and operating a diversity of oil and gas properties in western Canada, the IPC is one of the 50 largest oil and gas companies in Canada.

Along with our work in western Canada, the IPC retains a focus on our lands in the North. Significant oil and gas reserves have been discovered on these lands near the communities of Inuvik and Tuktoyaktuk. Proven oil and gas reserves on our lands are estimated at 100 million barrels of oil and 300 billion cubic feet of gas. Put another way: the size of our lands and the amount of our petroleum resources are larger than those of Prince Edward Island and New Brunswick combined.

In 1986, we concluded an Oil and Gas Concession with Esso and its partners on the Tuktoyaktuk lands. In 1992, a similar agreement was concluded with Shell Canada for the Inuvik lands. Both provided Inuvialuit with substantial royalties and the prospect of further benefits for us.

The Inuvialuit Development Corporation

The Inuvialuit Development Corporation (IDC) was established prior to the signing of the IFA. Today it is a diversified development corporation active in transportation, real estate, manufacturing, wholesale food supply, surveying, retailing, construction and environmental services.

Again, we have established partnerships and joint ventures with interests outside of the Inuvialuit Settlement Region. For instance, the largest component of the IDC group is Norterra Incorporated. Norterra, which is 50% owned by the Inuvialuit and 50% by the Inuit of the Eastern Arctic, transports supplies and equipment into the North via the Mackenzie River and Hudson Bay. Norterra also has a trucking division, a pipeline valve manufacturing company, and the largest mobile home manufacturing company in Canada. Norterra annually achieves revenues in excess of $50 million.

The Inuvialuit have been able to use our ownership and control of land and resources in co-operation with our business corporations to advance the interests of the Inuvialuit on major government and industry projects in the Western Arctic. From 1989 to 1993, IDC has successfully completed more than $20 million worth of contracts on site construction of the North Warning System facilities for the Department of National Defence. During the past year, additional DND projects have proceeded with the very substantial involvement of IDC and other private Inuvialuit businesses.

Land Development Outside of the ISR

Notwithstanding the considerable lands the Inuvialuit hold in the Western Arctic, we have also pursued land developments in other parts of Canada. IDC's early initiatives were in land development, primarily small apartment buildings and office complexes, in our own communities.

As our experience grew, we looked beyond the Settlement Region. In 1987, we developed a commercial residential complex in Vancouver. In less than a year this project was sold at a healthy profit. Since then, we have pursued further real estate investments in New Westminster, Surrey, Port Moody and Vancouver, including the purchase of over 800 acres of undeveloped land in Nanaimo. A development plan and the first stages of an industrial subdivision have been completed in Nanaimo. It is hoped that once this project is fully developed Inuvialuit will receive substantial profits in the millions of dollars.

In addition to being attractive investments, the real estate development projects have helped us achieve the important objective of diversifying our business enterprises. Although we recognize the necessity of using our capital to support economic development in the Western Arctic, it has been equally important to ensure that our investments are profitable, protected and secure.

Wildlife Institutions

It has also been important to us to ensure that wildlife is conserved and our environment protected. Although many Inuvialuit are wage earners and owners of small businesses, virtually all of us continue to hunt and fish. We believe that our own future well-being is inseparable from the health of the land and its wildlife.

The Inuvialuit Game Council was established in 1979 in anticipation of the IFA to represent the collective Inuvialuit interests in wildlife. With representatives elected from each of our communities, the Game Council is the prime Inuvialuit organization for dealing with government on wildlife management plans, the designation of harvest quotas, the review of policy and legislation affecting the Inuvialuit interest in wildlife, and the presentation of Inuvialuit concerns with respect to any project or undertaking that affects our interest in wildlife and wildlife habitat.

Alongside of its recognition of the Game Council, the IFA established a system of co-operative management between Canada, the Inuvialuit and the governments of the Northwest Territories and the Yukon. This means that collectively we share equally decision-making responsibilities regarding the management of our renewable resources. Wildlife management has changed in a rather dramatic fashion since 1984 because of the IFA and other events such as the *Sparrow* case. Most wildlife managers now recognize that wildlife management is a co-operative process. This was not the case prior to the IFA when co-operative management from a government perspective meant: we'll manage, you co-operate.

International Co-operation

As with our development activities, Inuvialuit have reached beyond the Settlement Region to build partnerships and achieve agreements that will ensure our future well-being and that of our land and resources. The Settlement Region is neither an economic enclave, nor a protectorate under the watchful eye of government. Like our business activities and development initiatives, our land and wildlife are affected by decisions and events external to where we live and hunt and fish. Here as well, we have sought to exert our influence beyond the specific provisions of the IFA and the boundaries of the Settlement Region.

For example, in 1988, the Inuvialuit and the Inupiat of Alaska signed an international agreement for the management of polar bear. Developed pursuant to the International Agreement on the Conservation of Polar Bears and Their Habitat (1976), our two user groups worked together to develop a management agreement to maintain a healthy and viable population of polar bear across our shared international boundary.

Our joint Alaska-Inuvialuit beluga management plan is attempting to accomplish much the same objective for beluga whales through the self-regulation of harvesting, and conservation, protection and research guidelines.

Environmental Screening and Review

With government we also share a responsibility for screening and reviewing development projects to assess the significance and nature of their impacts on the environment, wildlife, and harvesters. This includes developments outside of the Settlement Region which could have impacts within the claims area.

The approach of the IFA-based environmental screening and review process has set a new and defensible standard for environmentally responsible development. Some of these standards have been adjusted over time in recognition of changing public expectations, comfort and confidence with respect to certain forms of development and their related impacts.

The Environmental Impact Review Board conducts public reviews of development projects. It recommends to the authorized government authority whether or not the project should proceed and, if so, under what conditions. The Review Board's hearing in 1990 on Gulf Canada Resources' application to undertake a multi-well drilling program in the Beaufort Sea was controversial because of the scope of the hearing and its outcome (the Board turned the application down).

It should be remembered that the Kulluk hearings were held shortly after the *Exxon Valdez* tanker spill. This combined with a long-standing lack of trust in the federal government's regulatory process had a significant effect on the review itself. In response to the review, the Minister of Indian Affairs and

Northern Development established a task force to review all the issues relating to government preparedness for an oil spill resulting from an oil well blowout in the Beaufort Sea. The recommendations of the Task Force, if implemented, will go a long away to establishing an improved level of public comfort for this and other similar developments in the future.

It is our view that we have built an environmental regime for development in our area which will stand as a model of certainty, fairness and effectiveness. This is good for the environment and development. It is of importance not just to the Inuvialuit, but to all northerners and Canadians.

Relationship with Government

The IFA has defined the framework and basis for a new relationship between the Inuvialuit and government. Establishing this relationship has not been easy, nor without its challenges. The IFA does not guarantee government co-operation and support. It does not dictate corporate attitudes and government behaviour. We have learned much in this area over the course of implementing our claim – most notably that the land claim in itself will not ensure successful working relationships and outcomes.

The failure of government at any level to support and work with us will seriously hamper our ability to achieve significant benefits. Even with a land claims agreement, we cannot walk alone. Like any other private corporation, we are all too aware of the serious obstacles government can pose in implementing a project that has both political and public approval. The Tuk Gas Project is a case in point.

The Tuk Gas Project

In 1986, on the basis of an independent evaluation, the federal Minister of Energy announced a $9 million contribution to assist the Inuvialuit in developing a small scale gas project for local use and benefit. The purpose of the funding was to provide a form of bridge financing that would allow a small gas project with high local value to proceed during a period of depressed world prices until such time as a healthier economic climate made the project viable.

For two years after the announcement, we attempted to negotiate a contribution agreement with the same government that promised support. We were unsuccessful. Federal civil servants negotiating the agreement effectively halted the project on the basis of three requirements that we found untenable. First, they insisted, after the fact of the Minister's announcement, that the $9 million contribution was taxable. Second, they stipulated that if the economics of the project changed, the agreement would be terminated. Third, they insisted that the Minister could ask for his contribution back at any time.

I do not know of any private company that could operate in an industry that is inherently risky under such strict and narrow conditions. On the basis of a promise of $9 million by the Government of Canada, we spent $350,000 to see the Tuk Gas Project implemented. The termination of this project as a result of bureaucratic complexities, and the imposition of unreasonable funding conditions was a serious loss to the Inuvialuit. We remain convinced that the use of the clean gas resources to supply the community of Tuk would have been a good project for the Inuvialuit and Canada. Unfortunately, at this point, there does not seem to be a viable way to launch this project.

From our point of view, the Tuk Gas Project points to the need for a more realistic appraisal by government of the terms and conditions under which northern development can proceed. It is a good example of the costs that the private sector must bear if government is not clear in its thinking and approach to economic development. It demonstrates that in the North the public sector must reconsider its role as a supporter of private initiative. If government is not prepared to share the risks of northern development in an economy substantially different from those to the south, I suggest that the growth and benefits to people outside the large city centres will be limited and frustratingly slow.

Challenges of Claims Implementation

The challenges of implementing our land claim to achieve the objectives I have referred to are a reminder that even an agreement that has been enacted by Parliament and entrenched in the Canadian Constitution cannot alone ensure future well-being. The corporate culture of government is slow to respond to the requirements for institutional reform demanded of government by our land claim agreement. Government procurement policies, bidding and tendering procedures, and policy and program reform and design often appear resistant to the requirements of the IFA. The IFA itself recognizes that "institutional prejudice" within government may be an obstacle to implementing a number of economic measures established in the agreement. It provides for a public review in the year 2000 to assess the effectiveness of government in fulfilling these provisions. This is well and good, but in the meantime the challenge of achieving these institutional changes and building a new relationship with government remains.

Global Challenges

Many of the challenges we face in the Western Arctic are the same challenges that others face across the country. They are increasingly global in nature, not regional. They force us to re-examine our place in the world as a people that has long depended on our land and resources for our social and economic well-being. We hear that Canada as a nation of "hewers of wood and drawers of water" is fast changing in response to global "mega-trends" over which we have little control.

The rapid pace of technological change, the growing importance of information technologies, increased trade in high-value goods and services and less in resources, globalization of trade and markets, attempts to reduce protectionism and trade barriers, the growth of the Asia Pacific region, the integration of Europe and North America into continental trading blocks, and Soviet disintegration – all these trends demand that we change if we wish to compete and if we wish to participate in the national and international economies.

The health of our regional economy depends to some extent on our ability to compete and participate in economies beyond the Settlement Region. Our successes in these other economies, which often takes us well beyond our land and resources, also provides us with the means to build and invest profitably in our regional economy. For instance, our significant investment in major commercial renewable resource projects in the Western Arctic and our knowledge of markets as far away as Japan and Germany are very much tied to our development and investment initiatives and returns in other parts of Canada and the world.

Ownership of Land and Investment in People

Our ownership and management of land and resources in the Inuvialuit Settlement Region have given us a good foundation from which to build our regional economy and promise a stable economic future to our children. We are well prepared to take advantage of new resource development projects in our region. But land and resources alone, like our land claim agreement, will not guarantee this future.

We recognize that to take maximum advantage of these opportunities, we need to continue to make a tremendous investment in the education and training of our people. Without new and improved skills and knowledge, our ability to participate and compete in the national and international economies will be as limited as our ability to start new businesses and reap maximum advantage of regional employment opportunities and benefits.

A healthy stable economy depends on the sustainable use of land and resources. It also depends on the capacity of people to participate fully and freely in it, if it is to be more than an "economy in waiting." The training and education of our people are likely the most difficult challenges we will face, and will ultimately be the true measure of our success in implementing our land claims agreement and moving beyond it.

Historical Use of Land and Resources

*Lester Lafond**

The Pre-Reserve Period

Pre-European Era

For thousands of years, Aboriginal peoples were the sole occupants of the vast lands now known as the continent of North America. This immense land base provided a full range of climatic zones and an abundance of aquatic, wildlife and vegetation resources.

Survival was largely governed by the laws of nature. Although resources were abundant in many areas, the harsh environment, disease, poor diet and predators all contributed to maintaining a natural balance between man and his environment.

The economy of Aboriginal peoples has appropriately been described as "traditional"; that is, the economy was based upon the land and its capacity to provide a continuous supply of natural, renewable resources. The variety and abundance of the resource provided a degree of self-sufficiency, so that people were able to provide for their basic needs such as food, clothing, shelter, warmth, and safety.

Although some Aboriginal peoples developed sophisticated agricultural skills, others resorted to a nomadic existence to assure the replenishment of scarce

---

* P.M. Associates Ltd.

resources and to provide for the variety of raw materials required to fulfil their basic needs. Small communities or bands offered a degree of collective protection and allowed for some division of labour as well as for the pusuit of social, cultural and spiritual interaction. The size of these bands was a function of the productive capacity of the lands within their control. Where appropriate, trade occurred between the groups to balance resource inequities. This was a simple existence based upon the natural food cycle. Man lived in harmony with his surroundings, not in domination of them. The laws of nature prevailed, and even though it was a harsh existence, it did provide the basis for self-sufficiency.

This early existence offers considerable insight into the current economic problems facing Canada's Aboriginal peoples. Although much has changed over the past 500 years, there remains a strong cultural and spiritual link with the traditional ways of the past.

Post-European Era

Prior to the arrival of the explorers and settlers, the First Nations and Inuit were a self-sufficient people, their well-being predicated on these basic principles:

- A "traditional" economy founded on the sustainable use of a natural and renewable resource base – simply put, the collective activities of hunting, fishing, trapping, and gathering. This also included limited agricultural activity (cultivation, livestock domestication) and some trade. For the most part, this early economy provided for a collective self-sufficiency evidenced by the survival and growth of Aboriginal peoples.
- A "nomadic" existence necessitated by the need to seek new resources and to allow for the natural replenishment of those left behind. The laws of nature prevailed and man was not excluded from its harsh judgements.
- The concept of "land ownership" was foreign to these early people. The lands could not be owned but were provided for the collective use and benefit of all living creatures. There was a natural order, a harmony between all living things, what is now referred to as the "balance of nature."
- A total "dependency" on the land. Land was not a mere commodity, it was a gift from the Creator. It has, and will always have, a special and distinct place in the cultural, spiritual and economic well-being of the Aboriginal peoples.

In the early days of the explorers, there was little change from that which prevailed for centuries before. The visitors were few in number and more of a curiosity than a threat.

In the time before active settlement, exploratory visits turned to exploitation of land and sea resources. The material-based economies of Europe were driven by the need for ever-increasing goods and services to support their growing and urbanized populations. In addition, there was a new emphasis on wealth accumulation, made possible through trade with Indigenous trading partners in the New World.

The European traders instituted some fundamental changes in the traditional ways of life. New health problems arose with the introduction of new diseases and unfamiliar foods and beverages. The Aboriginal peoples were introduced to new cultures and religions that would eventually impose their dominant influence, with a view to eradicating the Aboriginal way of life. Lastly, the traders paved the way for a new economic order. They introduced production economics, encouraging the local population to exploit the resources in exchange for highly valued, mass-produced goods. This was the first step away from the traditional lifestyle, creating a new dependency on an array of products external to the natural environment.

As settlement advanced, the bands were forced to give up ever-increasing tracts of productive land. The migration patterns were altered, and, as the population density increased, food and other raw material shortages resulted. As access to the resources diminished, Aboriginal populations declined in numbers. In time, however, Aboriginal people began to adopt the agriculture practices of the new settlers in order to enhance the productivity of an ever smaller land base. With the introduction of this new technology came more permanent residence and a resignation to the new order.

The Post-Reserve Period

The Early Years

In the latter part of the nineteenth century and into the twentieth, the newly formed Dominion of Canada pursued treaties with the Aboriginal peoples, establishing the current reserve system. The intent and interpretation of the treaties is the subject of considerable debate, but it is safe to say that the two parties were not of the same mind when the agreements were executed. The concept of land ownership was the essential issue, and the intent of the new government was to extinguish Aboriginal title to the land so that settlement and other forms of development could take place. This ownership concept was foreign to the Aboriginal people, their perception being more a sharing of the lands with the newly arriving settlers.

While the rapid depletion of the buffalo caused widespread starvation on the prairies, a degree of self-sufficiency was maintained in the more remote areas. The bands were small and much of the country was sparsely populated. The traditional endeavours, combined with new agricultural practices, offered a means of survival for these small communities. However, the treaties, combined with new unilateral legislation, imposed considerable restrictions on Aboriginal activity, particularly in the economic arena. These external impositions would contribute to the deterioration of the reserve economies and an ever-increasing dependency on government support.

The Homestead Years

By the turn of the century, immigration was showing signs of growth, with particular emphasis on settlement in the rural areas. The influx of new immigrants further reduced access to the lands surrounding reserves, removing the last vestiges of mobility and all but ending the traditionally based economies, excepting those in the most remote areas.

Along with mass immigration came the agricultural revolution. Mechanized farming, combined with new production technologies, forever changed the rural landscape. In addition, new technologies increased the use of other renewable resources including fishing, forestry and wildlife. At the outset, the Aboriginal people readily adapted to these new technologies and, during the early decades of the twentieth century, many bands were able to maintain living standards similar to those of the new arrivals.

As technology advanced, however, the need for new skills and higher levels of investment increased. The lack of education infrastructure and the limited access to financial resources sealed the fate of these communities. In a few short decades, these self-sufficient and independent peoples became totally reliant on a new economic order based on transfer payments and other non-productive income sources.

Current Situation

Canada's reserve economies are in ruin. In general, these communities suffer from excessive levels of poverty and unemployment, their well-being dependent on welfare, unemployment payments and other transfers from government. Education and skill levels are low and social problems are abundant.

A current indication of the economic self-sufficiency of reserve economies might employ a measure of trade balance; that is, the net monetary flow between one jurisdiction and all others. With the exception of the resource-rich reserves, these communities are largely net importers of goods and services and, for the most part, have little in the way of exports, except for some limited primary production associated with their lands and the surrounding resources.

The producing capacity of the existing reserve lands is limited and cannot support the ever-increasing levels of population. The current resource base provides some potential for agriculture, forestry, and trapping but, with the exception of a few communities blessed with access to abundant, high value resources, the majority of these communities must seek alternative means to develop their economic futures. The options are simple:

- Maintain the status quo.
- Relocate to non-reserve communities.
- Re-structure the reserve economies.

In the past, the first two options have prevailed, although governments have expended considerable effort to promote new economic activity in reserve communities. The successes are few and the initiatives have had limited impact on improving the well-being of these communities. The efforts have focused on the service sector, with little in the way of new investment aimed at wealth creation and employment generation founded on real value added exports.

What can be done to change this situation? If anything has been learned, it is that short-term, piecemeal approaches don't work. There is no single answer, but to understand the traditional ways and to recognize the realities of the current situation can provide some direction, even though the potential solutions may be limited and long-term in nature.

The current situation is typified by an isolation from the mainstream of the Canadian economy. The legislative constraints arising from the *Indian Act* that restrict enterprise in reserve communities are not well understood by the non-Aboriginal business community. To add to this, the cultural and economic shock imposed on the Aboriginal people forced them to seek sanctuary, and the reserves provided the only safe haven to maintain the last vestiges of their cultural and spiritual traditions.

The isolation period is coming to an end, and the reserve communities are seeking new economic initiatives to improve their way of life. Apart from this, the non-Aboriginal business community has taken an ever-increasing interest in the market and resource potential of these communities, which have been enhanced by land claim and treaty settlements.

The reserves exist within a complex and advanced consumer-based economy which is highly competitive and profit-motivated. Every jurisdiction competes for new investment and value added opportunities, and each attempts to attract new ventures by creating and promoting unique, competitive advantages which are attractive to investors and business operators alike. Encouraging conventional investment and business development within the reserve communities will necessitate the identification, development and promotion of realizable competitive benefits, while at the same time affecting a change in perceptions arising from the long period of economic and cultural isolation.

Potential Solutions

This paper will discuss land and resource base issues with a view to building new economies in the Aboriginal community. The development of new ventures in a highly competitive environment is a difficult task at best, and the Aboriginal communities are further burdened with low levels of skills development, minimal management capacity, inadequate infrastructure, limited access to financial resources and a unique jurisdictional situation that is not well defined and very much misunderstood by the non-Aboriginal community.

This does not present a pretty picture, but there are some innovative ways to address these problems so as to create new opportunities and to provide the necessary elements for profitable business development.

Jurisdiction – The Competitive Advantage

The special status afforded reserves has historically had a negative impact on the economic development process. Restrictions on land tenure and security for loans have severely limited the potential for development.

The existing legislation affecting reserves may well provide for some unique and advantageous opportunities. Much work is now being done in the area of taxation, and this area provides the basis to effect a real competitive advantage. New policy and legislative changes will be required, but the existence of distinct and definable geographic areas provides the basis for the creation of incentives to encourage investment, offset development costs, and reduce business risks, both real and perceived:

- Current taxation practices can provide benefits to investors. Properly structured, there are legal avenues that can reduce the tax burden on non-Aboriginal investors but they are complicated and, more important, they are perceived to be short-term and subject to question by Revenue Canada.
- To induce investment/lending on reserves by way of tax incentives may well be more effective than the limited and restrictive implementation of government programs. At a minimum, it could support such programming and would certainly be more cost-effective than the current dependence on transfer payments.

It is possible to provide appropriate incentives to encourage external investment in reserve communities. Options range from more liberal zoning laws to the provision of special tax incentives for investment, lending, employment creation and the like. There is little doubt that a competitive advantage can be created, but appropriate measures are required to assure its effectiveness:

- Suitable policy and/or legislation is required that would clearly outline the incentives and guarantee their enforcement and continuity. Ideally this would take the form of providing full jurisdiction over all taxation matters to First Nations, but in the interim it could be implemented through amendments to existing tax legislation.
- The First Nations must provide appropriate and enforceable legislation to secure the confidence of investors with respect to access, use and securability of lands and assets.

The issue of jurisdiction is fundamental to the creation of new opportunities. It provides the basis for new legislation to induce and secure investment in new, value added industries which can generate new wealth through increased export sales. The concepts are not new in Canadian tax legislation; governments have used such incentives to induce investment in housing, research, resource exploration and the like. Given a clear and definable geographic location, it is possible to introduce appropriate mechanisms to induce equity/debt investment in these communities. No doubt, there is risk and cost associated with investment in under-developed communities but, in the long run, it is a far more active approach than the current transfer payment system.

Integration – Toward a Complete Economy

Given the current legislation and investment limitations, it is difficult to move beyond primary producing enterprises. In recent years, there have been land designations to effect new financing and development, but the cases are few and the process of implementation onerous. This is further compounded by the traditional association to the land; there is an inherent fear of alienation from the land and a mistrust of the *Indian Act* and its intent.

With the exception of a small number of resource-rich reserves, most communities are rural-based with a limited primary production capacity. The expectations associated with these resources are far beyond the capacities, so new initiatives are required to enhance economic development. The traditional economy gave way to the primary production-based economy, but this alone cannot provide for sufficient levels of activity to support ever-growing populations. The achievement of some degree of self-sufficiency can only come from new value added activity, the creation of new opportunities to use the human resource potential within these communities.

In our ever-expanding global market, one jurisdiction can import raw materials, provide value added services and export the same to distant market places. To be successful at this endeavour requires the mobilization of capital, human resources and technology such that the process and/or product achieves some competitive advantage over that accruing to other jurisdictions. On a status quo basis, Aboriginal communities will have some difficulty competing with their more developed non-reserve counterparts, thus incentives are required to induce new activity. Given the appropriate environment, Aboriginal communities can develop new manufacturing and processing employment opportunities, independent of the quantity and quality of their primary resource base.

Joint Ventures – a Partnering Approach

Each business venture is founded on some common elements, although the importance of each will vary with the enterprise:

- an opportunity;
- financial resources;
- management input;
- product, technology and/or a resource base;

- labour skills;
- marketing/distribution channels;
- special considerations.

Any organization can assess its relative strengths and weaknesses in each of these areas and, having done so, can elect to proceed as follows:

- maintain the status quo and attempt to strengthen its position by building from within;
- join forces with other parties whereby each complements the resources of the other.

Why would First Nations want to pursue a partnering arrangement? Obviously, any organization with the capacity to provide for all the requirements of an enterprise has no need for a partnering arrangement. On the other hand, where parties can complement each other's resources and/or bring other unique considerations to the table, it offers an opportunity to strengthen a business venture that might otherwise be of questionable viability.

Let us review some possible cases:

- The simplest situation exists when one organization has all the requirements except sufficient financial resources to fulfil its growth objectives. Such a firm would likely seek a financial partner, either on a short- or long-term basis. In turn, there are individuals and/or organizations that have financial resources but no other inputs, and these entities seek organizations in need of funds in return for potential profits.
- An Aboriginal community might well have labour resources, natural resources and/or other special considerations that are generally unavailable in other jurisdictions. These may well complement the resources of another organization which has financial, management, marketing and technological capacity.
- Many Aboriginal communities have unique locations for markets but lack other capacities to gain access to them. This may well provide the basis for partnering opportunities.

There are a variety of reasons to join forces, the most obvious being the mutual benefit accruing from an identified opportunity. This in itself forms the basis for a partnering arrangement, but, more specifically, the parties join forces because individually they do not have the capacity to exploit the opportunity.

- They may come together to increase their financial strength through increasing equity, borrowing power and/or bonding capacity.
- They may co-venture to provide management capacity which is unavailable to one or more of the parties.
- Parties often unite to combine and/or share individual strengths in the areas of product development, production technology, research and development, marketing, labour resources, tax advantages, natural resources, distribution

systems and the like.

- Combining knowledge, resources and other inputs may well allow for much needed diversification and/or improved economies of scale.
- Partnering may well enhance the benefits associated with government purchasing policies.

Generally, a combination of factors is involved, but a workable arrangement can only be achieved where the contribution of each party complements that of the others and therefore strengthens the new venture.

The strengths of individual reserves will vary, as will the opportunities. Where high value resources are available the options are more apparent, but the provision of special jurisdictional incentives will provide all Aboriginal communities with the much needed competitive position to attract those resources required to achieve their development goals.

Land Entitlement – The Urban Option

Recent settlements have precipitated new land additions, and some selections have been made in urban locations. This provides new access to large markets and further increases the potential for joint venture arrangements.

Over the years, the Aboriginal populations in Canada's urban areas have been increasing. Urban reserves provide an excellent opportunity to attract and develop Aboriginal-owned enterprises while retaining the jurisdictional benefits afforded these lands.

With recent taxation rulings, the value of such locations might well provide for unique tax-exempt zones with exclusive market rights to urban Aboriginal populations. The creation of this market niche acts much like an anchor tenant; it provides the necessary traffic to attract additional enterprises seeking access to growing markets, special tax concessions and a work force motivated by exemptions not available in adjacent jurisdictions. In addition, these commercial activities can provide new tax revenue opportunities for First Nations.

Métis Lands and Resources

*Clem Chartier**

The Importance of Land for Indigenous Peoples

For Indigenous peoples' continued existence – throughout the world – land is a prerequisite. It is essential because Indigenous peoples are inextricably related to land: it sustains our spirits and bodies; it determines how our societies develop and operate based on available environmental and natural resources; and our socialization and governance flow from this intimate relationship. Because of that intimate relationship, the land is rendered inalienable: it is a natural right, a right essential for the continued vitality of the physical, spiritual, socio-economic and political life and survival of the Indigenous peoples for generations to come.

Lands Historically Occupied by the Métis

The Métis – descendants primarily of the Cree, Dene and Ojibwa nations – are geographically located in western Canada, with the southern portion of the traditional Métis homeland extending into part of the northern United States. Although it is a separate and distinct Indigenous nation, the Métis nation evolved with close ties to the Cree, Dene and Ojibwa. The central economic activity around which this distinct community of people developed was the fur

* Métis Society of Saskatchewan.

trade. As a consequence, Métis communities grew along the fur trade and freighting routes in the Northwest, as far north as the Mackenzie River.

During the early years of the fur trade, the Métis readily adapted, and thus economic, social and religious institutions grew in those communities. After 1750, the Métis became a dominant force in the fur trade, as well as in the social and political life of the Northwest. By the late 1790s there were approximately 10,000 Métis.

By the late 1700s a small number of Métis settled on river lots along the Red River. After 1821, a steady stream of Métis arrived at the Red River community from all parts of the Northwest. Consequently, Red River became the economic, cultural and educational centre for the Métis Nation.

When Great Britain transferred Rupert's Land and the Northwest Territories from the Hudson's Bay Company to Canada in 1869, the Métis objected, invoking nationhood status and rights as a people indigenous to the land. They again invoked nationhood status and Indigenous rights at Batoche in 1885, and we are empowered today by those same rights.

Summary of the Recognition of Métis Lands

Manitoba

With the formation of the 1869 Red River provisional government, the Métis expressed inherent and national rights to land and government. The Government of Canada, consequently, negotiated the terms of the Métis Nation's entry into Confederation. The result of these negotiations led to the *Manitoba Act, 1870* which provided for the admission of Manitoba as a province into Confederation. The Métis view this agreement and Act as a solemn and binding treaty with the Canadian government.

Although they wanted to retain ownership and control of public lands, Métis negotiators were convinced the Dominion would maintain ownership in order to generate financing and resourcing necessary for settlement and commerce in the West. However, Métis negotiators were assured that a portion of the land to be included in the new province would be left in Métis ownership.

The result was section 31 which provided that 1.4 million acres of land be set aside for the Métis toward the extinguishment of their Indian title. Lands were to be distributed to the children of the Métis (half-breed) heads of families. It also provided that the Governor General in Council grant lands to the children in "such mode and on such conditions as to settlement," as determined from time to time.

> S. 31 And whereas, it is expedient, towards the extinguishment of the Indian title to the lands in the province, to appropriate a portion of such ungranted lands, to the extent of one million four hundred thousand acres thereof, for the benefit of the families of the half-breed residents, it is hereby enacted, that under regulations to be from time to time made by the Governor General in Council, the Lieutenant Governor shall select such lots or tracts in such parts of the province as he may deem expedient, to the extent aforesaid, and divide the same along the children of the half-breed heads of families residing in the province at the time of the said transfer to Canada, and the same shall be granted to the said children respectively, in such mode and on such conditions as to settlement and otherwise, as the Governor General in Council may from time to time determine.

The negotiators were assured that that provision had the same effect as the previous agreement which provided them with ownership of some of the public lands that were to be included within the new province.

In addition to section 31, section 32 provided that the people currently holding freehold or less than freehold lands would have their ownership confirmed. This meant that the Métis – who made up approximately 85% of the population in Manitoba – would have their river lot ownership guaranteed because section 32 provided for occupancy and peaceable possession of lands.

Because it was uncertain whether the new Canadian government could pass legislation to create new provinces out of newly acquired territory, Prime Minister John A. Macdonald referred that matter, as well as ratification of the *Manitoba Act, 1870* to the British Parliament. Thus, the British Parliament enacted the *British North America Act, 1871* which confirmed the *Manitoba Act, 1870* and by section 6 provided that neither Parliament nor the provincial government of Manitoba could unilaterally make amendments to the Act, thereby protecting the land rights of the Métis recognized therein.

The Northwest Territories

After 1870 there was a major dispersal of Métis from Manitoba to communities in other parts of the Northwest, and a series of petitions emerged requesting the government to recognize their rights.

As a result of Métis political activity and the desire of the government to populate the West with non-Aboriginal people, the government included a provision in the *Dominion Lands Act, 1879* which granted lands in extinguishment of their Indian title.

> S. 125 The following powers are hereby delegated to the Governor in Council...
>
> e. To satisfy any claims existing in connection with the extinguishment of the Indian title preferred by half-breeds resident in the Northwest Territories outside of the limits of Manitoba, on the fifteenth day of July, one thousand eight hundred and seventy, by granting land to such persons, to such extent and on such terms and conditions as may be deemed expedient...

No action was taken on that provision and in 1883 the section was amended to extend the recognition of the right to Métis living outside Manitoba, "previous" to July 15, 1870 as opposed to "on" the 15th day of July 1870.

> S. 81 The following powers are hereby delegated to the Governor in Council...
>
> e. To satisfy any claims existing in connection with the extinguishment of the Indian title, preferred by half-breeds resident in the Northwest Territories outside of the limits of Manitoba, previous to the fifteenth day of July, one thousand eight hundred and seventy, by granting land to such persons, to such extent and on such terms and conditions as my be deemed expedient...

These two sections clearly recognize Indian title rights of the Métis. In 1885 action on these provisions finally materialized when the Métis engaged in armed resistance in response to the loss of their rights and lands.

Although there was clear recognition of the Métis right to land, the federal government did not safeguard or protect Métis land rights. The federal government, in fact, acted in a manner that ensured the divesting of Métis land, although it had a fiduciary obligation by virtue of the 1763 Royal Proclamation, sections 91(24) and 146 of the *Constitution Act, 1867* and section 31 of the *Manitoba Act, 1870.*

Summary of the Methods of Allocation of Métis Lands

Manitoba

The *Manitoba Act* provided for three kinds of land grants:

- the "half-breed" reserves for children;
- title for the "half-breeds" to river lots and other lands of which they were in possession and on which they resided; and
- the settlement of common land rights.

Contrary to the recognition of rights in the *Manitoba Act*, government officials began analyzing sections which resulted in both federal and provincial legislation setting out a self-serving implementation process. Subsequent legislation, regulations and orders in council reflect the government's hidden agenda, which included divesting the Métis of their lands as quickly as possible.

According to government opinion, the only persons eligible for participating in the 1.4 million acres were Métis children under 21 years of age on July 15, 1870. Because of that interpretation, the federal government passed subsequent legislation providing for the allocation of scrip to so-called half-breed heads of families who were excluded.

Rather than lands set aside in large tracts and made inalienable – until at least the third generation – as requested by the Métis, the government issued land in fee simple, individual ownership. Once accomplished, the government knew it meant immediate loss of lands by the Métis.

In an effort to distribute land, a census was taken in 1871 which resulted in a determination that each allottee would be eligible for 190 acres. However, with the 1874 change of government the process had to start all over again.

A new census specified that each child would be eligible for 240 acres. Land allotments then commenced around existing parishes, and after another change of government in 1878 the remaining allotments were made by the issuance of scrip. Money scrip was issued in $20 denominations redeemable by the bearer for any open dominion lands in Manitoba.

With respect to the section 32 river lots, before the land patents could be issued, the lot had to be surveyed. However, government policy allowed surveys to cut across the river lot system in conformity with the federal survey system. As a result, many Métis lost parts of their lots or had them divided and allocated to others.

With reference to common lands – the two miles behind the river lots – government policy rejected Métis rights and encouraged settlers to take possession. After a Commission examined that issue, it was recommended that scrip for $160 be issued to the occupants of the adjacent river lots for the loss of the common lands. These lands were used primarily for haying and as a source of firewood.

The Northwest

Through legislation and subsequent regulations and orders in council, the federal government embarked on a unilateral course of action which involved issuing of scrip to the Métis. This unilateral activity ignored all constitutional rights, equitable procedures, and principles which were meant to govern Canada's dealings with the Aboriginal peoples, including the provisions contained in the

Royal Proclamation of 1763 and incorporated within section 146 of the *Constitution Act, 1867*.

Based on the Manitoba experience, the federal government avoided use of land reserves in distributing land to the Métis. This was done even though some Métis petitions specifically requested a land reserve distribution process.

Throughout the Northwest, money scrip – the issuance of a bearer bond specifying a set amount of money exchangeable for only the purchase of open dominion Crown land – became the preferred method of land distribution (at that time Crown land was worth $1 an acre). Based on that preferred method, the initial orders in council directed the 1885 scrip issue be money scrip. Money scrip was popular with land speculators because it ensured a quick method of passing Métis land entitlement to other persons.

The Métis in the Qu'Appelle Lakes area, however, refused to accept money scrip. As a result the order in council was amended to provide a choice between land scrip or money scrip. Several hundred orders in council followed which dealt with the issuance of scrip provisions, establishment of Half-breed Commissions, reviewing of individual cases, special classes of cases and provisions for regulations governing the process for issuance of scrip and its use.

The major orders in council in 1885, 1898, 1900, 1904, 1906 and 1921 provided for issuance of scrip in areas where treaties had been entered into with Indian Nations, or were about to be entered into.

The method of distributing scrip was through appointed Commissioners who dealt solely with the Métis; however, starting with Treaty 8, the Commissioners dealt with the Métis and Indians at the same time.

Summary of the History of Métis Lands

Manitoba

Métis lands were quickly lost as a result of the influx of settlers which had been part of the federal government's hidden agenda when it negotiated the entry of the Métis into Canada. The Métis' provincial status when joining Confederation marked the only time Indigenous peoples entered into a nation-to-nation arrangement, based on what is now known as non-ethnic government. The Métis felt comfortable with this kind of arrangement because they made up about 85% of the population.

Shortly after the Terms of Union – as reflected in the *Manitoba Act* – became operational and legally binding, the federal government sent troops to Manitoba. Ostensibly for the added protection and security of the new province, the troops became an occupation force which facilitated Canada's dispossession of Métis land and government.

As a consequence, a virtual state of lawlessness developed, coupled with physical and psychological terrorism. The subsequent racism and adverse government rulings prompted many, particularly the seasonal inhabitants, to leave Manitoba lands. Those Métis headed west where they were able to maintain their lifestyle and be among friends and relatives.

Speculators, encouraged to buy Métis lands very cheaply, played a very significant role in the loss of Métis lands. In addition, fraudulent methods were used to obtain scrip in the name of persons who had long since left the Red River. Other irregularities in land distribution and registration occurred with the active co-operation of federal land agents and officials.

The final result of the government's application of the *Manitoba Act* was the dispersal of members from a thriving community from their homes and land.

The Northwest

Métis lands were lost primarily through the scrip system. Because of the enormity of the geographic area, as opposed to the original postage-stamp province of Manitoba, the government was encouraged to adopt other strategies. Although it still promoted settlement, large numbers of settlers were required to facilitate that objective; thus, the government encouraged the creation of land colonization companies.

In any event, the scrip system was the vehicle by which the government dispossessed Métis of lands and their right of self-government. They became a colonized people/nation, and Métis prime lands were quickly lost once the scrip system was implemented.

In northern areas where scrip was not redeemable (because the areas were not surveyed), Métis were victimized by the same fraudulent methods. However, they remained in their communities and traditional areas – carrying on their way of life – until government regulations and laws around the mid-1900s began adversely to affect their right to land use, hunting, trapping and fishing. Even today, gathering rights are seriously impaired.

As a result of the scrip imposition process – through a unilateral federal government decision – the Métis became the sole people in British North America totally dispossessed of land and, in the opinion of government, of any other rights that flow from Indian title.

The Land Situation of the Métis Today

Manitoba

Currently, the Manitoba Métis do not have a legally recognized land base. There is, however, a significant Métis population living in more than 50 communities north of the principal agricultural belt. Also, they are almost always in the majority and on average make up two-thirds of the population.

In south and mid-Manitoba, there are an estimated 10 to 20 communities with a major Métis population. Métis as a numerical minority live in numerous other rural communities, as well as in urban centres.

The Manitoba Métis still use traditional areas and other areas of access to hunt, trap, fish and gather. These activities, however, are strictly regulated by the government.

The political organization representing the Manitoba Métis is currently engaged in legal proceedings that challenge the purported extinguishment of their land rights. In addition, in a recent provincial court decision (*R* v. *McPherson and Christie*) it was held that Métis have subsistence hunting rights by virtue of section 35(1) of the *Constitution Act, 1982*. That decision is under appeal and cross-appeal.

Saskatchewan

The Métis in Saskatchewan are also without a legally recognized land base. However, in the early and mid-1900s parcels of land were set aside to train Métis in agriculture. Those lands were designated as Métis farms.

To date, the farms are under the authority of the provincial government, except for the Métis Farm at Lebret which was turned over to The Lebret Farm Land Foundation Inc. in 1987. The government maintains that the land was transferred to Métis control for economic development and because of the attachment the Lebret Métis felt toward it. According to the government, the Lebret Farm transfer was not a land claims settlement.

In respect to the Métis community of Green Lake, political and legal researchers are examining ways to return 12 townships which had originally been set aside for the Métis by order in council in the mid-1940s. Also at stake is a community sawmill, which is not operational because of the dispute over land and resources.

In northern Saskatchewan, the Métis still use land to hunt, trap, fish and gather, just as their ancestors before them. In regard to the numerous traplines that cross the North, the Saskatchewan government maintains that trappers have no rights but merely privileges which can be removed in favour of resource extraction. Fishing is subject to the same arbitrary government decisions which are slowly forcing out Métis fishermen in favour of tourism and sports fishing. Hunters' traditional areas are being closed to Métis because of the creation of parks and game preserves (including hundreds of miles of Road Corridor Game Preserves). The government has also set aside a large tract of land for military use such as bombing experiments.

Alberta

As a result of political activism in the late 1920s and 1930s, Métis in Alberta convinced the Alberta government to address the issue of Métis lands. Resulting from that political activism Métis Settlements were created: originally there were 12 but currently there are 8.

The government, when it examined the issue through the Ewing Commission, made it clear that setting aside Métis lands was only a response to social and economic problems and not based on Métis legal right to land. Nevertheless, 5,000 to 6,000 Alberta Métis are currently in possession of approximately 1.25 million acres of land.

Through the constitutional reform process, and a civil suit in Alberta, the provincial government agreed to entrench those Métis lands in the *Alberta Act*. Limited protection has thereby been achieved through the *Constitution of Alberta Amendment Act, 1990* assented to by the Alberta government on July 5, 1990. Acting under section 45 of the *Constitution Act, 1982*, the province amended its own Constitution. Once these lands are constitutionally protected by Canada, the Alberta provision will be repealed.

British Columbia

Although the traditional/historic Métis Homeland extends into northeastern British Columbia, the Commissioners did not distribute scrip in that portion of Treaty 8. As a consequence, the land rights of the Métis communities and people of that area have yet to be dealt with. Added to that, a significant number of Métis have moved to other parts of the province; their land and resource rights need to be dealt with.

Ontario

The practice of land grants and scrip allocation began in Manitoba and moved westward. However, in 1875 the half-breeds of Rainy River signed an adhesion to Treaty 3 and were allocated reserve land and treated as Indians for the purposes of the *Indian Act*.

The other half-breeds residing in the area which became part of northwestern Ontario were not dealt with as Métis. To date, no identifiable Métis land holdings remain in northwestern Ontario. It is therefore critical that land be made available to the Métis of northwestern Ontario, as well as to the Métis who have moved to parts of the rest of Ontario.

The Northwest Territories

With the signing of Treaties 8 and 11 in 1921, the Métis were each given $240.00 cash as a continuation of the 1870 so-called extinguishment of Indian title. Fortunately, the government is currently negotiating land claims agreements with both the Dene and Métis peoples within the N.W.T. A Métis land and resource base in the N.W.T. should be the result of these negotiations.

What is Meant by a Métis Land Base?

Indigenous peoples the world over had territorial lands and resources prior to their dispossession. Although dispossession occurred in every corner of the earth, some Indigenous peoples have regained their "land base" and some form of self-government or autonomy.

Reference to a "Métis Land Base" basically means returning sufficient lands and natural resources to the Métis: lands and resources that will enable our people to survive (as a distinct people) and retain our culture, traditions, customs, livelihood, languages and dignity. A land base is our inalienable, natural right as self-determining Indigenous peoples.

In this context, Article 27 of the International Covenant on Civil and Political Rights has been of limited use.

> Art. 27 In those states in which ethnic, religious or linguistic minorities exist, persons belonging to such minorities shall not be denied the right, in community with other members of their group, to enjoy their own culture, to profess and practise their own religion, or to use their own language.

By comparison, a preliminary report to the Sami Rights Committee (established by the Norway government to investigate the situation of the Indigenous Sami people) concluded that when Article 27 was applied to the Sami, it required recognition of the traditional land base because land is the material foundation of Sami culture.

In the case of Sandra Lovelace, an Indian women who lost her rights upon marriage to a non-Indian, the Human Rights Committee held that Canada violated Article 27 because Lovelace was barred from living on the reserve and Canada denied her right to enjoy her culture which was connected to the land (reserve). In this sense, Article 27 instructs governments to respect and allow minorities to enjoy their culture by group. In the case of Indigenous peoples, including the Métis, this means – as a minimum – a secured land base to which culture is inextricably tied. Because land and culture go hand in hand, denying the Métis a land base is a continued violation of international law.

What is the Purpose of a Land Base?

A Place to Live

Primarily, a land base enables Métis people/communities to exist as Indigenous people. Those lands legitimize resource use necessary to sustain a traditional way of life. Essentially, a land base provides a place for our people to live and prosper according to our own ways.

An excerpt from a September 1986 presentation to the Métis National Council General Assembly by representatives from Métis communities in northern Saskatchewan best describes the need for a land base:

> For over two hundred years now, the Métis of northern Saskatchewan have lived in harmony with our land and its resources. We have made use of the land, the trees, the wild plants, the waters, the fish and the game – taking what we needed for our livelihood. During this time we built strong values, strong families and strong communities.
>
> These communities, communities such as Ile-a-la-Crosse, were not just a small patch of land defined by some bureaucrat who defined a set of village boundaries. No, until recently Ile-a-la-Crosse was much more than that – it was much more than a few square miles of land. Ile-a-la-Crosse was, and still is, all those things which go to make up a northern Métis community – it includes the trap lines of our families – it includes the lakes and the fish which support our people – it includes the wild game which feeds our people – it includes the wild fruits which we harvest – it includes the wild rice which we harvest both commercially and for our own use – it includes the trees which we use to build our homes and which we also harvest commercially – and, most important, it includes the people and that spirit of the Métis community that can't really be described in words we learn in school.
>
> The spirit, the community soul, that probably can only really be described in Cree... This is not past. It is true that in recent years the soul of Ile-a-la-Crosse has been dimmed and the spirit of some of our people has been covered over – covered, but not lost.
>
> We are fortunate, you see, because we have not been removed from our traditions for several generations – as has happened to many of our people who have lived in the cities of the south for several generations. Many of us, who live in northern Métis communities, still make our living in the traditional ways – and

> almost all of us remember the days when we had control of our own lives, the days when we used our resources for our needs and processed these resources in our own communities. Today most of us remember, today we understand.
>
> But in two or three generations who will understand – if we don't regain control over our own lives? What will become of our people and our way of life, if governments are allowed to continue to take control of our traditional sources of livelihood, then give control of these resources to the big companies – the government power companies, the timber companies and the mining companies?
>
> What am I trying to tell you about Ile-a-la-Crosse and other Métis communities of northern Saskatchewan? I guess the most important thing I am trying to help you understand is that we are still Métis communities – Métis communities with strong and deep roots in the Métis traditions and our way of life. We have not lost our roots and our goals must be seen as a continuation of our long-standing, traditional way of life.
>
> In short, when the people of northern Métis communities talk about our goals for the Constitutional negotiations we are not talking about fine-tuning a few government programs. What we are talking about is obtaining an agreement that fully respects our right to self-determination – our right to maintain a way of life which has served our people and communities well for many generations, though we expect that we may make adjustments to the economic base of our community – our right to make our own decisions, within our own community, about those matters which affect our daily lives – in a few words, the right to control our own futures, our own destiny.

That expressed need for a land base holds equally true for all Métis people and communities in various parts of the Métis Homeland. It received unanimous support by all representatives at the Assembly who represented such Métis communities and interests.

As an Economic Resource

What about Métis who would not use land for residential purposes? Perhaps it is possible, in areas of the province where it is not feasible or possible for sufficient lands to be set aside for self-sufficient residency, that land could be acquired for economic purposes.

For example, turning over the Lebret Farm to the Métis Farm Land Foundation has economic initiatives as one of its objectives. That land base should assist the

Lebret area Métis to enter into agriculture/livestock-based activities which can generate employment and possibly revenue for programming purposes.

There are several other Métis farms and lands (Crown lands) which could be made available for this purpose. Potentially, lands in the North, not selected by Métis communities, may be negotiable and could enable Métis organizations (local/regional/provincial) to enter into land use arrangements for economic development. The specific geographic area would be set out and the land reserved for economic opportunities to the Métis signatories.

As a Symbol of Nationhood

Symbolism, standing alone, is not for the Métis people. Indeed, there can be no substitute for the return of sufficient Métis lands as a place to live and be self-sufficient.

However, not all Métis can be accommodated under present circumstances, particularly in the southern parts of Canada. Nevertheless, there has been expressed desire for some identifiable territory or land for the Métis Homeland. Thus, it has been decided that the Métis must have ownership of land at Batoche, Saskatchewan, which symbolizes the last major Métis resistance and is a sacred shrine to Métis martyrdom. Over the past century, the Métis continued that association with Batoche and have thus maintained a strong spiritual, cultural and national affinity. The people now aspire to develop a Métis cultural/political centre at Batoche. It is envisaged that future Métis Nation governing assemblies will take place at Batoche.

Methods of Acquiring a Land Base

At the present time the primary land acquisition method is through a comprehensive or specific land claims process. That process represents the only available forum currently provided by the federal government.

In December 1986 the Minister of Indian Affairs and Northern Development announced amendments to the comprehensive claims policy. As expected, the policy continues to exclude Métis National Council constituents (with the exception of the Métis of the N.W.T.). That exclusion, presumably, is based on the 1981 Justice department opinion which instructs that by the supremacy of Parliament, Métis title was extinguished by the land grant and scrip process.

> In outlining the new comprehensive land claims policy, I should begin by stating that the federal government remains committed to the settlement of claims in those areas of Canada where Aboriginal title based on traditional and continuing use and occupancy of the land has not been dealt with by Treaty 8 or *already superseded by law*. (Emphasis added.)

It is interesting to note that although the Task Force to Review Comprehensive Claims Policy did not recommend inclusion of the Métis, they nevertheless made passing reference to the Métis and that the injustices inflicted upon the Métis should be remedied and new relations established.

> The history and current situation of most Métis and non-status Indians is quite different from other Aboriginal peoples. With the exception of the Constitutional discussions and Alberta's provisions for Métis Settlements, most Métis and non-status Indian groups have been excluded from the processes, such as Treaty renovation and self-government negotiations with the federal government. *Therefore, a separate policy and process should be developed by the government so that Métis and non-status Indians can negotiate with the government to remedy past injustices and to establish new relations.* (Emphasis added.)

Arguably some Métis could attempt to have their right to land re-examined, based on circumstances peculiar to their area. For example, it may be possible for the Métis in the Treaty 10 area to put forward a specific claim to land on the basis that their lands could not have been retained. In their case the scrip system dictated that if they wanted to own land – according to colonial concept – they would have had to move out of their traditional lands/territory to surveyed land in southern Saskatchewan (of course, they could not do so). That avenue has not yet been pursued because the current federal position vis-à-vis the comprehensive claims process is not acceptable to the Métis.

As stated above, the Métis have generally been excluded from comprehensive claims because of the Department of Justice's legal opinion that Métis rights were extinguished. The Métis, therefore, can challenge this opinion in the courts. If the Métis pursued court action and a ruling was made in their favour, they would have a better chance to access the Comprehensive Claims Policy.

In the absence of such, the Métis (since 1982) participated in the constitutional/political process hoping to enlighten governments about Métis rights to a land base. Had the Métis been successful in having their rights constitutionally protected, the Métis could have entered into negotiations with governments for land and resource acquisition.

For the Métis those processes could take the form of tripartite discussions or negotiations, with the federal government assuming the major responsibility and role because it is the government entrusted with the trust and fiduciary responsibility for dealing with Aboriginal peoples as a matter of British and Canadian policy and law. As well, it was the federal government which was instrumental in the dispossession of the Métis from their lands. There are still federal Crown lands available in western Canada for that purpose. In any event, the federal government can assist in the purchase of lands for the Métis or compensate the provinces for loss of provincial Crown lands.

The 1992 constitutional process is a good example of how the Métis land and resource issue could begin to be resolved. Although not the perfect solution, the proposed constitutional amendment on the inherent right of self-government, coupled with the commitment to negotiate such matters as land and the proposed Métis Nation Accord, providing a Métis land claims process, would have placed the Métis on a level playing field with the other two Indigenous peoples.

The prairie provinces must also be involved because the majority of Crown lands, as of 1930, belong to the Crown in right of the province. As such, provincial Crown lands would be turned over to the Métis. The province must also be involved in the social and political process leading to acquisition of lands and/or where there are third-party interests.

The non-constitutionally based tripartite discussions now under way could lead to a number of options for land base acquisition. The first and preferred option is direct transfer of title to Métis collectives in fee simple. Safeguards, however, must be in place so that the land, whether held collectively by Métis government or by individuals, could not be lost through taxation or other legal processes.

A second option would be a combination of direct land transfers and leases, or resource use agreements on surrounding lands. These leases or agreements would address such matters as hunting, trapping, fishing, gathering and other renewable or non-renewable resource use; it could include forestry, mineral development and tourism arrangements under co-management arrangements.

A third option would see arrangements based on long-term leases without any transfer of land. The leases could be specific in nature depending on the area of implementation. For example, leases could address forestry, mineral resources and wild rice. There could also be provisions made for co-management arrangements over fisheries, trapping, hunting and tourism. This option, although it offers a form of Métis jurisdiction with respect to land use, is not the Métis' currently expressed option. As an interim measure it may have some possibilities, particularly in view of the ever-increasing encroachment of outside interests on Métis resources. Blockades against forestry companies in northwestern Saskatchewan in December 1986 and January 1987 attest to the ever-increasing encroachment.

Arguably, if the land in existing Métis communities were transferred to residents, perhaps additional options of long-term leases could be viable. However, when leases are terminated the communities may suffer severe hardships. Thus, greater safeguards are necessary. As such, options one and two remain most preferred.

A fourth option could address situations where Métis who do not live in identifiable communities want to engage in economic or resource development. For example, Métis Economic Development Corporations in mid- and southern Saskatchewan may want to engage in economic initiatives like forestry, oil and gas or tourism. Thus, those provincial areas should be identified for specific economic use and short- or long-term leases depending on the resource use, as well as the quality and quantity of resources contained in the land area under lease. Those leases would be accompanied by land or resource use agreements.

How to Establish Quantities on Land and Compensation Required

Under the scrip process, land was distributed to Métis by a pre-arranged formula. As indicated previously, 240 acres of land were allotted to each Métis person eligible to participate in the land distribution. The land, however, was issued in fee simple to individuals and did not form any kind of discernable Métis land base.

In comparison, particularly in western Canada, the treaty formula specified one square mile for every family of five or 128 acres per person. The land was collective in nature and forms the land base of current Indian reserves.

Today it is more difficult to calculate and determine a formula for lands to be returned to the Métis. Issues such as use of traditional Métis lands, as well as temporal and demographic issues, complicate and frustrate an appropriate settlement.

From a practical perspective, an enumeration of Métis must be undertaken, with particular emphasis on Métis communities seeking a land base upon which to continue living. An enumeration could lead to a tripartite process encouraging community involvement to determine necessary self-sufficient land and resources (including water). The quantum of land should therefore be determined by the number of people who would live on the land base, as well as the quality of that land.

It may also be possible to add to the land base surrounding lands upon which the Métis could have the continuing right to hunt, trap, fish and gather, and guaranteed rights to economic development like forestry, mining, tourism and other renewable and non-renewable resource initiatives. In addition, non-Aboriginal resource development agreements would provide for royalties, tax and/or resource revenue sharing to be paid to Métis governments.

Where adequate lands or resource revenue/royalty sharing is not available due to resource depletion, governments must compensate the Métis for the loss. Compensation could basically be in the form of transfer payments to Métis governments and/or economic development financing turned over to Métis Economic Development Corporations for the use of Métis beneficiaries.

In areas where land is not available and off-land based Métis self-government is established, compensation for land and resource loss could include financial resourcing of Métis government programs and services. It could also involve economic development financing, royalties, and revenue sharing from the surrounding vicinity's economic activities to that Métis government.

In circumstances where land is available for economic development purposes only, the amount of land should again be based on the number of Métis who could potentially benefit and the quality of the land to be transferred or leased to the Métis for that specific purpose.

The Relationship of Métis Government Institutions to Métis Land and Resources

To ensure that future Métis lands are not lost again, some form of land tenure/ownership must be put in place. As the Métis are also speaking of self-government, as well as the acquisition of land, the lands must be tied to Métis government bodies and institutions which will emerge.

Métis generally agree that land must be collectively held to ensure continued ownership and control. Thus, while there is a need for a provincial Métis jurisdiction to ensure Métis rights and protection for potential land loss, ownership of lands must be vested in the hands of residents.

In the case of the Métis of Saskatchewan, ownership must devolve to Métis governments and their constituents. As cited previously, that local land base will in all probability be situated in and around existing Métis communities.

Although the land would be collectively owned, provincial Métis policy could provide that each local Métis government could pass legislation or regulations. That legislation could enable individual ownership of land, on the condition that any potential future sale (at fair market value), be available only to another member of the collective or to the Métis government's land department. This ensures that land remains with Métis owners and that any investments/work by members be fairly compensated.

With respect to lands or land use set aside for Métis economic development initiatives, the provincial Métis government (organization representing the interests of the Métis province-wide) would be vested with ownership and/or control of the initiatives and utilization of the resources.

To facilitate variations that could develop, like land-holdings and land-use agreements, a provincial Métis land policy and master plan must be developed which can then be translated into future provincial Métis government legislation. That legislation would have to be general in nature and provide land/resource ownership and control by local Métis government units.

Conclusions and Options for Pursuing Métis Lands

Land Claims Process

The likelihood of Métis inclusion in the land claims process – the only tool for the extinguishment of Aboriginal title – is negligible. To date, the federal government maintains Métis Aboriginal title was extinguished and therefore have not included Métis in the revised land claims policy. This, however, does not mean that the policy should not change to specify Métis inclusion.

Arguably some Métis areas could explore potential specific claims, such as Métis in the Treaty 10 area of Saskatchewan and/or Métis in the Treaty 8 area of Northeastern British Columbia. However, this approach has been rejected because Métis participation would signify acceptance that their Aboriginal title rights were extinguished.

Court Action on Original Land Grant Provisions

The Manitoba Métis Federation is currently pursuing this option. This is a wise tactic because the majority of the Métis – as represented by the Métis National Council – are pursuing a political solution through the constitutional process. A positive ruling in favour of the Métis would greatly enhance our bargaining position at the constitution-related tables, including the existing tripartite processes. On the other hand, a negative ruling shouldn't harm our political agenda as we are approaching it from a forward-looking position which could only benefit both the Métis and Canadians generally.

The other members of the MNC could entertain the possibility of using the courts under section 35 of the Constitution in the event that we fail in the constitution/political processes. Success in the courts could open the door for us to the Land Claims Process described above.

A Court Reference to Determine which Level of Government has Jurisdiction or Responsibility for the Métis and Whether this Responsibility, if in the Nature of a Fiduciary Duty (Trust), was Adequately Discharged

At the present time we can arguably maintain that the federal government under section 91(24) of the *Constitution Act, 1867* has the jurisdiction and its corresponding responsibility to deal in a fair and reasonable manner with the Métis. Indeed, the federal government has a trust and/or fiduciary duty to safeguard the land rights of the Métis. Added to that, rather than protect the Métis interest vis-à-vis Métis lands, the government callously paved the way for the dispossession of the Métis from their lands. That fiduciary duty was also breached with respect to their obligation as provided for by section 31 of the *Manitoba Act, 1870*. Successful court action would encourage access to the land claims process, especially with the fiduciary breach on the part of the federal government and would be helpful with a section 35 legal battle, if we must engage in it. Otherwise, within the constitutional or tripartite processes, we should be able to move forward with negotiations once we get beyond the impasse created by the jurisdiction and responsibility issues.

Constitutional Amendment (New Constitutional Provisions)

The Métis National Council has always maintained that its primary existence is to facilitate the entrenchment of a Métis Nation land base and self-government. The Métis have engaged in this process and continue to negotiate the recognition of the right to a land base through the political process.

The MNC has consistently argued that the specific right to land must be made as an amendment to the Constitution, in addition to the self-government amendment. The two rights are interrelated and in the ongoing negotiations under the general rubric of self-government, the location, quantity and quality of land and resources would be negotiated, not the right itself, which will already be recognized and entrenched. Although the 1992 proposed amendments did not fully accommodate this, it came sufficiently close to enabling the Métis leadership to endorse the Charlottetown Accord.

Although the section 38 amendment process is not available at this time, this does not foreclose the potential of section 43 or section 45 amendments to the Constitution, particularly as they relate solely to the Métis Nation. Under that approach, an amendment could be made for the whole of the Métis Nation, or by province, such as in the case of entrenchment of Métis lands in the province of Alberta by amending the *Alberta Act*. If this can be done for language rights in New Brunswick, why cannot the same approach be used for Métis Nation rights in one or more provinces, given that it would not affect all provinces?

By Political Agreement

Tripartite Agreements

In the absence of the constitutional process, it is possible for negotiated movement on Métis rights to take place. As was agreed to in 1985, tripartite negotiations between the federal government, relevant provinces, and the Métis provide an opportunity to develop concrete examples of what is meant by Métis self-government, as well as address land issues specific to self-government and/or economic development.

The current process involves a province-by-province approach. However, there is nothing preventing a Métis Nation approach, as reflected in the draft 1992

Métis Nation Accord. (All that is required is the adoption of a new title, along with removal of references to constitutional amendments.) By taking that approach, it should be possible to salvage the following Accord provision:

> **Land and Resources**
>
> Within the context of self-government negotiations,
>
> - Canada and the Provinces agree, where appropriate, to provide access to lands and resources to Métis and Métis self-governing institutions;
> - Where land is to be provided, Canada and the Provinces... agree to make available their fair share of Crown lands for transfer to Métis self-governing institutions;...
> - Canada and the Provinces agree to enter into discussions with representatives of the Métis Nation on the establishment of a land negotiation process.

Economic Development

In the absence of self-government and land agreements, there still would remain the potential for agreements based on economic development. Agreements could be entered into that would enable Métis communities or Métis Economic Development Foundations to exercise a degree of jurisdiction over land and resources for economic purposes. Through the use of leases or land use arrangements the Métis could enhance their conditions and livelihood through using the forests, lakes, mineral resources, agriculture, wild rice, tourism and other resource or economic opportunities. These leases, coupled with potential co-management arrangements over the fisheries, trapping, hunting and tourism, and so forth, would provide the Métis with some security knowing that they have a role in the control and development of resources surrounding their communities. Although not a preferred approach, it does offer an alternative for the interim or short term.

Modern Aboriginal Economies: Capitalism with an Aboriginal Face

*David R. Newhouse**

In March 1993, Victor Buffalo, Chairman, Peace Hills Trust Company, spent a few days with us as our Distinguished Visitor. He spoke to several classes and gave a public lecture about the Samson Cree Nation, the problems that it faces, and the role that Peace Hills Trust plays in helping to resolve these problems. After one of the lectures, a few students approached me and my colleagues to express their indignation that Mr. Buffalo had been invited to speak. They explained that Mr. Buffalo was not an Indian because he had not once used the word "sharing" in his presentation, he was wearing a suit and he was exploiting his own people. The exploitation was the making of a profit through the loaning of money. Mr. Buffalo's company loans money to Indian bands on the basis of cash flow, using the contribution agreements of the government as a form of collateral rather than the usual collateral of plant, equipment and land. His company has been able to do things that non-Aboriginal bankers have been reluctant or unwilling to do.

A decade ago, I chaired, for a short time, the Department of Indian Affairs and Northern Development's Ontario Region Indian Economic Development Loan Board and saw many of the early attempts at business development on Indian reserves in southern Ontario. I remember being struck by the projects that I saw and their differences from mainstream businesses. On the surface the proposals looked the same, they contained cash flow and profit projections, investments in

* Associate Professor, Native Management and Economic Development Program, Department of Native Studies/Administrative Studies Program, Trent University, Peterborough, Ontario.

plant and equipment, the usual things that one expects to find in business plans. The heart of many of the proposals was not profit in the normal accounting sense but the creation of jobs. Profits were the way in which more jobs could be created and hence more people employed.

There have been enormous and significant changes within Aboriginal society within the last generation. We often do not reflect upon them in order to discern their meaning and impact. I present these stories as examples of the type of change of the last two decades as prelude to my topic. I have been asked to write on the unique perspectives that Aboriginal belief systems have for development, how these can be preserved, and what lessons these might have for future development efforts both within Aboriginal communities and the mainstream. These are difficult questions and I'm not sure that they can be answered satisfactorily in the short time available to prepare this paper. I want, however, to provide some clues to the answers and suggest, not that further research be undertaken in this area, but that the processes that are under way within Aboriginal communities be supported through the development of Aboriginal institutions.

The Modernization of Aboriginal Societies

My premise is that Aboriginal societies are undergoing a process of modernization. I have written about this process in a previous paper (The Development Of Modern Aboriginal Societies, October 1992). This process is resulting in the development of new identities, and new social, political, cultural and economic institutions within Aboriginal societies. These institutions, in my opinion, will be primarily western in nature and will be adapted to operate in accordance with Aboriginal traditions, customs and values. One only has to look at the rapid development of organizations over the last decade to see evidence of this process. The 1990 Arrowfax directory of Aboriginal organizations lists 3,000 for-profit business and 3,000 not-for-profit businesses. The 1992 edition of the same directory has shown a significant increase in the number of listings. Many of these organizations were not in existence a decade ago.

There are also other indicators of the modernization of Aboriginal society: a steady growth in the off-reserve population; continuing convergence of Indian birth rates and family size to the Canadian norms; adoption of English as a lingua franca; adoption of western-style elected governments (most evident in the band councils on Indian reserves); an increasing number of Aboriginal students attending secondary and post-secondary education institutions; and a move towards textual transmission of knowledge rather than oral transmission. There are now two generations of Aboriginal people who have not lived on-reserve and for whom reserve life is unknown. I don't know if this process of modernization is good or bad. Its rapidity will, however, cause a certain amount of social dislocation and problems. While the pace of change may be rapid, it would be unfair to say that it proceeds evenly across all Aboriginal communities.

The million or so Aboriginal people in Canada live in the midst of 25 million others. It is impossible for Aboriginal people not to be affected by this contact and not to be changed by it. Aboriginal people are also surrounded by a capitalist economy and because of its strength and appeal will be affected by it. The question I have been asked to address needs to be placed in a context. The result is a slightly different question: Given this context and given that capitalism is an adaptable system, what unique perspectives do Aboriginal people bring to the ongoing debate about the practice of capitalism? One could also pose a related question: What changes do Aboriginal people need to make in order to adapt to capitalism? My suspicion is that the second question is one that people simply do not want to ask at this particular time.

I call this resultant adaptation capitalism with an Aboriginal face, for nowhere have I seen an outright rejection of capitalism by Aboriginal people. In fact, I have seen a desire to adapt this particular political-economic system to work in accordance with Aboriginal belief systems. In addition, I see the adoption of policies and programs by all governments, both Aboriginal and non-Aboriginal, designed to further the development of this system within Aboriginal society.

What is Capitalism?

Capitalism is a way of life first of all and foremost. Then it's a worldview and finally it's a political-economic system. Many people focus only on the economic aspects of capitalism and believe, once they describe how this feature works, that they understand it.

At the heart of capitalism is a particular view of man and a notion of social progress. Man is viewed as a being who is continually striving to improve his material and social well-being. Progress is measured through a continual improvement in individual material position. Most important, this progress occurs as the result of the actions of individuals, each of whom engages in this constant striving. It is the collection of individual effort which results in improved collective well-being. Individuals possess capital or labour that can be used to produce profits or surpluses. The goal of every individual is to produce an economic surplus that can be saved for use at a future date, spent on consumables, or invested in order to produce additional surpluses. Individuals may pool their surpluses and use them for that group's good, or governments may appropriate them in the form of taxes in order to produce public goods which are available for all.

This notion of individual effort and social competition is important for it is what drives capitalism. Without it, much of the gains would not be possible. One could argue that the work of this Royal Commission is paid for through the collective surpluses of individual workers.

Capitalism has proven to be a remarkably adaptable and versatile system and currently appears to be the preferred economic system throughout the world today. Cultures as varied as Japan, the United States, India and now members of the former U.S.S.R. are adapting it to their various cultures. Many are also involved in the search for a solution to one of capitalism's most difficult problems: achieving an equitable distribution of wealth in a society.

Aboriginal people in Canada appear to have accepted the fundamental premises of capitalism: the notion of progress as defined through social competition and the notion that one possesses either capital or labour, which can be used to produce surpluses.

There is no fear that capitalism cannot be adapted to Aboriginal realities. In fact, it is being done throughout Canada where economic programs, community infrastructure and education programs are encouraging its adoption. Individuals are being encouraged to use their own capital to establish enterprises to make profits, the rules of access to capital are being examined and revised, capital investment institutions (trust companies, caisses populaires, co-operatives, Aboriginal capital corporations) are being established, governments are setting up small enterprise assistance programs for Aboriginal individuals and communities, and some First Nations governments are tentatively thinking about some form of taxation and user fees on individual and corporate incomes.

It has been a popular belief in recent years that Aboriginal people did not engage in economic activity, that somehow this type of activity was inconsistent with Aboriginal culture and values. The historical record shows a much different picture: Aboriginal people were active in the fur trade, assumed a major role in it (the Hurons were said to have been responsible for 50% of the fur trade in the 1600s), and were good traders. One of the names of the Micmac was "Taranteens", which meant trader and which reflected their role as excellent middlemen between the hunters of the North and the agriculturalists of the south. Cree businessmen in the late 1800s in northern Saskatchewan were excellent business people, so good in fact that many of the surrounding business people wanted to restrain their ability to trade. In fact, throughout the whole of contact, Aboriginal people have engaged in trade with those who arrived here and, prior to that, with each other. For example, Oolichan grease was traded far into the interior of the country along trails which became known as "grease trails." In the present day, one has only to examine the huge powwow circuit that has grown up over the last few years or the rapid growth in the sale of cigarettes on Indian reserves to see the great increase in the number of people who are engaging in trade and making a profit, that most fundamental of capitalist activities.

The questions to be asked become clearer: What can Aboriginal belief systems contribute to the practice of capitalism in Aboriginal communities, what adaptions will be made to it, and what can governments do to assist in this adaption process?

Aboriginal Belief Systems

In 1991, the Manitoba Public Inquiry into the Administration of Justice and Aboriginal People reported:

> Aboriginal peoples do not adhere to a single life philosophy, religious belief or moral code. Indeed, there are and have been considerable differences among tribes. That the Aboriginal peoples of North America, for the most part, hold fundamental life philosophies different from those of the dominant European-Canadian society is now taken for granted.

At the core of Aboriginal belief systems is a difference in the perception of one's relationship with the universe and the Creator. In the Judeo-Christian tradition, which is arguably the philosophical basis for much of European-Canadian society, there is the notion that humankind (mankind in some interpretations) was to fill the earth and to have dominion over it and all that was contained within it. In Ojibwa thought, which is taken to be representative of traditional Aboriginal thought in general, mankind does not have dominion over the earth and all its creatures but is dependent upon all parts of the creation for survival. In this view, man is the least important entity of the creation.

James Dumont in a 1992 presentation to the Royal Commission on Aboriginal Peoples argued for a set of generalized Aboriginal primary values which he defined as arising from vision; i.e., a special way of seeing the world as an Aboriginal person and a capacity for holistic or total vision. With this ability to see the whole comes respect; respect for creation, respect for knowledge and wisdom, respect for the dignity and freedom of others, respect for the quality of life and spirit in all things, and respect for the mysterious.

From this core of vision and respect, he argues that there arise seven primary traditional values:

- *kindness*: a capacity for caring and desire for harmony and well-being in interpersonal relationships;
- *honesty*: a necessity to act with the utmost honesty and integrity in all relationships recognizing the inviolable and inherent autonomy, dignity and freedom of oneself and others;
- *sharing*: a willingness to relate to one another with an ethic of sharing, generosity and collective/communal consciousness and co-operation, while recognizing the interdependence and interrelatedness of all life;
- *strength*: conscious of the need for kindness and respecting the integrity of oneself and others, to exercise strength of character, fortitude and self-mastery in order to generate and maintain peace, harmony and well-being within oneself and in the total collective community;

- *bravery*: the exercise of courage and bravery on the part of the individual so that the quality of life and inherent autonomy of oneself and others can be exercised in an atmosphere of security, peace, dignity and freedom;
- *wisdom*: the respect for that quality of knowing and gift of vision in others (striving for the same within oneself) that encompasses the holistic view, possesses spiritual quality, and is expressed in the experiential breadth and depth of life; and
- *humility*: the recognition of oneself as a sacred and equal part of the creation, and the honouring of all life which is endowed with the same inherent autonomy, dignity, freedom and equality.

These values should be interpreted and translated into community processes, institutions and codes of behaviour. Another important factor to consider is the collectivist orientation of Aboriginal society. While the interpretation of this value orientation varies quite widely, its usual interpretation is that the needs of the group, whether it be the family, clan or nation, take precedence over the needs of the individual. It is also important to realize that traditional Aboriginal people viewed life as a journey. The practice of capitalism within Aboriginal society will be affected by these factors as well as modernizing trends as described earlier. It is this worldview and value set that Aboriginal people bring to the debate about the practice of capitalism.

There is and will continue to be considerable debate about whether traditional values are indeed compatible with capitalism. Within the Aboriginal community, there is a considerable effort under way to ensure that traditional values are understood and made the centre of Aboriginal life again, a process which sociologists call revitalization, but which I call retraditionalization. It is this process of relearning and reinterpreting traditional values which is at the heart of the modernization process. If Aboriginal people had not bought into the fundamental premises of capitalism, I would have argued that it may have been possible to develop a new economic system based to a larger extent on Aboriginal values, and this issue should be explored in greater depth. Since the fundamental premises appear to have been agreed to by Aboriginal people, the question is moot and one can only examine what the result will look like.

What Will this Form of Capitalism Look Like?

Aboriginal values and worldviews will affect the practice of capitalism and hence the process of economic development in the following ways:

- The concept of personal and social development will be much broader. Using a holistic view, development will be viewed as encompassing four dimensions: physical, mental, emotional and spiritual, the same dimensions as contained within the Cree Medicine Wheel. The development process will have to include all four elements at the same time and not just along the economic (physical) dimension.

- Development will be seen as a process and not a product. Based on the Aboriginal view that life itself is a journey, the development process will be seen as a journey, not as an end state to be achieved. This is not to say that movement along the journey cannot be measured but that the emphasis will be upon the quality of the journey rather than the specific place to be reached. This view of development may mean that there will be a willingness to pursue long-term results over short-term improvements.
- Development will be seen as a joint effort between the individual and the collective and its institutions; in this case, the community and government. The process will tend to be collaborative rather than competitive. One can see this happening in the manner in which individuals who attempt to start businesses without the legitimizing support of either community or governments are treated or dealt with.
- In addition to the notion of joint effort – and, somewhat along the same lines – development will be seen as a partnership between the individual and the world. In a world in which the fundamental value is respect, one needs to have permission of the world in order to change it, to transform it into something else. If one sees oneself as an integral part of the world, indeed as its least important creation, then one would hesitate to act in a way that shows a lack of respect. This will affect the choice of development projects engaged in and the type of technology employed.
- The development effort will emphasize human capital investment rather than individual capital accumulation. This focus on the human aspects of development will cause developers explicitly to consider the effects of their activities upon the quality of life which includes the environment and will affect development choices. Decisions may be reviewed by councils of elders. Decision criteria may be established that explicitly require an analysis of these aspects.
- Traditional wisdom as interpreted by the elders will be used to guide planning and decision making. Elders may be accorded a formal place in planning and development efforts through a variety of mechanisms: councils of elders who must approve plans, advisory councils which sit at the same table as councillors, or as advisers to individuals.
- The issues surrounding wealth distribution will be tackled using Aboriginal values of kindness and sharing. There will be expectations that individuals who have or who are accumulating wealth will somehow share it with community members.

Indeed, the current notion of success as defined by capitalism in material terms will be challenged and broadened. The adaption of capitalism will also alter traditional systems for determining social status. At present, elders who possess knowledge and experience of traditional lifeways are highly revered. The continued use of a material definition of success in Aboriginal society may change this hierarchy as those who have material wealth move to the top of the social scale.

- The economic institutions that are established will be primarily western in nature with adaptions to ensure that they operate in a manner which is appropriate to the local Aboriginal community. This means the development of a wide range of western-looking organizations: co-operatives, individual proprietorships, partnerships, corporations owned by individuals and governments, joint ventures – in fact, the myriad ways in which economic activity can be undertaken.

  In addition to this infrastructure primarily of economic institutions, there will develop a whole range of secondary economic support institutions such as development agencies, management advisory groups, loan funds, etc., whose primary function is not economic activity itself but increasing the efficiency of the economy.

- The desire to arrive at decisions by consensus will guide the development of community and organizational structures and processes which are consistent with this value. This has implications for the development planning process. Planners and decision makers will not be able to proceed with plans unless consensus, using an acceptable process, has been reached that this is what should be done. In addition, decision makers will not be able to make decisions without ensuring that broad community consensus exists for a particular direction and course of action. The current business approach to decision making which is based on "number crunching" – that is, quantitative information – will be broadened.
- The notions of honesty and respect will result in a heightened sense of accountability for economic institutions and decision makers. This accountability will be focused on two issues: adherence to the direction as consensually approved; and adherence to Aboriginal notions of holism and development.

Much of this is happening now. A quick glance at recent developments within Aboriginal society will show evidence of these developments:

- an increasing number of primary and secondary economic institutions;
- increased involvement of elders in decision making;
- adoption of community economic development models with their broad notions of development and the subsequent development of indicators to permit communities to gauge their movement;
- continued and expanded use of programs designed to provide Aboriginal people with the skills, knowledge and capital to participate in the broader Canadian economy.

The recentness of these developments, the general lack of understanding of the workings of Aboriginal economies, and the tentative acceptance by Canadians of the notion of Aboriginal self-government are indications of the fragility of modern Aboriginal economies. Great care needs to be taken in the choice of interventions by governments and outside agents.

What Can the Royal Commission Do?

The process of modernization and the adoption of capitalism as the dominant political-economic system within Aboriginal society is well under way. It would be sheer folly to attempt to reverse the process or to attempt dramatic shifts in direction. I would argue that the forces of modernization are much too great to resist, especially in this area. The question, however, remains: What should the Royal Commission's overall strategy be and what can it reasonably do to influence the future course of events?

There are, in my opinion, three possible courses of action:

- The Royal Commission could do very little at this time. It could take the view that the process is under way, Aboriginal people are gaining access to the Canadian economy and are participating in it in increasing numbers in contrast to the recent past when economic participation was legally ruled out. The adoption of this approach, given the fragile nature of Aboriginal economies would, I think, prolong the current situation for an indefinite period. Development would continue, but at a very slow pace not keeping up with the demand for an improved quality of life. In addition, Aboriginal values would probably have a difficult time surviving given the highly competitive nature of the Canadian and global economy.
- The Royal Commission could recommend that the level of effort within existing programs be increased. The reasoning would be that an increased level of effort will directly result in a quicker improvement in the quality of life for Aboriginal individuals. The adoption of this approach would permit an increased level of economic activity but does not do much to support Aboriginal values and worldviews.
- The Royal Commission could adopt a strategy of institution building within Aboriginal society; i.e., it could make its focus the building of institutional capacities within Aboriginal communities that could then begin to deal with the various problems and issues of Aboriginal life.

This is the course of action that I suggest for the economic development area (and for the Royal Commission in general).

Although this should be the focus of the Royal Commission's work, it should also take steps to ensure that the various adjustments to the economic development programs are made, for they are important parts of the solution. These adjustments are beyond the scope of this paper and are discussed in other reports.

A society's values are reflected in its institutions just as much as in its day-to-day practices. In fact, institutions assume a large role in the preservation and transmission of culture and values. Much of the thinking that needs to be done with respect to Aboriginal economic development and values needs to be undertaken by Aboriginal people. On an individual and collective basis, Aboriginal people are making daily decisions based on their understanding of their values. Much needs to be done to support that decision making.

It would be useful to establish an economic research and policy development institute whose main function is to identify issues such as those I've raised in this paper and to research them on behalf of Aboriginal individuals, communities, organizations and governments. It would develop the culturally appropriate tools and make them available for use by individuals and communities. It would also be able to provide policy analysis and advice to Aboriginal governments using Aboriginal perspectives and values.

At the present time, an institution of this sort does not exist. This is not to suggest that there is little being accomplished in this area. In fact, there is a considerable amount of research and experiential learning that is taking place. Much of this needs to be captured and fed back into the community in a form that is usable and viewed as legitimate. An institute of this sort could do that.

The question, then, as I see it, is not one of preserving Aboriginal worldviews and values but finding ways to assist in the creative interpretation of these worldviews and values in the contemporary reality, a process that is already under way.

References

Byrnes, J. *Aboriginal Enterprise Development: Themes and Issues*, 1989.

Dickason, O. *Canada's First Nations, A History of Founding Peoples from Earliest Times*. Toronto: McClelland and Stewart, 1992.

Dumont, J. *Aboriginal People and Justice*, Presentation to Royal Commission on Aboriginal Peoples, Canada, 1992.

Hamilton, A.C. and C.M. Sinclair. *The Report of the Aboriginal Justice Inquiry of Manitoba, Volume 1*, 1991.

Langdon, S. *Contemporary Alaskan Native Economies*, University Press of America, Inc, U.S.A., 1986.

Lockhart, R.A. *Issues Perceived as Critical to the Construction of Native Management and Economic Development Models*, 1992 for The Working Group on Native Management.

Merrel, J. H. *The Indians' New World: Catawbas and their Neighbours from European Contact Through The Era of Removal*. W. W. Norton and Company, 1989.

Newhouse, D.R. *From the Tribal to the Modern: The Development of Modern Aboriginal Societies*, Presentation to Royal Commission on Aboriginal Peoples, Canada, 1992.

Ruffing, L. *Navajo Economic Development Subject to Cultural Constraints*, American Indian Policy Review Commission, date unknown.

Stanley, S. *American Indian Economic Development*. Paris: Mouton Publishers, Paris, 1978.

Vecsay, C. and R. Venables. *American Indian Environments: Ecological Issues in Native American History*. Syracuse: Syracuse University Press, 1980.

Wien, F. *Rebuilding the Economic Base of Indian Communities: The Micmac in Nova Scotia*, The Institute for Research on Public Policy, Canada, 1986.

Strengthening Traditional Economies and Perspectives

*Simon Brascoupé**

It is the traditional economy, living on the land and with the land, that brings meaning to Aboriginal peoples. All culture comes from the land, the relationship with the environment, and a people's sacred duty to all creation. Today, the traditional economy needs to be strengthened and supported. This paper argues for a change in attitude and perception of traditional economies, for supports and programs for traditional economic activities, and for research to improve our understanding of traditional economies.

What is the Traditional Economy?

The traditional or subsistence economy is not well understood. Traditional economies in Canada are not one, but several "economic systems" which evolved for several thousand years to provide material goods and specialist services in a renewable fashion. The systems are based on Indigenous knowledge and systems that constitute storehouses of knowledge about the environment, animals, birds, fish, medicines, land, fauna and specific ecologies. Thomas D. Lonner describes subsistence economies in *Contemporary Alaskan Native Economies* as follows:

* Professor, Department of Sociology and Anthropology, Carleton University, Ottawa.

> Internationally, "subsistence" refers to those economic activities (hunting, fishing, gathering, farming, herding, crafting, trading, toolmaking, transportation, skill training, storage, energy development, and so on) which are relatively self-contained within a community or region, which are not conducted primarily for profit-maximization, which aim primarily for present consumption, and which are governed by traditional patterns rather than market conditions or immediate needs. A subsistence farmer, for example, is one who consumes most of what he produces, sells little in the cash market, buys few items for production and consumption, uses little non-family labour, employs non-capital demanding technology, possesses a limited standard of living, and whose decision making is dominated by family survival (Wharton 1971). Subsistence is, in this way, a system of production for both use and exchange. Its objective is not total self-sufficiency, not capital formation but an endless flow of goods, services, and other products (Sahlins 1971). (Langdon 1986)

Contemporary Aboriginal artisans, it could be argued, operate under a subsistence economic system, sometimes referred to as a cottage industry. The system has operated the same way since contact. For example, most artisans have only one price for wholesale and retail sales. It is not entirely true that Aboriginal artisans do not understand marketing, but rather they choose not to participate in the market system. This behaviour can be witnessed in the Sante Fe Market, a $3 million market held each August, where Pueblo potters will sell their products to gallery owners and consumers at the same price. Artisans are not profit maximizers through this action, but are motivated by short-term economic survival.

In Canada, a significant part of the traditional economy is traditional arts. The traditional arts have continually survived from pre-contact to the present. Traditional artisans masterfully used available materials and tools to produce goods of lasting value and beauty. In early contact and through the colonial period, Aboriginal people produced "crafts" for trade or sale. During this period, many Aboriginal people survived on country foods and locally produced crafts. Throughout Canada, wherever a market existed, Aboriginal artisans produced and sold art and crafts to an available market. In recent years, a significant market exists in the souvenir, crafts, fine crafts and fine arts.

Today, this significant sector in the traditional economy plays an important role in self-government and the redefining of Aboriginal culture. In a project to study Indigenous learning in "crafts", Adri Kater (Veldhuis 1993) intended "to obtain insight into the process by which skills are acquired for crafts that play a significant role in the economy of the people concerned." Research on this traditional activity could have far-reaching effects on training and education of Aboriginal people.

> Most difficult was the part on the acquisition of knowledge and skills. The learning processes are often so much a matter of course that the people concerned are not conscious of them. They never discuss these processes among themselves and find it difficult to verbalize them. (Veldhuis 1993)

Many of these skills survive today and play a significant economic and social role.

Threats to the Traditional Economy

Threats to the continuation of traditional ways life come from within Aboriginal societies because of public policies, but western societies' perceptions of traditional societies are equally threatening. This section explains the basis of these erroneous perceptions of traditional economies and societies as "primitive." A brief review of economic development, using the World Bank policies related to Indigenous peoples as a case study, argues for involvement of Indigenous peoples in development decisions, local control and support for Aboriginal governments (Bodley 1988). Finally, to perpetuate and counter the history of unthinking policies related to traditional economies, the emerging research in Indigenous knowledge must be furthered to fill the knowledge gaps in the economic system and knowledge base. The development of Indigenous knowledge will also be vital for the future determination of economic and social impacts and the benefits of this knowledge to sustainable development and a sustainable future.

To begin our exploration of the traditional economy the first question to be asked is: "What are the forces that threaten the continuation of traditional ways of making a living, and what steps need to be taken to support, rather than undermine, the traditional economy including the role of Aboriginal men and women?"

The Erroneous Image of Traditional Ways of Life

Western society's perceptions of traditional societies, through stereotypes and images of traditional life, are clouded by three images – the traditional way of life as harsh, primitive, and dying.

Marshall Sahlins clearly demonstrated in his seminal work, *Stone Age Economics*, that the egalitarian life is not "nasty, brutish, and short", but is highly efficient from economic and ecological perspectives. It is also a very social way of life. Sahlins and others have demonstrated conclusively that hunting and gathering in many Indigenous cultures can take only two and a half days per week, leaving plenty of time for social interaction. This has been a successful way of life for thousands of years. In comparison, the world that we know as "civilized" is largely unproven. Colin Turnbull, in *The Human Cycle* (1988), says that "civilization is very much an immature and ongoing experiment, the success of which is by no means yet proven." Turnbull wonders why in our world "so many of us find so much of life to be unsatisfactory." Because "there is so much potential for beauty and goodness at every stage of life, in any culture; so much potential for living life better by living it for others as well as for ourselves." Egalitarian societies like the Bushman believe life lived well is a lasting joy to us all. When comparing the "benefits" and the exploitation caused by economic development, it is hard to justify progress in these terms.

One of the most serious threats to the survival and well-being of traditional economies and way of life are public policies that do not comprehend the traditional way of life. To understand this issue we can examine past economic development policies of the World Bank related to tribal peoples. The official policy statement of the World Bank on Tribal Peoples was prepared by Robert Goodland in 1982 (Bodley 1988). The policy is based on some very questionable assumptions, which by omission are at the core of Canadian economic development policy:

- all tribes will inevitably be developed;
- development will benefit tribal peoples;
- tribes will be allowed a choice; and
- tribes must become ethnic minorities.

Bodley, in his paper, "The World Bank Tribal Policy: Criticisms and Recommendations" (1983), clearly refutes all the false assumptions that form contemporary economic development and World Bank policy.

The inevitability of development assumes that tribal peoples are integrated into national economies because their traditional economies were lost because of specific national development policies. The benefits of development are clearly suspect. Development policies weaken tribal autonomy and reduce tribal control over their resources, leading, as Bodley puts it, to detribalization. Bodley recommends that "the World Bank should not fund projects that would disturb or displace isolated, fully traditional tribal groups."

The World Bank policy states that tribes have a choice, but the policy does not ensure freedom of choice for tribal peoples. Bodley recommends that full discussion is necessary for "how the choice process can be implemented for partly integrated tribal peoples." There must be a process whereby tribal peoples can reject economic development projects.

The World Bank policy is directed at making "citizens" or ethnic minorities of tribal peoples. It has been conclusively shown that the process results in social disruption, disease, loss of subsistence economy, and loss of identity for tribal peoples. Bodley recommends that the World Bank refuse funding projects where tribes have no voice in national development projects affecting them and their lands. Finally, Bodley advocates that "the World Bank policy should be subject to critical review by a panel of tribal political leaders" and other authorities to ensure a wide range of perspectives. World Bank policy reflects the national development and social policies of Canada which are based on the same assumptions. A successful rebuff of the World Bank policy will weaken the national economic development policy arguments in North America.

In recent years we have witnessed several very large development projects and disastrous land settlements in North America. The Alaskan Native Claims Settlement Act (ANCSA) of 1971 created several corporate-style institutions, many of which have since failed. For compensation of 90% by the state, Aboriginal people received $962.5 million – about three dollars per acre. Berger, in *Village Journey* (1985), concludes: "Now that ANCSA has failed Alaskan Natives, it is not surprising that they have begun to look for new ways of strengthening the subsistence economy and the village way of life." Berger's Commission report was released in 1985. In 1986, Steve J. Langdon, in the introduction to *Contemporary Alaskan Native Economies* wrote: "It is hoped that through these efforts [Commission Review], Alaskan Native people will be given the opportunity to forge the lifestyles and cultures which they envision and are striving to attain."

Richard F. Salisbury says, in *A Homeland For The Cree: Regional Development in James Bay 1971-1981* (1986): "In July 1971 the chiefs of the seven Cree villages and several younger Cree met in Mistassini to discuss the recent announcement by the Quebec government of a $5.6 billion hydro-electric project on their lands." In 1974, an Agreement in Principle was signed compensating the Cree with $90 million for settlement. This included royalties and the right to retain all benefits provided to Status Indians. The difference between ANCSA and the James Bay and Northern Quebec Agreement (JBNQA) of 1976 is that the Cree wound up developing regional unity from their eight village-band societies and achieved regional autonomy.

But why did the ANCSA fail where the JBNQA is a qualified success for the traditional economy? Both Aboriginal economies were largely subsistence and remote. The JBNQA was unique because it provided an income security program for Cree hunters and trappers (Section 30). Whereas the ANCSA's poorly conceived regional policies, such as limited access to fisheries policy in Bristol Bay, caused hardship in the local rural community rather than benefiting it as intended. The resulting alienation of Native Alaskans from their subsistence economic system separated Aboriginal society from the land. This relationship was the core of Native Alaskan culture. Berger found subsistence to be more than survival:

> Alaskan Natives now realize that ANCSA has failed them and that its goals are at cross purposes with their own. Today they are trying to strengthen their subsistence economy and to restore

> their tribal governments. We must understand the historical legitimacy and the present value of these goals. These aspirations are not anachronistic, they are not absurd, they are not an impediment to progress. They are, quite simply, the only means whereby the future of village Alaska can be protected.

Salisbury says that "the Cree example suggests that a viable local subsistence economy is important." The income security program for hunters and trappers provides incomes "that are comparable with, or better than, what can be earned from unskilled manual wage-work." It has stopped Crees turning "from hunters to proletarians", as I. E. LaRusic wrote in 1968 (Salisbury 1986).

In conclusion, why did the Crees successfully create regional unity and regional autonomy when the Alaskan Natives were unable successfully to maintain the subsistence way of life and manage their regional corporations? Salisbury asks:

> Even if the balance sheet of the emergence of Cree regional society is generally a favourable one, it remains to consider whether their experience is one that provides a precedent for future use, either by other native groups, by other politically powerless regions, or by central governments wishing to be more effective in delivering services to outlying areas. What are the external conditions that were necessary, and without which the emergence of Cree regional society could not have occurred?

What were the crucial steps in the process of emergence that made it a success? Salisbury identified several factors leading to Crees' success:

- One clear external condition was the goodwill of the Canadian and Quebec governments, and their readiness to decentralize government powers to the region.
- A second possible external condition is that the Cree, in 1981, appear as a unified, culturally homogeneous group, constituting an overwhelming majority of the population of the regional government's jurisdiction.
- The "crisis" of 1971, though it was unpleasant and could have been followed by the death of Cree society, is the obvious factor that created regional unity.
- A further requirement for the emergence of a regional society is that the personnel was made up of local Cree.
- The Cree leaders actively supported a strengthening of the basic Cree hunting economy, and did not focus exclusively on either the service sector or the involvement of the Cree in work outside the local economy.
- The final factor is predictability. The energies of the Cree administration have not been consumed in trying nervously to justify a base budget or planning for programs that may never materialize if the budget is not provided.

If cultural values, beliefs and practices are ignored in development, social experiments and economic development will fail. Aboriginal peoples will pay a high price for their way of life. However, if Aboriginal peoples' culture and values are respected, forming part of public policy, and Aboriginal/white relations are based on both subsistence and market systems, Aboriginal peoples' culture and society can be protected when economic development projects occur on their lands.

Animal Rights Lobby

Public attacks on the traditional way of life by the animal rights lobby is based on similar perceptions and erroneous beliefs about hunting and trapping. These misconceptions come from the same stereotypical images of traditional peoples. When lobbyists do not see any value in a traditional way of life in contemporary times they assume that Aboriginal people living in a traditional economic system want to join the "rat race." Large anti-fur campaigns against the Canadian fur industry have resulted in untold hardship on thousands of Aboriginal families. Traditional hunting and trapping across Canada, not to mention non-Aboriginal families and the fur industry, are under severe stress to survive.

Fur lobbyists do not understand that once Aboriginal families lose contact with the land through the loss of the fur market, the results are long-term and serious. The social and economic impact is similar to those associated with the dislocation of Aboriginal peoples through megaprojects like the James Bay Hydro Project, and the flooding of the inter-lakes in Manitoba. The effects were thought to be short-term, lasting only a few years, but in reality they are sustained for several generations. A high price is paid when Aboriginal peoples' sacred relationship and link with the environment is misunderstood.

To understand the underlying structure of the relationship of Aboriginal culture to the environment, and the severe impact of removing these communities from their natural world, one must understand Aboriginal society and spiritual relationships with all of creation. Aboriginal peoples' values and culture emerge from their relationship with the environment; this is also true for other Indigenous cultures. Different environments create subtle and obvious differences in such things as social structure, religion and economy. Scholars from various disciplines have developed methodologies for comprehending cultures. Christopher Vecsey, in *American Indian Environments* (1980), summarizes these approaches:

> Ecologists examine the day-to-day, pragmatic interrelations between humans and their ecosystems. A student of comparative religion is more likely to look at the ideal human views of nature (or geosophy), as found in myths, prayers, ceremonials, and other religious phenomena.

The study of culture can be understood anthropologically, according to Vecsey: "Anthropologists attempt to understand the cultural base of religious and environmental relations." Thus, all cultures and values derive from a people's relationship to their environment.

In Canada some northern bands have been relocated, resulting in considerable social destruction. Does the resulting social crisis have to do with Aboriginal persons' relationship to the land? Are there other factors to be aware of in analyzing the problems created by removals? What has happened to the culture? It has been said that Aboriginal persons are assimilated to our Mother the Earth. A change in that status will cause considerable social disruption, particularly when Aboriginal peoples are separated from their traditional "sharing" relationship, and their symbolic relationships seem permanently changed during the resulting confusion.

American Aboriginal persons achieve an integration between environment and the sacred, explains Vecsey in *American Indian Environments*. Economic anthropologists might say a change from subsistence economy to a market economy during relocation causes social disruption. Vecsey says there are three types of interrelated integration between environment and religions among Aboriginal peoples:

- **Primary integration**: The religious core is moulded by environmental relations. Hunting rituals in which Aboriginal hunters tried to call in game and apologized to animals upon killing them, are examples. The seasonal cycles of agricultural rituals in which planting activities are combined with prayers also illustrate primary integration. The fertilization rituals of the Pueblos or Eastern Woodland farmers promoted life in humans, plants, animals, and the world at large.
- **Secondary integration**: Aboriginal peoples' social structure was partly moulded by environmental interactions, and the religious structure reflected the social structure. Aboriginal farming societies, for example, tended to have organized priesthoods because their way of subsistence allowed, or perhaps needed, a hierarchical structure of society. Hunting cultures in native North America resembled atomistic shamanism; the individualism of hunting extended to an individualism of religion.
- **Morphological (or symbolic) integration**: Aboriginal persons' religious symbols in words, designs, and motions reflected the surrounding environment. It is well known that Aboriginal peoples' myths contain innumerable references to natural phenomena. They are largely about natural phenomena. Natural materials shaped their designs to the central core of Aboriginal peoples' culture. The basis of their philosophical difference with European culture is the relationship between Aboriginal peoples and Mother Earth. "Nature: that's our religion, our way of life", says Leon Shenandoah, Tadodaho of the Six Nations in *American Indian Environments*. In the same collection, Oren Lyons writes:

> In our perception all life is equal, and that includes the birds, animals, things that grow, things that swim. All life is created equal in our perception. It is the Creator who presents the reality, and as you read this singularly... you are a manifestation of the creation.

In summary, human/nature analysis may indicate whether decisions and actions made by society are in harmony with nature. There are three possible human/nature relationships to conquer, harness and change. Indigenous peoples have cultural values which favour humans in harmony with nature. Humans are part of nature, not outside it. Jim Lovelock proposed the Gaia Hypothesis that the biosphere behaves like a living organism and operates its own "life-support" systems through natural feedback mechanisms. If society does not achieve harmony with nature, it could conclude it must conquer nature, or face being conquered by nature. Of course this is an anthropomorphic viewpoint. Humans have always been part of nature – at no point have humans risen above natural laws.

Understanding the subsistence economy helps us understand traditional Aboriginal persons' views of the economy and economic development. Even though the subsistence economy has proven itself over thousands of years, today it is thought of as "primitive". This view has much to do with contemporary myths about progress and evolution. For most people it is difficult to envisage any different economy than the present. In *Economics Explained*, Heilbroner and Thurow reflect that "many people speak about capitalism as if it were as old as the hills, as ancient as the Bible, implying that there is something about the system that accords with human nature. Yet, on reflection, this is clearly not the case." In *Contemporary Alaskan Native Economics*, Thomas D. Lonner paraphrases Sahlins' work. "Subsistence is, in this way, a system of production for both use and exchange. Its objective is not total self-sufficiency nor capital formation but an endless flow of goods, services and other products." Thus is explained the difference between the subsistence system based on plenty, "an endless flow", compared to the patriarchal capitalist system of scarcity created by a market system, where "commodities" are scarce because capital is unequally distributed.

Indigenous Knowledge

Indigenous knowledge is one of the most exciting and newly emerging fields of Indigenous studies. Warren et al. (Veldhuis 1993) have identified important contributions in a number of academic disciplines and fields such as ecology, soil science, veterinary medicine, forestry, human health, aquatic resource management, botany, zoology, agronomy, agricultural economics, rural sociology, mathematics, management science, agricultural education and extension, fisheries, range management, information science, wildlife management, and water resource management. New fields of study in Indigenous knowledge include ecology, mediation, healing and arts.

Indigenous knowledge is really local knowledge and Indigenous science passed down since time immemorial. Its impact has been felt in many areas of the world since contact and will continue to influence all fields of science in the future. One of the leading researchers and proponents of Indigenous knowledge, D.M. Warren, defines it as:

> ... local knowledge – knowledge that is unique to a given culture or society [ecology and territory], Indigenous knowledge contrasts with the international system generated by universities, research institutions and private firms. It is the basis for local-level decision making in agriculture, health care, food preparation, education, etc. (Warren, page 9)

There is a new research ethic emerging as scientists study and document Indigenous knowledge: participatory, community-based and -controlled research. Martha Johnson, in *Documenting Dene Traditional Environmental Knowledge*, writes:

> The Dene Cultural Institute Pilot Project has provided some preliminary insights into the nature of Dene TEK [Traditional Environmental Knowledge] and the system of traditional resource management. It is clear from the research that Dene TEK is a valuable resource for assessing the environmental impacts of development projects and understanding environmental change. It is also clear that the successful documentation of TEK is dependent upon Dene to conduct the research themselves, in collaboration with western scientists. Successful integration of Dene TEK and western science depends upon the ability of both groups to develop an appreciation of and sensitivity to the strengths and limitations of their respective knowledge systems. However, only through a change in the present power structure will Dene TEK take its rightful place in future resource management. (Akwe:kon Journal, page 79)

To study Indigenous knowledge adequately, Aboriginally controlled institutions will have to be established. These institutions could establish partnerships and collaborations with the already proliferating Indigenous knowledge resource centres. Today, there are 11 formally established Indigenous knowledge resource centres in the Netherlands, the United States, Sri Lanka, Mexico, Nigeria, the Philippines, Ghana, Indonesia, and Kenya. There are several more centres being developed in Benin, Namibia, Zimbabwe, Burkina Faso, Costa Rica, Venezuela, Colombia, Peru, Bolivia, South Africa, Tanzania, Nepal and Australia. Both the Dene and the Inuit in Canada have been contributing to the international dialogue on Indigenous knowledge.

The Indigenous knowledge centres would strengthen the traditional economy by dispelling myths about the subsistence economy being "primitive" and harsh.

Research on traditional knowledge would provide some answers to questions like: "To what extent can wildlife resources in the North support the numbers of Aboriginal people wishing to live a traditional lifestyle?" There is currently very little specific knowledge regarding the traditional subsistence economy. There is very little known about other aspects of the Aboriginal traditional economy like the informal economy, the arts economy, and micro-enterprise, which all arguably have roots in the traditional economy.

These centres, in addition to strengthening the traditional economy, would also serve the purposes of self-government. As Aboriginal people increasingly control programs, they will attempt to merge both traditional concepts and values with western concepts and institutions. Knowledge on how this process would work, gleaned from Indigenous knowledge research, would be a substantial contribution to Aboriginal self-government and management of programs and policies.

Indigenous knowledge will substantially contribute to perceptions of traditional societies and economies. The public and scientists are developing a new respect based on the remarkable success of traditional medicines, technology and concepts. These successes include medicines for childhood leukaemia, and some forms of cancer. *Time* magazine, in an article, fears that, "Today, with little notice, more vast archives of knowledge and expertise are spilling into oblivion, leaving humanity in danger of losing its past and perhaps its future as well." In the article, Eugene Linden compared the loss of traditional knowledge to the great library in Alexandria burning down 1,600 years ago. Linden also realizes that if Indigenous cultures are lost, so is the knowledge. The article argues strongly to protect and maintain Indigenous cultures in order to preserve the traditional way of life and the Indigenous knowledge embedded in these societies.

Strengthening the Traditional Economic System

There are several alternatives for government and Aboriginal peoples to strengthen the traditional economy. The question that will be addressed here is "through what means can access to the land and resource base for traditional economies be assured?" Issues related to the land's ability to support traditional economies will be addressed, and the alternatives open to Aboriginal peoples who opt not to pursue traditional subsistence will be discussed. This latter question is important because of the perception that Aboriginal people in remote and isolated regions of Canada have few options except relocation. The employment options for Indigenous peoples in the North will be explored in the latter part of this paper.

- **Aboriginal rights, self-government, land claims**: Aboriginal traditional economies and systems must be recognized and affirmed as an Aboriginal right, based on treaties, historical rights and the Canadian Constitution.

- **Research on Indigenous ecological knowledge**: Aboriginal institutions that study Indigenous knowledge should be supported to document, preserve, publish and teach. This would support Canada's international commitments under Agenda 21, contribute to new ecological and other fields of knowledge, and support Aboriginal governance and programs.
- **Establishment of traditional resource regimes and agreements**: Agreements, memoranda of understanding, and co-management regimes among Aboriginal peoples, federal and provincial governments, and other relevant stakeholders to manage collectively resources in traditional, disputed and claimed lands of Aboriginal peoples. Indigenous knowledge of natural resources must be an integral part of these agreements.
- **Integration of the traditional into local economic plans**: Economic and other resource-based plans should incorporate elements of the traditional economy. The traditional economy is often poorly understood; therefore, Aboriginal communities should be encouraged to include elements related to the traditional economy in economic, human resource, and natural resource planning.
- **Conference, workshops, publications and research**: Support should be directed to understanding and sharing of information regarding that part of the Aboriginal economy. Existing research, reports and studies should be collected, documented and disseminated in the form of bibliographies and research papers.
- **Training and education**: Indigenous economies and knowledge interest Aboriginal persons. Aboriginal people desire education and knowledge related to the entire range of Indigenous knowledge. The educational component has implications for self-government, resource management and program management. Indigenous knowledge and economic systems should be available at all levels of the school and post-secondary system. This knowledge could achieve the objectives set out in *Our Common Future* in educating a new generation of citizens to respect the natural world through Aboriginal perspectives. Training in collecting and documenting affects other areas of research and would contribute to increased capacities in Aboriginal communities for resource management.
- **Traditional economies and megaprojects**: Indigenous knowledge and its applications will assist Aboriginal peoples, government, and the public in understanding the environmental impact of megaprojects. Indigenous peoples should be involved in the planning and development of megaprojects to mitigate environmental problems.
- **Environmental degradation**: There are several threats to the traditional economy as a result of environmental degradation, water quality, acid rain, loss of habitat, the ozone hole, mercury and other poisons, infestations, tourism, and mining practices. As the threats to the environment increase, it is becoming more important for Aboriginal peoples and Canada to develop mechanisms to study these impacts on the natural environment. They threaten

not only the traditional economy, but future generations of Canadians who would potentially benefit from the maintenance of a healthy environment.

- **Resource and administrative policies**: There is generally a lack of program support to the traditional economy. Aboriginal people in conjunction with the federal and provincial governments should establish programs and policies which support the traditional economy, research on Indigenous knowledge, and contribute to increased understanding of the traditional sector and its benefits to Aboriginal people and society.
- **Jurisdictional issues**: The lack of co-ordination and policy harmonization poses a considerable threat to resolving effectively any of the issues, problems and concerns of Aboriginal people who live off the land, or desire to manage the resource base in their region. Jurisdictional issues can be solved through various methods: land claims settlements, self-government regimes, co-management agreements, administrative instruments, and programs and policies. However, without the political will to resolve jurisdictional issues very little can be accomplished. The importance of resolving these jurisdictional issues related to resource management and control should become a priority for government and Aboriginal peoples in all discussion regarding relationships and agreements.
- **Resource management**: Co-management, shared responsibility regimes and principled management of resources should be the objective of government and Aboriginal peoples. Resource agreements should consider keeping Aboriginal subsistence families on the land rather than relocating these families. In the case of major projects, such as forestry, planning should cause the least amount of disruption to the traditional economy. Plans should also be in place to provide hunters and gatherers a choice to live on the land, return to the land after development has ceased, and to provide compensation for any adverse economic or environment damage caused by development.

Competing Uses of Traditional Hunting and Gathering Lands

One of the greatest threats to the traditional economy is the growth in competing uses for land. These threats are tourism, development, sports hunting and fishing, real estate, and recreation. The question here is: "To what extent and in what ways can traditional uses of the land be combined with other uses?"

Traditional uses of the land can only be combined with other competing uses by ensuring Aboriginal people have control in managing land and resources. Co-management can be employed where government and Aboriginal peoples make joint plans and decisions regarding lands and resources. More recently, provincial governments have been piloting projects where Aboriginal people have principal control over managing the resource, based on a resource agreement. Research on resource management where government has imposed a management regime often fails because Aboriginal people and their institutions are misunderstood. Therefore, by situating management of resources in Aboriginal control, the problem of inappropriate and misguided policy is mitigated, and the issues of rights are resolved.

The Carrying Capacity of the Land

It is frequently implied that Aboriginal people, even if they wanted to, could not make a living off the land, even if they wanted to, because the population is too large. It would be useful to know how many persons could live off specific land and water resource regimes using Indigenous harvesting techniques, but a clear answer does not exist. To answer the research question, "To what extent can wildlife resources in the North support the numbers of Aboriginal people wishing to live a traditional lifestyle?", four types of information are required. First, how many Aboriginal people wish to live a traditional lifestyle, assuming in a mixed or purely subsistence economy? Second, what is the carrying capacity of the various land and water regimes to provide an endless flow of resources from different environments. This means the number of people who can live off a hectare of land varies according to climate and land regime. Third, to what degree is the animal and fish habitat threatened by development and other harvesters in the region? Competing demands will lower the amount of country food available to the subsistence hunter and gatherer. Fourth, to what degree do Aboriginal people rely on the market for other foods and income? This will affect the total number of persons that can live a traditional lifestyle.

The following will explore the question of how various researchers have examined the questions of this land's carrying capacity, and the economic benefits of subsistence economic activities.

Case Study: Northeastern British Columbia

The traditional economic system is complex and sophisticated. Hugh Brody, in *Maps and Dreams* (1981), says of the traditional economy: "But they [maps] cannot do justice to the sophistication of an economic system involving patterns of movement at different times of year, shifts from one kind of resource harvesting to another, and the knowledge of the land – and its animals – whose richness is astounding." Brody was able to demonstrate the relationship between wild meat and furs and the Aboriginal economy in the northeast of British Columbia.

> The present strengths and weaknesses of the Indian economy come from a mixture of income and resources that is closely bound up with a seasonal round. Over the past fifty years this round has changed in detail, but not in broad outline. It can be divided into five activities: the fall dry-meat hunt, early winter hunting and trapping, late winter hunting and trapping, the spring beaver hunt, and summer slack. Each of these has its own

pattern and its own areas of land use.

Brody also studied the separation and overlapping nature of men's and women's work.

> The separation has several aspects. Men hunt large game animals; women hunt smaller species. Men's work is concerned with killing and butchering; women's work is centred on distribution and preparation of food and cannes. Men hunt very intensively for short periods; women work all the time – and have complete responsibility for young children.

In many Aboriginal communities, families rely on several forms of income to make a living: hunting, trapping, wage employment and transfer payments. Brody attempted to value country food production to compare the returns with other kinds of activities, to determine its economic viability. Brody set out to establish a value using the following method:

> Setting dollar equivalence to meat is not easy. Hunted meat has no real or hypothetical market value.... the only way to arrive at equivalence is to assess the cost to Indian families of buying produce of the same nutritional value, using, for example, the price of beef as the value equivalent of wild meats.

Annual values from various sources of incomes were calculated for wild meats, fur and handicrafts, guiding, and cash income (wages, child allowance, and unemployment insurance). The table below shows Brody's adjusted annual value per household (in 1979 dollars) of meat harvest:

Adjusted Annual Value per Household (in 1979 dollars) of Meat Harvest

Reserve	Total
East Kits	3,182.97
Cannes	3,388.83
Blueberry	5,648.35

Case Study: Kotlik fishers, hunters, and gatherers

In a study completed in the mid-seventies, Robert J. Wolfe (Langdon 1986) attempted to study "more precisely the mechanisms accounting for the apparent successful integration of hunting-fishing-gathering and market economies in certain Alaska Eskimo [western Alaska Yup'ik] communities." The estimated harvest levels of local food resources and other forms of income are important aspects of this case study. Wolfe characterized the local economy as follows:

> The major source of monetary income for most households was

> commercial salmon fishing during the summer. In addition, some adult women and adolescents worked for commercial salmon canneries and on freezer ships along the southern pass during summer. Occasionally, money was earned by construction, longshoring, and fighting fires. During fall, winter, and spring, many men harvested furbearers such as mink, land otter, fox, beaver, and muskrat for commercial sale. Sources of monetary income generally were seasonal, sporadic, and at levels insufficient to solely support a family's food and material needs.

The study found that household cash incomes ranged from $920 to $10,551, including welfare payments. Household production of subsistence food consisted of salmon, smelt, beluga, various fish, seal, waterfowl, ptarmigan and hare. Monthly catches varied from 813 pounds per month in summer, the most productive time, to 37 pounds per month in the spring and winter, the least productive time. Fall months average 586 pounds, except for November when 1,169 pounds of subsistence food were harvested. Besides clearly showing the annual cycle of reliance on wage and subsistence economies, this study revealed that the "interaction of monetary income and subsistence output argues against a conceptual polarization of a "subsistence economy" and "market economy" as mutually exclusive and antagonistic production systems." Rather than competing, Kotlik people were able to blend the two systems into a mutually supportive mixed economy. The research demonstrates that rather than the market economy overtaking and replacing the subsistence economy, both economies can be mutually supportive.

The subsistence economy and resources are important too because "subsistence is a principal characteristic of the economy, culture and way of life" in Alaska. According to a recent article in *The Northern Review*, "The Regulation of Subsistence in Alaska: The State's Current Dilemma," (1992) a Subsistence Advisory Council was appointed in 1990 to develop a plan that would satisfy subsistence requirements without changing the Alaska Constitution. A subsequent bill introduced in 1992 attempted to address issues of competing uses of resources as follows:

> The state's proposed plan attempts to provide a preference for rural subsistence users as required by ANILCA [the Alaska National Interest Lands Conservation Act], while allowing for the possibility for non-rural residents to qualify as subsistence users.
>
> It establishes additional criteria besides place of residence for determining who qualifies as a subsistence user. These criteria can be grouped into three categories: customary dependence on subsistence; proximity of residence to subsistence resources; and, ability to obtain alternative foods.
>
> It does not define a subsistence user simply on the basis of

quantity of subsistence resources used or simply on the basis of economic need. Natives and others have argued that subsistence as a way of life must be valued and protected by the law.

In Alaska custom, modern human migration and recent legal actions have generated considerable debate over the subsistence economy's priority over resources. Aboriginal peoples are finding themselves in this situation in many regions of Canada. Aboriginal peoples argue for rights and jurisdiction, while other users compete for claim over use. Attempts to balance this, in the face of other threats to the traditional economy, only make it more important to understand the traditional economy in terms of the biological, social and economic context of traditional life.

Case Study: Kitigan Zibi Anishnawbeg

It is difficult to determine the economic value, but this is significant for facilitating a comparative value of "country foods" to these goods in terms of the western market and wage economy which is characteristic throughout Canada. The economic impact of the traditional economy across Canada ranges from almost total dependence to significant economic and social impacts. Many Aboriginal communities live within a traditional economic system. Research conducted by the Kitigan Zibi Anishnawbeg (Brascoupé 1990) found that almost all families consume some country foods on a daily basis. Country foods in this First Nations community includes moose, deer, beaver, rabbit, muskrat, partridge and various fish. The total replacement value of country foods was estimated at $600,000 in 1988, or $1,715 per household. Forty-five per cent of the Kitigan Zibi Anishnawbeg households considered the traditional economy very significant to their overall economic livelihood.

Employment Options in the North

As stated earlier in this paper, it is generally believed that northern residents have limited economic options. Transportation and other costs make competing in the Canadian economy very difficult for northerners. So the question, "for those Aboriginal men and women who cannot be, or do not wish to be, accommodated in traditional pursuits, what options do they have for employment in northern communities?", is not easily answered. Because the northern economy is unforgiving, Aboriginal communities must have a diversified economic and employment strategy. The following identifies the five economic opportunity areas for northern Aboriginal communities:

- **Aboriginal government**: As with most Aboriginal economies band government is the major employer and contributor to the local economy. Employment and wealth generated from this sector are key to a stable and growing economy. There is a potential to establish new private businesses to provide services to band government and programs within existing funding. However, Aboriginal government should develop plans to reduce dependency on government funding.

- **Provision of local goods and services**: Most Aboriginal communities have an underdeveloped private sector to provide local goods and services. This situation results in considerable economic loss. Income which comes into the Aboriginal communities is almost immediately spent on goods and services purchased outside Aboriginal communities. Only about 10% of the reserve incomes are spent in Aboriginal communities. Not only is this a loss of potential wealth, but also a loss of jobs. Starting businesses in Aboriginal communities creates jobs and facilitates the circulation of cash within the local economy.
- **Regional/external market**: All economies develop by having new money coming into the economy from external markets. The external market contributes to local wealth creation and helps circulate money through the local economy. Business opportunities exist in tourism and the primary sectors. Tourism is one of the fastest growing sectors of the Canadian economy. Tourism directed at Aboriginal destinations attracts both the domestic and foreign markets. The primary sector, specifically forestry and minerals, are potential opportunities, keeping in mind that this sector, like the other primary sectors, is going through major restructuring. Restructuring means an overall shedding of jobs for fewer, but higher paying technical occupations.
- **High growth and emerging industries**: The economy and jobs of the future will be dominated by computers, technology and communications. This sector has been the fastest growing area of Canadian and international markets. The Canadian economy is dominated by the service sector which includes these emerging, high growth industries. It was once thought that the manufacturing sector fuelled the modern industrial economy. The new "information" industries appear to be competing with manufacturing and displacing the primary sector from its central role in the Canadian economy.

References

Berger, Thomas R. *Village Journey: The Report of the Alaska Native Review Commission*. New York: Hill and Wang, 1985.

Bodley, John H. *Tribal Peoples and Development Issues: A Global View*. Mayfield Publishing Company, 1988.

Brascoupé, Simon. *River Desert Band Economic Research Study*. River Desert Band, 1990.

Heilbroner, Robert L. and Lester C. Thurow. *Economics Explained*. A Touchstone Book, 250 pages, 1982.

Johnson, Martha. *"Documenting Dene Traditional Environmental Knowledge."* Akwe:kon Journal, Cornell University, winter 1993.

Langdon, Steve J. (ed.). *Contemporary Alaskan Native Economies.* University Press of America, 1986.

Nakazawa, Anthony, Francis Mitchell, and George Goldman. "The Regulation of Subsistence in Alaska: The State's Current Dilemma." *The Northern Review*, Number 8/9 - summer 1992.

Sahlins, Marshall. "Stone Age Economics", in *Studies in Economic Anthropology*, edited by G. Dalton, American Anthropological Association, Washington, D.C., 1991.

Salisbury, Richard F. *A Homeland for the Cree: Regional Development in James Bay 1971-1981.* Kingston and Montreal: McGill-Queen's University Press, 1986.

Turnbull, Colin. *The Human Cycle.* Triad Paladin, 1985.

The World Commission of Environment and Development. *Our Common Future.* Oxford: University Press, 1987.

Vecsey, Christopher, and Robert W. Venables (eds). *American Indian Environments: Ecological Issues in Native American History.* Syracuse: Syracuse University Press, 1980.

Veldhuis, Marijke. *Indigenous Knowledge & Development Monitor.* CIRAN, The Hague, The Netherlands, Volume 1 number 1 1993.

Creating a Climate of Confidence: Providing Services within Aboriginal Communities

*Corinne Jetté**

The fundamental questions surrounding the provision of business and professional services by and for Aboriginal people are directly related to a number of key issues that also arise in the overall discussion of Aboriginal economic development. This paper focuses on specific root causes for the inadequate or nonexistent delivery of services, and explores potential strategies to address the problem.

The document is prepared as an instrument for prompting discussion in conjunction with the National Round Table on Aboriginal Economic Development and Resources convened by the Royal Commission on Aboriginal Peoples on April 27-29, 1993 in Ottawa. It is a written response to questions provided by the Royal Commission, and seeks to promote open discussion of a number of delicate issues that still remain unresolved throughout Aboriginal communities across Canada.

The five questions formulated by the Royal Commission in this segment of the round table discussion could each be the subject of volumes of writing. Or, on the other hand, each question could be answered succinctly in a line or two. But since the guideline for writers suggests that participants in the round table "seek creative solutions based on their knowledge and expertise in the field", the writer anticipates that round table participants are already well informed of the obvious answers to these questions. For the purposes, however, of having a mutual understanding and a common perspective on the situation, brief commentary in

* Assistant Professor, Faculty of Engineering and Computer Science, Concordia University.

response to the questions is provided in the Appendix. The body of the paper examines five issues that contribute to the problem; it is followed by five strategies designed to respond to each of the issues identified.

Issues raised are limited to those crucial factors that impinge on the development and delivery of business and professional services within remote, rural, and urban Aboriginal communities. Geographic circumstances may differ, but fundamental problem areas are similar.

Although any discussion of national strategies implies some level of political involvement, the scope of the discussion remains limited to matters of economic development and, as such, precludes any direct call for political action by any specific governing authority. Rather, the ideal framework for this discussion exists within Aboriginal communities where community members commit themselves to the principles of self-determination, to address the current problem areas, and to seek creative, workable solutions that will benefit generations to come.

The scope of background material provided in this document is not derived from empirical research or quantifiable data; rather, the issues raised are directed findings from anecdotal evidence and experience compiled from the author's research activities in the areas of employment and education practices as they relate to Aboriginal communities in Canada.

Statement of the Problem

Throughout "Indian country", the phenomenon of economic, political, and social dependence and its ensuing socio-economic morass has for decades been documented again and again by Aboriginal and non-Aboriginal writers. Statistics have been compiled and profiles drawn to support the reality faced by Aboriginal peoples from coast to coast. Government departments and agencies have issued thousands of pages of analysis, all concluding that a state of crisis exists across the nation. And yet, the situation remains basically unchanged. Some effort has been dedicated to the matter of economic development by a number of organizations: papers have been written, studies have been financed, and resources have been allocated through several programs at various government levels.

But in spite of these efforts, few examples exist of Aboriginal entrepreneurs delivering profit-oriented services within their own communities; service delivery within Aboriginal public sector agencies is often below acceptable levels; few practising Aboriginal professionals serve Aboriginal clients; and few young people can envision a future engaged in such activities. As well, the level of service that is provided is often inefficient, non-standard, and, at best, sporadic in its effectiveness. It is not surprising therefore that the proportion of Aboriginal people involved in providing services is not showing any significant progress.

A number of the studies and reports referred to earlier have looked into the reasons underlying the inability of Aboriginal communities to plan, implement, and sustain sound economic activity. And in some cases, clear statements have been issued that define the specific root causes for this reality. But such reports usually focus on one or two areas that need improvement, and often lack the macroeconomic perspective that might provide the framework for long-term strategies for success. In fact, by concentrating so much energy on the leaves and the trees, it's little wonder that analysts have lost sight of the forest. Aboriginal people in Canada are in the midst of an abrupt transition from traditional societies to the free-wheeling, anything-goes ambience of a fully developed consumer society devoid of culturally relevant business practices.

In fact, Aboriginal people in Canada are on the brink of an abrupt transition from the position of being considered wards of a paternalistic state, having little say in the conduct of their own affairs, to the position of being considered masters of their own destiny, having clear jurisdiction over matters related to prosperity and self-determination that must be determined by their own leadership.

Just as the transition from rural to urban society often produces disastrous effects on Aboriginal individuals, and just as the transition from non-verbal familial communication to the world of high-tech video communication produces equally debilitating effects on Aboriginal children, Aboriginal economies are struggling with the pressure to respect tradition and, at the same time, move ahead into a productive future of economic stability.

By way of explanation, one might explore the problem from one of the most basic premises of economic theory. Quite simply, the fundamental laws of supply and demand have not driven Aboriginal communities to produce a service sector that is economically sustainable or profitable. In fact, the demand for many consumer services common in non-Aboriginal society may not even exist in Aboriginal communities. Where a potential demand does exist, potential suppliers often do not have the resources, infrastructure, or expertise to seize the opportunity. The concepts of consumer confidence, consumer risk, and business confidence are, for the most part, unknown in the majority of Aboriginal communities. Market-driven economies have not been established, and some degree of mainstream consumerism exists only in those communities close to urban centres.

So, why don't Aboriginal people operate profit-oriented, service-type commercial establishments such as the following?

- hairdressers/barbershops
- optician/audiology services
- dry cleaner/laundry
- hotel/tourism
- babysitting/daycare
- electronics sales/repair
- shoe repair
- carpet cleaning
- dressmaking/tailoring
- housecleaning/home repair
- appliance sales/repair
- lawn mowing/snow removal

In some cases, the demand simply may not exist or the skills necessary for certain services may not be sufficiently developed. Many residents of Aboriginal communities don't need services that they have the time and the desire to do themselves. Others may not be able to afford to pay for external services, and still others do not make use of such commercial services because of the existence of an extensive informal, 'underground' economy. For whatever range of reasons, demand for services may fall short of supply. Demand for public sector services, however, is high; therefore, the need for efficiency in these areas is critical.

It is not uncommon for residents of Aboriginal communities to have long-established sources for any number of services that are required, therefore precluding the need to patronize local commercial establishments. Often, family members trade services as a means of supporting each other. The existence of bartering and exchange plays a role in discouraging the establishment of service enterprises.

Moreover, ever-present internal community conflicts often mitigate against the success of service industries because of the likelihood that some residents would prefer to travel some distance (often outside the local community) to non-Aboriginal businesses than to access the same service from individuals with whom a source of conflict or rivalry exists. People simply do not have sufficient trust or confidence in the capacity of their neighbours to perform a specific task. This phenomenon deters progress in establishing new ventures and consequently impedes the progress of developing a skilled work force.

Furthermore, since the entrepreneurial spirit is often clearly identified with non-Aboriginal materialistic values, a degree of conflict may also be presented by an individual business operator who could be seen as compromising his or her traditional culture by becoming profit-oriented. Similarly, other individuals would simply dismiss any involvement in operating a service-type establishment because of a lack of interest in pursuing 'capitalist' ideology.

Any and all of these phenomena discourage the formation of a strong service sector and delay the employment and training of Aboriginal people. Several other factors compound the problem of lack of progress in the delivery of business and professional services within Aboriginal communities. Some of these factors are now presented for the purpose of initiating discussion.

Lack of Strategic Planning

Present-time orientation among most Aboriginal people hinders the capacity to plan for the future. We have all heard the articulation of this fact from members of our own families and communities who comment without hesitation, "Let's not think about next year or even next week... Let's look after today; tomorrow will look after itself."

Because of this learned survival tactic, strategic planning or critical path planning are foreign concepts among many community leaders who invariably face a range of urgent matters on a daily basis. As dominated, oppressed peoples, members of Aboriginal communities have been forced to rely on outside agents to provide life support for so many years that the prospect of self-directed strategic planning is practically outside their human experience. In some instances, attempts to initiate planning at the community or individual level have been circumvented or derailed by these same outside agents.

So the prospect of developing effective strategic plans for the future economic development of Aboriginal communities is still outside of the grasp of most young Aboriginal people and, in most cases, they do not have a base of knowledge or expertise to build on as they pursue their own options for the future. It remains for these future leaders to learn planning skills and develop their own strategic plans.

Since planning is not routine, Aboriginal employers don't usually consider human resources development as a priority. Long-term professional development of employees is overlooked and therefore contributes to the lack of progress in the proportion of Aboriginal employees providing service within Aboriginal communities.

Lack of Education

Appropriate labour market skills or entrepreneurial skills are practically nonexistent because of the historical non-participation of Aboriginal people in formal post-secondary educational programs.

To a certain extent, access to recognized educational institutions has been difficult for Aboriginal people, but the more pressing issue is the absence of motivation among young people. Because so few role models exist, and because parents and grandparents received little or no formal education, children are often discouraged at the prospect of leaving their communities to pursue post-secondary studies. Added to this fact is the sense of futility experienced by young people who are surrounded by unemployment and who may already be caught up in the welfare cycle.

As well, the experience of the residential school system and its devastating impact on Aboriginal communities contributes to the level of disenchantment with formal educational opportunities. As parents come to terms with the negative effects that these experiences had on their own childhood, it is little wonder that many do not exert pressure on their own children to travel to major centres for post-secondary education.

Added to these factors, one must consider the many cultural variables that make entry into university life extremely traumatic for many young Aboriginal people. Even when basic literacy and numeracy skills are adequate, the academic culture and demanding pace of university studies often prove to be insurmountable obstacles to good levels of success. High dropout rates, and low graduation statistics are often directly related to the lack of support services for Aboriginal students, combined with the fact that they often arrive at university ill-prepared to cope with the demands of academic programs, and ill-equipped to deal with the realities of life in the city away from family and friends. Hence, lack of higher education remains one of the primary obstacles in the development of an Aboriginal work force that can provide services within communities.

Lack of Communication

Although some highly successful service industries exist in Aboriginal communities, very little opportunity exists for information sharing among those communities. Communication practices and vehicles are not well managed, and as a result, some of the 'best practice models' are also some of the 'best kept secrets'.

Many factors inhibit the free flow of information both between and within Aboriginal communities. Communication strategies, like planning strategies, are not based on sound organizational principles. Often, access to crucial types of information is limited to a small inner circle of people who have ready access to incoming data, but who are not willing, or are not properly trained, to disseminate information. Management of information is haphazard, and is further mishandled because of improper or nonexistent organizational communication policies.

Cutbacks in the Aboriginal communications industry are also responsible for the limited range of audience contact that exists across the nation. Even though news of a social or political nature travels quickly throughout a given community, communication breakdowns frequently occur when information is channelled through the wrong institutions at the community level.

Resource centres, on-line retrieval systems, electronic bulletin boards, audio-visual material, and video sources are of little use to people who have historically relied on oral traditions, have faltering English/French language skills, have limited access to the technologies, and who have not kept pace with the technological revolution of the last 20 years. Some encouraging efforts are being made to improve this situation, but better training and education opportunities are still required to enhance opportunities for communities to communicate freely with each other.

In addition, attitudinal changes are also required with regard to the sharing of useful practices and procedures that facilitate better communication. Until significant changes take place in the communication of information regarding client services, customer service, and consumer awareness specific to Aboriginal communities, this issue will remain a contributing factor to the low rate of participation of Aboriginal people in the provision of services within Aboriginal communities.

Lack of Gender Equity

Services within Aboriginal communities are provided to a large extent by the women of the community. As providers of daycare, catering, communication, transportation, education, budgeting, tailoring, sewing, cleaning, gardening and hairdressing, thousands of Aboriginal women currently occupy positions and offer service within the 'underground' economy referred to earlier.

Whether organizing fairs, raising money for community or family gatherings, holding arts and crafts sales, supervising activities, or co-ordinating sports or cultural events, Aboriginal women often provide the community with the much needed social and cultural glue that holds the community together. In fact, many women have clearly defined roles as 'entrepreneurs' even though they do not formally operate businesses. Many households are supported by the various informal 'entrepreneurial' activities carried out by the wives, mothers, sisters, grandmothers, and daughters of the family. And yet most women do not endeavour to formalize their operations for two primary reasons: they don't feel that such formal steps to open a business are necessary to maintain their livelihood and lifestyle, and they know that their efforts to establish commercial establishments would likely meet resistance from the established local community authorities or from members of their own families. Of course, there are, no doubt, several other secondary reasons why women don't formalize their entrepreneurial activities.

If a woman provides homecare, hair styling, catering or craft manufacturing within the context of her 'traditional' role as mother and homemaker, why should she challenge accepted convention in her community by entering into a quasi-competitive world of merchandising when the entire process would more than likely pit her against the strength of male-dominated structures that operate from a perspective of clearly defined gender roles? If women in Aboriginal communities were truly equal partners in the decision-making processes of the communities themselves, they would be more likely to pursue opportunities that would strengthen the economic base of the community. As the current situation stands, many Aboriginal women are excluded from decision making, and therefore cannot be expected actively to pursue opportunities to expand the service sector in local Aboriginal economies.

Simply put, men occupy most positions of power and control within Aboriginal society, and when women aspire to these roles, they are frequently dismissed as incapable, overly assertive, or even presumptuous for thinking that they could make a contribution. When all else fails, men often turn to matters of 'tradition' as a means of discouraging women from joining the decision-making process. The irony of such a tactic is exacerbated as men sit in offices surrounded by fax machines, cellular phones, laptop computers, and other trappings of modern life as they invoke ancient ancestral gender role definitions in their efforts to maintain the exclusionary practices that are so entrenched in Aboriginal communities.

Although there is evidence that women are becoming more involved in local decision making through their participation in various 'governing' bodies, as well as through the roles they play in directing social service, education, and community health initiatives, for the most part, exclusionary attitudes and behaviours still persist within Aboriginal communities. Historical sexist ideologies imported by European conquerors and religious missionaries still play a part in gender role stereotyping to such an extent that Aboriginal children lack the positive message that gender equity will contribute to self-sufficiency of Aboriginal communities.

The role played by women in pre-contact societies varied among many Aboriginal nations, but in every case women made significant contributions to the welfare of the group. Similarly, as the issues surrounding Aboriginal economic development are explored, women must be seen as key players in the growth of self-sufficiency. As 50% of the adult population, women must participate in the growth of the service sector, specifically because it is in this area where much of their knowledge and experience lies.

Lack of Trust

One of the key elements in any discussion of the growth of the provision of business and professional services in Aboriginal communities is the matter of trust.

Trust can be defined as the feeling of confidence that one holds in a person because of the qualities that are perceived. Or trust can be defined as the ability to accept something as true; to have faith in the future; to rely on a person's capacity to produce an expected result. However one understands the concept of trust, it is an essential component in the process of building stronger economies, and it is integral to any effort designed to encourage Aboriginal communities to support local business and professional services.

Aboriginal communities, for the most part, have been robbed of the capacity to trust in anyone or anything. Years of manipulation, broken promises, and outright deception have produced a nation of individuals who hold very low tolerance for what they perceive to be risky ventures. Cynicism, sarcasm, and skepticism are the hallmark qualities of both the leadership and grassroots membership of Aboriginal communities. Without any conscious decision to do so, Aboriginal people naturally tend to question the validity of promises of economic stability or economic development. And, taken a step further, this tendency to question the potential for success should be seen as a major impediment to growth in the business sector.

This inability to trust is also reflected in the phenomenon of Aboriginal community members travelling outside their own community to access services that may be available in their own neighbourhoods. Consider the example of a small reserve located within 10 kilometres of a small rural town. Even though two grocery outlets exist on the reserve, residents still travel to the town grocer to buy staple food items because a perception exists that the Aboriginal shop owner isn't honest. The bread and eggs still carry the same price, but residents prefer not to do business with their neighbour whom they are unable to trust. The reserve entrepreneur may operate within a personal standard of ethics, but rumour and negative perceptions may be working against his or her success.

Or consider the example of a resident of a reserve where a branch of a major bank has recently opened. The resident refuses to open an account on the reserve and travels about 20 kilometres to a nearby town to do her banking at another branch of the same bank. In this case, the lack of trust lies in the perception that the bank's tellers will not respect their oaths of confidentiality. So rather than encourage the local employer and employees by showing trust in their banking operation, the resident travels the greater distance. Of course these examples are only simple illustrations of a far more serious and all-pervasive problem.

This lack of trust is not limited in any way to a discussion of economic development. It also characterizes the interaction between clients and people who may wish to establish commercial enterprises within Aboriginal communities. Since many individuals still insist on classifying Aboriginal people according to federal government definitions under the *Indian Act*, trust also breaks down when potential clients question the right of the entrepreneur to engage in a commercial enterprise on reserve territory. If there is any question of the entrepreneur's 'status' this frequently mitigates against their potential for success. As well, the whole area of band membership and self-identification often contributes to heightened tensions in the area of trust.

The entrepreneurial spirit is inextricably linked to risk taking. If the entrepreneur lacks formal education and training in managing a business, the element of risk is far greater and the potential for success is significantly reduced. Similarly, trust issues are directly related to the concepts of consumer risk and consumer confidence. If the person delivering a business or professional service does not enjoy the trust of the client, then the entire system breaks down. If Aboriginal employees are not suited to their position, are insufficiently trained, or do not project an image of professionalism, the all-important ingredient of trust cannot be established. Consumer confidence is based on trust, and business confidence within Aboriginal communities cannot be achieved without it.

The growth of a strong service sector, then, is prevented in large part because of weaknesses in the areas of strategic planning, education, communication, gender equity, and trust. So it is within these spheres that strategies should be developed to effect change. The following section of this document addresses possible strategies for consideration.

Strategies to Address the Problem

By identifying the underlying factors that inhibit growth in Aboriginal economies, concrete strategies can be developed to address them. It is of the utmost importance, however, that these strategies be designed within a global perspective that will benefit Aboriginal societies as a whole. Care and attention must be maintained toward the overall goals and objectives of building strong, productive, sustainable development. Effective leadership is essential to ensure that cultural values are respected, that minimum standards are established, that clear goals and objectives are defined, and that checks and balances are maintained throughout the process of implementing these strategies. Creating a climate of confidence in the calibre of employees and service industries is predicated on these requirements.

Developing a Strategic Planning Culture

Planning for the short and long term is the first order of priority in encouraging the expansion of business and professional services within Aboriginal communities. Existing business operations and public service organizations should, of course, be included in planning for the future with a specific focus on methodologies to improve levels of service delivery through in-service training and upgrading of skill levels for the Aboriginal work force.

As local, regional, and national strategic planning takes shape, the leadership and community membership must develop a strong commitment to follow through on decisions taken for the benefit of all. This 'buy in' by all key players will facilitate the achievement of common goals and objectives.

The initial phase of planning activities should include a detailed analysis of the organizational development of existing establishments, including a summary of the past five years of operational and program activities, employment practices, financial management and performance, communications policies, and professional development opportunities. The second phase would then chart a course for the next five years of operation and development.

Developing a Learning Culture

Education and training must play a fundamental part in all areas of community development including, of course, measures directed at economic self-sufficiency. Without the concerted effort to upgrade the skill levels of all participants in the economic life of the community, little change will occur. Professional career programs and post-secondary education must be demystified for all age groups. Partnerships with committed educational institutions should be established immediately to address the crucial issues of access and success. Although distance education and the use of high technologies can improve access, strategies should be developed to improve the availability of course offerings even to the most remote communities.

Development of curriculum that responds directly to the most immediate needs of local communities should begin immediately with the input of informed Aboriginal people.

Over the short and medium terms, Aboriginal communities must endeavour to establish a 'learning culture' where education is celebrated, learning is encouraged, and commitment to the importance of education and training becomes universally recognized and promoted. Initial steps in this process would involve public statements by leadership from all levels within the communities.

Whether perceived or real, barriers to educational opportunities must be completely eliminated. If necessary, all forms of education and training should be supported and regulated to ensure consistent levels of quality education that respect cultural values and learning styles specific to Aboriginal people. To accomplish this task, assessment of the level of awareness and sensitivity to Aboriginal culture within educational institutions should be conducted.

Particular emphasis should be placed on opportunities to acquire knowledge and skills that will be directly transferable to service sector establishments to ensure the support of economic development initiatives. To this end, skills related to business management, finance, communication, science, and technology should be ranked as priorities for the short term. Where potential students lack the basic literacy and numeracy skills, special upgrading courses that are accessible to local Aboriginal communities should be created and implemented.

To deal with the real impediments facing students studying outside their own communities, partnerships with specific post-secondary institutions should be established and nurtured to ensure ongoing realistic support bases for students having difficulty with the transition to urban centres. Aboriginal community leadership should identify those institutions that already have such support mechanisms in place, and should bear the responsibility for building these partnerships.

Bridging programs and opportunities for career education must be enhanced so that 'at risk' students or very young children are not discouraged from pursuing higher education because they lack role models. As well, students should be informed at a very early stage of the wide range of career possibilities that will be required for the growth of economic development in their own communities, and to avoid over-enrolment in currently popular programs such as law, social work, and community health nursing.

Developing Open Communication

With the use of emerging technologies, the goal of open communication among Aboriginal communities is within reach. Provided any attitudinal barriers to the free flow exchange of ideas and models are eliminated, the benefits of shared experience can be enjoyed by all Aboriginal communities, regardless of their levels of sophistication.

Communication tools should be readily available to permit entrepreneurs and professionals to identify the most effective organizational management practices. 'How to' manuals and interactive instructional video kits and documentation should be at the disposal of all members of Aboriginal communities, and workshop facilitators should be available to provide practical advice to anyone who expresses a serious commitment to establish small businesses within their communities, and thus provide additional employment and training opportunities to other Aboriginal individuals.

Again, through effective national leadership, a 'clearing house' of effective Aboriginal management practices and procedures could provide local entrepreneurs with much needed employment, training, production, marketing and promotional strategies.

Effective communications standards and practices would also help to dispel the myths surrounding the negative attitudes toward a profit-oriented economy. By establishing guidelines for minimum standards of communication, leadership would communicate its own commitment to the goals identified in the strategic planning process.

By taking advantage of existing networking opportunities, the so-called 'moccasin telegraph' could become a highly useful means of communicating success stories and could contribute significantly to overall economic development in Aboriginal communities.

Developing Gender Inclusiveness

As the present generation of Aboriginal children moves through the early years of education, they must be provided with positive messages with regard to the role women play in contributing to Aboriginal self-sufficiency. They must not be subjected to real or perceived examples of the marginalization of respected members of their community.

Any expression of ambition on the part of young women should be encouraged, and not dismissed as 'inappropriate behaviour' for an Aboriginal woman. Since all adolescents experience a certain degree of ambiguity with regard to their career orientation, a great deal of sensitivity is required to reassure young women that choosing a 'non-traditional' career path does not mean that they would be abandoning their traditional cultural roles as mothers and caregivers.

At the same time, young Aboriginal men must also be encouraged to pursue higher education as preparation for their contribution to the future of their communities. And this encouragement must be coupled with the positive message that their female peers will also play an equally important role in the pursuit of self-sufficiency.

Since young people are extremely perceptive of exclusionary or discriminatory behaviours, they must be provided with opportunities to see gender-inclusive decision making at all levels of Aboriginal society. By dispelling myths of the inferiority of women, young people will mature within a healthy environment that will nurture their own attitudinal and behavioural development. Such positive reinforcement will contribute as well to more harmonious adult relationships than they have witnessed in their own childhood communities.

Developing Business/Consumer Confidence

Low levels of self-esteem that characterize some Aboriginal people often result in debilitating influences that prevent risk taking and consequently prevent the development of entrepreneurial activity. This reality must be addressed with strategies designed to instill confidence in future entrepreneurs. By recognizing the need to establish trust at many levels, leadership within Aboriginal communities will encourage the development of a standard of professional service delivery within a context of professional ethics.

This step in the process of organizational development is a crucial strategy to address the lack of trust that permeates many communities, hinders development of local economies, and blocks progress in the growth of the proportion of Aboriginal people who deliver business and professional services.

By building a sense of communal pride, tied closely to the notion of pride in one's cultural identity, clients and entrepreneurs alike will develop a strong commitment to local economic development. The restoration of trust between individuals, and the ensuing growth in business confidence, can influence the prospects for sustained, productive local economies. Communities would then establish the important conviction that is so essential for success in the delivery of business and professional services.

A Vision for the Future

Aboriginal communities in the 1990s face the tremendous task of building a productive thriving economy from scratch. Isolated examples of successful business ventures do exist and have marked the path for generations to come. As well, a number of talented, ambitious entrepreneurs have succeeded in the challenging world of business, and they too have provided direction for future generations of Aboriginal people.

But in every case, the success stories of Aboriginal entrepreneurs across the nation are appended with painful experiences caused by poor management decisions, lack of formal education, inadequate support systems, and insufficiently skilled support staff. As the participants in the National Round Table on Aboriginal Economic Development and Resources approach their important discussions, they will no doubt open their minds to these valuable lessons and explore other findings that the experiences of seasoned entrepreneurs will provide.

Probably one of the key lessons to be taught by these pioneers would be the importance of having the best product in the best market at the best time and at the best price. Although any number of other lessons could be taught, these are the fundamental principles that spell success for any business person.

All of the difficulties in operating a successful enterprise are too numerous to list here, but the factors outlined in this paper provide an overview of the specific contextual problems and the potentially successful strategies that are related to Aboriginal communities. Perhaps by combining these issues and strategies with the experiences of successful Aboriginal entrepreneurs, a vision will emerge of how Aboriginal communities can address the need to expand the business and professional service sector, as well as the need to involve a greater number of capable Aboriginal people in the delivery of those services.

Conclusion

Aboriginal communities and individuals throughout the nation must develop a shared vision of developed economies where products and services are delivered within a context that is positive, ethical, productive, efficient, and professional.

Whether the client requires service from a housing contractor, a teacher, a clerk, a hairdresser, or a peace officer, the service must be delivered in such a way that the client feels satisfied with the level of service quality that is expected and that is being received. Once this client, or consumer, confidence is established, the cycle of business confidence is initiated. Given the consequent effects of a sound service sector, additional resources can then be directed to maintaining the level of professional training and development for other Aboriginal employees.

This paper has reviewed five problem areas identified as impediments to the progress of providing services to Aboriginal communities and has offered strategies that Aboriginal leaders may adopt in response to them. The first priority lies in defining strategic planning initiatives to chart a course for the future. Once plans are developed, a concerted effort is needed to promote the concept of a 'learning culture' throughout Aboriginal communities that will value and celebrate increased levels of education for all members of the communities. By developing partnerships with educational institutions, Aboriginal society will ensure that relevant, quality education is made available to young people.

The next area of concern is the need to develop open communication attitudes, policies, and vehicles to ensure that information is shared on the most effective management and organizational practices available for Aboriginal communities.

Finally, efforts must be directed to the subtle areas of interpersonal relationships within Aboriginal society. Since all members of Aboriginal society are stakeholders in the development of productive community economies, no one group should bear all the responsibility for its success. Similarly, no one group should be excluded or marginalized in the process of developing sustainable self-sufficiency. Trust must be established on many levels within communities across the nation, starting with the acceptance of Aboriginal women into the circle of leadership.

Appendix

Commentary on Questions Formulated by the Royal Commission

Question 1

Why is it that only slow progress is being made with respect to increasing the proportion of Aboriginal people in the provision of business and professional services, even when it comes to the provision of such services to Aboriginal people?

- Low percentage of *employees* because:
  - knowledge and skill levels are low;
  - low motivation/incentives from family or leadership;
  - effects of welfare dependency;
  - shyness, discomfort dealing with the public;
  - non-verbal orientation produces poor communication skills;
  - risk of dramatic change to lifestyle/pattern of living;
  - other priorities such as family/ recreational/ or social activities.
- Low percentage of *entrepreneurs* because:
  - knowledge and skill levels are low;
  - capital financing is complicated/impossible to access;
  - non-materialistic value system;
  - poor track record of predecessors (learned experience);
  - avoidance of potential for increased stress;
  - avoidance of risk (personal and financial);
  - perception/reality (?) that empowerment rests with select few;
  - other priorities such as family/recreational/ social activities.

Question 2

To what extent is the root of the problem found in problems accessing and completing appropriate education and training programs?

- To a medium extent, *access* is a problem because:
  - geographic distance from community;
  - low level of basic academic skills (pre-college or pre-university);
  - improper career guidance;

- low standing in competitive admission process;
- misunderstanding of affirmative action measures/programs;
- lack of financial support (particularly affects single parents);
- zero tolerance of academic culture/bureaucratic procedures;
- inadequate information distribution on various available programs.

- To a greater extent, *completion* is a problem because:
  - repeated shifts in career/program direction;
  - absence of support structures (social and academic);
  - insensitivity of mainstream educators and educational institutions to Aboriginal culture;
  - poor performance in initial term of study (early dropout);
  - low self-esteem;
  - family/community pressures take precedence
  - exposure to city life;
  - absence of time management/stress management/study skills;
  - lack of sufficient incentive/motivation to complete program;
  - high demand (and high salaries) for positions in home communities/Aboriginal organizations.

Question 3

To what extent is the root of the problem found in barriers related to the employment decisions made by school boards, health organizations, or social service agencies?

When Aboriginal candidates do not meet the minimum educational requirements imposed by licensing agencies, regulatory bodies, funding sources, or accreditation boards, barriers do exist. And in some instances, discriminatory hiring practices result from the ignorance or prejudices of selection committees. But the more likely factor is the need for organizations like those mentioned to insist on consistent levels of excellence in service delivery.

Employment decisions must be made on the basis of ensuring delivery of the best available service to clients. Minimum standards of performance are essential; therefore, minimum qualification standards must exist. Candidates lacking proper credentials, but having relevant, exceptional life experience should be employed, but in auxiliary capacities.

Question 4

What successful examples can be noted, and what steps need to be taken?

(Case studies are to be presented by participants in the round table discussions.)

Question 5

What steps need to be taken to improve the conditions of employment and training for personnel who hold public sector positions in Aboriginal communities?

- require strong management skills for managers;
- hold organizational planning sessions regularly;
- offer summer employment opportunities to students;
- offer incentives to employees who upgrade skill levels;
- offer rewards for human resource development plans;
- articulate roles and responsibilities clearly;
- ensure workload distribution is fairly assigned;
- provide frequent opportunities for training;
- use positive, detailed performance evaluation procedures;
- develop mentoring and monitoring for new hires;
- cultivate participatory work environment;
- handle nepotism practices with care;
- create consensual management practices;
- require minimum standards for client service;
- define and respond to employee needs (daycare/eldercare/etc.);
- cultivate open communication habits;
- encourage cultural component in operations;
- design flexible employment arrangements (shifts/job sharing);
- present clear policies on grounds for discipline/dismissal.

Retaining Wealth and Control in Remote Aboriginal Communities

*William Lyall**

As Canadians, we Inuit, Dene and Métis members of the Northwest Territories co-operative movement are the occupants of a territory which has sustained us as free and distinctive people for thousands of years. This land is the source of inspiration for our art and our lives. It has defined our society, culture and traditions. It has sustained us.

For the last half of this century, we have been a people in transition. Our new generations are facing challenges that our grandparents would never have dreamed of. We are making arrangements for our continuing stewardship of the land through our land claim agreements. At the same time, we are taking action to get control of the forces of change that are transforming our society.

In this brief, we intend to provide Commissioners with insight into the special difficulties of Aboriginal people who live in the North, especially as they relate to our participating in the economy of the Northwest Territories, and the success of the co-operative model in coping with those difficulties. Issues addressed in the presentation will include:

- an overview of the development and structure of the Northwest Territories co-operatives;
- a brief case study on the economic and employment benefits that have accrued to the communities of Pelly Bay and Pond Inlet through their co-operatives;

* President, Arctic Co-operatives Limited.

- a commentary on the development of financial services in the remote, Aboriginal communities of the Northwest Territories;
- a description of the unique role of co-operatives in Aboriginal community economic development in the Northwest Territories.

The Northwest Territories Co-operatives

The first co-operatives in the Northwest Territories were incorporated in 1960. During the 1960s and '70s, most Northwest Territories Aboriginal communities formed co-operatives as community-based member-owned businesses to provide community residents with services and employment opportunities. Today there are 35 co-operatives active in their communities providing a broad range of services beyond just retail. The Northwest Territories co-operatives affiliated over the years to form two co-operatively owned subsidiary service organizations, Arctic Co-operatives Limited and the N.W.T. Co-operative Business Development Fund. The combination of 100% local ownership and control with strong support services through their affiliations, has resulted in the co-operatives growing into a major economic and social force in the Northwest Territories.

The scope of business volume and activities of co-operatives are detailed further in this report.

Benefits Accrued to the Communities of Pelly Bay and Pond Inlet, Northwest Territories, Through their Community Co-operatives

Pelly Bay is a community of 410 people in 75 households located 1,300 air kilometres from the closest road link. The Co-op has an ownership base of 130 community residents. It is the only retail store in the community. In addition, it runs a small hotel facility, purchases carvings for resale in the south, and operates a heavy equipment contracting business. It also provides agency services for the telephone, airline, and for petroleum delivery.

The following statistics provide an overview of the financial impact of the Koomiut Co-operative for the five-year period 1988 to 1992:

		per household
Net Savings	$1.9 million	$25,000
Wages and Cash Dividends paid out	$2.1 million	$28,000
Re-investment in Fixed Assets	$1.1 million	$15,000
Increase in Owners' Equity	$1.2 million	$16,000

In 1993 the Co-operative issued T4 slips to 89 residents, which amounts to approximately 45% of the adult population. In the past year the Co-operative employed only one full-time non-Aboriginal person, the manager, and one part-time non-Aboriginal person.

Pond Inlet is a community of 970 people in 180 households located 3,000 air kilometres from the closest air/road link. The Co-op has an ownership base of 525 people. The Co-operative competes with southern-based Northern Stores in retailing, and runs a hotel facility, tourist lodge, agency services for petroleum and airlines, and operates a building leasing service for offices and accommodation.

The following statistics provide an overview of the financial impact of the Toonoonik Sahoonik Co-operative for the five-year period 1988 to 1992:

		per household
Net Savings	$1.2 million	$ 6,700
Wages and Cash Dividends paid out	$2.1 million	$11,700
Re-investment in Fixed Assets	$1.1 million	$ 6,100
Increase in Owners' Equity	$1.2 million	$ 6,700

In 1993 the Co-operative issued T4 slips to 64 residents, which amounts to approximately 13% of the adult population. In the past year the Co-operative employed only one full-time non-Aboriginal person, the manager.

These statistics demonstrate clearly, in simple form, the financial success and benefit of Aboriginal businesses in the Northwest Territories that have a broad community investor/owner base. What the statistics don't show is the development of our people in understanding and participating in their community economy through staff development and Board of Directors involvement. It is this people development factor that provides for the true long-term development of our communities.

Although it is important to recognize the local success of these businesses, it is equally important to note that they did not accomplish this alone. By combining their need for service with other Northwest Territories Inuit, Dene, and Métis people, they have built a support structure that they control. In this same five-year period, these two co-operatives have invested $480,000 in the form of share capital in their two central service organizations, building an infrastructure that has supported their continued success.

Environmental Constraints

Fully to understand the success of the development model we have used, it is important that the constraints under which we operate be understood.

The Northwest Territories community co-operatives are unique both in terms of the role they play as a vehicle for our peoples' participation in the Canadian economy and in terms of many barriers we have overcome through the use of our co-operatives in the North.

The majority of our communities have been formal participants in the Canadian economy only with the incorporation of the first Aboriginal businesses, locally owned co-operatives in the early '60s. Most of the economic activity in the Northwest Territories that has been owned and controlled by Aboriginal people is a result of our co-operatives. In this short period of time, the Aboriginal people of the Northwest Territories have built for ourselves, in the form of our co-operatives, the largest affiliation of locally owned Aboriginal businesses in Canada.

Geographic Conditions

Our geographic location influences every facet of our lives and imposes conditions on our business operations that exist nowhere else in the country. The Aboriginal communities we service are small, ranging in size from a low of 53 to a high of 1,700 people, are not accessible by road, and are separated from one another by large distances. Supplies are generally available by sea only once per year. In June, we must purchase and deliver to the southern dockside products that we will not see until September and that must last us until the following September.

The complete absence of any financial institution outside the major centres imposes a severe handicap on our ability to develop our personal financial management skills, on the ability of our businesses to function effectively, and on our quality of life. The geographic isolation provides no opportunity for our people to access personal financial advice, savings facilities, and personal loans. Our businesses are continually searching for ways to get deposits to the bank and to bring cash into our communities.

A resident of one of our communities will have to travel not less than 200 kilometres and as much as several thousand kilometres to find a financial institution.

Economic Conditions

Before 1950 our people lived in a cashless society and as a result have not had the experience or the opportunity to amass capital.

Through our co-operative businesses we have been able to develop local assets of over $49 million and build our equity in the businesses to $13 million. We are the people who benefit from the profits of our own businesses – profits that would otherwise have gone to enterprises owned by people who are not the residents of our small communities and are generally non-Aboriginal people. Economic development in our communities has been greatest where co-operatives have been strongest.

There have been increased wages and other sources of income for our people in the last 20 years; however, there has been no opportunity for our people to develop personal financial management skills and wealth. These skills will be critical to the economic development of our communities and our people over the next 20 years and can be accomplished only through locally available financial services.

Socio-Cultural Conditions

Co-operative associations represent the primary economic institutions of the Aboriginal people of the Northwest Territories. They are also the only Aboriginally controlled economic organizations that have provided a structure for Aboriginal people of Inuit, Dene, and Métis ancestry to work together for the betterment of all groups. They are consistent with our traditional values and have provided a viable means for achieving our financial independence. Co-operatives are important institutions in the Arctic because they are one of the few organizations that we have a direct ownership in and that we can use to improve our socio-economic status.

The extension of this co-operative model to community-owned financial institutions will be necessary if our people are to see improvements develop in our socio-cultural conditions. We cannot be forced to depend on outside influences to develop and control our financial infrastructure. Financial control and independence are a key element of social and cultural development. We are not talking about the need for instant teller services, but the need for the opportunity to develop our full understanding and management of our personal and business finances.

We are the first people in the history of mankind who have been obliged to travel from the stone age to the space age in one generation. This transition of an entire culture from a hunting and gathering society to a producer and consumer society has been facilitated by the co-operative model. This transition is not complete without reasonable access to financial services, and the co-operative financial model – credit unions – will be the only vehicle we can use to complete the process effectively and with our input and control.

Co-operatives and Community Economic Development

Over the past 30 years the scope of co-operative business activity has changed dramatically. The co-operatives have evolved from being primarily a resource and arts and crafts-based business organization. Today in the Northwest Territories members of the co-operative movement number close to 10,000; we control assets in the communities valued at $49 million. We also control assets valued at $29 million in our two central organizations, Arctic Co-operatives Limited and the N.W.T. Co-operative Business Development Fund. Our co-operatives employ over 650 people directly in our communities. In addition, income payments to artists, craftspeople and primary producers amount to an additional $2 million or more each year. Over 250 directors participate regularly in business decision making in our communities. That experience has helped many people, who served in co-operatives as staff or directors and have chosen other careers in civil administration in the communities or the territorial and federal governments. Many also serve in positions of authority in our own political organizations. There are, of course, many of us who have remained in the co-operative movement and continue to guide the economic affairs of our people.

Co-operatives are locally owned, financially and structurally independent businesses. The information that follows is a consolidation of the operations of our co-operatives and should not be understood to detail a single corporate entity.

The following is a list of the services delivered by the our Co-ops today in the Northwest Territories communities:

Number – 37	**Membership – Over 9,900**
Retail	37 Co-operatives
Hotel	20 Co-operatives
Arts & crafts	26 Co-operatives
POL	19 Co-operatives
Restaurants/coffee shops	25 Co-operatives
Contracts/agencies	13 Co-operatives
Taxi	4 Co-operatives
Cable TV	5 Co-operatives
Building leases	4 Co-operatives
Commercial fisheries	2 Co-operatives
OPERATING RESULTS 1992	
Total Volume	$58 million
Total Savings	$ 2 million
Total Assets	$49 million
Total Equity	$13 million

Absence of Financial Services

There is one essential component of economic development that still eludes us in our communities. Outside of the regional centres in the Northwest Territories, there are no financial services available. Residents in Pelly Bay, for example, have to travel thousands of kilometres by air to get to the closest financial services. This lack of financial services, together with the environmental constraints detailed already, serves to demonstrate the remarkable achievements of our co-operatives.

Although the co-operative business infrastructure has developed ways of coping with the difficulties, the development of micro-businesses and individual personal financial development has been limited significantly. The following statement, made at a workshop held to assist in the preparation of this brief, sums up the frustration many of us have had when dealing with the few banks which do exist in the regional centres.

> I know three people in our community. All of them earn over $40,000 per year. When they went to the bank to get a loan, none of them received satisfactory service.

Because of this frustration, our people have given the mandate to our co-operatives to take the initiative to establish financial services in the form of credit unions in our communities. Our co-operatives have been encouraged by the support for this initiative that we have seen demonstrated in communities where organizing efforts have begun; by the support of both the Credit Union Central of Canada and the Canadian Co-operative Association; by the results of studies and reports that have been completed with the support of government; by the acknowledgement of our own political organizations and the endorsement of our elected politicians in the territorial and federal governments.

Supporting Documents

A list of the studies and reports that have indicated the probable success of providing financial services through credit unions in the Northwest Territories includes:

- a needs assessment – *Banking Services in the Northwest Territories: A background Study prepared for the Northwest Territories Legislative Assembly's Special Committee on the Northern Economy* (Core/Net Consulting Limited),
- a feasibility study – *Feasibility of a Credit Union System in the Northwest Territories* (Core/Net Consulting Limited),
- an economic benefits study – *Benefits Arising from Small Scale Credit Unions in the Northwest Territories* (Richard A. Eckert),
- a business plan for implementation – *Planning for Credit Union Development in the Northwest Territories* (Richard Eckert).

These documents are all available on request from the N.W.T. Co-operative Business Development Fund or Arctic Co-operatives Limited.

In addition to these reports/studies, reference to the desirability of providing financial services through credit unions is contained in the *Final Report of the Working Group on Inuit Participation in the Canadian Aboriginal Economic Development Strategy* (CAED), sponsored by the Inuit Tapirisat of Canada, and *A Study of Diversification Opportunities for Aboriginal Capital Corporations*, prepared for Industry Science and Technology Canada by Dr. E. Wayne Clendenning.

The following Aboriginal organizations in the Northwest Territories are on record as supporting the development:

- Inuit Tapirisat of Canada
- Sinaaq Enterprises Limited
- Tungavik Federation of Nunavut
- Inuvialuit Development Corporation
- Pauktuutit Inuit Women's Association
- Kitikmeot Regional Council
- Keewatin Inuit Association
- Baffin Regional Inuit Association

There have also been letters of support and interest from a number of municipalities, organizations and individuals.

Role of Government

Governments have played a key role, with varying degrees of success, in facilitating community economic development in Aboriginal communities. Co-operatives in the Northwest Territories have been one of the most successful vehicles for development in our communities.

Many of those early federal government employees who were community animators in the process of co-operative development, although they could not foresee the movement among our people for self-determination, were involved in the process of expediting it.

> The mission statement of Arctic Co-operatives Limited is to be the vehicle for service to and co-operation among, the Northwest Territories Co-operatives; hence, providing leadership and expertise to develop and safeguard the ownership participation of the northern people in the business and commerce of their country, to assure control over their own destiny.

With the announcement of the CAED Strategy and the overwhelming support of Aboriginal business and community leaders, our co-operative initiatives seemed to be especially appropriate for support, given the objectives of the strategy.

The broad objectives of the strategy were stated as follows:

- greater Aboriginal participation in the design of and control over the delivery of economic development programs and services;
- strengthening Aboriginal financial, sectoral and local development institutions;
- decentralization of program delivery;
- harmonization of federal programs;
- removal of barriers within federal programs;

- increased involvement with Canadian business and investment interests; and
- active participation and support from provincial and territorial governments.

From the beginnings of the implementation of the CAED Strategy, those departments participating were informed of the importance of co-operatives in the Northwest Territories economy. The need for financial services in the form of credit unions was emphasized in the final report of the working committee on Inuit participation in the CAED Strategy. Our Aboriginal leaders from our own political organizations, economic development organizations, land claim bodies and sitting in our Parliament and territorial legislatures have also supported the development.

If we are not able to effect a change in the design of economic development programs with this level of support from our communities, it is hard to believe that we have greater participation in the design of programs, and we surely do not have control over them. The CAED Strategy has not met its first objective in the context of Northwest Territories Aboriginal people.

The credit union system in southern Canada, with assets of over $50 billion, must be considered by Canadian business and investment interests. Their willingness to support and participate in this development, financially, technically and with training, will be wasted if this development doesn't happen. This would seem to be particularly appropriate and desirable in meeting the sixth objective of the strategy. How many opportunities like this can be lost if the development of our community economies is to be achieved?

It is difficult to understand the absence of support for our co-operative initiatives from the federal government. It is amazing to us as Aboriginal people, when funds can be found to support credit union development in the Ukraine or Third World countries in Africa or the Caribbean, that no funds are available for our underdeveloped communities in our own country. It is especially so when the establishment of financial services through community credit unions is so clearly within the framework of the stated objectives of the CAED Strategy.

One evaluation of co-operative programs delivered by the Department of Indian Affairs and Northern Development included the following statement:

> If the federal government places value on the achievements of co-operatives which it has nurtured, then it has an obligation to see that native organizations adopt the same respect for twenty years of sacrifice and hard work...of native-owned co-operatives in the field of economic development...at the community level.

Community economic development through the co-operative model has proven to be highly successful and effective in the Northwest Territories. This may not be the case in other parts of Canada and that fact may have compelled the federal government to implement the CAED Strategy at the national level. It would have potentially permanently damaging results in our communities if the federal government refuses at this time to acknowledge the value of co-operative achievements. When a national strategy is implemented, regional sensitivities have to be considered. Where limited or nonexistent partnerships may have been the case in some Canadian communities, it has not been the case in the Northwest Territories. The partnership between our people and the federal government through our co-operatives needs to be continued in the field of economic development at the community level.

Conclusion

Co-operatives, as the first Aboriginal development corporations in the Northwest Territories, continue to be the most effective vehicle for community economic development. This is demonstrated by the results achieved by our co-operatives – financially in assets under our control and equity invested by our people; second, as agents for human resource development and most important, as the single largest business owned and operated by Aboriginal people in our Northwest Territories communities. Initiatives such as the effort by the co-operatives over the past five years to develop community-based financial services through credit unions indicate clearly the co-operatives' commitment to broad community and personal economic development.

- **For this reason, we are recommending that the federal government departments involved in the CAED Strategy officially recognize our Co-operatives as Community Economic Development Organizations (CEDOs).**

The provision of financial services in our communities is essential to the development of our people individually and to our economy generally. There is a demonstrated lack of access by our people to financial services through their absence in our communities, and frustration in attempting to deal with officials of the banks that do exist in the regional centres of the Northwest Territories. Access to financial services through credit unions will provide individuals with valuable experience and training in managing finances. According to the economic benefits study on developing credit unions, completed in partnership with the federal government, 12% of local households in the communities would participate as staff, directors or on committees of the local credit unions. This represents an opportunity for our people to learn financial skills through participation at a time when those skills are in urgent demand with the implementation of land claim agreements.

Credit unions also make investments through loans in small businesses which are the key to the continued development of our local economies. They can also provide financial services to existing businesses, increasing efficiency and saving dollars in small local economies.

- **We are recommending that the federal government provide direct and adequate financial investment to allow for the establishment of financial services in our communities through the development of community credit unions.**

In closing, I would like to return to some of the broad objectives of the CAED Strategy and indicate our perception of the government's progress in implementing the strategy.

- **Greater Aboriginal participation in the design, control and delivery of programs and services.**

The co-operative movement has brought forward a proposal for the development of locally owned financial institutions – credit unions – in full consultation and with the full support of local, regional and national Aboriginal organizations. There has been no positive response by the federal government departments on this issue.

- **Strengthening Aboriginal financial, sectoral and local development institutions.**

From the very beginning the co-operatives have supported the development of regional and national CEDOs to assist with community development and animation. At the same time we emphasized that the Northwest Territories co-operatives are unique in Canada in their proven success at providing for community development, and that recognition of their central organization as a sectoral CEDO must be provided. Instead we have seen the decline and elimination of support for our development work. The program has resulted in the withdrawal of support for sectoral development institutions.

- **Harmonization of federal programs.**

In the years we have been working on the development of credit unions for our communities, we have been constantly bounced back and forth between different levels of government and different departments and programs. There has been no harmonization between governments or departments on this issue.

- **Removal of barriers within federal programs.**

On the credit union issue we have been told that a development of this nature does not fall within policy, or within mandates. Despite the significant support of Aboriginal individuals and groups at all levels, from the local communities to the national level, there has been no effort on the part of the government to remove barriers to this development.

- **Increased involvement with Canadian businesses.**

The credit union and co-operative movement from across Canada has already contributed over $200,000 in development funds and support to the development of credit unions in Aboriginal communities of the Northwest Territories.

There is a further commitment of a one-time $1 million contribution, and further commitments of ongoing technical support from the co-operative and credit union system. I challenge the government to find any other example for this kind of support with no return to the donors. Despite this, there has been no support from government on this initiative.

Our closing message to the Commission is that the government needs to:

- live up to the stated objectives of the CAED Strategy;
- review the programs and policies to ensure they are responding to proposals in the spirit in which the programs were created;
- review the unique needs and developments of the Northwest Territories in terms of financial services and co-operatives as community development organizations and revise their programs and support accordingly.

Expanding Employment in the Canadian Economy

*Peter George and Peter Kuhn**

It is generally known that there exists a sizeable employment rate gap between Aboriginal people and non-Aboriginal people in Canada, and recent empirical investigations have determined that there is a significant wage gap between the two groups, too. In this paper, we begin by examining briefly the statistical record on Aboriginal education and labour market activity in Canada, and then we review some recent empirical studies of the Canadian labour market and Aboriginal earnings and employment. Finally, we discuss some of the principal policy issues confronting the Royal Commission in its consideration of future Aboriginal employment in Canada.

We have two principal emphases:

- our examination of the recent experience of Aboriginal and non-Aboriginal people in the Canadian labour force indicates that the wage gaps that exist between Aboriginal people and whites may be partly explained by differences in personal characteristics, including education and age;
- the economic returns to education are significant, and the positive relationship of educational attainment to future Aboriginal earnings and employment prospects warrants serious attention.

---

* Professors George and Kuhn are members of the Department of Economics, McMaster University, Hamilton, Ontario. Peter George is also President, Council of Ontario Universities.

Post-Secondary Education and Aboriginal Employment: The Record

Public expenditures on Aboriginal education have risen significantly, and Aboriginal enrolment rates in post-secondary education have increased dramatically over recent years. The statistical record is summarized in the Department of Indian Affairs and Northern Development's *Growth in Federal Expenditures on Aboriginal Peoples* (1993: pp. 13-17), and in Patrinos and Sekellariou (1992: Table 1, p. 258). Since 1964, the number of Aboriginal students enrolled in post-secondary programs has increased from 60 to 21,300 in 1990-91 and an estimated 24,240 in 1992-93, with most of the increase concentrated in the past decade. Meanwhile, post-secondary education expenditures have grown from virtually none to more than $200 million.

The employment record of Aboriginal persons in Canada has been bleak in comparison with that of non-Aboriginal people. Aboriginal people are less likely than non-Aboriginal people to participate in the labour force, more likely to experience high rates of unemployment, and more likely to have lower earnings. Nevertheless, studies based on the 1986 Census do show high returns from educational attainment for Aboriginal peoples.

According to the DIAND figures, drawn from the 1986 Census, 6.2% of registered Indians had some university education, compared with 18.5% of non-Indians; 1.3% of registered Indians had earned a university degree, compared with 9.6% of non-Indians (Armstrong, Kennedy, and Oberle, 1990: pp. 12, 41). One of the factors explaining these lower participation rates for Indian persons is their relatively low completion rates of high school diplomas. Even when Indian people do register at university, they appear to be less than half as likely as non-Indians to complete university degree studies.

The general correlation between years of education and various indicators of economic well-being is well known. Table 1 summarizes some of the DIAND data on employment and earnings by educational level. Labour force participation rates, employment rates, and incomes are higher, and unemployment rates are lower, at successively higher levels of educational attainment. Armstrong, Kennedy, and Oberle present data on these indicators for four educational levels (less than high school; high school diploma; non-university certificate or diploma; university degree) for both Indians and non-Indians. Take labour force participation rates for example. For Indians, the rates increase from 37.9% at the lowest educational level to 86.9% at the highest level; for non-Indians, the comparable increase is from 50.6% to 87.1%. Employment rates behave similarly. For unemployment rates, the decrease for Indians is from a high of 38.9% for those of low educational attainment to a low of 11.8% for those with university degrees. Unemployment rates for non-Indians also decrease with education, but within a smaller range.

Table 1

Aboriginal Labour Force Activity and Income, 1986 Census

	Registered Indians	Non-Indians	Ratio, Non-Indians/Indians
1. Less Than High School			
Labour Force Participation Rate	37.9	50.6	1.3
Employment Rate	23.1	43.9	1.9
Unemployment Rate	38.9	13.3	0.3
Median Income	$ 9,694	$14,587	1.5
2. High School Only			
Labour Force Participation Rate	63.5	72.2	1.1
Employment Rate	46.3	65.1	1.4
Unemployment Rate	27.1	9.8	0.4
Median Income	$10,836	$16,834	1.6
Percentage Above $20,000	15.5	29.2	1.9
Percentage Above $40,000	1.8	5.0	2.8
3. Non-University Certificate			
Labour Force Participation Rate	77.5	81.1	1.1
Employment Rate	58.5	74.2	1.3
Unemployment Rate	24.5	8.5	0.3
Median Income	$12,764	$19,277	1.5
4. University Degree Holders			
Labour Force Participation Rate	86.9	87.1	1.0
Employment Rate	76.9	82.3	1.1
Unemployment Rate	11.8	5.4	0.5
Median Income	$21,275	$30,016	1.4
Percentage Above $20,000	50.6	62.6	1.2
Percentage Above $40,000	12.6	29.5	2.3

Source: Armstrong, Robin, Jeff Kennedy, and Peter R. Oberle. *University Education and Economic Well-being: Indian Achievement and Prospects* (Ottawa: Department of Indian Affairs and Northern Development, October 1990), p. 41

Similar results also obtain for median income comparisons by educational level for Indians and non-Indians: Indians with university degrees have a median income of $21,275, non-Indians $30,016; for those with high school only, the median income levels are $10,836 and $16,834 for Indians and non-Indians respectively; and for those reporting less than high school completion, the figures fall to $9,694 and $14,587 respectively. In brief, these results suggest that labour force activity increases with education for both Indians and non-Indians, and that the differences in labour force activity between the two groups decline with education. This suggests relatively greater returns to educational level for Indians than non-Indians. Some of the differences in labour force activity and incomes are attributed by Armstrong, Kennedy, and Oberle to barriers to gaining work experience which confront Indians, partly because of fewer opportunities to participate in labour force activity on reserves and in remote regions. A useful review of many economic and non-economic factors, which may influence Indian participation in the labour force, is presented by Peters and Rosenberg (1992).

Given the apparent differences in labour force characteristics of Indians and non-Indians reported by Armstrong, Kennedy, and Oberle, it is useful to look at some studies that inquire into the determinants of earnings and employment for Aboriginal people and non-Aboriginal people. These studies examine the contributions of personal productivity-enhancing characteristics to earnings, and search out wage gaps that are not readily explained by human capital endowments and which might be a function of discrimination or cultural factors (e.g., living in a remote region with elements of traditional lifestyle). Our purpose is to help answer whether the increasing participation of Aboriginal people in education, especially post-secondary education, will remedy some past wage differentials between Aboriginal people and non-Aboriginal people. This is especially important because of growing numbers of off-reserve Aboriginal persons and the large numbers of young school-age population in Aboriginal communities.

The Canadian Labour Market and Aboriginal Employment: Recent Empirical Investigations

Banerjee, Alam, and De Civita (1991)

In an unpublished paper, based on data from the 1986 Labour Market Activity Survey (LMAS), the authors measure Aboriginal/non-Aboriginal earnings differentials and assess the influence of various socio-economic factors to explain the differentials.

Their regression results indicate that, on average, Aboriginal people earned about 26% less than non-Aboriginal people. Both experience and education variables are significant and positive, implying that higher wages, associated with marketable skills and knowledge and hence greater labour productivity, are related to greater experience and education. Overall, about 58% of the Aboriginal/non-Aboriginal wage gap is "explained" by differences in human capital (e.g., experience, education, unionization), and the remaining 42% is "unexplained" and is accounted for by such factors as "barriers to entry, culture, remoteness, and racial discrimination."

They proceed to examine more closely the impact of education. An additional year of education leads to a 10% increase in earnings of Aboriginal people, and to a 7.5% increase in the earnings of non-Aboriginal people. If Aboriginal people are assumed to have the same educational level as non-Aboriginal people, the wage differential falls from 26% to 17%. A similar analysis lowers the differential from 26% to 22% when Aboriginal people are assumed to have the same levels of experience as non-Aboriginal people. When both education and experience are held equal, the wage gap falls to 12.5%.

Although these appear to be interesting preliminary results, there are problems of interpretation in this study. The dependent variable is variously called "wages", "earnings", and "income", but is never defined. The LMAS reports Total Annual Earnings from all jobs, and this is probably what the authors are examining. But it cannot be interpreted as wages, since it has two components – hours worked and wages per hour. Is any measured "gap" in earnings a gap in "wages" or in "hours worked", or both? The solution is to use hourly wage data, or to restrict the analysis to full-time, full-year workers (as do George and Kuhn (1993); see below). Also, the LMAS is somewhat limiting as a data base, in that it does not distinguish between registered and non-registered Indians and it does not cover Indian reserves.

Drost and Eryou (1991)

The authors examine the impacts of education and training on the employment experience of Aboriginal and non-Aboriginal people, using data on the labour force status of trade/vocational school leavers two years after graduation (National Graduates Survey (NGS) 1984) and of a random sample of the total Canadian population, 15-54 years of age (1986 Census). For the NGS sample, the unemployment rate for both Aboriginal and non-Aboriginal people is higher than the national average rate for Aboriginal and non-Aboriginal people aged 15-54 years, likely reflecting the relatively low educational attainment of the NGS sample. In May/June 1984, the unemployment rate for Aboriginal people was higher by 6.7% than for non-Aboriginal people (30.0% compared with 23.3%), but the differential falls as educational attainment level increases, to a low of 3.7% for vocational school graduates with some university education or a university degree (22.2% compared with 18.5%). This result may suggest a higher return to educational attainment for Aboriginal persons than for non-Aboriginal persons (see George and Kuhn (1993), below). The authors also report unemployment rates by field of vocational training, and speculate on the possible reasons for differential impacts on Aboriginal and non-Aboriginal persons in highly cyclical and seasonal industries characterized by low employment stability, and in local labour markets with limited absorptive capacity.

The regression results suggest that unemployment is more affected by the major field of study than the level of education, and that previous work experience has a positive impact on post-training employability, especially for Aboriginal respondents. Also important is the finding that Aboriginal graduates who have themselves financed their training programs have a lower chance of being unemployed, whereas the funding of training by the federal or provincial governments seems to have a strong disincentive effect on subsequent employment.

We turn now to Drost and Eryou's analysis of the 1986 Census sample. Not surprisingly, the labour force participation rate rises and the unemployment rate falls as educational attainment level increases for both Aboriginal and non-Aboriginal persons. The lowest rates of unemployment for both Aboriginal and non-Aboriginal are for those with university degrees (9.1% and 6.3% respectively). Aboriginal males had higher unemployment rate differentials relative to non-Aboriginal males than did Aboriginal females vis-à-vis non-Aboriginal females at all but one level of schooling. Again, the differential between Aboriginal and non-Aboriginal persons was smallest for those with university degrees. The regression results give powerful testimony to the positive impact of any post-secondary education or training on employment for Aboriginal women, and of a university degree for Aboriginal men, when compared with completing a secondary school graduation diploma.

Drost and Eryou alert us to the importance of studying men and women separately: they demonstrate that the impacts of educational attainment on unemployment are quite different for Aboriginal men and women, especially for education beyond the secondary school level. Their similar findings for non-Aboriginal men and women suggest that gender differences may not be entirely the result of labour market conditions specific to Aboriginal persons. Finally, Drost and Eryou recommend a review of the policy implications of sources of training funding and income for Aboriginal participation and success in the labour market, and consideration of the impacts of alternative institutional delivery mechanisms.

Patrinos and Sekellariou (1992)

This is a recently published paper that examines wage gaps between Indians and non-Indians using the 1986 Labour Market Activity Survey, as did Banerjee, Alam, and De Civita (1991). Again, the basic approach is to decompose the differences in wages into "explained" and "unexplained" components, the "explained" elements being identified with human capital endowments that enhance productivity and hence earning capacity, and the "unexplained" elements reflecting unobserved factors, including discrimination.

Patrinos and Sekellariou employ a standard methodology for decomposing the difference in wages into the "explained" and "unexplained" components. The sample characteristics of Indians and non-Indians are as expected. Indians, on average, earn less than non-Indians, and have a lesser endowment of the personal characteristics normally expected to influence employment earnings, including fewer years of schooling and experience. A higher proportion of Indians are in manual labour and are non-unionized, and a lower proportion in managerial and professional employment, than is the case for non-Indians.

The earnings function results are very interesting. As the authors report, the average returns to years of schooling are higher for non-Indians than for Indians, as are the returns to labour market experience. As a result, non-Indians are found to have a distinct earnings advantage. (This result is actually misreported in Patrinos and Sekellariou, p. 262.) Differential endowments of productive personal characteristics of individuals explain about 41% of the wage differential between Indians and non-Indians. The remaining 59% is "unexplained", and may be because of unobserved characteristics (e.g., ability, health, culture) and/or by discrimination.

The authors' conclusions are important for our present purposes. In terms of personal endowments, much of the earnings gap of Indians compared with non-Indians can be explained by Indians' disadvantageous educational attainment, labour force experience, and occupational attainment. But education and experience are no guarantee of earnings equality; the "unexplained" component is very high in Canada among full-time male workers. The authors cite results for a similar United States study that finds only 10% of the earnings gap to be "unexplained". In other words, much of the earnings differential in the U.S. would disappear if Indians' education and experience were brought up to the level of non-Indians. This suggests that "discrimination" accounts for very little of the differential in the U.S. In Canada, according to Patrinos and Sekellariou, almost 60% is "unexplained", and hence possibly accounted for by discrimination. They adduce lower quality of schooling at Indian schools on-reserve and cultural differences leading to lesser attachment to the labour force, both of which cannot be modelled adequately, as likely causes of the size of the "unexplained" differential. Even after allowing for the endowment of Indians with the same productive characteristics as non-Indians, Indians are paid less in Canada.

The principal policy recommendation by the authors is that investment in education and training to increase human capital are important for Indians, because such productivity-enhancing characteristics are positively related to earned income. They also recommend affirmative action efforts to recruit Indians into high-wage, high-skill occupations, which will improve the returns to Indians for their acquisition of productivity-enhancing characteristics.

One of the limitations of this study is that it investigates only gross wages for males employed full-time. Moreover, the LMAS is limited to off-reserve status and non-status Indians, and excludes those on-reserve as well as Inuit and Métis. The Survey also excludes the Yukon and Northwest Territories. These deficiencies are satisfied in the George and Kuhn (1993) study.

George and Kuhn (1993)

As with the Patrinos and Sekellariou (1992) paper, we employ standard techniques in the earnings function literature to decompose wage differentials between Aboriginal people and non-Aboriginal people into their "explained" and "unexplained" components. The primary focus of our study is also Aboriginal persons living off-reserve and outside the Yukon and Northwest Territories, because there are some important differences in wage structure on reserves and in the Territories and because there are legitimate concerns about the representativeness of the on-reserve data owing to incomplete participation in the 1986 Census.

There the similarity ends, for we make use of Statistics Canada's Public Use Sample Tape from the 1986 Census, which allows for a much larger sample of Aboriginal people than either the LMAS or NGS. (Using LMAS, Patrinos and Sekellariou (1992) have 359 Aboriginal people in their data set; we have 5,832 Aboriginal people of whom 1,535 are full-time full-year workers off-reserve and in Canada outside the Territories.) We also use two definitions of Aboriginality in our paper: the first, more *inclusive* definition, includes all respondents reporting *any* Aboriginal origins, possibly in combination with non-Aboriginal origins, where Aboriginal origins includes North American Indian, Métis and Inuit; the second, more *exclusive*, definition includes those respondents reporting *only* Aboriginal origins.

Our results for off-reserve full-time full-year workers living outside the Yukon and Northwest Territories can be summarized briefly. We find a relatively small raw wage differential between Aboriginal and white Canadians at 11%, which grows to 17.6% when the sample is restricted to persons with exclusively Aboriginal origins; by comparison, we find a raw wage gap of almost 35% between white men and women in our data set. Interestingly, the gap varies with gender and degree of Aboriginal self-identification: for women reporting any Aboriginal origins, the gap is only 6.5%, whereas the male gap is 11.6%; when restricted to persons reporting exclusively Aboriginal origins, the women's gap rises to 10.8% and the men's to 18.1%.

Differences in observable personal characteristics, such as education, language and region, are readily apparent. Aboriginal people are, on average, younger, more likely to live in the west, and less likely to live in Census metropolitan areas. Aboriginal people are less well educated than non-Aboriginal people, but Aboriginal women are considerably better educated than Aboriginal men. Among whites, 24% of men and 23% of women have at least some university education; among Aboriginal people, these numbers are 7% for men and a surprisingly high 17% for women. Aboriginal people also report less non-university training than non-Aboriginal people.

Our wage regressions report some of the standard results common in the literature. For both whites and Aboriginal people, wages rise with education and training. There are considerably greater returns to education for non-Aboriginal women than for men: while well-educated women still earn less than comparable men, they do much better relative to men than do less educated women. The returns to education for Aboriginal men are very similar to those for white men, and there are very large returns to education for Aboriginal women, exceeding even those of white women in the sample. Finally, there doesn't appear to be any clear regional pattern in the Aboriginal-white wage gap.

In calculating the share of the overall Aboriginal-white earnings gap that can be attributed to observable personal characteristics, we are able to explain about 50% of the overall Aboriginal-white wage gap for those declaring exclusively Aboriginal origins, and about 20% to 40% of the gap between our broader definition of Aboriginal people and whites. For this group, raising the education and training levels of Aboriginal people to those of non-Aboriginal people could eliminate about 30% of the Aboriginal-white wage gap for men and 40% for women, according to our estimates. The higher number for Aboriginal women is the result of a higher marginal return to education for Aboriginal women than for Aboriginal men in our sample. The remaining differences could also result from differences in productivity-enhancing characteristics that are observed by employers but not measured in the Census, but given the number of documented cases of labour market discrimination seen in forums like the Canadian Human Rights Commission, it seems likely that discrimination plays some role here as well. If so, our analysis suggests that labour market discrimination is stronger against Aboriginal men than women.

We also study Aboriginal people who live on-reserve and in the Yukon and Northwest Territories. Aboriginal people who live on-reserve earn considerably less than Aboriginal people who live off-reserve. Men with exclusively Aboriginal origins earn 14% less on-reserve than off-reserve; such women earn 9% less on-reserve than off-reserve. Lower wages on-reserve could be caused by a number of factors, including differences in the observed and/or unobserved qualifications of on-reserve Aboriginal persons, differences in the structure of earnings on-reserve and off-reserve, and differences in wages resulting from compensating differentials for the tax benefits of living and/or working on-reserve, or from a lower local demand for labour. Based on our estimates, unlike the case for off-reserve Aboriginal people, there is a lack of any detectable return to education for people living on-reserve, whether male or female. This finding is consistent with differences in the structure of earnings and employment opportunities on-reserve and off-reserve, with relatively few full-time full-year wage employment opportunities in the rather thin labour markets characteristic of most reserves and their vicinities, especially in remote areas. In addition, there is the possibility of income-augmenting traditional activities for those living on-reserve, the results of which affect real income but do not usually enter into measured earnings differences.

Aboriginal/non-Aboriginal wage gaps are much larger in the Yukon and Northwest Territories than in other parts of Canada. For men with any Aboriginal origins, the gap rises from 11.6% in the rest of Canada to 16.1% in the Territories; for women, the gap increases from 6.5% in the rest of Canada to 29.2% in the Territories. This does not reflect lower wages for Aboriginal people in the North than in the south; rather it results from a smaller wage premium for working in the North among Aboriginal people than among non-Aboriginal people. The raw data suggest that the northern premium is about 5% for Aboriginal persons of both sexes, about 11% for white males, and an astounding 39% for white females, which persists when all observable personal characteristics are controlled for. This might reflect differences in real costs of living for Aboriginal people and non-Aboriginal people in the North, and the distinct possibility that Aboriginal people are deriving real income supplements to wage earnings from their unmeasured economic activities on the land (e.g., hunting, trapping, fishing, fowling, and gathering).

We are somewhat more optimistic about the economic position of Aboriginal people in the Canadian labour market than are Patrinos and Sekellariou (1992). Certainly there is evidence of serious unemployment problems among Aboriginal people, and these can be attributed in part to barriers to entry into the labour market, including the lack of employment opportunities in or near Aboriginal communities and to discrimination in the education system and job market. On the other hand, when those barriers have been overcome and Aboriginal persons are working full-time full-year in the labour market, Aboriginal people incur wage gaps that are small and returns to education that are high when compared with other, much-studied disadvantaged groups in the same situations (e.g., women and U.S. Blacks). This suggests that full and effective integration into mainstream Canadian labour markets of Aboriginal people living in Canada, and especially Aboriginal women, may not be an unrealistic goal in the future. Whether this kind of integration is desired by most Aboriginal people in Canada is a very different question.

We have restricted our analysis to full-time full-year workers because of the nature of the earnings question in the Census survey instrument. Reliable estimates of wages are available then only for full-time full-year workers, and we restricted our sample to persons working 48 weeks or more and who report doing so full-time. This excludes from our estimations of wage gaps those workers who choose to be part-time part-year or seasonal workers, and as a consequence excludes many Aboriginal people. In many remote areas, for example, Aboriginal people may prefer part-time or seasonal work, because of their participation in traditional activities. Among some Aboriginal people, there may well be a preference for jobs that represent combinations of lower wages plus greater flexibility and non-measured bush income, and our study doesn't allow for this possibility. Hence, our neglect of part-time wage earnings may be unfortunate. Again, we have not looked at earnings gaps by occupational group. Many

Aboriginal people appearing in the Census sample who report full-time full-year employment may well be employed in the bureaucracy and in education; if true, our aggregative approach might distort the earnings comparisons with non-Aboriginal people by concealing the disproportionate representation of Aboriginal people in these sectors and disguising some greater earnings differentials in other occupational groups.

Finally, we believe that it is important that a follow-up study of the kind we have completed with the 1986 Census data be undertaken with the 1991 Census data, including the special Aboriginal Survey, as a matter of highest priority. Canadians need to know the real state of affairs about whether there is fair and equitable treatment of Aboriginal people in Canada who are actively engaged in the Canadian labour market.

The Canadian Labour Market and Aboriginal Employment: Some Policy Issues

In this section, we comment on some of the major policy issues surrounding the employment of Aboriginal people in the Canadian labour market. We take as our starting point the five questions posed by the organizers of the Round Table.

> To what extent are portions of the Aboriginal labour force particularly vulnerable to displacement from existing patterns of employment, due to the development of new labour-saving technologies, the impact of competing markets, and so forth? What can be done to assist these groups better to adjust to the changing conditions of the Canadian labour market?

If we interpret "displacement" broadly as simply being unemployed, then it is clear that the unemployment rates of Aboriginal people in Canada are much higher than among non-Aboriginal people. Unemployment is slightly higher among Aboriginal men than among women, much higher on-reserve than off-reserve, and generally declining with age. Not only is the average Aboriginal unemployment rate high, there is also considerable variation within the Aboriginal population in terms of its vulnerability to unemployment.

If we interpret "displacement" as permanent job loss as a result of industry- or plant-level economic conditions, then there are to our knowledge no studies of the particular vulnerability of Aboriginal people. There is, however, some work on displacement *per se*, from which we can probably infer some things about Aboriginal people. Regarding the incidence of displacement, Farber (1993) in one of the few studies of this topic finds that, like unemployment in general, displacement is decreasing with age and education. Since the Aboriginal population is younger and less educated than the general population, this makes Aboriginal people likely to be more vulnerable to displacement resulting from industrial restructuring, at least conditional on their being employed in the first place. It should be pointed out, however, that for people who are unemployed to begin with, this kind of restructuring-induced displacement is rather meaningless: the unemployed were never players in the "old" system, so the collapse of that old system (high-wage, blue-collar union jobs for unskilled and semi-skilled males) is, although quite painful for some, not really an issue for these people.

Regarding the costs of displacement for those who are displaced, it is well known that both the durations of unemployment and the wage losses associated with displacement are, like the incidence of displacement, greater for poorly-educated workers. This makes Aboriginal people more vulnerable again. These same costs of displacement are *lower* for younger workers, as it is the senior, not the junior workers who experience major wage losses on displacement. Being younger, on average, actually helps Aboriginal people in this regard.

> What has been the employment experience of the large number of Aboriginal graduates of post-secondary programs over the last two decades? Has the investment in higher education paid off and is it likely to continue to do so in the future? Does the experience of Aboriginal men and women differ? How well equipped is the Aboriginal labour force to participate in a Canadian economy that is increasingly based on advanced technologies and the processing of information?

We have reviewed the employment rates of Aboriginal persons with post-secondary education, and the beneficial effects of higher education seem clear. There are many studies attesting to the high private returns to investment in higher education. Regarding earnings of the more-educated Aboriginal people conditional upon employment, our study (George and Kuhn, 1993) shows very substantial returns to education of Aboriginal people, primarily for those off-reserve and especially for women.

All indicators in the labour market show that, compared with 10 years ago, education is much more important than before. In a recent study by Kuhn, Lemaitre and Picot (1993) for Statistics Canada, on the demographic distribution of unemployment in Canada from 1977 to 1992, the group that experienced the largest increase in unemployment over the period was men with a primary education, aged 25-44 (i.e., the traditional, unskilled, middle-aged, blue-collar male). This group's unemployment rate was 8.9% in 1977 and 21.8% in 1992. (By contrast, women aged 15-24 with some post-secondary education saw their unemployment rates fall from 11.4% to 10.5% over this period.) Anything that moves Aboriginal people out of this most vulnerable group will certainly help, and education and training are the primary instruments for doing so.

Government programs aimed at increasing participation rates in post-secondary education, such as DIAND's Post-Secondary Education Assistance Program and

Ontario's Aboriginal Education Strategy, are, in principle, steps in the right direction. But the evidence on the Post-Secondary Education Assistance Program is somewhat mixed to date: participation rates of Aboriginal people in post-secondary education have increased significantly, but success and completion rates have lagged, and this raises questions about program design. (See Armstrong, Kennedy, and Oberle (1990: pp. 37-39), and Drost and Eryou (1991: pp. 11-15).) Moreover, greater Aboriginal participation in post-secondary education continues to be challenged by the low rates of participation and completion of secondary school diplomas which remain the principal route for admission to post-secondary education.

> To what extent and in what ways do Aboriginal women face distinctive problems in the Canadian labour market, and what should be done about them? To what extent do Aboriginal youth face distinctive problems in the Canadian labour market, and what should be done about them?

There are particular labour market problems associated with being a single parent, or a mother alone. According to our paper, Aboriginal women are less likely than white women to be married, more likely to be widowed, divorced or separated, and have more children. We do find evidence of high returns to education for Aboriginal women in our study, and this remains the best corrective to the adverse impacts on earnings and employment and welfare dependency of marital breakdown. Similarly, for Aboriginal youth, who suffer extremely high rates of unemployment relative to non-Aboriginal people, the importance of increased education and training is axiomatic.

There are some important differences arising from off-reserve versus on-reserve residence. According to our results, education produces higher benefits to off-reserve Aboriginal people than to on-reserve Aboriginal people. On-reserve Aboriginal people start from lower levels of educational attainment, but there is also the matter of differential in-kind earnings opportunities, especially from bush-related activities on-reserve, that may distort the on-reserve, off-reserve earnings comparisons.

We need also to reflect on the extent to which the major labour market conditions discussed in this paper are peculiar to Aboriginal persons, and to what extent they are gender-based and independent of Aboriginal/non-Aboriginal differences. We have presented some evidence, for example, that Aboriginal males have greater difficulty in matching training/skills to employment opportunities than females. Moreover, we suspect that these problems are exacerbated by the regulatory environment represented by the *Indian Act* and in certain provincial jurisdictions, which induce educated, skilled Aboriginal people to engage in rent-seeking rather than directly productive activities. Indeed, devolution and self-determination will provide more jobs at the local level for rent-seekers but also permit greater community influence on resource allocation decisions. In our view, decentralization is necessary but not sufficient to increase the well-being of Aboriginal communities: improvement of community economic prospects will require as well the reduction of regulatory constraints that inhibit investment and participation in directly productive activities in Aboriginal communities.

Concluding Remarks

By all the standard measures, Canada's Aboriginal population is economically disadvantaged. Aboriginal people in Canada have a high proportion of dependent population, and their widespread spatial distribution, especially the rural orientation of Status Indians and the remote locations of many reserves, pose serious challenges for accessibility to employment, capital and consumer markets, and to the full range of social services provided through government programs.

Labour force data are particularly telling. A high proportion of registered Indians of labour force age, both on-reserve and off-reserve, has effectively withdrawn from the labour force. Labour force participation rates are very low for Indians compared with non-Indians, and the lowest participation rates are found for Indians on-reserve. Similarly, unemployment rates of First Nations and other Aboriginal people are high relative to non-Aboriginal people; again, they are highest for Indians on-reserve. The employment rate (the percentage of working age population employed) is about one-third for Indians on-reserve, about one-half for Indians off-reserve, and about two-thirds for non-Aboriginal people. Indian youth employment rates are low everywhere. In part, employment rates in remote areas (e.g., for northern reserves) are low because few local employment opportunities exist, and because traditional non-wage economic activities are not included in Census calculations. Nevertheless, two conclusions are inescapable: first, Aboriginal peoples, including registered Indians, take up available jobs and achieve respectable employment rates when employment opportunities exist, although at levels that appear to be somewhat lower than for non-Aboriginal people living in Canada; second, Indians on-reserve suffer from extremely low levels of employment and from a preponderance of less stable, low-paying forms of employment, with a heavy reliance on part-time and seasonal work, some of which admittedly may be by choice.

As a consequence of their more tenuous labour force connections, Aboriginal peoples are disproportionately represented in the lowest ranges of personal incomes and in their greater dependence on transfer payments. Levels of educational attainment tend to parallel the findings on labour force and personal income, with which they are highly correlated. Compared with non-Aboriginal people, Aboriginal peoples, especially registered Indians, are likely to have low levels of education.

This remains a gloomy picture, but it is one that is showing distinct signs of improvement, as some of the findings reported earlier in this paper attest. Indeed, the results of recent empirical studies accord with our "common sense" view of the basic factors in Aboriginal/non-Aboriginal employment and earnings experience, and our conviction about the income- and employment-augmenting effects of education. As a result, we believe that Commissioners should assign high priority to increasing Aboriginal participation in the completion of education and training programs. To enhance the impact of investment in education and training on employability, particular attention should be paid to such proven benchmarks of educational attainment as secondary school diploma and university degree completion. Then, given the decision to participate in the labour market, more education and training will help Aboriginal people (and non-Aboriginal people for that matter) to adjust better to displacement in the shrinking sectors of the Canadian economy and to capitalize on expanding employment opportunities in the growing sectors, especially among knowledge-based industries and services.

Nevertheless, the empirical studies reported here also deny the implicit assumption that parity in earnings and employment would follow on greater integration into the labour market. Given the George and Kuhn (1993) results, even when restricting our analysis to those Aboriginal people who are off-reserve, full-time, full-year wage-earners, there is still a large, unexplained residual after differences in human capital endowments are accounted for. Job equity may well begin with education, but even after full policy attention has been directed to the ameliorative effects of greater Aboriginal participation in educational and training opportunities, Commissioners will still need to give close consideration to equity and affirmative action policies to eradicate persistent earnings differentials that can be laid to discrimination.

References

Armstrong, Robin, Jeff Kennedy, and Peter R. Oberle. *University Education and Economic Well-being: Indian Achievement and Prospects*. Ottawa: Department of Indian Affairs and Northern Development, October 1990.

Banerjee, A.K. Paul, Jahangir Alam, and Paul De Civita. "Wage Gap Between Aboriginals and Non-Aboriginals in Canada: An Empirical Analysis," paper presented to the Annual Meeting of the Canadian Economics Association, Kingston, June 2-4, 1991.

Department of Indian Affairs and Northern Development. *Growth in Federal Expenditures on Aboriginal Peoples*. Ottawa: February 1993.

Drost, Helmar, and Tim Eryou, "Education/Training and Labour Force Status: A Cross-Section Study of Canadian Natives," paper presented to the Annual Meeting of the Canadian Economics Association, Kingston, June 2-4, 1991.

Farber, Henry S., "The Incidence and Costs of Job Loss: 1982-1991," Princeton University Industrial Relations Section, Working Paper No. 309, January 1993.

George, Peter, and Peter Kuhn, "The Size and Structure of Native-White Wage Differentials in Canada," revised version of McMaster University Department of Economics Working Paper No. 92-12, February,1993.

Kuhn, Peter, G. Lemaitre, and G. Picot, "Employment, Unemployment, Hirings and Layoffs during the 1981-82 and 1990-92 Recessions," paper presented at the Statistics Canada/CERF Conference on Comparing Labour markets during the Last Two Recessions, March 5, 1993.

Patrinos, Harry A., and Chris N. Sekellariou, "North American Indians in the Canadian Labour Market: A Decomposition of Wage Differentials," *Economics of Education Review*, 11 (1992), 257-66.

Peters, Evelyn, and Mark W. Rosenberg. *Indian Attachment to the Labour Force.* Ottawa: Department of Indian Affairs and Northern Development, August, 1992.

Aboriginal Peoples and Employment Equity

*Renée Dupuis**

This working paper, which was prepared at the request of the Royal Commission on Aboriginal Peoples, is the result of reflections based on my 20 or so years of experience with various Aboriginal groups. It attempts to answer questions raised by the Royal Commission concerning employment equity for Aboriginal peoples and the adjustments that will be required for the employment of Aboriginal people outside their communities. These are complex questions and, unfortunately, it is difficult to provide simple answers. We shall attempt here to cast some light on these questions that will help us toward a better understanding of the issues.

Since the 1970s various groups representing women and a number of minority communities have demanded government action to improve their position in Canada's work force. The adoption of the *Canadian Charter of Rights and Freedoms* as part of the Canadian Constitution in 1982 is certainly not unrelated to the increased pressure exerted by groups that feel disadvantaged in order to improve their position in Canadian society. In the view of these groups, one of the means of achieving this is to ensure that the work force reflects the make-up of Canadian society.

* Commissioner, Canadian Human Rights Commission. Renée Dupuis teaches law at the École nationale d'administration publique and acts as counsel to the Quebec Department of Justice. Starting in 1972, she also acted as counsel to several Aboriginal groups. She is author of *La Question Indienne au Canada*, published in Montreal by Éditions du Boréal in 1991.

Moreover, section 15 of the *Canadian Charter of Rights and Freedoms*, guaranteeing the right of every individual to equality before the law, is counterbalanced by the possibility that a so-called affirmative action program may be implemented "that has as its object the amelioration of conditions of disadvantaged *individuals* or *groups*" and involves discrimination on grounds such as sex, race, ethnic origin or disability.

The Supreme Court of Canada recognized the validity of such programs in 1987, when it upheld the decision of a federal human rights tribunal ordering an employer, Canadian National, to hire women for positions traditionally reserved for men until a specific percentage was achieved.

The object of the employment equity legislation and programs adopted by various levels of government is to achieve equality in the work force so that nobody will be deprived of opportunities that are related to competence and, in order to achieve this, to rectify the disadvantages to which various designated groups are subject. Essentially, these target groups are women, people with disabilities, Aboriginal peoples, visible minorities and cultural communities.

This objective, which is designed to guarantee equitable participation and representation for the various groups making up society, has two components:

- An *individual component*, namely, to give any competent person an opportunity to obtain employment or promotion and to retain such employment. The aim is to ensure that no person is penalized in respect of his or her employment for discriminatory reasons such as race, sex, ethnic origin, etc. that are unrelated to his or her competence.
- A *collective component*, namely, on the one hand, to identify and eliminate discriminatory conditions affecting the designated groups and, on the other hand, to make particular adjustments that will promote participation by members of the designated groups. Thus, it is not sufficient simply to act in a manner that is not discriminatory; rather, it is necessary to take the initiative to achieve adequate representation of the designated groups in the work force that reflects their representation in society as a whole.

How effective are federal and provincial employment equity and affirmative action programs for Aboriginal peoples?

As a member of the Canadian Human Rights Commission since 1989, I have paid particular attention to developments in the situation at the federal level.

The *Employment Equity Act*, which was passed in 1986, governs some 365 private sector employers that are subject to federal jurisdiction and have more than 100 employees. In 1990 there were more than 632,820 employees in this sector.

Federal government departments and agencies are governed by a Treasury Board policy adopted in 1983. In 1990 the staff of the 44 federal departments and agencies numbered more than 218,328.

The federal government has also instituted a program governing federal contracts under which employers with more than 100 employees who conclude contracts with the federal government for sums greater than $200,000 must agree to take appropriate measures to implement employment equity. If an employer fails to comply with this undertaking, it may be liable to penalties that can include a ban on tendering in the future.

An analysis of the annual reports issued by departments and public agencies and by private sector employers generally shows that Aboriginal people are under-represented throughout the Canadian work force from every point of view:

- Overall, the figure for Aboriginal people is less than 2.1%, which, according to data from the 1986 Census, corresponds to the rate of their representation in the Canadian work force. It should not be forgotten that several Aboriginal communities did not take part in the Census. The data obtained at the time of the Census must accordingly be analyzed with a certain amount of care.

  Aboriginal representation in the private sector increased from 0.7% in 1987 to 1.0% in 1991. The same period saw an increase from 1.8% to 2% in the public sector. It is worthy of note that one-quarter of Aboriginal people working in the public sector are employees of the Department of Indian Affairs and Northern Development (19.4%) and of Health and Welfare Canada (4.8%), which are directly responsible for providing services to the Aboriginal peoples. If we exclude the department of Indian Affairs, total representation of Aboriginal people in the public sector declines to 1.7%.

- Aboriginal people are also under-represented in all the provinces and in all major Census metropolitan areas (Calgary, Edmonton, Halifax, Montreal, Regina, Toronto, Vancouver and Winnipeg).

- Although it increased between 1987 and 1991, Aboriginal representation in all sectors of industry does not reflect their numbers in the population as a whole: banking (from 0.7% to 0.8%), communications (from 0.6% to 0.8%), transportation (from 0.7% to 1.1%) and "other" (from 1.0% to 1.7%).

- Aboriginal people are under-represented in all categories of employees (full- and part-time).

- Aboriginal people are under-represented in all occupational groups, especially at all levels of management and among professionals and, although their representation increased in several occupational groups in the public sector between 1987 and 1991, it declined from 2.0% to 1.3% in the professional and scientific group. In the private sector they were under-represented in the 12 occupational groups in 1991, and the vast majority of them (66%) fell within the office and manual labour groups.

- Aboriginal people are more likely to be found in lower-paying positions in most occupational groups. Aboriginal women suffer a dual handicap. Although the average salary of a full-time Canadian worker in the private sector was $38,198 (men: $42,715 and women: $31,538) in 1991, the average salary of Aboriginal workers was $33,101, or $36,817 for men and $27,602 for women.

  In the public sector the average salary was $40,453 (men: $44,734 and women: $36,697) while the average salary of Aboriginal public servants was $36,227 (men: $40,086 and women: $33,848). The difference between the average salary of Aboriginal women and that of women generally was less marked here than in the private sector.

- A particular problem for Aboriginal people is that of remaining in their jobs. In fact, statistics show that the percentage of Aboriginal workers who quit is generally higher than that for all workers in both the public and the private sectors.

  Furthermore, the proportion of Aboriginal workers who quit is greater than that of workers as a whole. In 1991, for example, 50% of job terminations among Aboriginal people were the result of resignations while the percentage for government employees as a whole was 34%.

  Moreover, statistics seem to suggest that a smaller percentage of Aboriginal public servants remains on the job until retirement. In 1991, for example, 7.6% of Aboriginal employees terminated their employment by retiring as compared with 25.6% for all public servants who terminated their employment. It should also be noted that the percentage of job terminations for Aboriginal employees in the private sector was equal to or greater than the percentage of those hired; this figure has been increasing since 1987 (from 0.5% to 1.2% in 1991). The result is a net decline in their representation in this sector.

An examination of these statistics suggests a number of conclusions concerning the stated objective of ensuring equitable representation for Aboriginal persons in the work force.

As far as the individual component is concerned, the Aboriginal recruitment rate in the private sector has remained lower than their rate of representation in the work force, despite a slight increase. Efforts have been made to recruit Aboriginal people but the results cannot be described as satisfactory. Although recruitment rates in the public sector have exceeded the rate of Aboriginal availability, the net figure for their representation still does not reflect their numbers in the population as a whole.

As far as the collective component is concerned, it must be noted that, despite the efforts made, the overall representation of Aboriginal people remains below their availability rate.

In its annual report, tabled last March, the Canadian Human Rights Commission notes "the poor results achieved following five years of effort" in the employment equity field, especially with respect to Aboriginal people.

What should be done to increase the effectiveness of these programs?

In 1991, a House of Commons Special Committee proceeded to examine the *Employment Equity Act* and its application following its enactment in 1986. Several organizations testified before the Committee concerning their experiences.

It must be noted that even today there is still no consensus on the need to strengthen the mandatory nature of legislation of this kind, whether it be the existing obligation for employers to report on their activities in this area, the eventual obligation for employers to disclose their plans to promote employment equity, the eventual obligation for employers to adopt uniform methods of collecting data and analyzing their employment systems or the establishment of an independent agency to monitor the application of the Act. In other words, those who are in favour of strengthening the legal obligations do not see eye to eye with those who would like to see these obligations eased, although both would like to improve the effectiveness of these programs. No matter what the outcome of this debate is, a number of comments can be made at this point.

There is still a great deal of reluctance to implement employment equity and it takes on various forms:

- prejudice where there is a refusal to see the discrimination that existed and still exists toward members of the designated groups and that consequently creates an impression that employment equity does not depend on the competence of individuals but rather on their membership in a "privileged" group;
- a lack of commitment in the management of organizations;
- a refusal by individuals to identify themselves as members of a designated group out of fear that this will compromise their possibilities of promotion within their organization;
- resistance on the part of labour unions;
- resistance to change in terms of both structures and attitudes.

It seems to me that a crucial factor in improving the effectiveness of employment equity programs would be a clear and formal commitment on the part of the managers of organizations. Such a commitment would be decisive in allowing real work to be done within the agency. Both the existing documentation on the subject and experiments that have been conducted with a certain amount of success identify the commitment of management as a crucial factor.

Not only must management be convinced of the need to achieve employment equity but it must inform all levels of the organization, both by means of specific communications strategies (memos, brochures, etc.) and by including employment equity objectives in the organization's strategic plan. Although it is not a panacea, communication is decisive in dealing with prejudice and showing that the organization does not tolerate discrimination. There can be no hope of overcoming resistance to change if the example is not set, above all, by the decision makers.

Another important factor is to place the individual responsible for employment equity at a sufficiently senior level to make management's commitment in this regard clear.

A further important consideration is the integration of the employment equity program in human resources management: analysis of availability, analysis of the organization's employment systems so as to eliminate direct and indirect (systemic) discriminatory barriers, and development of an employment equity plan to rectify the shortcomings noted.

It will be noted that employment equity remains a theoretical notion in many organizations where there is little understanding of how it might be integrated into the organization's management. Human resources management methods have not yet come to grips with what is still viewed as yet another constraint in labour relations management, the scope of which is misjudged.

Moreover, a great deal of importance must be placed on the analysis of organizations' employment systems, recruiting practices, selection and assessment methods, not to mention training and development programs.

It will be seen that traditional recruiting practices are not suitable, for example, for recruiting Aboriginal employees. Use of the national media means that they cannot be reached when most of them are located outside the major urban centres. In some cases, businesses have realized that they obtain better results if they use local or Aboriginal media or work with Aboriginal groups (band councils, Aboriginal employment services, etc.).

The analysis of duties is essential in eliminating conditions that are not directly related to the needs of the job to be performed and that create unnecessary barriers to Aboriginal recruits; for example, academic requirements.

Just as important is an examination of possibilities of providing training and development within the organization in order to "deghettoize" certain types of employment. In fact, some types of employment do not provide real opportunities for development and do not allow incumbents of positions to move into other areas of employment that offer potential for promotion within the organization.

Special support mechanisms must be established within the organization in order to help Aboriginal employees adjust to their new environment.

Finally, a special effort must be made to provide better documentation of what seems to be a problem unique to Aboriginal people: the high quitting rate. It is far from clear that, even if Aboriginal people were recruited en masse, better overall results could be achieved.

One theory may explain the particular situation of Aboriginal people as compared with the three other designated groups: women, people with disabilities, and members of visible minorities. Unlike these three groups, the members of which wish to be integrated into the work force, it may be that Aboriginal people are torn between aspirations that they find mutually contradictory. Given the lack of documentation on the issue, an attempt should be made to examine further some of the data obtained in studies of job retention in the public sector and the phenomenon of quitting among Aboriginal employees.

The study of job retention in the federal public service conducted by the Public Service Commission of Canada in 1991 allows us to draw a number of conclusions that need to be confirmed by further research. We saw earlier that the quitting rate among Aboriginal people far exceeds the quitting rate for public servants in all professional categories and at all levels of the organization.

Interviews with Aboriginal people conducted as part of the above study show that one of the factors motivating Aboriginal people who join the public service is a desire to defend the interests of their community by taking part in the government decisions that affect them. They claim to be disappointed that they cannot actually participate in the development of policies affecting their communities.

They say that they find themselves in a very uncomfortable position: they are subject to both the demands of the government and those of the Aboriginal clientele. Caught between the imperatives of the programs they are required to apply and the dissatisfaction of the Aboriginal clients for whom these programs are intended, they decide to quit because they can no longer endure this "buffer" role. They have the impression that, for the government, they are token Aboriginal people, while other Aboriginal people consider them to be "traitors", mere messengers for the government.

We conclude from this that, as individuals, Aboriginal people have aspirations that prove to be contradictory since they are caught between their personal desire for development within Canadian society and the image of "traitor" that the other Aboriginal people apply to them, between the desire to defend the interests of their community and the disillusionment they feel on realizing that they are simply cogs, often only symbolic, in their view, in a bureaucratic machine that does not place any importance on the aspirations of what is, in the eyes of this bureaucracy, simply one client group among many.

They see employment equity programs as providing a further encounter for them with racism and the "ghettoization" of positions occupied by Aboriginal people. In any event, these positions are not wanted by non-Aboriginal people, and Aboriginal people feel that this merely helps to ostracize them further. In their view, there is a tendency to consider the experience they acquire in these positions as not being transferable to other parts of the public service. It should not be forgotten that the Department of Indian Affairs and Northern Development is by far the main employer of Aboriginal people in the public service.

Furthermore, other factors seem to contribute to the increase in the numbers of Aboriginal people who quit their jobs. Some of them see their time in the public service as an opportunity to acquire experience and knowledge that they then choose to place at the service of their communities. They do not see themselves as having careers in the public service but view their time there as simply a passing phase. Others oscillate between the public service and jobs in their communities in line with political changes in those communities. Finally, one factor that may play a considerable role is the fact that income earned from jobs done on a reserve, unlike that earned from employment in the public service, is not subject to income tax.

What action should be taken by government (local and other) to plan for and accommodate Aboriginal people looking for work in urban areas in the southern part of the country?

Governments should at least provide inter-cultural training for their non-Aboriginal staff. It is still felt that non-Aboriginal personnel required to work in an Aboriginal environment or to provide service to Aboriginal people do not need any specific preparation, and this is true of those working in the legal field (judges, lawyers, etc.) as well as the medical and other fields.

Governments should establish support mechanisms for the employees recruited in the form of sponsorship by a third person either within the organization or from outside.

A system of equivalence could be developed to enable Aboriginal people holding positions in their community, for example, to gain access to higher education (as already happens in the case of managers of public and para-public organizations).

Training programs could enable Aboriginal people to undertake training periods in equivalent positions in business or public organizations (municipal government, hospitals, etc.).

Programs to facilitate the exchange of municipal and Aboriginal officials could encourage better mutual understanding while enabling Aboriginal people to gain experience in a non-Aboriginal setting.

Forms of business sponsorship could enable non-Aboriginal business to help Aboriginal people in the establishment and management of businesses in their community. For example, the establishment of Aboriginal credit unions on certain Indian reserves in Quebec has helped give these communities a community development tool and enabled the individuals working there to benefit from the training and support provided by the Desjardins Movement.

Joint government-Aboriginal committees could be set up at the federal and provincial levels with a mandate to develop employment strategies for Aboriginal people. Needless to say, the mere existence of such committees would not achieve results overnight. On the one hand, however, it is important to involve Aboriginal people in the creation of strategies that affect them. On the other hand, Aboriginal people alone cannot determine how their members can join the work force. We are not thinking here of advisory committees that would enhance bureaucratic thinking but rather of joint committees that could be given responsibility for developing employment policies for Aboriginal people.

Above all, however, governments must emphasize education. No employment equity program can make up for inadequate training in the long term. In order to place appropriate emphasis on this factor, government must attempt seriously to make Aboriginal people comfortable with the idea of school.

For many Aboriginal parents, school is a symbol of dispossession. They have lost control over the education of their children by sending them to school. The values inculcated at school have cut the children off from traditional forms of knowledge. School has allowed feelings of incompetence to develop among parents: traditional values were supplanted by values conveyed at school since the parents were not familiar with the new types of knowledge or the language in which this knowledge was conveyed.

A band leader explained to me recently that he was in an uncomfortable position because his parents felt that he betrayed his people by going to university. A pejorative term is used in the language of his people to describe individuals who have "sold out" to the world of the whites.

Another band leader, who has been trying for a long time to have the school calendar changed to include instruction for students in traditional activities during the winter, explained that he refused to give his daughter cigarettes. Given the dispute with the school and enraged that she wished to attend school, he told her that she should ask the principal for cigarettes.

Governments and Aboriginal people must deal with the need to make up for lost time in this area. Aboriginal people must accept school, which is still too often regarded as a tool for depriving them of their culture. Moreover, once school is accepted as being adaptable to their own cultural characteristics, then it must give Aboriginal students training equivalent to that given to other Canadian children. Many Aboriginal communities have ambivalent feelings in this regard.

They want responsibility for their own schools but they are afraid that the training given there will not be as good as that provided by non-Aboriginal people, while they aspire to the best possible training so that their children can join the country's work force. They do not want the self-government to which they aspire to "ghettoize" them more than is already the case.

Conclusion

Aboriginal people are not merely isolated geographically; it could even be said that they are outside Canadian society. It is important that Aboriginal people wish to be a part of Canadian society but it is even more important for governments representing this society to establish nodal points at which Aboriginal people can be integrated into Canadian society. In this sense, even if they achieve full Aboriginal self-government, joint mechanisms would have to be created to ensure that they were not merely members of independent communities but also had the possibility of integrating into Canadian society if that is what they chose for themselves as individuals.

Hitherto we have been dealing with two worlds that have existed side by side. They share the same national territory but do not really know each other. In this respect it is significant that the vast majority of individuals consulted in 1991 by the Citizens' Forum on Canada's Future was not able to come up with solutions to the problems of Aboriginal people because it claimed that it was not familiar with their situation or their problems.

How can a valid solution ever be found if these two worlds cannot succeed in carrying on a dialogue with each other?

Education, Training, Employment and Economic Development

*Del Anaquod**

> ...a disproportionately large number of able bodied Indians of working age are unemployed or underemployed....To facilitate the transfer of large numbers of these into more skilled or better paid fields of employment having the most favourable prospects of expansion, will require an extensive, and intensive program of education, training and conditioning of Indian workers.
>
> *Hawthorn Report, 1966 (p. 102)*

Ironically, 30 years later, conditions have not changed. The issues today, which I am addressing in my discussion paper, were the challenges of yesterday. How then do we avoid them becoming the continuing problems of tomorrow? Is it possible?

Ever since the introduction of the "farm instructor" in the 1880s to the "rotating herd" concept of the 1940s and 1950s, strategies are continually being devised to make Aboriginal people self-sufficient and self-reliant. The rotating herd mentality is still with us today. The program entailed a herd of cattle rotating from reserve to reserve with the idea that a band kept any newborn calves – to build their own herd – before the herd moved on to another community. I relish the stories of some of our elders who would humorously recall the Indian agents searching for their herds, only to find they had mysteriously disappeared. In later years, the Department of Indian Affairs and Northern Development

* President, Anaquod Traders International, and Associate Professor, Saskatchewan Indian Federated College.

would revive the concept with its "Revolving Indian Loan Fund". Same idea –Indian businesses would borrow and later repay – replenishing the Fund so others could borrow as well. The loan loss rate of that idea was 80%. It was not until the mid-1980s that the government had the wisdom to fund Aboriginal capital corporations. The loan loss rate plunged to less than 10% and in some cases under 5%. Why?

Education, Training, Employment and Economic Development

We cannot separate education, training, employment and economic development. They are interrelated. To treat these issues in isolation from the governance, social, health, culture and other conditions would also be considered irresponsible. However, on this understanding and with some apprehension, I will attempt to cover the material while remaining in the general guidelines of the issues identified above.

Before proceeding with my own observations and recommendations regarding education, training, employment and economic development, I would like to dispense with two background topics. The first is the theoretical approach to labour market participation (or lack of) by Aboriginal peoples. Rather than regurgitating academic theories of why our people are unemployed and under-represented in the economic sphere, I've appended a brief summary of the various ideologies. Those so inclined may refer to Appendix A.

Second, I would like to draw a little more attention to the elements I believe are the requirements for our Aboriginal communities to become more self-sufficient and self-reliant. These elements must be understood in order to recognize why we have high unemployment and why we will always be on the economic periphery of this country. What is the use of education and training, if there are no jobs? The elements are:

- land and natural resources;
- capital and financing;
- geography;
- governmental environment (Aboriginal, federal, provincial, municipal);
- organization; and
- human resources.

A full coverage of these would require a major presentation. However, I cannot miss the opportunity to give my personal views on such key components of our employment and economic thrusts. I will cover some elements in more detail than others. The balance of my discussion paper will concentrate on the last point – human resources and their development.

Land and Natural Resources

With the possible exception of some recent and pending land settlements, the vast majority of First Nation reserves and Aboriginal communities are small and of marginal economic value. Our once great empires have been reduced to islands of poverty surrounded by a sea of plenty. Governments have taken our land and resources and we are now being told to take care of ourselves and become "self-sufficient". The hypocrisy of it all. Let me illustrate this by giving two examples. First, in Brian Titley's book entitled *Narrow Vision*, he writes about Duncan Campbell Scott, who worked for Indian Affairs from 1880 until 1932, the last 20 years as Deputy Minister.

Titley quotes Scott, who in 1905 was talking about preparations for the signing of Treaty 9 and about the vast wealth in Northern Ontario:

> This vast territory contains much arable land, many million feet of pulpwood, untold wealth of minerals, and unharnessed water-powers, sufficient to do the work on half the continent (p.62).

Initially signed in 1905, and again in 1928, the beneficiaries of Treaty 9 received $40,000; however, the author, Titley, goes on to state:

> The silver mines at Cobalt which had started all the excitement, produced in excess of $206,000,000.00 of the precious metal during their first eighteen years of operation. Knowing that the budget for the first round of Treaty negotiations was less than $40,000.00, makes the magnitude of the "bargain" clear. And Cobalt was no exception (p. 73).

Duncan Campbell Scott, the Deputy Minister, was rather proud of his accomplishment and role in signing Treaty 9. He thought it was a good deal for the Canadian government.

The second example of the role of land and resources and their importance to economic development and employment of our people is closer to home in my province of Saskatchewan. I see parallel experiences. Like Northern Ontario, we also signed treaties; under those treaties, the federal government and Canadian people were given over 160,000,000 acres of land. I've outlined below in more detail how some of the land was dispersed:

Total Provincial Area	**160,000,000 acres (est)**
Homesteads	30,000,000 acres
Railways (all told)	15,000,000 acres
Hudson's Bay Company	3,300,000 acres (£300,000)
Road Allowances	1,500,000 acres
Parks	1,500,000 acres
* Indian Reserves	1,500,000 acres (<1%)

*Note: This amount has diminished to approximately 1,250,000 acres as a result of land frauds, the *Veterans' Land Act*, forced selling, etc.

Since the 1870s, when treaties on the prairies were signed, one can well imagine the billions of dollars that have been extracted in resources. A project recently undertaken by the Federation of Saskatchewan Indian Nations, was a "Treaty Audit." The well known auditing firm of Coopers & Lybrand was contracted to conduct an evaluation/audit on the beneficiaries of treaty. The results are not for public consumption; however, it highlights the difference in magnitude of what First Nations in Saskatchewan received between 1873 and 1990 and the amounts non-Aboriginal governments and their citizens acquired. The difference annually is in the hundreds of millions. To reiterate my point – resources run governments. As a side note, government dollars from personal income taxes (if the Government of Saskatchewan is an example) make up less than 24% of total government revenue.

If land and resources are so important for Aboriginal people and we don't have any – what do we do?

I believe what is needed in this country is major land reform surpassing even that of land claims and entitlement. In Saskatchewan, there is a major agreement to settle outstanding land entitlements which may add another 1.7 million acres. After the selection process is completed, the total acreage under First Nation government control will total 2.9 million acres. This is only 1.8% of the Saskatchewan land base – Aboriginal people at present make up 9% of the population (86,695 – 1991 Census).

To me, availability of land is not the issue. With over 80% of Canadians living within 100 miles of the American border (almost huddling with the Americans on the one hand, and screaming they are distinctly Canadian on the other), the vast majority of land is "unoccupied" (except for us). If we lived in France, I can see a problem. However, we do not – we live in the largest country in the world.

Land, then, is not the issue. The problem is the lack of political will. Deep down, Canadian leaders are still daydreaming we will first integrate, second, assimilate, and third, disappear. Providing land and resources as a foundation for our Aboriginal governments goes against that grain. The only exceptions are some of the more recent settlements that look generous today; however, in hindsight 50 years from now, they will pale, just like our treaties. It is my proposition that the gravest tactical mistake the Canadian government ever made was giving us our reserves. In the beginning, they were used as a method of removing us out of the way; instead, the reserve became the cornerstone of our survival – a collective island that has withstood the forces of assimilation.

To conclude, we may be heading into an "information era"; however, the economic foundation of resources and land still remains the future for Aboriginal and non-Aboriginal peoples in Canada.

Capital and Finance

Aboriginal Government Support

Mark Malone, in his booklet entitled *Financing Aboriginal Self-Government in Canada* (Queen's University, 1986) outlined succinctly the various methods that could be used to raise revenue. To summarize his conclusion, he laid out two broad sources of financing Aboriginal governments and their economic endeavours.

Own Source:

- Taxation
- Resource Revenue-Sharing (i.e., Royalties)
- Profits from Aboriginal Development Corporations

Other Source:

- Unconditional Transfers
- Conditional Transfers
- Recourse to Federal and Provincial Spending Powers

To show the impact of government transfers on Aboriginal people, I've included on the following page, DIAND's recently released (February, 1993) "Federal Expenditures for Aboriginal Peoples". The total for 1992-93 is $5,040,000,000. Divide this by the number of people who identified with their Aboriginal identity in the 1991 Aboriginal Peoples Survey, which is 625,710 (Statistics Canada – Cat. No. 94-327) and you come up with a figure of $8,057. This is how much the federal government spends on every Aboriginal man, woman and child. Add to this provincial expenditures and other related costs, such as corrections, and you have an interesting study on "Aboriginal People as Big Business." Something is definitely wrong!

Another point to be noted is the over-reliance of Aboriginal economies on the public sector, versus the private. At present, jobs in our communities revolve around the initiatives of the band council – education, social, public administration, make-work programs. Many are seasonal and part-time and all have been created with the transfer of federal programs and services to First Nation communities. Jobs previously controlled by DIAND are now controlled by the First Nations. DIAND estimates that there are over 16,000 people employed in the Indian public sector. I don't foresee a dramatic increase of employment in the public sector, as in the past, since 80% of all programs have been transferred. Nevertheless, there is still considerable opportunity for Aboriginal employment, since I calculate 25% of all employees in the Aboriginal public sector are non-Aboriginal people.

The third concern I have regarding the financing of Aboriginal governments is my personal belief in a mixed economy of Aboriginal Crown corporations and

Approximate Federal Expenditures for Aboriginal Peoples[1]

Year	Annual Departmental Expenditures for Aboriginal Peoples[2] ($ Millions)								Yearly Growth
	DIAND	NHW	EIC	CMHC	ISTC	SS	Other	Total	(%)
75-76	587	74	–	3	26	13	–	703	–
76-77	707	97	–	7	30	14	–	855	21.6
77-78	816	109	3	8	31	16	2	985	15.2
78-79	858	115	3	83	34	18	5	1,116	13.3
79-80	933	125	3	83	42	19	6	1,211	8.5
80-81	1,134	155	57	58	44	23	4	1,475	21.8
81-82	1,252	174	70	77	47	28	4	1,652	12.0
82-83	1,423	220	100	124	27	32	3	1,929	16.8
83-84	1,683	261	180	146	35	46	10	2,361	22.4
84-85	1,900	302	200	146	38	50	14	2,650	12.2
85-86	1,990	341	159	156	15	53	22	2,736	3.2
86-87	2,212	399	151	89	49	58	14	2,972	8.6
87-88	2,282	434	133	104	49	55	17	3,074	3.4
88-89	2,527	428	126	125	68	56	20	3,350	9.0
89-90	2,813	481	145	157	84	54	22	3,756	12.1
90-91	3,081	578	152	199	85	45	22	4,162	10.8
91-92	3,412	639	200	240	79	62	42	4,674	12.3
92-93	3,647	706	200	272	76	51	89	5,041	7.9

1 Federal departments and agencies with Aboriginal programs include Indian and Northern Affairs Canada; Health and Welfare Canada; Employment and Immigration Canada; Canada Mortgage and Housing Corporation; Industry, Science and Technology Canada; Secretary of State; Solicitor General; Fisheries and Oceans; Public Service Commission; Justice; and National Defence.

2 1991-92 and 1992-93 figures are from *Main Estimates*. Figures include spending on Aboriginal employment equity programs, but do not include spending on programs available to all Canadians, such as Old Age Security and Unemployment Insurance.

private enterprise. I see a proliferation of First Nation Crown corporations in our economic development plans. Why? This could be for a number of reasons: absence of private Aboriginal entrepreneurs; a reflection of First Nation cultural values of sharing and communal ownership; perhaps they were developed by Aboriginal political organizations and they want to maintain control; or are we merely replicating community development models imported from elsewhere. My concern is that Aboriginal governments *must* also provide an atmosphere to allow private Aboriginal enterprises to flourish. In this environment, they would create jobs, keep the money circulating in the Aboriginal economy, and further develop other opportunities. Although there may be benefits to the Aboriginal community, what benefits would there be for the Aboriginal government? None, unless they decide to tax these private corporations. However, that is a discussion for another place and time.

Aboriginal Business Support

I don't want to dwell on this topic too long, because the issue is amply covered elsewhere. Since we lack land and resources, where else can an Aboriginal business obtain money? Government programs such as CAEDS and DIAND's Economic Development, or even the 32 Aboriginal financial institutions established across this country, are certainly sources. As well, and unless you're from Alberta, taking over and managing your trust funds will only have minimal impact. Of the $1.1 billion in the consolidated revenue fund for "Funds and Estates", over 93% is destined for Alberta bands. Why don't they control their own trust funds ? I don't know – since they could obtain a better return on their investment than they are receiving from the federal government.

I believe it is also imperative that Aboriginal communities ask for their share of federal and provincial government contracts. To paraphrase Premier Bourassa – we want our share of the pie! If we had contracts, we wouldn't need grants.

Geography

Location, location, location! We live in a global community that is becoming more competitive with a freer market economy, and Aboriginal businesses must not only survive but thrive in this environment. Aboriginal leaders must realize that we live in a capitalist society, and why build a manufacturing plant if you're not near your major market?

Governmental Environment

Previously I alluded to the fact that the governmental environment would determine our march toward full employment, economic development and self-sufficiency. What did I mean?

The best way to illustrate this point, is to refer to the "United States Presidential Commission on Indian Reservation Economics" which was conducted in 1984. The findings of that Commission could almost in total apply to our situation in Canada. One of the major tasks was to identify the "Obstacles to Indian Reservation Economic Development". Rather than reciting their findings verbatim, I've included the actual graphs from the report on the following pages. A similar exercise, if not already done, should be done in Canada.

Composition of Tribal Obstacles to Indian Reservation Economic Development

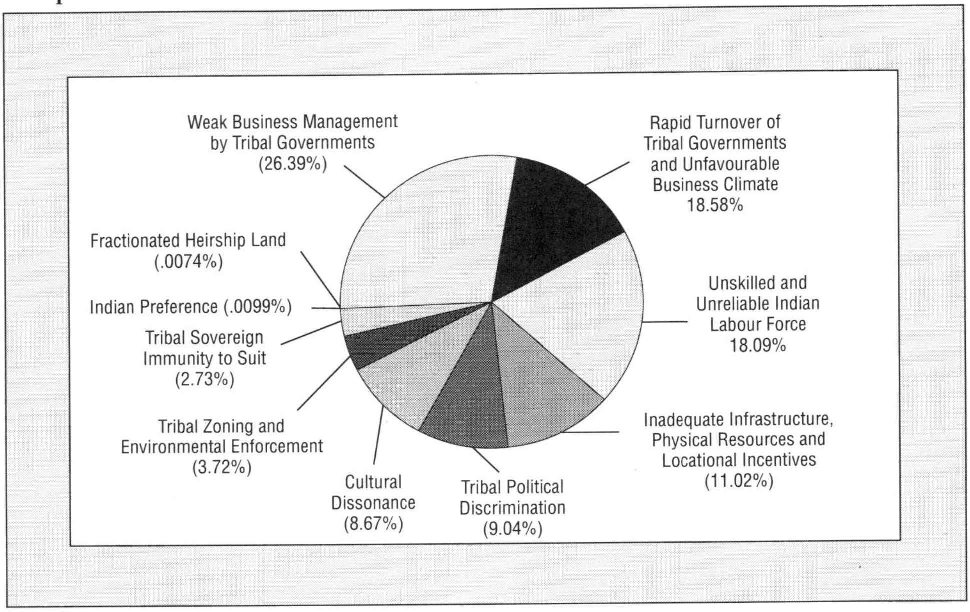

Composition of BIA Obstacles to Indian Reservation Economic Development

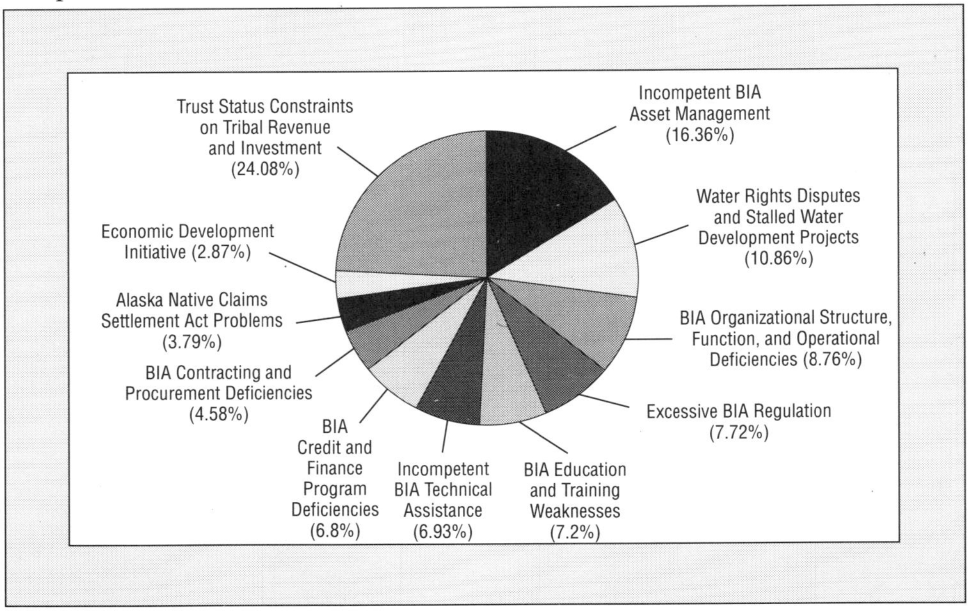

Composition of Federal Obstacles to Indian Reservation Economic Development

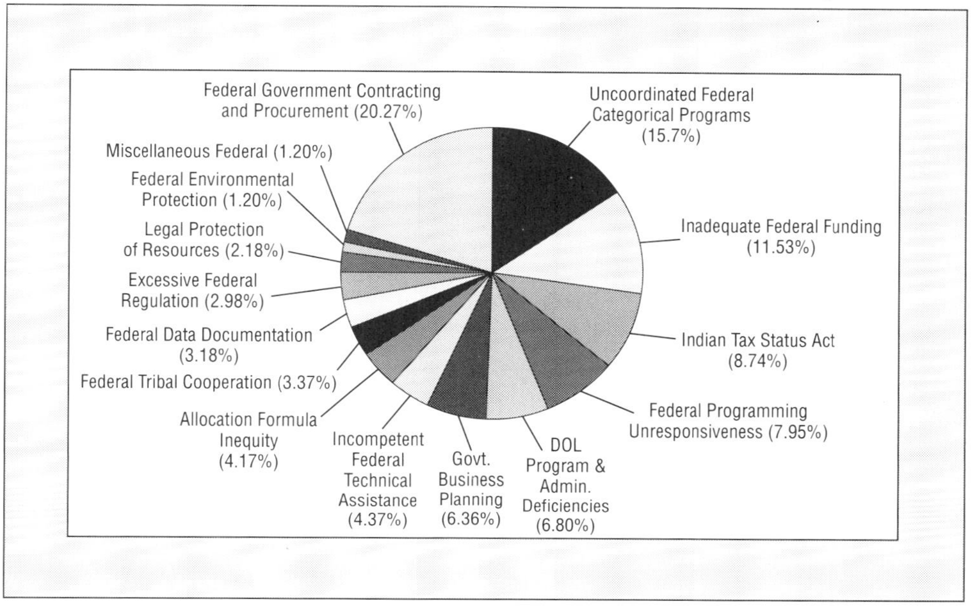

Composition of State and Local Government Obstacles to Indian Reservation Economic Development

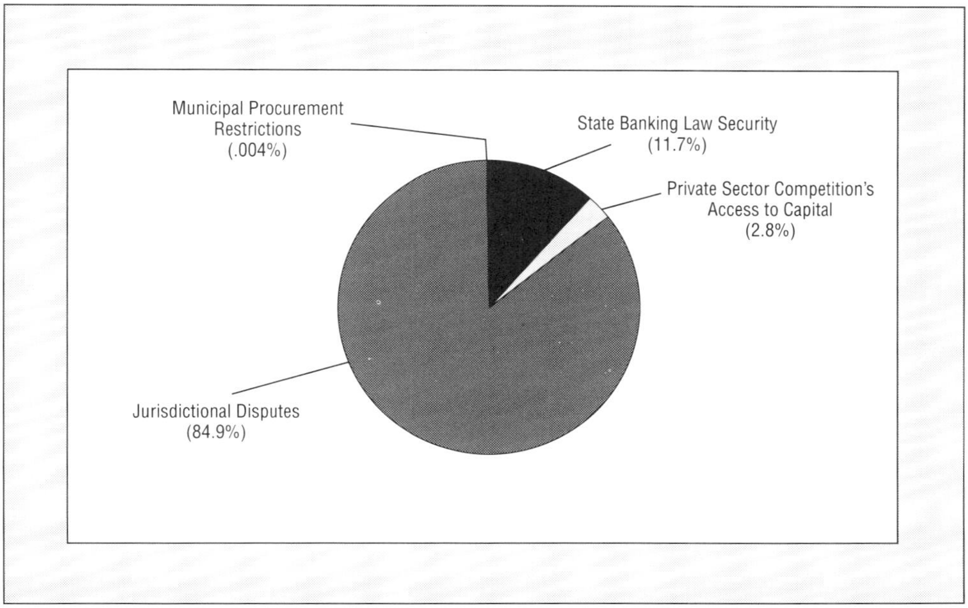

Organization

The graphs on the previous pages lead to my final point of Aboriginal people and their governments achieving some aspect of economic self-sufficiency – organization. It is fair to say that governments and business have different agendas. Many times, band-run businesses focus on the "big picture" such as providing jobs, rather than profits as a goal. Employment and business development are two separate functions. One provides jobs, the other attempts to make profits. These functions must be separated.

Another problem is the myriad government programs and their civil servants who often themselves don't understand concepts of sales and rates of return. Each feeds on the other. If governments are going to give grants, then give grants. If they are going to give loans, give them to national Aboriginal banks. You cannot have an environment that attempts to do both.

I am also worried about the direction of our community economic developers. Many have replaced the function and attitude of DIAND, which is to help communities prepare proposals for funding rather than producing sound business plans. Compound this with the proliferation of consultants, and no wonder some of our communities are so screwed up. Many times, consultants feel their job is to obtain funding for their clients and when this is accomplished, they're finished. Where a project or corporation fails, they are nowhere to be found. I strongly believe they should be held accountable for their projections, calculations, market analysis, etc. and eventually the success or failure of the enterprise.

If governments want to play a useful role, in addition to providing capital and training dollars, they should recognize the need for creating Aboriginal research and development corporations that will identify market opportunities, private financial sources, human resources and generally long-term opportunities. These corporations should be under Aboriginal control, but at arm's length from governments, particularly Aboriginal governments. Their only job would be to make a profit which can then be returned to the Aboriginal communities. To do this, one must have the proper organization.

Human Resource Development – Education and Training

Existing Financial Sources For Aboriginal Education and Training, With Recommendations

Secretary of State

Established Programs Financing (EPF)
- post-secondary education;
- health; and
- Canada Assistance Plan.

Last year, the federal government transferred over $70 billion to provincial governments to assist them in these three areas. This is a contentious point with some Aboriginal groups, because part of the calculation is based on the overall provincial population, including Aboriginal people. Since these areas are under provincial jurisdiction, provincial governments argue EPF is an unconditional grant to be spent as they see fit and not necessarily for the areas identified by the federal government.

When Aboriginal institutions approach the federal government, they are advised to apply to their provincial government, since the money has already been transferred.

Language Training and Support
Over $250 million is provided for Official Languages support, mainly French. An additional $50 million is provided for heritage languages; Aboriginal languages support is less that $1 million.

Canada Student Loans
Like other students, Aboriginal students are eligible to apply. There have been recent discussions about privatizing the fund, because of heavy loan loss rates. The Fraser Institute in B.C. has calculated that every $1,000 loaned by the federal government, costs $600, including interest subsidy costs, administration and defaults. Last year, the federal government paid out more than $100 million to collection agencies. DIAND's investment in the Post-Secondary Student Support Program (PSSSP) looks like a bargain when compared to these costs.

Department of Indian Affairs and Northern Development

Post-Secondary Student Support Program
In 1977, DIAND introduced the E-12 guidelines (Post-Secondary Education Assistance Program), which provided for the support of First Nations students attending post-secondary education programs. In its first year (1976-77) the program assisted 2,684 students nationally, at a cost of $8 million; in its last year (1987-88), over 14,000 were enrolled with a financial commitment of $93.7 million.

The E-12 guidelines were replaced in 1988 with the new Post-Secondary Student Support Program (PSSSP), which placed restrictions on student months eligibility and removed such features as daycare and rent subsidies. In 1990, the program was capped; listed below are the projected annual financial commitments for 1991-96:

1991-92	$190.0 million
1992-93	$201.4 million
1993-94	$213.5 million
1994-95	$226.3 million
1995-96	$239.9 million

Approximately 25,000 students were funded under the PSSSP in 1992-93 and this will not increase significantly, if at all, because of the capped funding. Over 85% of PSSSP students are now funded under First Nations' control and most bands and tribal councils are being forced to say "no" to their students, putting many in an awkward position.

Although DIAND funds the program as "discretionary", many treaty First Nations see it as a treaty right. Unless the issue is resolved quickly, in the political arena, in all likelihood the matter will end up in the courts. Both DIAND and the FSIN in 1989, established an "Office of the Treaty Commissioner", to address the issue in Saskatchewan and it is expected a final resolution is still a year away.

If the matter is legally challenged and (in my opinion) based on the principle of the treaty right to education, the federal Crown will lose. At a minimum, the courts will rule that First Nations, under their understanding and interpretation of the treaties to assist them in surviving and flourishing in a new society, must have available to them the ongoing resources (financial and otherwise) to accomplish this end. The measurement for this will be such factors as similar university and technical attainment for treaty First Nations, as the general population. Other indicators could include high school completion rates, literacy levels, language retention, skills comparability. Are PSSSP and, in particular, student funding, a treaty right? The answer is a resounding yes, because it assists First Nations in achieving those things set out above.

Indian Studies Support Program

Twelve per cent of the overall PSSSP is reserved for the support of First Nations-controlled programming. The most well known and only recognized national First Nation institution is the Saskatchewan Indian Federated College (SIFC). Started in 1976 with 9 students, the SIFC has grown to 1,100 with over 600 graduates in its brief history. A success story! However, the SIFC, like other emerging Aboriginal-controlled institutions, is caught between federal and provincial jurisdictional responsibilities and limited fiscal resources, in an era of dramatically increasing enrollments.

In Stuart Smith's national and well publicized report commissioned by the Association of Universities and Colleges of Canada (AUCC) and entitled "Commission of Inquiry on Canadian University Education" (1991), he brings together, in a concise manner, the plight of the SIFC:

> ...The Saskatchewan Indian Federated College at the University of Regina is a special experiment for which the federal government deserves a great deal of credit, in the view of the Commission. Unlike the other programs, which try to integrate native students into non-native educational experiences, the SIFC approach is similar to those of the tribal colleges in the United States....

> ...The Commission was dismayed to learn of federal-provincial wrangling over the funding of SIFC. It seems that the province would like the federal government to pay the entire cost for the operation of this educational institution, presumably not otherwise needed by the province. The federal government, on the other hand, is used to paying only the incremental costs (fees, etc.) for native students at other universities and balks at paying the total cost at this particular college. While the battle goes on, the college is in jeopardy and the students may suffer. It is the hope of the Commission that the two governments could accept, "without prejudice", an interim shared funding solution, while appointing an arbitrator to settle the matter...

Stuart's reference to tribal colleges in the United States brings to mind an evaluation of those institutions by the well respected Carnegie Foundation for the Advancement of Teaching. In their report, "Tribal Colleges – Shaping the Future of Native America" (1989), they overwhelmingly recognized and supported the tribal college system:

> During the conduct of this study, we were struck by the capacity of tribal colleges to cope with resources that are painfully restricted. At almost all of the institutions, salaries are far too low, libraries are shockingly underfunded, and administrators struggle to operate with day-to-day budget constraints that other higher learning institutions would totally reject. Although a few of the colleges have accommodating campuses, many are getting by with mismatched trailers or unsuitable buildings converted from other uses. Still, faced with difficult conditions, tribal colleges have managed not only to stay alive, but also to expand their services and creatively serve their students and their communities.
>
> Tribal colleges are truly community institutions. After years of brutal physical hardship and disorienting cultural loss, Native Americans – through the tribal college movement – are building new communities based on shared traditions. They are challenging the conditions that plague their societies and continue to threaten their survival.
>
> But if we have learned anything from our relationship with the American Indian, it is that people cannot be torn from their cultural roots without harm. To the extent that we fail to assist Native Americans, through their own institutions, to reclaim their past and secure their future, we are compounding the costly errors of the past.

Recommendations

- Aboriginal-controlled universities and technical institutions should be encouraged and financially supported, because:
  - Aboriginal-controlled institutions create a learning environment that builds self-confidence and greater participation by their students than do non-Aboriginal institutions. They feel wanted and welcomed and their chances of success are greatly enhanced;
  - Aboriginal colleges celebrate and help sustain our rich Aboriginal languages and cultures.
  - Aboriginal colleges and Aboriginal-controlled programs provide essential services that enrich the communities they serve.
  - They are excellent centres for research, development and general scholarship.
  - It is a treaty right – schools were promised.
- Funding of ISSP should be separate from funding of student support. Put them in the same pot, cap the dollars, and conflicts and competition arise.

Nominal Student Rolls up to 21 years

DIAND now funds elementary/secondary students on a "cost" times "nominal" roll basis. Funding is based on some "formula" – the overall basis, no one knows. A common DIAND expression is "it's in the formula funding". Problems in this area are complex, however, there are some areas of major deficiency which need to be flagged:

- lack of curriculum development dollars;
- need to fund early learning children's programs to give our children a head start;
- need to fund second and third level services properly (tribal council and regional level);
- need to include on the nominal rolls students over 21 years old, who may be part of a retrieval program to complete high school. The alternative is creating ABE and GED programs which are more costly.

Economic Development

Over the years, DIAND has gradually extricated itself from its responsibilities to provide training (as well as literacy) to First Nations. The last remaining areas are hidden in the economic development dollars which are transferred to First Nations. Included in those measly amounts, are on-the-job training moneys. Such a policy causes conflicts within many of our communities.

Industry, Science and Technology (ISTC)

Who knows what programs are available for training? When the Canadian Aboriginal Economic Development Strategy (CAEDS) was first announced, a major recognized component was the need for training and other support. Somewhere, somehow, it never materialized.

Health and Welfare Canada

Indian and Inuit Health Careers Program has five main components:

- bursaries/scholarships
- health careers promotion
- career-related employment
- institutional programs
- community-based programs

Justice/Solicitor General

The Aboriginal Policing Program was transferred in 1992 from DIAND to the Solicitor General. A major component of the program was targeted for training. In addition, smaller amount are identified for individual projects, scholarships, etc.

Provincial Governments

Education and training dollars vary from province to province. For example, in Saskatchewan, the government provides institutional support moneys for both the Gabriel Dumont Institute and the Saskatchewan Indian Federated College. As well, the Non-Status Indian and Métis (NSIM) Program, receives $4,000,000 annually to assist those students in furthering their education. On the other hand, Status Indian students are not eligible to apply for a Saskatchewan Student Loan.

Foundations and Corporations

Generally, this is an untouched area. However, if we are to be innovative in our education and training programs, we must initiate employment development agreements with corporations. For example, why train mechanics? Technological change is such that by the time a person graduates, his or her training is redundant. Besides, major auto manufacturers are squeezing out the independent garage owners with their factory-backed, five-year warranties and roadside service. Our technical institutions should be hooking up with a "Toyota" to guarantee our graduates jobs. The ideas for employment development agreements are endless. Existing technical and university institutions must re-evaluate their role in society – the ones who fail to readjust will be the losers.

Canada Employment and Immigration Commission

Of all the federal programs providing dollars for training, CEIC is the most asinine. Its myriad programs requires a full-time consultant to keep tabs. Central to all of this is Pathways, or commonly known to some as the "highway to hell". To try to explain the confusion of Pathways and how it operates, I've drawn a schematic of Saskatchewan operations, as an example.

However, before that, I've summarized as best as possible the various programs offered by CEIC:

- Pathways
  - Project Funding – uses Consolidated Revenue Fund;
  - SEED – summer student employment;
  - START – funds projects to keep students in school;
  - Purchase of Training (POT) – funds to purchase training slots in training institutions;
  - Outreach – separate from Pathways allocations and primarily service extensions;
  - Co-op Education – support administration costs for secondary and post-secondary employment experience;
  - UI – Unemployment Insurance connected;
  - SAR – Social Assistance.
- Local CEC Walk-In Services – a portion of the Pathways dollars have been retained at the local CEC office:
  - POT (Purchase of Training) seats;
  - Section 25 – applies to community projects that allows an individual to collect UI while continuing to use their skills;
  - Section 26.1 – section of UI Act which supports UI recipients in retraining;
  - SEED;
  - START;
  - Special Initiatives – funding on a project-by- project basis, using the local CEC manager to sort/seek out funding within a variety of hidden pots of money at the regional and national level;
  - Employer-based – subsidizes an employer for up to two years at a minimum of $7.50/hour if the trainee gets a permanent job.
- Regional CEC Programs
  - Community Futures/Business Development Centres;
  - Industrial Adjustment Services (IAS) – Administrative dollars to examine and plan for labour force adjustments;
  - Co-op Education.
- Labour Force Development Boards – supported by UIC programs.
- Each province has established boards comprised of union and business representatives, to plan long-term strategies for Labour Force Development. They have a major influence over how hundreds of millions of dollars are spent in each region.

Recommendations

- Clean up CEIC programming for Aboriginal people. Dispense with all the rules and regulations and give money direct to Aboriginal groups to do their own thing.
- Recognize that, in Canada, an attitude is surfacing that the days of paying someone (i.e., UI) to sit at home are over. I suspect UI benefits in the future,

Case Study: Pathways in Saskatchewan

Total Saskatchewan Allocation – $23,859,000.00 (1992-93)

CEIC Regionally Controlled Moneys

$1,349,000.00
IAS + CO-OP ED
Community Futures

CEIC Locally Controlled Moneys

Walk-In Services	$4,085,000.00
CRF	2,500,000.00
SAR	585,000.00
UI	500,000.00
YOUTH	500,000.00

Aboriginal Controlled Moneys

*Treaty First Nations – $10,993,00.00

CRF	7,738,000.00
SAR	783,000.00
UI	1,500,000.00
SEED	198,000.00
START	204,000.00
CO-OP ED.	60,000.00
OUTREACH	510,000.00

*Métis – $7,432,000.00

CRF	5,092,000.00
SAR	522,000.00
UI	1,000,000.00
SEED	132,000.00
START	136,000.00
CO-OP ED.	40,000.00
OUTREACH	510,000.00

*Note: Both groups in turn have regional management boards and LIMBS (Local Indian Management Boards) and LAMBS (Local Aboriginal Management Boards).

will be more directly tied to retraining. Under the existing Pathways program, the policy is to decrease Consolidated Revenue Fund money and use more UI dollars. Since our people don't have jobs, this will only limit our training opportunities and further marginalize our people.

- Recognize that, in Canada, and, in particular, in Aboriginal communities, we will continue to experience a job shortage, not a skills shortage for the short term (less than five years). Furthermore, the growth occupation areas will either be in the highly skilled (17+ years education) or low skilled (less than 12 years) with few jobs in the intermediate skills.
- Aboriginal labour market conditions and change will continue to be affected from a variety of sources.
- Support more local education/training programs. Once our people leave for education and training, many never return. An added benefit is that when a local program is offered, the whole community benefits.
- We must promote self-employment as the major opportunity for employment growth. Of the G-7 countries, Canada is the lowest in the percentage of its labour force that is self-employed. In Aboriginal communities, it is almost nonexistent.
- The Aboriginal labour force will continue to explode with approximately 15,000 Aboriginal youth entering the labour force each year. Where are the jobs coming from? This will place increased demands on Aboriginal institutions and communities, many of whom will be unable to respond, because of a lack of infrastructure.
- The best opportunity for creating jobs is in the Aboriginal private sector. The non-Aboriginal public sector is downsizing, and initiatives such as "employment equity" will be a tough sell with unions who are out to protect their members.
- The Aboriginal public sector, particularly First Nations, is almost saturated. The transfer of programs from the federal to First Nation governments is almost complete, except for a few areas such as policing, health and child welfare. The only major opportunity for growth in this area is to replace non-Aboriginal employees with Aboriginal graduates.
- Aboriginal people must leap-frog general society. As a strategy for Aboriginal national building, we should promote university over technical training.

Elementary/Secondary Education and its Role in Employment Development

Does Aboriginal Control of Education Work?

In 1972, the forerunner of the Assembly of First Nations, the National Indian Brotherhood, announced its "Indian Control of Indian Education". Twenty years have passed and great strides were made. However, much work still needs to be done – we have yet to control fully the education of our children. How have we fared so far? To illustrate that Indian control of Indian Education has been successful to date, I would like to refer to the data on the following page and the accompanying graph. Using Saskatchewan as an example, the table on the following page shows the nominal rolls by grade of First Nations students living on reserve for the years 1981-1992. Added to the table is the number of students by age, residing on-reserve. For example, in the year 1981-82, we noted that the number of youth between the ages of 14 and 17 years was 3,678. Students in this age bracket would normally be in grades 9-12. Instead, for this age bracket, only 1,698 were enrolled. When we compare these two figures (1,698/3,678), we arrive at a retention rate of only 46.2%. As we go down the chart, we notice that the retention rate gradually increases to 87.6% in 1992.

The subsequent table shows the number of federally and First Nations-controlled schools for the period 1981-1992. As the number of federally controlled schools decreases, we note a corresponding rise in the number of First Nations-controlled schools; today we only have one school that is being run by DIAND.

Using this data, we produced the graph to illustrate that as we take over the running of our schools, we see the retention rate of our students rise. There is no other explanation for this but to conclude that Indian control of Indian Education has been successful, very successful.

Future Directions

Since we only have "administrative control" of our schools, I see "Indian Control of Indian Education" moving into a new phase in our developments. Because of the consistent high dropout rate of our Aboriginal youth in the urban setting, we must take similar Aboriginal control initiatives to deal with the problem. In addition, we must also gain control over all aspects of Indian education from teacher accreditation, certification, curriculum, standards and general jurisdiction now enjoyed by the provincial governments. How then would we be different from the existing educational system? I would propose the following:

- a year-round school system, rather than the present one which is based on an outmoded agricultural economy;
- raising the compulsory school age from 16 to 18 years of age;
- increasing the number of school days from the national average of 180 days per year to 215 school days annually;
- have no grading until grade 4;
- provide for a younger head-start program;
- implement a truly bilingual program;
- stress science and math and young business skills;
- combine co-op work study and other work-related experience for high school students;
- instill adaptability to change;

DIAND - Saskatchewan Region First Nation Education Nominal Rolls 1981-1992

YEAR	Kinder 4	Kinder 5	Gr. 1/4 Age 6/9	Gr. 5/8 Age 10/13	Gr. 9/12 Age 14/17	Gr. 1/12 Age 16/17	Total Student
81/82	601	958	5351	4348	1698	11397	12956
			3836	3854	3678	11368	
Gr: Age			139.5	112.8	46.2	100.3	
82/83	437	788	4366	3741	1877	9984	11209
			3770	3849	3780	11399	
Gr: Age			115.8	97.2	49.7	87.6	
83/84	618	1019	4601	3874	1265	10640	12277
			3847	3850	3819	11516	
Gr: Age			119.6	100.6	56.7	92.4	
84/85	600	856	4283	3620	2195	10098	11644
			3913	3842	3846	11601	
Gr: Age			109.5	94.2	57.1	87.0	
85/86	698	919	4718	3826	2373	10917	12534
			3998	3854	3860	11712	
Gr. Age			118.0	99.3	61.5	93.2	
86/87	673	1017	4558	3821	2477	10856	12546
			4142	3813	3867	11822	
Gr: Age			110.0	100.2	64.1	91.8	
87/88	818	1042	4633	3911	2529	11073	12933
Gr: Age							
88/89	859	1100	4524	3883	2643	11050	13009
			3942	3630	3626	11198	
Gr: Age			114.8	107.0	72.9	98.7	
89/90	935	1053	4523	3898	2922	11343	1331
			4079	3674	3592	11345	
Gr: Age			110.9	106.1	81.3	100.0	
90/91	992	1110	4730	4058	3351	12139	14241
			4459	3901	3717	12077	
Gr: Age			106.1	104.0	90.2	100.5	
91/92	1118	1140	4835	4055	3354	12244	14502
			4624	4117	3829	12570	
Gr: Age			104.6	98.5	87.6	97.4	

First Nations and Federally Controlled Schools in Saskatchewan

Year	Federally Controlled Schools	First Nations Controlled Schools
1981/82	39	24
1982/83	30	23
1983/84	31	34
1984/85	30	37
1985/86	24	44
1986/87	24	45
1987/88	20	49
1988/89	16	51
1989/90	9	55
1990/91	5	60
1991/92	1	62

Saskatchewan On-reserve High School Student Retention Compared to the Change in the Number of First Nation and Federally-controlled Schools

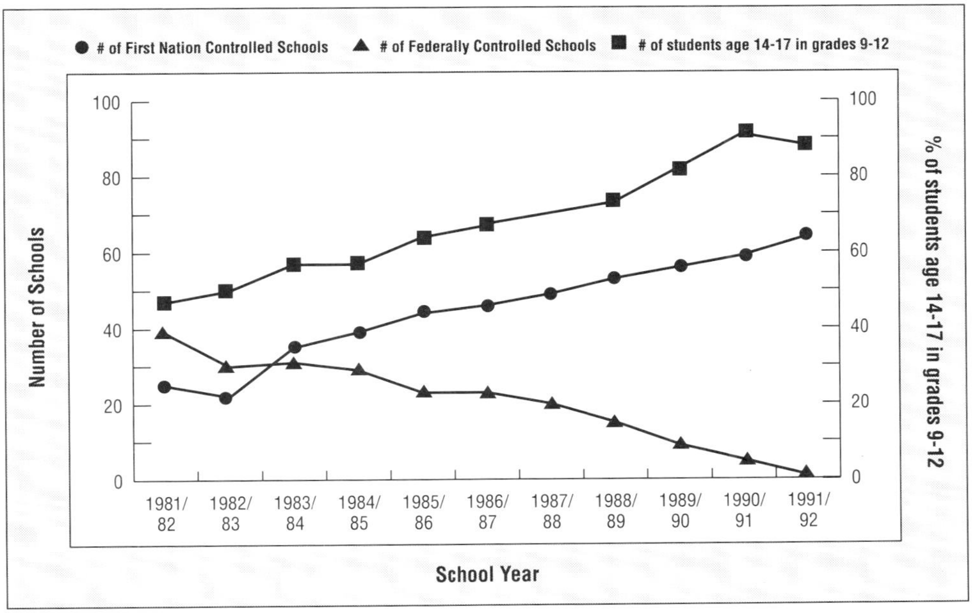

- foster management skills; at one time, we had a shortage of information, now we have an over-abundance. All must also learn to manage change affecting their personal life and the lives of others.

Such a system would be based on the following principles:

- Education and training is a lifelong process.
- Educational processes and institutions must address the intellectual, spiritual, emotional and physical development of our students.
- Beneficiaries of education should include individuals, their families, communities and future generations. With education rights come obligations and responsibilities.
- We must recognize the legitimate needs of contemporary Aboriginal people to function in several worlds, often with several different languages and with skills and knowledge drawn from several cultures.
- The responsibility for quality and success in education and training is shared among students, educational institutions, parents, families, communities and various levels of government.
- We must recognize that Aboriginal people, regardless of where they live or their previous educational experience, have the right to educational institutions which foster and support employment opportunities, the development of positive self-concepts and cultural and linguistic identity.

Need to Promote Sciences

A recurring theme that we often hear, particularly from the business community (besides returning to the 3Rs), is the need to promote sciences in our schools. For Aboriginal people, this is crucial if our future generations are going to participate fully in Canadian society. Such a plan could easily be implemented that would yield significant economic and employment benefits not only for our people but for the broader Canadian community. For example, if more Aboriginal people became doctors, nurses, engineers and agrologists, this would not only provide greater opportunities for employment but would provide a pool of highly trained Aboriginal people to assume leadership roles within Aboriginal communities. Under strong leadership, economic enterprises, health services and facilities could be established that are viewed as a component of the Aboriginal community.

As can be noted on the following tables, First Nations people are severely under-represented not only in science and technology areas requiring university degrees, certificates and diplomas, but also in the non-university technology based fields. For First Nations people to have proportionate representation in these fields by the year 2006, we must graduate 19,160 at the university level and another 57,985 at the technical/trades level. Is this possible and how would we accomplish this?

Number of People With University Certificates, Diplomas, And Degrees in Certain Science-Based Fields And Number of First Nations People Required to Hold These Credentials for Proportional Representation In 2006* In Canada and In Saskatchewan

	CANADA		SASKATCHEWAN	
	Number In General Population	Number Of First Nations People For Proportional Representation	Number In General Population	Number Of First Nations People For Proportional Representation
Agricultural Science	31,610	830	4,055	475
Architecture	14,955	395	200	25
Biological Sciences	60,420	1,590	1,650	195
Chemistry	27,935	735	575	70
Dentistry	14,735	390	360	40
Engineering	187,080	4,925	3,995	470
General Science	26,680	700	610	70
Geology & Related Fields	16,955	450	465	55
Household Science	25,180	665	1,070	125
Mathematics	67,605	1,780	1,900	225
Medicine	55,215	1,455	1,780	210
Nursing	86,065	2,270	3,340	390
Other Engineering & Applied Sciences	19,245	510	455	55
Other Health Sciences	50,640	1,335	1,220	140
Pharmacy	20,865	550	1,100	130
Physics	16,185	425	360	40
Veterinary Medicine	5,865	155	325	40
TOTALS	**727,235**	**19,160**	**23,460**	**2,755**

* Medium First Nations population projection for the year 2006 used; Canada 671,526, Sask. 118,934: From *Population Projection of Registered Indians* 1986-2011, Shirley Lob, Populations Projections Section, Demography Division, Statistics Canada, January 1990.

* Data compilation credit to Office of Education, Federation of Saskatchewan Indian Nations, "A Strategic and Operational Plan to Increase The Number of First Nations People In The Science Based Professions" (February, 1993).

Number of People With Non-University Certificates, Diplomas, And Degrees in Certain Science-Based Fields And Number of First Nations People Required to Hold These Credentials for Proportional Representation In 2006* In Canada and In Saskatchewan

	CANADA		SASKATCHEWAN	
	Number In General Population	**Number Of First Nations People For Proportional Representation**	**Number In General Population**	**Number Of First Nations People For Proportional Representation**
Agricultural & Biological Technologies	81,180	2,135	2,910	340
Engineering & Applied Science Technologies	1,481,885	39,020	50,490	5,940
Household Science Technologies	103,475	2,725	2,615	310
Mathematics & Physical Science Technologies	44,215	1,165	930	110
Medical Laboratory & Diagnostic Technologies	25,785	680	1,015	120
Medical Treatment Technologies	49,825	1,310	3,410	400
Nursing	236,415	6,225	10,455	1,230
Nursing Assistant	133,965	3,530	6,405	755
Other Health Related Technologies	45,365	1,195	1,020	120
TOTALS	**2,202,101**	**57,985**	**79,250**	**9,325**

* Medium First Nations population projection for the year 2006 used; Canada 671,526, Sask. 118,934: From *Population Projection of Registered Indians* 1986-2011, Shirley Lob, Populations Projections Section, Demography Division, Statistics Canada, January 1990.

* Data compilation credit to Office of Education, Federation of Saskatchewan Indian Nations, "A Strategic and Operational Plan to Increase The Number of First Nations People In The Science Based Professions" (February, 1993).

The strategy is straightforward:

- To foster in our young children a "desire to be" and to provide the encouragement to become an engineer, a doctor, a nurse, an agrologist, etc. Currently, for a variety of reasons, few Aboriginal children even consider the possibility of entering science-based professions and occupations. Creating this "desire to be" will require the support and encouragement of their families and communities. Universities, technical colleges, Crown corporations, and private sector companies also have a role to play in establishing opportunities for Aboriginal children to see and experience first hand what it might be like to learn and work in a science-based field.
- To increase the number of Aboriginal students graduating from high school with a solid foundation in mathematics and the sciences, thus enabling them to pursue science-based careers in the health-care professions, engineering, agriculture, the natural sciences and related technologies, if they so choose. More Aboriginal students are completing high school than ever before, but the number graduating with a solid foundation in mathematics and science is still relatively low. Correcting this situation will require special programs and the co-operation of many agencies and individuals, particularly those involved in teacher training and in the teaching of science and mathematics.
- To establish a better learning environment for Aboriginal students to make the transition successfully from high school into the first or second year of a science-based degree or diploma program. The adjustment First Nations and other Aboriginal students must make to succeed in a traditional post-secondary learning environment is much greater than that required of their peers. Studies have shown that about 25% of the First Nations students who commenced university studies earned a degree, compared to 55% for the general student population. However, it has also been shown that by creating a better learning environment, particularly in first and second year, minority engineering students, for example, can be retained at higher than the average rate for all students and at three times the rate for minority students in a traditional learning environment.
- To facilitate the entry into, and the successful completion of, a science-based degree or diploma program by Aboriginal students. Most science-based programs have enrolment limits. To ameliorate the problem this causes, it is proposed that a network of universities and technical institutes be established that would:
  - admit into their regular science-based professional diploma and degree programs, with an appropriate transfer of credits, Aboriginal students who have successfully completed the transition program;
  - provide a hospitable educational environment for First Nations and Aboriginal students to acquire the necessary credentials to become practising professionals. The co-operation and support of the science-based colleges/faculties in a number of universities is required to achieve this objective,

but one university in particular will be required to take a lead role and set an example.

To conclude, if we don't take the initiative now, to prepare our students properly in these areas, another generation of Aboriginal people will be relegated to the sidelines.

Appendix
Participation Theories of Aboriginal People in the Labour Force

The following is a synopsis of various theories of participation of Aboriginal people in the labour force. They attempt to analyze the possible barriers and constraints to Aboriginal employment. For further reader, see Peters and Rosenberg's study on the "Indian Attachment to the Labour Force" (DIAND, August 1992).

Indian Attachment to the Labour Force

Theory One – Dual Economy

It is argued that there are two separate labour markets in Canadian society, and each operates by different behavioural rules. One can be called the primary labour market with its stable employment, high wages and more long-term security. The other is the secondary labour market with its low wages, instability and low skill requirements. It is proposed that the structure of the labour market to which an individual belongs, rather than an individual's qualification or characteristics, determines whether he or she participates in one or the other. It is concluded that discrimination prevents Aboriginal people from participating in the primary labour market.

Theory Two – Dependency Syndrome

Dependency theorists propose that relationships develop in a capitalist system between the exploited and the exploiter, usually because of colonization. Discussions about development are usually made by the exploiter (external) rather than meeting local needs. In addition, capital never accumulates in the hands of the exploited. Capital is drained away and employment opportunities for local people are usually low status, short-term and few in number.

Theory Three – Marxist Approach

A combination of a variety of approaches, incorporating some of the underlying themes of the first two theories. They propose a class structure with the majority (proletariat) being controlled by the bourgeoisie. What can one say, except the U.S.S.R. has fallen apart.

Theory Four – Individual Characteristics

The most commonly held and practised. Their approach is to change an individual's attributes (skills, education, etc.) to increase their opportunities in the labour force.

There are four approaches/theories to achieve this:

- Economic theory: presupposes that individual Aboriginal people enter the labour market with a set of productive characteristics (training, attitudes) and individual preferences and, because of these, make rational decisions regarding choice of jobs and salary. Therefore, there is an emphasis on formal education, vocational and on-the-job and other training, since these will improve his or her chances.
- Culture and poverty theory: explains why successive generations of some poor adapt to their marginalized position in a society by creating a culture that makes it impossible for successive generations to break out. Characteristics such as inferiority, family disintegration, welfare dependency, hatred of established institutions and rejection of middle class values, underlie this culture. Therefore, this cultural attitude in itself becomes an obstacle. How does one then change an individual's character?
- Sociological approach: concentrates on an individual's background – sex, parental education and occupation, race, age, attitudes and values. Any of these could affect an individual's chances of participating in the labour force.
- Modernization theory: views western attitudes and values as prerequisite to economic well-being. They argue that traditional economies represent major obstacles to be overcome if development is to proceed.

Toward Strategic Management of Self-Sufficient Aboriginal Economies: A Holistic Vision

*Richard-Marc Lacasse**

> We are living in the Time of the Parenthesis, the time between eras. Although the time between eras is uncertain, it is a great and yeasty time, filled with opportunity. If we can learn to make uncertainty our friend, we can achieve more than in stable eras.
>
> *John Naisbitt*

Aboriginal communities are living in a time of crisis. Too many Aboriginal peoples are still outside the circle. The disintegration of the family, the fragmentation of traditional values, the distorted economy, the erosion of spirituality seem to have no remedy. Classical models of economic development have shown themselves inadequate to meet the current crises. We need to identify the structural changes that need to be made. We must explore new directions in order to build the self-sufficient economies of the future. The problems are systemic, which means that they are interconnected and cannot be understood within the fragmented methodologies of our academic disciplines and government agencies. We believe that transformations are necessary en route toward self-sufficient Aboriginal economies. For the Chinese, living in a time of crisis (*wei-ji*) has two meanings: danger and opportunity. It is time to work on socio-economic opportunities for Aboriginal communities.

This paper does not present a classical view of economic development. The source of inspiration comes from many sages, from A.T. Ariyaratne in Sri Lanka

* Department of Economics and Management, University of Quebec at Rimouski.

to S. J. Augustine in Big Cove, New Brunswick. Scholars like Dr. Harold Bhérer enlightened us with cutting-edge research on Aboriginal entrepreneurship. Field work with indigenous peoples of the Americas (from the Quichuas and the Otavalians in the Andes to the Innu and Micmac in Eastern Quebec) has also provided insight into the exploration of new avenues.

A New Vision of Aboriginal Socio-Economic Development

To meet the challenge of the twenty-first century, a new way of thinking must be developed. This involves a profound reconditioning of our attitudes toward controlling socio-economic development. Can we still talk of values and economic planning in Aboriginal communities? Can we mix faith, hope, tolerance and charity with economic development? Can we work toward economic health without confrontation?

When we talk about intervention regarding economic planning in Aboriginal communities, we must continually take into consideration an ever-present set of values which includes the preservation of language, culture and spirituality. Native American spiritual traditions teach that Earth is a Mother to be nourished, celebrated and respected. Future Aboriginal socio-economic development must be congruent with this precept.

In the past, economic planning for Aboriginal peoples was kept in the hands of experts and bureaucrats isolated in ivory towers. In the future, all planning should be based on the collective input of the parties involved. Strategic planning must viewed as something done *by* Aboriginal communities, not *for* Aboriginal peoples by consultants. This reflection on current Aboriginal problems (exploring new paths) involves the implementation of a new vision, replacing outdated conceptual models. We must develop systemic thinking with recourse to communal intelligence and creativity. We must elaborate a *how-to* arsenal accessible to all Aboriginal communities. It is time to work on a *how-to* approach to the development of an *intrapreneurial* culture within Aboriginal communities.

Mending and Healing the Broken Circle

For millennia, the circle has been at the heart of the everyday life of Aboriginal peoples. From daily gatherings to symbolic ceremonies, from poetry to spiritual encounters, the circle has illustrated the bonds that determine the healthy community life of these peoples. There was a physical and spiritual equilibrium in the relationship between them and their world. The arrival of the European nations in America disrupted the traditional Aboriginal way of life, breaking the mighty circle of dignity, pride and spirit among the Aboriginal peoples. They lost touch with each other, they lost their connection to Mother Earth, they lost the control of their destiny: they have been systematically conditioned to depend upon people outside their own population.

The circles of talking and sharing should be the main forum used to reach a consensus regarding socio-economic planning. Let me cite a Micmac historian:

> Today, if our leaders are guided by the wisdom of our elders, if they are concerned about the views of the young people and are guided by these concerns, and if they are listening to the lessons of our mothers to learn to share and care and cooperate, they could never make a bad decision. The reason for this is that a decision which reflects the values and morals of the community is a decision that cannot be wrong in the eyes of our community.[1]

In Aboriginal strategic planning, we must respect the wisdom and knowledge of the elders; we must listen to the lessons of the mothers; we must respect the young and their vision of the future.

The Sarvodaya Movement in Sri Lanka

An analysis of this movement can be of help to us in our attempt to preserve traditional values within economic development. Professor Ariyaratne has transformed the lives of hundreds of thousands of villagers in Sri Lanka (4,000 villages) by his vast program of self-sufficiency and self-reliance based on six different aspects: the social (co-operative betterment); the economic (producing goods with appropriate technology by co-operative methods with minimum damage to the eco-system); the political (decentralization of power and decision making free from coercion); the moral (ethics); the cultural (recognition and nourishment of cultural heterogeneity); and the spiritual (maintaining the spirit of the ancient culture). The Sarvodaya movement's strategy is to foster the intelligence, the competence, the confidence and the co-operativeness of villagers so that they can really help themselves. The structure is non-hierarchical with balanced numbers of men, women and young people. The community development program is a social learning experience: the process, as a human experience, is as important as the final product. Professor Ariyaratne believes that the villagers themselves know best what it is they need. The role of outside experts is to listen with respect, then facilitate the emergence of collective intelligence within the community. Listening to the community builds individual and collective self-esteem, reawakens dormant energies, and uncovers neglected and under-exploited capabilities.

Involving Aboriginal Peoples in Socio-Economic Development, a Reality

Some Aboriginal communities in Canada have developed economic strategies, projects and institutions that are contributing to improvements in their local economy. Allow us to present briefly two programs that have demonstrated the capability of Aboriginal communities in the planning of socio-economic development.

The Labour Adjustment Program

This program establishes a committee (*Comité d'adaptation de la main-d'oeuvre*) whose aim is to prevent labour layoffs and ensure a more stable economy within Quebec's Aboriginal communities. It also encourages the establishment of socio-economic task forces in Aboriginal communities. These task forces identify the difficulties in the community and implement solutions to these problems. The committee is usually made up of members from the band council (politicians) and from the Aboriginal community (elders, women, youth, spiritual leaders). Both parties choose a task force chairperson. The team generally benefits from technical expertise and financial aid from several government organizations: the *Ministère de la main-d'oeuvre et de la securité du revenu du Québec*, Employment and Immigration Canada, Indian and Northern Affairs Canada, the *Secrétariat des affaires autochtones du Québec*, the *Office de planification et de développement du Québec*, etc. Usually, the task force progresses through five major steps:

- The pre-analysis of the Aboriginal community: the economic development agents, the government representatives and members of the band council analyze the socio-economic situation and consider the need for a labour adjustment committee.
- Setting up the committee: all parties sign an agreement to create a task force. The band council, the Aboriginal community and government representatives meet to establish the mandate and structure of the task force. A chairperson and a treasurer are selected. Usually, the chairperson is an animator with solid socio-economic experience in local and regional development. The committee members establish a decision-making process and define the roles of participants.
- Analysis of the Aboriginal community: the task force must prepare a diagnostic study of the community. A responsibility chart is then drawn up. Usually advisers are hired to help the committee. The committee reviews the results of the study.
- The problem-solving plan: following the diagnostic study, the task force establishes an economic recovery plan with the assistance of advisers. The committee also examines ways of implementing the plan.
- Evaluation: the committee evaluates the results of the work. A final report with recommendations is prepared. The report is submitted to the band council for approval.

Through interviews and reports from different Aboriginal socio-economic development planning experiences in 20 Aboriginal communities in the province of Quebec, different socio-economic strategic planning models were analyzed.[2] We were pleasantly surprised by the creative and visionary approach to socio-economic development evidenced in these Aboriginal communities.

The Community Futures Program

Another program was adapted by two Quebec Aboriginal communities: the Community Futures Program. This federal government program allows communities with difficulties to be the innovators, leaders and managers in solving their long-term employment problems. Through Community Futures, Employment and Immigration Canada (EIC) forms a partnership with non-metropolitan and smaller communities in crisis. Community Futures participates in local endeavours to assess economic problems, identify opportunities and achieve long-term employment stability, growth and adjustment.

The Community Futures Committee (CFC) is the agent responsible for the community's economic development plan. The CFC assesses the community's development and adjustment needs and develops a strategic plan. The CFC brings the community together toward the common goal of community development. The success of this program and its strength lie in having the community assume control of the development and implementation of the strategic plan.

The Community Futures Committee is usually responsible for:

- involving the private sector and various levels of government in the assessment of community problems and the design of suitable remedies;
- developing an overall local economic development plan and proposals for short- and long-term solutions to labour market problems;
- co-ordinating self-help initiatives at the local level;
- recommending appropriate Community Futures options;
- monitoring the appropriateness of the strategic plan over a period of time;
- updating the plan on an annual basis;
- evaluating program implementation.

Empowering Aboriginal Communities to Take Control of their Socio-Economic Development

The overall mandate regarding socio-economic development of Aboriginal communities should be to establish a strategic plan that will revive the traditional sense of dignity, pride and spirit in Aboriginal communities. Any Aboriginal economic development strategy should take into consideration the seven physical and spiritual needs identified by Aboriginal historians: food, clothes, medicine, shelter, tools, travel and spirit.

The methodology should be flexible, creative and culturally relevant. The preparation of a socio-economic strategic plan requires eclectic research-action techniques: documentary research (especially on the lazy circle and/or broken circle and historical research on past heroic sagas and legendary exploits); communal encounters; healing ceremonies; nominal group techniques (NGT); and workshops on visions of the future (elders, women, teenagers, dropouts). These approaches empower the community to release an enormous quantity of human energy not available when Aboriginal peoples are constrained to act as passive recipients of expertise and supervision. The community must be the local arena in which change is implemented. The main steps of these communal mandates could be:

- diagnosis of obstacles, of threats and of opportunities regarding socio-economic development of the community;
- conception of a plan of action clearly identifying the strategic choices and priority interventions required to create self-sufficient economies in Aboriginal communities;
- implementation of short-, medium- and long-term projects;
- definition of specific tools of appraisal for the objectives set up in the plan of action.

Toward a Holistic Model

We will now discuss a strategic planning process that could be used by Aboriginal communities. This holistic model is both eclectic (inspired by Aboriginal people of the Americas and by the Sarvodaya Movement in Sri Lanka) and ideal (presenting the best elements identified in these experiences). This socio-economic development model is a social learning encounter for any Aboriginal community: the process, as a human experience, is as important as the final product. Chart 1 describes the process.

First, authorities and Aboriginal community representatives study the pertinence of establishing a strategy to improve socio-economic development (phase 1). Then both parties agree on setting up a committee (phase 2). The task force recruits an experienced facilitator who will support the planning, organization and co-ordination of the committee's work. This facilitator should have solid socio-economic experience in local and regional development. The facilitator's main role will be to stimulate communal input and creativity en route to solving the community's problems. One of the committee's first tasks is to inform the Aboriginal community of its past and present socio-economic situation in order to solicit proposals for a community development plan (phases 3 and 4). Generally the scope of the task at hand requires hiring advisers (phase 5).

The task force and the community prepare a socio-economic profile and a spiritual-cultural profile (phase 6) and examine strengths and weaknesses of the community base (phase 7). A wide variety of participatory techniques will be required to release the enormous quantity of human energy and creativity: communal encounters, healing ceremonies, synectics, nominal group techniques, delphi process, workshops on visions of the future (elders, women, teenagers, dropouts), role playing techniques, etc.

Chart 1

Strategic Management of Self-Sufficient Aboriginal Economies: A Holistic Model[4]

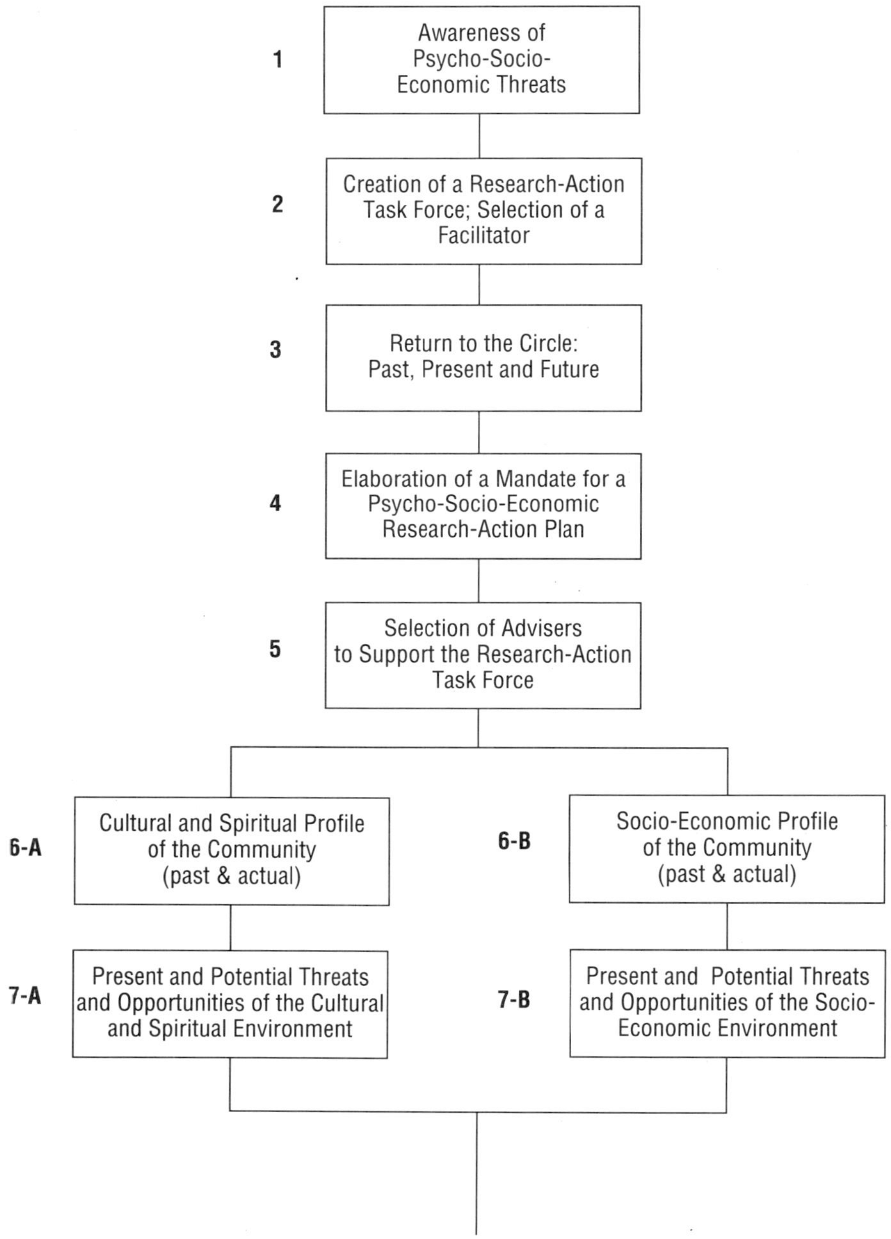

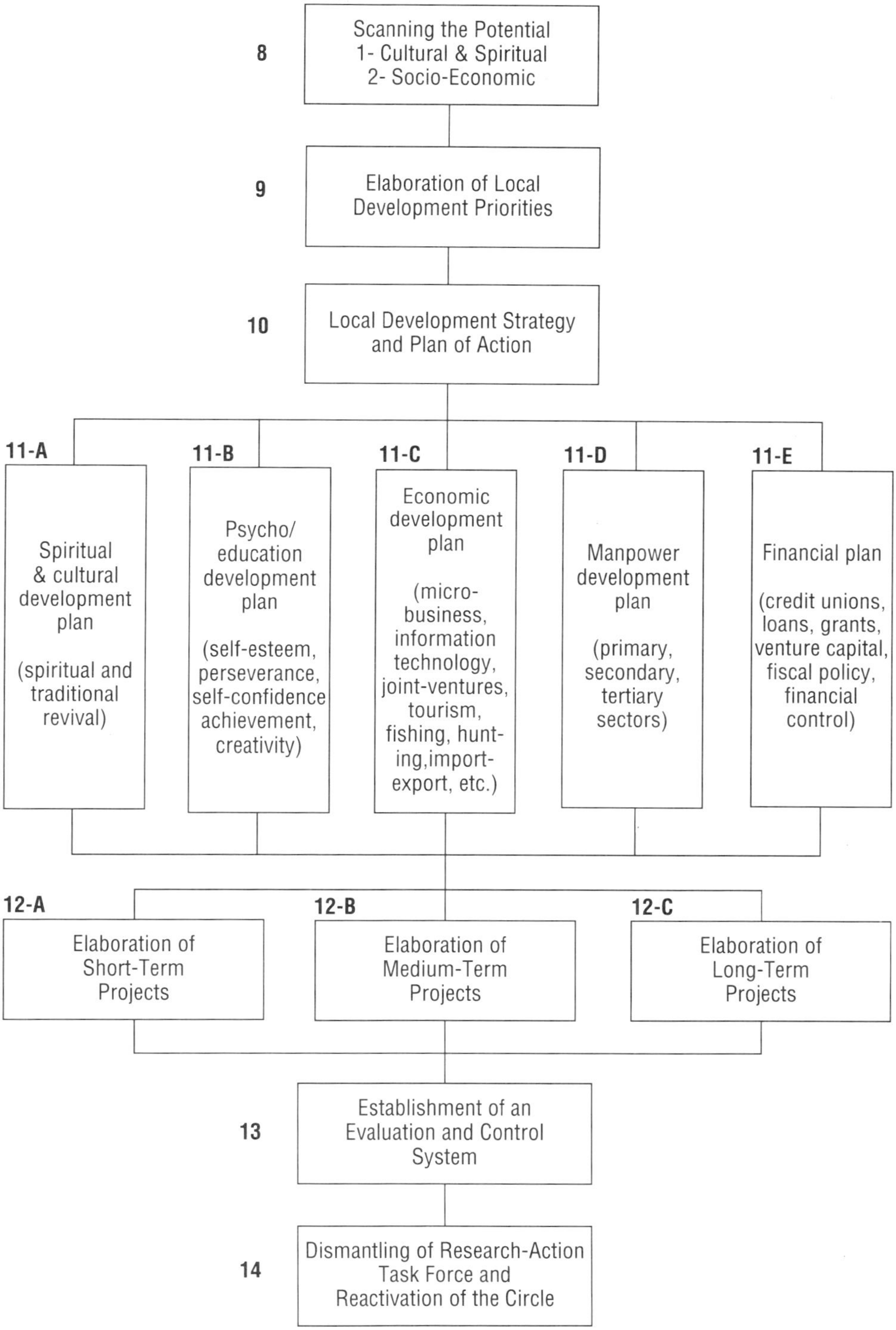
8
Scanning the Potential
1- Cultural & Spiritual
2- Socio-Economic
9
Elaboration of Local Development Priorities
10
Local Development Strategy and Plan of Action
11-A
Spiritual & cultural development plan
(spiritual and traditional revival)
11-B
Psycho/ education development plan
(self-esteem, perseverance, self-confidence achievement, creativity)
11-C
Economic development plan
(micro-business, information technology, joint-ventures, tourism, fishing, hunting,import-export, etc.)
11-D
Manpower development plan
(primary, secondary, tertiary sectors)
11-E
Financial plan
(credit unions, loans, grants, venture capital, fiscal policy, financial control)
12-A
Elaboration of Short-Term Projects
12-B
Elaboration of Medium-Term Projects
12-C
Elaboration of Long-Term Projects
13
Establishment of an Evaluation and Control System
14
Dismantling of Research-Action Task Force and Reactivation of the Circle

A detailed overall analysis of phases 6 and 7 gives the committee a better grasp of the Aboriginal community's potential and the entrepreneurial potential of its human resources (phase 8). Based on this data and with nominal group techniques, the Aboriginal community then prepares a list of priorities for socio-economic development geared to the strengths and weaknesses of the community (phase 9).

Then the facilitator and the Aboriginal committee prepare a local development strategy (phase 10). This strategic plan deals with the spiritual and cultural development (spiritual and traditional revival); psycho-education development (self-esteem, self-confidence, junior achievement programs); economic development (micro-business, information technology, joint-ventures, tourism, fishing, hunting, arts and crafts, import/export, etc.); plans for manpower training (primary, secondary and tertiary sectors); project financing (credit union, loans, grants, venture capital, fiscal, financial control). Regarding the effective support of the growth of Aboriginal businesses, specific considerations are presented in the Appendix. This overall plan (phase 11) must be congruent with the cultural and spiritual ideology of the community.

The following step (phase 12) will result in the preparation of a list of short-, medium-, and long-term projects. The logical next step is to establish an evaluation and follow-up system (phase 13). Finally, the facilitator oversees the dismantling of the Task force and the activation of a permanent local socio-economic development agency.

> Many spiritual and healing traditions use visualization in order to heal. To heal ourselves means to contact this wholeness, this holiness, to visualize human futures that embrace all of what we are and can be, the light, the dark, and the other shades.
>
> *Anonymous*

Conclusion

The promotion of socio-economic autonomy is a relay race sustained by a series of torch bearers: the family, the spiritual leaders, the educators, the business networks, the government authorities. The seeds of achievement are nurtured in the family nest. Parents have an important mission: they must impress upon their children the traditional sense of dignity, pride and spirit. Fathers and mothers must stimulate and maintain the *feu sacré* of their children's self-confidence. Then the *credo* of self-reliance must filter through the educational system: nursery and primary schools, colleges and universities. Educators must propagate and consolidate the *intrapreneurial* culture through the school system. At the local level, band councils, educators, social workers, entrepreneurs must diffuse successful role models, restore past heroic sagas, promote joint ventures at local, regional, national and even the international level.

The threats, obstacles and opportunities that Aboriginal communities face can be dealt with through strategic socio-economic planning; the management of the present *wei-ji* involves trade-offs between individual and collective values, compromises between the local culture and the global village. The common denominator of the creation of wealth in Aboriginal communities will be collective intelligence.

In the future, the long route toward self-sufficient Aboriginal economies will not necessarily depend on muscle and physical effort; it will probably be an amalgam of environmental scanning, collective intuition and creativity, know-how, self-confidence and strategic management of interpersonal networks.

Appendix
Developing an Entrepreneurial Culture

Designing a model to identify the entrepreneurial initiatives of new business ventures is a complex exercise. The particular field of Aboriginal entrepreneurship calls for a type of reflection capable of remaining open to every possible avenue. Various aspects (economic, historical, spiritual, psychological and sociological) must be considered in dealing with problems related to the emergence of small enterprises in the context of a local Aboriginal environment.

Our inspiration is drawn from the following paradigm: "Entrepreneurial formations are the results of interacting situational and cultural factors." The principal elements of our model are composed of psychological, social, economic and situational variables which influence the potential entrepreneur, *pushing* or *pulling* her or him toward the entrepreneurial event. We can identify different types of entrepreneurial events: business start-ups, purchase of an existing firm, family business inheritance and access to an existing firm by invitation. In Aboriginal communities, special attention must be given to communal projects.

Main Variables

For the purpose of this paper, the variables were grouped into five blocks (Figure 1). The selected variables are: the sociological variables, the situational variables, the potential female or male entrepreneur, the access to resources and the entrepreneurial event.

Sociological variables: To further explore the social components, studies in the field prompt us to retain the following variables: family context, education background, work environment, role models, traditional values, local environment and integration to networks. These variables can generate an entrepreneurial culture which will push the potential Aboriginal entrepreneur to form a new business.

Figure 1

Building an entrepreneurial culture[4]

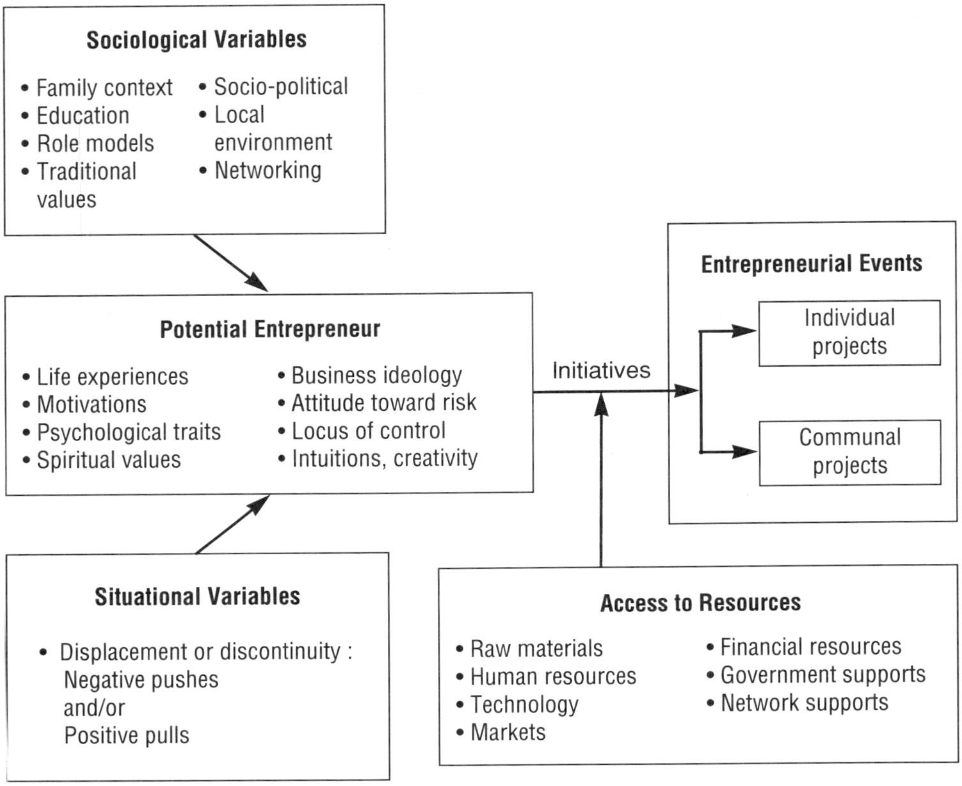

Situational variables: We believe that many cases of business start-ups result from upsettings or tumultuous events in the course of a person's life. Literature on the matter and our own previous findings legitimize the presence of situational variables in our model. They are classified under two types: *negative pushes* and *positive pulls* events.

Potential female or male entrepreneur: The individual can also be an explanatory variable of the entrepreneurial event. The potential entrepreneur variable includes the individual's life experience, motivations, psychological and spiritual characteristics, business ideology, attitude toward risk, locus of control, intuitions and creativity.

Entrepreneurial event: This dependant variable is the centre of interest of the model. The individual ventures can take place in different ways: business start-up, purchase of an existing firm, access to ownership by invitation and finally, access to a family business by inheritance. Communal projects are also entrepreneurial events.

Access to resources: In addition to favourable situational and social vectors, the potential entrepreneur needs resources to initiate entrepreneurial action. Our field work on the subject has led us to identify the following basic resources: raw materials, qualified work force, access to technology, access to markets, risk capital and support from governments and networks.

Specific considerations for the development of entrepreneurship in Aboriginal communities

The implementation of social and economic development of Aboriginal entrepreneurs through the ownership of a small business should take into account the following aspects:

- The promotion of entrepreneurship is a relay race sustained by a series of torch bearers: the family, the educators and the spiritual leaders, business networks, public authorities, international organizations, etc.
- The germ of an entrepreneurial culture must be nurtured in the family nest. Parents have an important mission: they must show their children that entrepreneurial ventures are not limited to the white man's world. Fathers and mothers must stimulate and maintain the feu sacré of their daughters and sons, encouraging self-reliance through entrepreneurship.
- Then the entrepreneurial credo must filter through the educational system: nursery and primary schools, high school, colleges and universities. Educators must propagate and consolidate the entrepreneurial culture through the school system. The implementation of curricula that encourage entrepreneurship should stimulate:
  - perseverance;
  - self-confidence;
  - self-reliance;
  - self-respect;
  - positive attitudes toward calculated risks;
  - achievement motives;
  - creativity and intuition.
- At the local level, social and business leaders must:
  - present successful role models;
  - promote joint ventures;
  - develop interlocking networks (suppliers, bankers and entrepreneurs);
  - implement micro-business incubators for potential entrepreneurs.

- Public authorities at the local, provincial and national levels must stimulate Aboriginal entrepreneurship. They must modify the image of the bureaucratic civil servant: he or she must be a counsellor and a mentor to the potential Aboriginal entrepreneur. Research centres must maintain contact with the Aboriginal businesses, share their technology and their know-how. The state departments must alter their image of entrepreneurial extinguishers and become synergetic units.
- At the international level, in the context of the globalization of the economy, organizations such as the Canadian International Development Agency (CIDA) and External Affairs and International Trade Canada must be more creative in their support of the diversification of Aboriginal economies through import/export programs.

Notes

1. Stephen J. Augustine. "Reviving the Traditional Sense of Dignity, Pride and Spirit." *Working Paper*, Big Cove, New Brunswick, March 1993.
2. Source of data: Analysis of internal documents from the *Secrétariat des affaires autochtones du Québec* and from the *Ministère de la main-d'oeuvre et de la sécurité du revenu du Québec*; analysis of mandates and reports from Aboriginal labour adjustment task forces; interviews with Aboriginal leaders, government representatives and economic development agents; correspondence with Aboriginal communities using the labour adjustment committees; press clippings.
3. Adapted from Lacasse, R. M., "Hacia la Automia Economica de los Pueblos Indigenas", *Working Paper*, Pontificia Universidad Catolica del Ecuador, Quito, Ecuador, Fe.1991.
4. Source: Lacasse, R. M., "Hacia la Automia Economica de los Pueblos Indigenas", *Working Paper*, Pontificia Universidad Catolica del Ecuador, Quito, Ecuador, Fe.1991.

A Brief Tax(on a me) of First Nations Taxation and Economic Development

*André LeDressay**

The Doomsday Scenario

In 1085 AD, in what is now modern day England, King William ordered a group of his commissioners to conduct a survey of his kingdom. Information about the population, amount of land held by individuals and quantities of livestock, tools and especially ploughs was recorded (Angresano, 1992, p. 73).

This exercise became known as the Doomsday Survey, because it was believed that a king would only conduct such an assessment of his kingdom in anticipation of Judgement Day. However, subsequent history indicates that Doomsday may well have referred to the ultimate intent of the survey – property taxation. In this regard, anyone conducting taxation research for First Nations has surely felt like the grim reaper.

Judgement Day

In the beginning there was section 87 of the *Indian Act*. In 1985 section 87 of the *Indian Act* was revised and now states, in part:

(1) Notwithstanding any other Act of the Parliament of Canada or any Act of the legislature of a province, but subject to

* Policy Analyst, Shuswap Nation Tribal Council.

section 83, the following property is exempt from taxation, namely,

(a) the personal property of an Indian or a band in reserve lands or surrendered land; and

(b) the personal property of an Indian or a band situated on a reserve.

(2) No Indian or band is subject to taxation in respect of the ownership, occupation, possession or use of any property mentioned in paragraph 1(a) or (b) or otherwise subject to taxation in respect of such property.

(3) No succession duty, inheritance tax or estate duty is payable on the death of any Indian in respect of any property mentioned in paragraphs 1(a) or 1(b) or for succession thereto if the property be taken into account in determining the duty payable under the Dominion Succession Duty Act (citation omitted) on or in respect of other property passing to an Indian (Strother and Brown, 1991, p. 16).

The scope of this discussion paper concentrates on the relationship between taxation and economic development within First Nations land. It is common knowledge that every discussion paper on First Nation taxation and economic development begins with the vaunted section 87 of the *Indian Act*. In fact some would suggest that the Act might be amended with subsection 87 (4) making this law for future discussion papers. These papers develop a number of detailed legal analyses of the implications of the partial taxation exemption[1] (see references). The consistent economic development finding from such papers implies a considerable comparative advantage for on-reserve First Nation businesses. The statistical evidence presented in this paper, however, indicates that this advantage is remarkably under used for economic development by First Nations.[2] The following text reveals answers to the "why".

The first section of this paper briefly presents the legal implications of the section 87 taxation exemption. Historically, case law determined the scope of application for section 87. Although a degree of certainty about the exemption's application may have previously existed, the recent Supreme Court ruling in the *Williams* case has clouded the exemption's application for many forms of off-reserve employment. Despite the current legal uncertainty about the parameters of the exemption, this section also discusses the comparative economic and business development advantages (and disadvantages) of the exemption provision for First Nations.

The second section of this paper presents household, government, and business case study evidence from six First Nation communities from the Shuswap Nation in the interior of B.C. One conclusion from these studies is an under-exploitation of the economic development opportunities afforded by the section 87 exemption. Discussions with interested individuals in other First Nations and cursory taxation base research from a number of First Nations suggest that this conclusion can be generalized for most, if not all, First Nations.

The third section of this paper argues that jurisdictional uncertainty on First Nations land offers one reason for the under-use of the section 87 exemption.[3] The recently released Canadian Department of Finance "Working Paper on Indian Taxation" provides a tentative federal step to address this uncertainty, especially as it relates to federal sales and income tax. Few First Nations[4] have developed policy positions on these taxation fields. This section presents taxation potential case study evidence from a number of First Nations and suggests that a revenue generating incentive may exist for First Nations to develop more encompassing (property, sales, income and resource) taxation schemes. Moreover, the development of such taxation systems could help clear the jurisdictional uncertainty surrounding First Nations and provide a more suitable climate to community based economic development initiatives.

87 Curse or Blessing

Earlier in this paper the section 87 exemption was referred to as a partial exemption because of a number of constraints on its application. Specifically three conditions must be met (Highlights Report, 1992, p 44).

- The tax must be enforceable by law.
- The claimant must be an Indian or a First Nation government as defined in the *Indian Act* (no corporations).
- The taxable Indian or First Nation government interest must be located on a reserve or surrendered land and/or the personal property of an Indian or First Nation government located on a reserve.

Interpretive difficulties arise with these conditions, and the entailing case law is a subject of Brown and Strother, 1991, and Morry, 1993. Below is a brief summary of some section 87 legal implications extracted from more detailed discussions.

The Implications

- The notwithstanding any other Act portion of section 87 supersedes any other federal or provincial law.
- Personal property which is exempt includes both intangible (electricity, income) and tangible (movable) property.
- For tangible property the litmus test for situs is generally its paramount location. This depends on the pattern of use and safe keeping of the property. For example, a car purchased on-reserve for use on- and off-reserve is paramountly located on-reserve and thus tax exempt.

- Intangible property like income tax is much more complicated. Until recently, if the employer was located on-reserve, the income of its Status Indian employees would be tax-exempt. The recent Supreme Court ruling in the *Williams* case, however, will allow the courts to consider other connecting factors such as where the employee provides her or his services.[5] For example, confusion arises in situations like the Assembly of First Nations whose head office is in the Territory of Akwesasne but a number of its status employees work in Ottawa.
- The *Williams* decision also clouded the exemption of business income located on-reserve. What are the important factors connecting the business income to the reserve? Is it:
  - the location of the head office;
  - the place where employees report for work;
  - the employee payment location;
  - the location of business transactions; or
  - the location of work activity?[6]
- Interest income on bank deposits is generally exempt if the bank branch is located on-reserve.
- The taxation exemption of bonds, bills of exchange and securities depends on the location of the paper representing the security.
- First Nation governments and "status" individuals are exempt from the GST if the property's purchase is made on a reserve or if the vendor or its agent delivers the property to a reserve. The notwithstanding any other Act clause means that these rules apply to provincial retail sales taxes as well.
- If cigarettes and gasoline are purchased on a reserve, these purchases should be entitled to an exemption from provincial gas and tobacco taxes.[7]

87 and Economic Development – The Good, The Bad and The Uncertain

The section 87 taxation exemption employed to its potential can be an effective tool in successful First Nations economic development.[8] It is unfortunately a double-edged sword, clearing a potential path to economic development with one edge, and creating confusion, tension, and red tape with the other. This section briefly reviews the role of the partial exemption in economic development.

The Good

The partial exemption offers several advantages to on-reserve First Nation businesses including the following:

- Exemption from GST, provincial retail sales taxes, and tobacco and fuel taxes means on-reserve First Nation businesses have a significant pricing advantage for their "status" customers. Assuming profit margins are high enough, and competition remains slim or nonexistent, this comparative pricing advantage could in theory be partially passed along to the larger non-status market in some First Nations.

- The income tax exemption for status employees could entail lower labour costs for on-reserve First Nation businesses and a subsequent comparative pricing advantage. This, though, is not a costless advantage, as discussed below.
- On-reserve corporations can distribute the business income to tax-exempt First Nation governments or individuals as a deductible fee, or possibly through dividends, thereby eliminating all its taxable income. This would provide such businesses with a comparative advantage since the opportunity cost[9] (true cost) of doing business is lower.
- If First Nations governments can be considered municipalities and they control over 90% of a corporation, then an exemption can be applied for under 149(1)(d)[10] of the *Income Tax Act*. The situs of the income is irrelevant for this exemption (Morry, 1993, p.17).
- First Nation partnership taxation exemptions will depend on the connecting factors of the business income. When the First Nation partner is tax-exempt, this particular business structure may act as an investment incentive[11] since some of the taxable income can be allocated to the tax-exempt partner. This, however, does not apply to joint ventures.
- Band-operated businesses are tax-exempt if the source of income is situated on-reserve or if it uses the *Income Tax Act* municipality provisions alluded to above. It should be cautioned that as an unincorporated entity, the band may unintentionally expose its off-reserve assets to its creditors.

The Bad and The Uncertain

The section 87 exemption, however, is not always advantageous to successful First Nation business and economic development. In fact at least one First Nation business person has suggested that its handicaps almost outweigh its advantages, and may explain its apparent under-use on First Nation land. "Another band of not inconsiderable wealth indicated that on a scale of 1 to 10, the tax exemption didn't even register." (Brown and Strother, 1991, p. 120) Below are listed a few reasons why this may be the case:

- Many non-First Nation businesses believe that First Nation businesses are unfairly advantaged because of the partial taxation exemption. The media often perpetuate the myth that members of First Nations do not pay tax. This may discourage potential First Nation business persons who feel unwilling to wage a political battle just for developing a business.
- The situs provisions in the partial taxation exemption discourage off-reserve business development and expansion to larger markets.
- Use of the income tax exemption for First Nation employees often creates tension when these employees compare their before-tax income with non-First Nation workers[12] doing similar work.
- The bureaucratic requirements of GST and provincial sales tax refunds from tax-exempt sales for on-reserve First Nation businesses (especially gas stations) can seriously affect these businesses' cash flow. Although the customer

avoids sales tax at the time of purchase, the retailer may have to wait up to three months to be reimbursed for the tax exemption.[13] For smaller businesses, obtaining these refunds often consumes a disproportionate amount of administrative time.

- There would appear to be a significant communication barrier between the methods for exploiting the section 87 taxation exemption and its effective economic application in First Nation communities. Interpretive difficulties such as the nature of an individual's property and the location of its acquisition complicate section 87. Beyond this the use of indecipherable legalese, economese, and bureaucratese seldom translates into First Nation community-based economic development action.[14] The uncertainty surrounding the *Williams* case only exacerbates these problems.[15]

Although it is undoubtedly true that the section 87 partial exemption provides a comparative advantage to First Nation business development, the case study statistical evidence presented in the next section clearly reveals its under-use. There are clearly other factors at work. It is the contention of this paper that a greater economic development yield could be attained through concentrating on these other factors. Once again jurisdictional uncertainty raises its ugly head.

Bungee Economics – A Case Study of a First Nations Economy

In order to understand the potential role between taxation and economic development for First Nations, it is crucial to comprehend the workings of a typical First Nations economy. To coin a phrase, most (if not all) First Nation economies are victims of "bungee economics." Money goes in and bounces right back out to the surrounding non-First Nation economy. Summary evidence extracted from "The Value of Co-operation – A Case Study of Six Shuswap Nation Tribal Council Communities"[16] describes below the extent of this monetary rubber band.

The Shuswap Nation Tribal Council (SNTC) officially launched its statistics program in 1991.[17] A component of this initiative was the collection of community-based economic development survey information. Appendix A contains a brief description of the information collection methodologies used for these research exercises[18] and the response rates for the studies referenced here.

The communities of the SNTC, for the purpose of this document, are considered representative of most Canadian First Nations (rural, urban, and isolated). Statistics Canada 1991 Census and Aboriginal Peoples Survey data[19] will be employed to validate these case study data nationally, as Statistics Canada releases the results throughout the current calender year. As such, this paper presents case study statistical evidence relevant to taxation and economic development.

The Empty Tax Net – Socio-Economic Indicators

The data below reflect some of the socio-economic indicators of the case study communities. They assume that these are not significantly different from most

First Nations in Canada.[20] Those statistics referring to the First Nation communities were gathered by the SNTC in 1991 and 1992. The statistics from Kamloops city were collected by Statistics Canada in 1990 or as projections from the 1986 Census.

Table I

Socio-Economic Indicator Statistical Comparisons

	Skeetchestn	Adams Lake	North Thompson	Canoe Creek	Kamloops
Persons per household	3.4	4.2	3.4	4.2	2.75
% UIC claimants*	29.5	30.3	30	49	8.7 (1990)
Mean Household Income**	$21,000	$22,500	$26,100	$14,000	$43,714 (1990)
% pop. > Gr.12***	18	26	31	14.3	37

Kamloops refers to the City of Kamloops.
* The % was calculated by dividing UIC claimants by the sum of all employed and UIC claimants.
** For the SNTC communities the mean was calculated from household income estimates where this information was provided, or from total household expenditure estimates where the direct response for household income was not given.
*** This is the percentage of the population (normalized from sample) that has completed either a university degree or a vocational program over and above high school.

Many First Nation leaders object to discussions on taxation because it may ultimately result in the removal of the section 87 tax exemption, and ultimately lead to the direct taxing of First Nation community members. It should be painfully obvious in the indicators above that even if First Nations did tax their own people, there is nothing to tax. Consider that mean household income in Canoe Creek[21] is but 32% of the average household income in Kamloops. Moreover, the percentage of UIC claimants is anywhere from 400% to 600% higher in the SNTC communities compared to Kamloops.[22]

The Department of Finance conducted taxation case studies in six First Nation communities in Canada. The study concluded in support of the evidence above; only a small portion of First Nation households would pay tax if the current Canadian taxation system were applied to them.[23] Most First Nation community members would receive tax rebates if they filed a tax return.[24]

The Leakage Problem – Household Expenditures

Table II summarizes the household expenditure behaviour (or in economists' lingo, leakages) of the case study communities. It should clearly indicate the scale of economic outflow from these First Nation communities. It assumes a similar economic reality for a number of other First Nation communities. The scale of the phenomenon should dispel any myth that First Nations do not contribute to the non-First Nation economy, and do not pay sales tax.

Table II

Economic Leakage Summary Table

	North Thompson	Kamloops	Adams Lake	Skeetchestn	Canoe Creek	Bonaparte
% Total expend. off-reserve*	83	85	77	73	68	89
% groceries off-reserve	99	99	100	77	75	100
% restaurants off-reserve	94	72	98	93	96	95
% auto care off-reserve	93	84	87	87	36	95
% clothing off-reserve	85	100	99	100	96	99
% recreation off-reserve**	88	97	95	87	98	80
% cultural off-reserve***	100		54	96	100	100
% leisure off-reserve****	100		31	93	68	100

Kamloops refers to the Shuswap people of Kamloops. Complete results were not collected for this community.

* These percentages were calculated using the following formula 100% - {(Exp. on-reserve Good X ÷ Tot. exp good X) x 100}

** Recreation refers to expenditures on rodeos and sports-related activities.

*** Cultural refers to expenditures on powwows, cultural gatherings and related activities.

**** Leisure primarily refers to expenditures on bingos and gambling activities.

Highlights from more detailed analysis of this data contained in the "The Value of Co-operation – A Case Study of the Six SNTC Communities" include:

- 81% of all expenditures from these six Shuswap communities (457 households) are spent off-reserve.
- The households of these communities contribute approximately $7.3 million[25] annually into the non-First Nation economy. This amounts to an expenditure of over $16,700 per household; average household income is only about $20,600.
- This substantial off-reserve expenditure also destroys a myth concerning the payment of sales tax by First Nation peoples, since there are no tax exemption provisions for many of these off-reserve expenditures. The lack of business development on-reserve limits the usage of the tax exemption by consumers. "It was (generally) felt that in most situations involving purchases of a value less than $500, the additional effort and cost of delivery outweighed the GST (exemption) benefit" (Brown and Strother, 1991, p. 119).
- The estimated household multiplier for these communities is 1.25 (standard Keynesian techniques). This implies that every $10 that lands into the lap of an SNTC household produces an additional $2.50 for the SNTC community-based economy. This points to a lack of economic co-operation among and between SNTC communities.[26]

The Rubber Band Syndrome – First Nation Government Expenditures

The monetary rubber band persists. First Nation government and household expenditures bounce right off-reserve into the non-SNTC economy. Although it is false to assert that all First Nations governments are theoretically identical, it is safe to assume – given the administrative requirements of the Department of Indian Affairs and Northern Development system – that there are more than a few expenditure similarities.

The data of this subsection have also been extracted from "The Value of Co-operation – A Case Study of Six SNTC Communities" Table III summarizes the expenditures by location of selected SNTC governments organizations. Highlights from this study include:

- The selected SNTC governments are the major source of on-reserve employment.[27]
- 52% of all SNTC government organization expenditures are made off-reserve[28] and the 48% on-reserve expenditure is primarily wages and salaries.
- Approximately 80%[29] of all household expenditures is spent off-reserve, This implies that about 90% of all SNTC government organization expenditures eventually occur off-reserve. The percentage translates to approximately $11.8 million into the non-SNTC economy. Add this amount to the household contribution and it translates to approximately $35,000[30] per household. Coincidentally, each household has an average income of just over $20,000 – hence the term bungee economics.
- Over 14% of SNTC government organization expenditures is for communications.[31]
- 11% of SNTC government organization expenditures is paid to outside consultants.[32]
- 39% of SNTC governmental organization expenditures is paid direct to on-staff employees.[33]

First Nation Economic Development and Taxation Jurisdiction

There are two conclusions relating to taxation from this case study analysis that might be generalized to other First Nations:

- The lack of a self-sustained reserve economy (reflected by the off-reserve expenditures by households and their governments) is undoubtedly a major cause of the well below average economic indicators for First Nations. These communities are clearly not exploiting the section 87 taxation exemption to its full potential.
- First Nations households and their governments significantly contribute not only to the non-First Nation economy but also to other governments through the payment of sales and income taxation.

Table III

Expenditure Summary of Shuswap Governments

Type of Expenditure	On-Reserve	Kamloops*	Other	Total
Stationery		$280,000		$280,000
Printing	$3,000	$67,000	$4,000	$74,000
Furniture		$10,000		$10,000
Computer Costs		$180,000		$180,000
Copier Costs		$210,000		$210,000
Fax Costs		$220,000		$220,000
Phone Costs		$265,000		$265,000
Equipment Purchase		$24,000		$24,000
Plumbing Supplies		$30,000		$30,000
Janitorial Supplies		$50,000		$50,000
Construction**		$2,800,000		$2,800,000
Vehicles		$320,000		$320,000
Electricity		$350,000		$350,000
Travel		$300,000	$300,000	$600,000
Postage		$10,000	$40,000	$50,000
Institutional Care	$40,000	$140,000	$10,000	$190,000
Post-Secondary	$750,000	$90,000	$50,000	$890,000
Insurance		$140,000		$140,000
Chief and Council Wages	$400,000			$400,000
Support Staff Wages	$2,800,000			$2,800,000
Oper. and Mainten. staff	$1,400,000			$1,400,000
Teacher/Instructor wages	$390,000			$390,000
Daycare salaries and operation	$140,000			$140,000
Accounting Fees	$50,000			$50,000
Legal Counsel fees		$80,000	$220,000	$300,000
Auditing fees		$90,000		$90,000
Pension Plan Contributions	$350,000			$350,000
Other Consultants***		$400,000	$200,000	$600,000
Total	**$6,323,000**	**$5,656,000**	**$624,000**	**$13,203,000**

These results are based on the estimates from the SNTC, SCES, Skeetchestn, Kamloops, Bonaparte, Canoe Creek and Adams Lake governments.

The numbers reported here are generally conservative and are not inclusive of all governmental expenditures.

* Refers to expenditures in the city of Kamloops.

** Construction includes expenditures on roads, community, buildings, and housing.

*** Other consultants include fees paid to engineering, economists, advertising, public relations and other professionals.

It would be easy to dismiss taxation as an important tool for First Nation economic development because few First Nations effectively exploit the section 87 tax exemption. This, though, would be premature and naive. It would assume that the partial tax exemption was actually meant for economic development.[34] From another perspective, the section 87 partial tax exemption is not an economic development creation of First Nations governments. Its existence is an implicit recognition of another government's jurisdiction on First Nation land.

> Taxation is an issue of jurisdiction ... it provides us with a mechanism to develop our own training and economic development initiatives. (Assembly of First Nations Grand Chief, Ovide Mercredi, March 30, 1993, addressing the special chiefs' assembly on taxation)

As such the section 87 exemption should not be over-emphasized in First Nation economic development. Evidence from the United States indicates that it was after certain First Nations exercised taxation jurisdiction that they were able to make economic gains and not before. Political sovereignty proceeded successful economic development.

> ...research says that if you want a viable economy, you first have to be able to assert effective sovereignty. ... self-government is one of the keys to solving poverty on reservations... (Highlights report, 1992, p. 33).[35] Moreover, "the tribe started exercising its governmental authority. The tribal leaders decided to develop and implement a tribal taxation system which would become the critical tool for economic development." (Highlights Report, 1992, p. 55, Truman Carter).

Slightly more esoteric is the economic development assertion[36] that government uncertainty (jurisdictional, administrative, political or other) is detrimental to interaction between economic agents. Bish (1993) raises the issue by asking what lending institution would interact with a First Nation government that it could not trust, or was uncertain about its recourse in the event of default. Confusion concerning the application of the section 87 partial exemption serves to aggravate this uncertainty surrounding First Nation jurisdiction, and by extension may be detrimental to economic development.

This need not be so. At the end of March 1993 the Department of Finance officially released its "Working Paper on Indian Taxation." Based on the contents of this paper, the metaphorical door for the exercise of such jurisdictional authority would appear to be opening up for First Nations.

> A new tax relationship [for First Nations] should be compatible with the overall approach to self-government...that is increased autonomy and self-sufficiency within confederation...Indian government taxation should be viewed as an avenue for devel-

> opment of independent revenues and the recognition of Indian government taxation powers should not be seen as an alternative to continued federal funding[37] for Indian people. (Working Paper, 1993, p. 13-14)

Should the Department of Finance's veiled commitment to First Nation tax systems bear fruit, First Nations could follow their own community consultative processes and develop a tax system that best serves their interests and aspirations. A First Nation tax system would define:

- who pays tax;
- how much tax they pay;
- when they pay;
- what type of tax they pay;
- methods for making them pay; and
- methods for appeal should they be unhappy with the taxes they pay.

For example, those First Nations who have developed property taxation by-laws specify whose property (general leased) is taxable, how the value of the land is assessed, what the tax rate is, how taxation collection will be enforced, and how one can appeal an assessment or tax bill.

The economic justification for the assertion of First Nation taxation jurisdiction would appear to be real. The next section reviews a number of taxes which First Nations may want to incorporate into their own taxation scheme. Specifically, it presents the tax-base potential for selected First Nations and a brief rationale for considering a number of taxes ranging from sales and income to property and resources.

The Path to Jurisdiction Authority – First Nation Tax Bases and Systems

Previous evidence illustrated the monetary seepage from the First Nation economy to the non-First Nation economy. Cursory evidence presented here demonstrates the level of taxation leakages from First Nations land or residents to non-First Nation governments. In so doing, it further illustrates the lack of taxation jurisdiction that First Nations currently have over their own lands.

Before proceeding, however, one must differentiate between tax paid by "residents" and tax paid on the basis of its source. This distinction is drawn so as not to restrict First Nation self-government models unduly.[38]

If one were taxed on the basis of residency, the tax would be paid on the basis of which government's land an entity (households, businesses, utilities, and others as defined by property tax guidelines) occupies. For example, this would include all sales tax and income tax paid by individuals living on a reserve (status or non-status). Taxation by residency is practised by all the provinces of Canada. This definition is taken from Thomas Courchene[39] in a paper proposing a First Nations Province.

For taxation by source it does not matter where the taxable entity resides, but where the taxable revenue is gained.[40] If the source of the taxation revenue is First Nations land, then First Nation governments using a tax by source system would collect the taxation. For example, the corporate tax paid by on-reserve businesses (non-status), and the income tax paid by non-status First Nation government employees would be collected by the First Nation government since the source of their taxable income was on First Nation jurisdiction (land). The practical difficulties surrounding the residence versus source issue will be discussed in slightly more detail in the next section.

For the purposes of providing a relatively complete overview of the First Nation tax-base potential, the discussion presents both jurisdictional contingencies (residence or source). It would not be surprising if most First Nations suffer some form of taxation leakage. Case study examples from selected First Nations provide a 'guesstimate' of the potential magnitude of this revenue source. Appendix B contains a methodological summary of some of these case study estimates.

Rebates and Tax Havens – Sales Tax (including GST)

By the residency or source definition, First Nations may wish to collect some or all of the sales tax from the following sources:

- Resident First Nation members purchasing and paying tax on goods and services outside the First Nation land should not pay sales tax under the provisions within the *Indian Act*. The collection of this tax entails a non-Indian government collecting taxes from Indians.[41]

  Six SNTC communities pay an estimated $500,000 of sales tax revenue per annum.

- For the identical rationale as above First Nation government expenditures for which sales tax was not rebated are also estimated.[42]

  The Meadow Lake Tribal Council located on the Flying Dust First Nation in Saskatchewan pays an estimated $300,000 in sales tax each year.

- A First Nation government should also collect a portion of the sales tax paid by non-First Nation members living in the First Nation community and purchasing goods and services outside the community. There are two reasons for justifying that a portion of this revenue be rebated to the pertinent First Nation.

  First, sales tax is used for a variety of governmental purposes, including service delivery and sustaining government infrastructure. This may be an appropriate funding source in as much as the self-government aspirations of First Nations require significant infrastructure development and enhancement of services delivered. After all, it is not important where tax is collected, but how and where it is used, especially as this relates to services and infrastructure within First Nation governments.

Second, if a portion of this taxation revenue is not rebated to First Nations, then an incentive exists to open businesses within First Nation boundaries to collect this tax. There is substantial potential to establish tax havens[43] within First Nations boundaries to attract businesses. A rebate could be considered the value for not fully using *Indian Act* provisions, and engaging in unfair competition or, if one prefers, a form of duty.

Since this is a rather contentious issue for taxation potential, and provisions for administration of this tax must be accounted for, an upper[44] (80%) and a lower estimate (10%) of the estimated taxation potential are provided.

For the Westbank First Nation[45] this would be between $2.2 million and $280,000 in sales tax paid by non-Aboriginal households.

- Purchases made at businesses on First Nation land for which tax was collected and given to federal and provincial governments should be the tax revenue of the relevant First Nation government.

  If the mall on the land of The Pas First Nation in Manitoba does approximately $20 million in business each year, then this would generate over $1 million in annual sales tax.

Widening the Net – Income Tax and Corporate Tax

Once again, applying either the tax by residency or tax by source definition, First Nation governments should collect all or a portion of the income tax from the following sources:

- Income tax paid by First Nation members working off-reserve should be paid to the First Nation government (if anyone). (A Working Paper on Indian Taxation, 1993, p. 29)

  In the Six Nations reserve near Brampton, Ontario, if only 300 people work off-reserve they would pay a lower bound estimate of $1.9 million in income tax.[46]

- Income tax paid by non-status individuals, whose source of income is a First Nation government, should be returned to that government as a recognition of an inherent right to self-government. This could be interpreted as the Canadian government taxing a First Nation government.

  In the Huron Village of Wendake, Quebec, if just 110 non-Aboriginal persons work directly for this First Nation government, then they would be paying approximately $700,000 in income tax.

- Income tax paid by non-status residents of a First Nation community should be estimated since this tax is used to provide governmental services that under most current definitions of self-government could be provided by the First Nation government. An upper (80%) and lower limit (20%) estimate is provided since some provincial and federal services will undoubtedly still be provided for these residents, and administrative costs should be covered.

  In the Westbank First Nation this would translate to between $5.1 million and $1.27 million per year in income tax.

- Income tax paid by employees of businesses located within the First Nation community and corporate taxes paid by the owners of these businesses are estimated because this income depends on those businesses being located on First Nation land. These individuals would by definition be part-time residents. Based on the extrapolations in "The Value of Co-operation – A Case Study of Six Shuswap Nation Communities" (p. 19), the businesses in the Mount Paul Industrial Park in Kamloops and their employees pay an estimated $12.3 million per year in income and corporate taxes to the federal and provincial governments.

  For argument's sake this could translate into an upper estimate (85%) of $10.5 million and a lower estimate (20%) of $2.5 million in income and corporate tax.

Property Tax

Property tax would be paid to a First Nations government when a non-status (government, business or household) interest occupies First Nation land. A number of First Nations currently collect property tax by means of the Kamloops Amendment (C-115) to the *Indian Act*. In practice, the value of these non-Aboriginal interests is assessed (value of land, value of business, size of property are some of the factors) and a property tax rate[47] applied to yield a property tax payment for each interest on First Nation land. To date, the Indian Taxation Advisory Board has concentrated its efforts primarily in the area of real property taxation by recommending First Nation property tax by-laws for the signature of the Minister of Indian Affairs and Northern Development.

There are many sources of property taxation that First Nations should consider. These include:

- non-Aboriginal households and business (including agriculture) that exist in Westbank, The Pas, Siksika, and Kamloops;
- utilities such as hydro (which generally have a high assessed value) and telephone lines crisscrossing most reserves in Canada;[48]
- transportation facilities such as railways, highways (where no right of way has been negotiated), and pipelines.

A number of First Nation governments are currently collecting property tax from non-Aboriginal interests. Examples of First Nations collecting or intending to collect property tax are provided below. The major source of their property tax revenue is in brackets:

Kamloops taxation revenue (non-status business)	$ 655,000
Westbank (non-status households)	$ 550,000
Siksika (pipelines, resource equipment, and hydro)	$ 116,628
Skeetchestn (pipelines)[49]	$ 340,000
Musqueam (households)	$ 884,429

Beneath the Land – Resource Taxes

This paper does not include every type of tax that First Nation governments may one day have jurisdiction over. Another "source" of considerable tax revenue potential is the tax generated from resource exploitation on reserve land. It is common knowledge that any taxation (stumpage, royalties, etc.) collected from resource exploitation on First Nation land would have been collected from the permittee or purchaser and returned to that First Nation's capital accounts.[50]

This is only a small part of the taxation story, because it deals only with the initial resource extraction[51] from the First Nation land. The real taxation revenue from resources comes from the income and sales tax collected in the process of its refinement or final sale. If one considers that the source of this resource was First Nation land, then a case can be made for sharing in the tax revenue that the resource generates. Applying this argument, the oil producing wells in the Siksika Nation (Alberta) generate an estimate of over $25 million of taxes for other governments as they develop, refine and sell this resource (see Appendix B).

This form of taxation scheme may be applicable to many more "isolated" First Nations with claims to resources. For instance there may be a number of resources that are currently exploited on or near First Nations land including: aluminum, copper, gold, silver, platinum, lead, zinc, nickel, gypsum, gravel, granite, oil, natural gas, hardwood, and softwood. These resources could be generating substantial tax revenue for federal or pertinent provincial government.

Land Claims and Other Taxes

There are at least two other tax base[52] issues that First Nations may be interested in discussing:

- Many if not all First Nations are in some stage of land settlement (claims) with the federal and/or relevant provincial government. Assuming jurisdictional issues[53] can be addressed in these discussions, the settlement of these claims would significantly enhance the resource and taxation potential for First Nations.

- As First Nation self-government infrastructure and jurisdictional authority develop, a variety of potential taxes may evolve. An example might be environmental taxes for damage to First Nations land.

It is clear that there is a revenue incentive exists for First Nations to evolve their own taxation systems. The federal government is willing to discuss First Nation taxation schemes:

> Where an Indian First Nation government wishes to implement a tax system, the federal government would be willing to explore ways in which the application of federal direct taxes can be co-ordinated with that system. (Working Paper, 1993, p. 25)

Furthermore, the assertion of such jurisdictional authority might serve to dismantle the institutional uncertainty barrier to First Nation economic development. What, then, are First Nations waiting for? The remainder of this paper discusses some, but certainly not all the possible constraints that First Nations interested in establishing their own tax systems must overcome.

Bingo and Bake Sale Revenue – Jurisdictional Constraints

Section 83 of the *Indian Act* outlines the mechanisms by which First Nations can raise revenue. In summary, and after digesting a number of Department of Justice interpretations of this section, Chief Strater Crowfoot of the Siksika Nation in Alberta described the limitations of section 83 by stating that "we can raise as much money as we want from bingos and bake sales, but that's the extent of our revenue-generating capacity."

Future research should involve a complete legal analysis and evaluation of a number of strategic plans[54] to surmount this substantial hurdle. Politically, this process will undoubtedly benefit from by co-ordinated collective support.[55]

Representing and Participation – Philosophical Constraints

First, a number of First Nations object to the principal of taxation for cultural reasons. It is for this reason that the concept of community developed taxation systems (as hinted at in the Department of Finance discussion paper) is so appealing. This would provide First Nations with a choice about their level of participation in the development of First Nation taxation systems. Mechanisms, however, should be evolved to ensure that these First Nations protect their interests in any taxation discussions.

Second, the extension of First Nation taxation jurisdiction to sales and income tax of non-status residents, and/or non-Aboriginal persons whose source of income is on First Nation land, will certainly raise concerns about taxation without representation. These taxpayers currently do not have a vote in First Nation elections. A number of alternatives must be explored such as setting up local tax boards to address this most volatile of issues. Interested First Nations should prepare for a public relations battle on this matter especially given the existing section 87 partial taxation exemption.

Self-Government in Harmony – Practical Constraints

Although the jurisdiction "battle" should be the political priority for those First Nations interested in pursuing this strategy, it would be foolhardy to concentrate all efforts on this issue. There will come a time when First Nations will be asked to present alternative taxation solutions[56] that show specific taxation systems. In this regard these initial First Nation tax systems will have to wrestle with at least the practical difficulties introduced below.

To begin, the level of jurisdiction received will ultimately determine the nature of a particular First Nation tax system. For example, jurisdiction similar to that of the provinces would mean First Nations could collect direct taxation (sales and income) but not indirect taxation (customs and excise).[57] A more "nation" level of jurisdiction[58] would allow the collection of customs duties at First Nation borders. Prototype First Nation tax systems should allow for these jurisdictional contingencies.

Second, the Department of Finance discussion paper brings up the issue of residence versus source for determining who and what to tax. Since all provinces currently collect taxes on the basis of the residence of the taxpayer, this may limit First Nations' ability to implement similar tax systems.[59] This might occur despite the possibility that a taxation by source system may be economically advantageous to a particular First Nation. It could be verified by conducting the appropriate research for the interested First Nation community. Subsequently, should a First Nation favour taxation by source, then an argument concerning double taxation for those affected will certainly arise (such as First Nation non-Aboriginal government employees). Innovative implementation methods could be derived to overcome this potential obstacle.

Third, perhaps the greatest fear of the Department of Finance is that First Nations will develop taxation systems that are not co-ordinated with the federal and/or provincial taxation system. The taxation lingo for this dilemma is "harmony." For example, would First Nations have lower sales tax on the reserve for shoppers, thus creating a made-in-Canada cross-border shopping phenomenon? Respect for this harmony concern would limit First Nation tax rates to being equal to or greater than existing tax rates.

This is a quandary for potential First Nations taxation systems. If taxes identical to existing federal and provincial apply, then it would be possible to develop taxation collection agreements[60] with the current provincial and federal (grim) reapers of this tax revenue. If First Nations, however, apply different tax rates, then they would likely have to develop their own taxation administration and enforcement mechanisms.

Fourth, most First Nations currently do not have the administrative and informational capacity to manage a taxation system. This is reflected by the paucity of computerized geo-referenced data about First Nation land. This information would be useful on Geographic Information System (GIS) software since it would allow a small number of people to manage a First Nation tax base. Moreover, most First Nation administrations do not have the expertise or the resources to manage a taxation scheme. A number of alternatives would have to be explored such as the development of First Nation GIS taxation applications, and the potential co-operation between a number of First Nations in geographical (and cultural) proximity.[61]

Finally, interested First Nations should realize that taxation is an effective policy tool. Positively, it can be used to prevent development in areas of high community value, or encourage business to locate on a reserve, or redistribute wealth.[62] Detrimental taxation policies could make businesses leave or create incentives for organized crime to develop. Taxation is seldom and perhaps never neutral. Interested First Nations must carefully evaluate the potential economic, social, and political impacts of any proposed taxation system.

There are, of course, a number of other hindrances that First Nations taxation schemes will face. These hurdles would appear worth overcoming. Jurisdiction over taxation (however defined) will create the necessary certainty and trust vital for economic development within First Nations. It is no coincidence that an overwhelming majority of Assembly of First Nations leaders and attending chiefs formally recognized the role of taxation in self-government on March 30, 1993. This is, after all, the historical starting place for self-governing nations. (Hicks, 1969)

Appendix A
Survey Methods Overview

This appendix provides a brief and painless summary of the methodologies used over the last two years to collect the survey data contained in this report. The collection vehicle for these surveys was a branch of the Shuswap Nation Tribal Council's statistics division called the Shuswap Information System (SIS).[63]

Perhaps the best method to summarize the methodology employed by the Shuswap Information System project team is to chronicle the experience with the term, "economic leakage." Although the term is well understood by economists, the twisted faces and groans of disgust that the SIS project team emitted upon hearing the phrase suggested a connotation problem. After much discussion and evidence provided by the SIS project team, the author and principal researcher (an economist) finally consented to use more appropriate community-sensitive terms in the survey exercises – community economic development studies, for example. After a period of rather painful ego shrinking, it dawned on the principal researcher that this was the difference between community-based information collection and production-based information collection.

This paper summarizes three distinct information collection exercises using three different survey instruments – A Household Economic Leakage Survey, Band government, SNTC and affiliated Organizations Economic Leakage Survey, and An Economic Development Study for the Business on the Kamloops Indian Reserve. A copy of each survey is available upon request. Although the methodology was different for each, ranging from multiple household visits for the household survey, quiet and persistent persuasion for the government survey, to hand delivery and extensive phone follow-up for the business survey, the philosophy of emphasizing the interviewee's (community's) benefit in participation was underscored in each collection exercise.

It is well beyond the scope of this paper or the patience of the interested reader to review all the methodologies used for collecting the information in this section of the document. Each referenced report contains the particular community study methodology should one crave more detailed discussions. A detailed "SIS Information Package and Household Survey Training Guide" is also available upon request for those interested in methodological review. As has been mentioned previously, the methodologies used for these studies will, at a later date, be statistically compared to methods used by Statistics Canada.

Suffice it for this section of the paper to review briefly some biases that may be present in the results section and to present a table summarizing the success of the information collection exercises.

As the results in this paper make reference to the normality assumption in the survey samples, it is important to be aware of any factors that may bias the aggregated results.[64] A list of the main biases that may be present in the studies referenced in this document are discussed below:

Seasonality

This occurs when a significant proportion of a survey population is not surveyed for reasons of seasonal employment, schooling and other reasons. This absent population could significantly affect the normality assumption. Since most of the household surveys were conducted in the summer, the potential for missing persons because of seasonal employment, hunting, and fishing exists. However, a number of students not normally on reserves may be present during this time, so it is difficult to ascertain the direction of this bias.

Table 1

Survey Response Summary

Survey	Date of Survey	Instrument	Potential Respondents	Respondents	Response Rate (%)
Adams Lake Household	July 1992	Household Expenditure and Human Resource Profile	72 Households	48 Households	67
Bonaparte Household	June 1992	Household Expenditure and Human Resource Profile	54 Households	35 Households	65
Skeetchestn Household	May 1992	Household Expenditure and Human Resource Profile	39 Households	31 Households	79
Canoe Creek Household	August 1991	Household Expenditure and Human Resource Profile	49 Households	34 Households	69
North Thompson Household	May 1991	Household Expenditure and Human Resource Profile	75 Households	45 Households	60
Kamloops Household*	September 1991	Department of Finance Taxation Survey	148 Households	118 Households	80
Shuswap	Feb. 1992 - Sept. 1992	Expenditure and Employment Survey	12 Governments	7 Governments	58
Mt. Paul Industrial Park Businesses	June 1992 - October 1992	Revenue, Expenditure and Employment Survey	121 Businesses	19 Businesses	16

* The Kamloops Survey represents an anomaly in this research since the survey instrument and methodology employed a more production-oriented technique as guided by the Canadian Department of Finance. For the interested reader, the Appendix contains a methodological review from the original report.

Reliability

This form of bias arises when a respondent, for a variety of reasons, does not provide accurate information. A primary objective of the SIS project team is to reduce dramatically this form of bias through more community-oriented information collection techniques. This, however, was a major concern in the Kamloops study and in the Mount Paul Business study, given the sensitive nature of the questions and the reputation[65] of the collection agency.

Interviewer

Many of the questions in these surveys involved interpretations which may vary from interviewer to interviewer. The SIS training manual was developed to eliminate this form of bias, but not until after the 1991 surveys were completed.

Instrument

The surveys used in this research may have contained questions which the respondents may have unwittingly misinterpreted. Several pre-tests and design critique workshops were held to reduce this form of bias. As the SIS team completed other projects this form of bias will undoubtedly continue to fall.

Without a number of further tests and comparative data (which will be supplied by Statistics Canada by June 1993), it is difficult to ascertain the magnitude and direction of these biases in the results below. The reader is, therefore, given the usual caution concerning over-interpretation and the formation of generalizations using this paper's results.

Appendix B

Brief Survey of Taxation Potential Estimate Methodologies

This appendix contains tax potential estimates of the Siksika Nation, the Shuswap People of Kamloops, and the Shuswap People of Bonaparte. These methods summarize the techniques used for the cited estimates. The following unpublished research (LeDressay, 1992) was used for the data that appear below.

A Preliminary Analysis of the Tax Base Potential for the Kamloops Community

A Preliminary Analysis of the Tax Base Potential for the Westbank Indian Band

A Summary Analysis of the Tax Base Potential of the Siksika Nation (Alberta)

A Summary Analysis of the Tax Base Potential of Six Nations (Ontario)

A Summary Analysis of the Tax Base Potential of the Flying Dust Band (Saskatchewan)

A Household Economic Leakage Study for the Shuswap People of North Thompson (1991)

A Household Economic Leakage Study for the Shuswap People of Kamloops

A Household Economic Leakage Study for the Shuswap People of Canoe Creek (1991)

Summary Household Economic Leakage Results for the Shuswap People of Adams Lake

Summary Household Economic Leakage Results for the Shuswap People of Bonaparte

Summary Household Economic Leakage Results for the Shuswap People of Skeetchestn

A Study of the Employment and Expenditures of Shuswap Governments

Summary Results of a Survey of the Mount Paul Industrial Park Businesses

A. Siksik Nation Taxation Potential Estimates

1. Sales Tax by on-reserve households

630 Households

average household expenditure[66]	$ 21,000
Expenditure off-reserve (CPI basket – on reserve services = 40%)	$ 8,400
Household GST (7%) expenditure (CPI Stats Can 62-533 = 70%)	$ 533
Sales tax estimate	$370,000

2. Income Tax paid by on-reserve individuals

310 individuals working off-reserve

Average employment income (Stats Can 93-114)	$ 19,677
Marginal Direct Tax rate (Stats Can 13-216)	20.73 %
Total income tax paid	$1 million

3. Non-Native Income Tax

Estimated # of employees	34
Average income tax paid	$ 4,700
Total Income Tax	$160,000

4. Income tax from Non-Native contracting

Value of contracting[67]	$500,000
Estimated Income Tax	$100,000

5. Property tax

Railways	$ 3,698.20
Hydro	$25,349.20
Telephone Lines	$ 4,965.20
Cellular (2 companies)	$ 6,062.20
Natural Gas Pipeline	$35,397.60
Resource Development equipment (oil and natural gas)	$41,157.60

6. Natural Resource Taxation

# of development wells (oil and gas) in Siksika	26
# of total wells in Siksika	120
# of development wells in Alberta (Stats Can 26-213)	1,888
# of total wells in Alberta	4,189
# Product share for Siksika oil and gas	1.2 - 3%

Expenditures by broad category in Alberta (1990 in $000s)

Exploration (16%)	2,016,360
Development (21%)	2,566,749
Operations (37%)	4,445,386
Royalities (26%)	3,085,000

Wages generated by oil and gas development in Alberta (1990 $000s)	1,624,536
Value of Marketable production (1990 $ 000s)	15,464,258

Income tax generated at 1.5% of total	$5.1 million
Royalities at 1.5% of total	$4.6 million
GST (7%) of 1.5% of marketable product	$ 16 million
Total conservative tax estimate generated from oil and gas	$ 25 million
Similar methods for sand and gravel (total tax estimate)	$20,000

Total conservatively estimated tax of Siksika Nation **$27.9 million**

Tax Potential for the Shuswap People of Kamloops

Sales Tax

1. Resident Kamloops members

Data collected by the Shuswap Nation Tribal Council on the income and expenditures of the resident Kamloops members and other SNTC communities were used for this estimate.

Annual off-reserve expenditures per person in Kamloops	$2,959.00
Conservative estimate % taxable using CPI basket (Stats Can 62-533)	50%
Conservative estimate of % for which no rebate was given	50%
Tax rate (GST + PST)	13%

Sales tax paid per person	$96.17
On-reserve population of Kamloops	20%
Sales tax revenue	$70,202

2. Kamloops government

Total expenditures ('91 audit) by Kamloops government	$5.84 million
Conservative expert estimate of expenditures involving sales tax	20%
Expert opinion of expenditures for which no rebate was received	5%
PST + GST	13%
Sales tax estimate	$7,592

3. Kamloops non-members residents

Average household income in Kamloops (Stats Can 98-116, 1986 unadjusted)	$33,079
Savings rate (composite estimate Stats Can 11-010)	10%
Marginal tax rate for Thompson-Nicola district (Stats Can 13-216)	15.56%
Resulting average disposable income ·	$24,621
Taxable expenditures from CPI reference paper 62-533) for GST	70%
Taxable expenditure from CPI for PST	505
# of households (Kamloops statistics)	221
GST revenue $24621 x. 7 x .07 = $1206.43 x 221	$266,620
PST revenue $24621 x .5 x 06 = $738.63 x 221	$163,237
Total revenue	$429,857

It should be noted that this estimate is likely biased downward since unadjusted 1986 income estimates were used.

4. Mount Paul Industrial Park Businesses

The data used for this estimate were taken from extrapolated sales data from A Model of Co-operation between the Shuswap People of Kamloops and the Businesses of the Mount Paul Industrial Park.

Total projected Sales (p5)	$130 million
Portion of Sales to consumers	33%
Conservative % of this taxable	50%
PST + GST	13%
Total estimate	$ 2.8 million

It should be noted that the Kamloops Exhibition Association is located on Kamloops land and has an estimated annual attendance at its horse races of 15,000 with wagers estimated at nearly $1 million. They did not respond to the survey. This likely biases the estimate downward.

Income Tax

1. Kamloops taxable government employees

T-4 summary data for income tax paid by Kamloops government staff	$125,251
Fees paid to consultants off-reserve (estimated from '91 audit)	$150,000
Marginal tax rate for Thompson-Nicola	15.56%
Tax paid by professional and consultants for Kamloops government	$ 23,340
Income tax paid	$148,591

2. Kamloops non-members residents

Average households income in Kamloops (Stats Can 95-116)	$33,079
Marginal tax rate for Thompson-Nicola	15.56
# of households	221
Income tax estimate	$1.million

Once again this estimate is likely biased downward since household income is unadjusted for inflation.

Tax Potential of the Shuswap People of Bonaparte

Sales Tax

# of households	67
average household expenditure	$ 27,453
expenditure off-reserve (90% see Leakage study)	$ 24,707
Taxable expenditure (CPI) 70%	$ 17,295
Provincial + Federal tax rate (13%)	$ 2,248
Household Sales tax estimate	$150,000
Bonaparte Government Expenditure	$2,500,000
Off-reserve expenditure (72%)	$ 1,800.00
Taxable expenditure – 60 %	$1,080,000
Government Sales Tax Estimate	$140,000
Non-Aboriginal households	6
Average Sales tax per year (Stats Can)	$4,300
Non-Aboriginal sales tax	$25,800

Income Tax

Bonaparte members working off-reserve	10
Average individual annual employment income tax	$4,600
Bonaparte member income tax	$46,000
Non-Aboriginal persons' employment for Bonaparte government	$ 9,200
Non-Aboriginal contractors for Bonaparte government	$92,000
Non-Aboriginal households	$47,250

Property Tax

School District 23 tax rates per km of railway - $2,300; per km of Hydro - $1,614; per km of telephone - $35

Km of railway on Bonaparte reserves	2
Property tax from railways	$ 4600
Property tax hydro	$ 27,438
Property tax from telephone lines	$ 1,190
Non-Aboriginal household average property tax	$ 595
Property tax from non-Aboriginal households	$ 3,570
Property tax from non-Aboriginal business (estimate based on averages)	$ 1,580
Total taxation estimate from Bonaparte reserves	$548,628

References

Arrow, Kenneth. "Gifts and Exchange," *Philosophy and Public Affairs*, 1, 4, 1972.

Barber, Bernard. *The Logic and Limits of Trust*. Rutgers: The State University of New Jersey, 1983.

Bish, Robert L. "Debt Financing for First Nations – A Discussion Paper," Taxation Workshop for Public Financing for First Nations Governments, Kelowna, B.C.

British Columbia Provincial Government, Ministry of Finance, Planning and Statistics Division, "Community Statistical Profiles" for selected B.C. communities.

Brown, Robert A. and Robert C. Strother. "Self Government and Taxation of Aboriginal People in Canada," Indian Governments and Tax, Whistler, B.C., 1991.

Courchene, Thomas J. and Lisa M. Power. "A First Nations Province", Kingston: School of Policy Studies, Queen's University, 1992.

Dasgupta, Partha. "Trust is a Commodity," *Trust* (ed. by Diega Gambetta). London: Cambridge University Press, 1986.

Department of Finance Canada. "A Working Paper on Indian Government Taxation," 1992.

Good, David. "Individuals, Interpersonal Relations, and Trust." *Trust*. London: Cambridge University Press, 1986.

Hicks, Sir John. *A Theory of Economic History*. London: Oxford University Press, 1969.

LeDressay, André. "Going in Style – A Tale of GIS in the Shuswap Nation." *GIS '93 Symposium*, Vancouver, B.C., 1993.

Morry, Howard L. "Taxation of Aboriginals in Canada. Manitoba Law Journal, Spring 1993.

Pirsig, Robert M. *Lila – An Inquiry into Morals*. New York: Bantam Books, 1991.

Unpublished SNTC Source Documents

Bin, Dianne and Louisa Celesta. *A Training Guide for the Shuswap Information System*. 1992.

LeDressay, A. *The Value of Co-operation – A Case Study of Six Shuswap Nation Tribal Council Communities*. 1992.

LeDressay, A. *A Model of Co-operation Between the Shuswap People of Kamloops and the Businesses of the Mount Paul Industrial Park*. 1992.

LeDressay, A. *A Study of the Employment and Expenditures of Shuswap Governments*. 1992.

LeDressay, A. *A Community Economic Development Study for the Kamloops Indian Band*. 1992.

LeDressay, A. *A Community Economic Development Study for the Shuswap People of Canoe Creek*. 1992.

LeDressay, A. *A Community Economic Development Study for the Shuswap People of Bonaparte*. 1992.

LeDressay, A. *A Community Economic Development Study for the Shuswap People of Skeetchestn*. 1992.

LeDressay, A. *A Community Economic Development Study for the Shuswap People of Adams Lake*. 1992.

LeDressay, A. *A Community Economic Development Study for the Shuswap People of North Thompson*. 1992.

Notes

1. Many First Nation leaders contend that section 87 of the *Indian Act* should be considered an immunity from taxation granted in respect of the sovereignty of First Nations on the basis of the 1763 Royal Proclamation, the numbered treaties and the Jay Treaty. Taxation immunity arises from "an absolute freedom from the tax laws of a sovereign authority, generally on the basis that the person or persons immune from tax are possessed of an equivalent sovereign authority." (Brown and Strother, 1991, p. 5) Although the argument may be legally justifiable, it is certainly not reflected in section 87 of the *Indian Act*. If there was a true taxation immunity for First Nations, then these governments could decide whether to grant a taxation immunity to federal government taxation on First Nation land. Immunity is an issue of sovereign jurisdiction.
2. There are exceptions to this rule such as Muskeg Lake, Saskatchewan, The Pas, Manitoba, Six Nations, Ontario, and Kamloops, B.C., among others.
3. The relationship between taxation and jurisdiction is well understood among First Nations. At an Assembly of First Nations special chiefs' assembly dedicated to taxation in late March 1993, a resolution was passed to proceed politically with the assertion of sovereign taxation jurisdiction on First Nation land.
4. According to the Indian Taxation Secretariat and The Indian Taxation Advisory Board, approximately 35 First Nations have developed property tax by laws (systems or policies). The Council for Yukon Indians' umbrella agreement, however, further addresses the issue of sales and income tax by selling the taxation exemption in exchange for something similar to provincial taxation powers.
5. Revenue Canada remission orders provide for a remission of taxes which are reasonably attributable to the employment of an Indian on reserve.
6. Income Tax regulations 400 and 2600 would seem to indicate this is the key connecting factor. The use of this connecting factor in subsequent tax years would have an enormous economic impact on a number of existing First Nation businesses and organizations.
7. Although providing an apparent comparative advantage to on-reserve First Nation businesses, a number of First Nation gas retailers have complained that the delay between claiming this tax rebate on purchases made by Status Indians and receiving it has caused serious cash flow problems.
8. There are, of course, many other factors to successful First Nation business and economic development other than effective use of the section 87 partial exemption. These are raised in other discussion papers.
9. Economic costs, unlike accounting costs, take into account factors such as sufficient compensation for the risk of business development. A First Nation corporation taking advantage of the section 87 exemption would not have to subtract its taxes from its expected return and could use this economic cost saving to its advantage in doing business.
10. Similar taxation exemption rules apply for non-profit organizations and/or charitable organizations.
11. Access to sufficient capital is an important hurdle for First Nation business and economic development.
12. This tension is also felt within First Nation governments employing status and non-First Nation persons where differential wages are paid to reflect the partial taxation exemption.
13. Stop-gap measures such as tax exempt quotas of gasoline or cigarettes have been implemented to deal with this problem in some provinces.

14. It should be noted that some more economically developed First Nations are intimately familiar with all the advantages of the partial taxation exemption and employ it in their economic development planning. This, though, is the exception rather than the rule.

15. Although well beyond the scope of this paper, research on effective methods for communicating legal, economic, and business information to First Nation communities would be invaluable (see LeDressay, 1993).

16. This report was completed by this author in January 1993 for the chiefs of the SNTC. It will eventually serve as a chapter in a Ph.D. dissertation. It is available for review upon request assuming respect for unpublished intellectual property.

17. The author was director of the statistics program from January 1991 until January 1993. This position is now held by one of the program's original researchers, a recent B.A. (Hons) graduate of the Simon Fraser University Secwepmc Cultural Education Society program located on the Kamloops reserve.

18. Detailed methodologies are contained in each community's specific study referenced in this document.

19. The Assembly of First Nations in conjunction with Statistics Canada is developing a similar comprehensive data base for all First Nations in Canada. Upon completion this national project will be invaluable for evolving a more indepth policy discussion paper.

20. If anything, these "representative" communities might be considered to be "advantaged" by Canadian First Nations standards.

21. As further indication of the state of this particular community's economy, the proportion of Cariboo region residents in 1986 that earned more than $25,000 was 24% compared to 0% for the Canoe Creek community in 1991. Canoe Creek is a semi-"isolated" community (department of Indian Affairs definition) along the upper Fraser River Canyon.

22. This evidence indicates that there are many pressing impediments to economic development that First Nations must address, including at least social problems and education.

23. This conclusion was drawn from the Department of Finance Kamloops study (the net income taxation revenue for all of the approximately 700 on-reserve Kamloops residents was a paltry $80,000) and extrapolated after conversation with individuals associated with the other case study communities.

24. A policy that at least one First Nation is considering after reviewing these results.

25. This assumes for demonstration purposes that the responses from these surveys can be normalized to represent all these six communities' population.

26.. Although not the topic of this paper, the author is conducting his dissertation research into the apparent lack of trust and co-operation within the Shuswap Nation. Given the generally small market size of First Nation communities, such co-operation would appear to be the only method for successful larger scale economic development.

27. See "The Value of Co-operation – A Case Study of Six SNTC Communities" (p 13). Clearly, not many on-reserve businesses exist as most household expenditure occurs off reserve. As such, if not employed by the government and still employed, SNTC community members are likely working off reserve and paying taxes.

28. This is calculated as follows: (Total exp - on-reserve exp) ÷ total expenditure

29. This is a simple calculation as .8 x .48 = .384 and when added to .52 equals approximately a 90% leakage. Most on-reserve government expenditures are for salaries, so the 80% leakage is likely an underestimate.

30. An estimate of the transfers from First Nation governments to households was made to avoid double counting.

31. Communications include expenditures on stationery, printing, computers, copiers, fax, phone, postage and travel.

32. Outside consultants include accounting, audits, engineering, legal, and other consultants (economists, researchers, and construction expertise – estimated at $400,000).

33. This includes chief and councils, support and operations staff, teacher/instruction and daycare staff.

34. "The exemption from taxation is derived from the federal government's fiduciary obligation to ensure that lands and entitlements obtained by Aboriginal people in exchange for acknowledgement of Crown sovereignty and the ceding of Aboriginal rights are protected from market forces and government action, including taxation" (Brown and Strother, 1991, p. 5).

35. This was extracted from Stephen Cornell's summary of the Harvard project on Indian Economic Development.

36. See any of a number of economic development studies such as Hicks, 1969, Dasgupta, 1986, or Arrow, 1972. For a personal example a recent trip to Costa Rica and Nicaragua demonstrated this theory. Costa Rica, perceived as stable and safe, was literally crawling with tourists while Nicaragua, perceived as unstable, was virtually devoid of "gringos." Perhaps more pertinent to the subject matter, a number of resource development companies in B.C. are postponing expansion or development plans pending First Nation land claims settlement.

37. It should be stressed that such tax systems could be considered as supplemental to other sources of self-government revenue such as the gross expenditure base equalization method in Coercion (1992) or Alternative Funding Arrangements (AFAs).

38. It should be noted that this section does not discuss citizenship models of taxation jurisdiction. As a number of First Nation members do not live on reserves, this model may hold considerable appeal for First Nations (Courchene, 1992).

39. "all residents, Aboriginal or non-Aboriginal, of First Nations (land) would be subject to First Nations laws, taxation, ... etc." (Coercion and Powell, 1992, pg. 7) .

40. In as much as the source of income (physical location) could be an important connecting factor in the Mitchell (1992) case, it would be rather ironic if a First Nation developed a taxation-by-source tax system.

41. The federal government has already expressed an interest in discussing taxation collection agreements for this specific source of taxation (like their existing provincial models). "The government is willing to enter into arrangements with Indian governments which would provide for the redirection of federal tax revenues raised from Indian individuals living on a reserve to the Indian government in question." (Working Paper, 1993, p. 20)

42. "Indian governments and corporations owned by them, should be exempt from income tax and .... should be eligible for a full rebate of GST" (Working Paper, 1993, p. 29).

43. The sale of cigarettes to non-status individuals in a number of Mohawk communities, such as Six Nations and Akwesasne, "smuggled" (see Jay Treaty) from the United States devoid of taxes is a text book example of a First Nation tax haven.

44. Taxation collection is administratively complicated. First Nations acquiring increased taxation jurisdiction may need to develop a taxation collection agreement with the current tax collectors (federal or provincial governments). As such, the upper and lower limits in this paper could be considered the bounds of these potential negotiations.

45. The significant number of non-status households in the Westbank community make it a rarity among First Nations. The Department of Finance speculates that only 12 First Nations have the potential to develop a relatively comprehensive tax scheme. This, though, does not reduce the application of a more sovereign taxation jurisdiction (Assembly of First Nations resolution concerning taxation) to all First Nations. The experience of the relatively economically disadvantaged Sac and Fox Nation in Oklahoma suggests that taxation jurisdiction preceded economic development (Highlights Report, p. 54).

46. Should a First Nation adopt a citizenship model of taxation, this estimate could be substantially higher. For example approximately half of the Shuswap Nation community members (3,500) live off-reserve.

47. Among the many factors that determine appropriate rates is the attractiveness of the rate to business, and the cost of services (fire, police, garbage, sewer, roads, etc.) that the property tax is intended to pay for.

48. In this regard, among its many initiatives the Indian Taxation Advisory Board (ITAB was originally established in 1988 to help First Nations enter the field of real property taxation) is concerned with providing First Nations with the ability to tax various rights of way through reserves. This includes the use of First Nation land by railway, hydro, and telephone corporations. These companies currently claim they are either exempt from taxes (as Crown corporations) or that the federal government actually allowed them to take the land. The ITAB attempts to assist First Nations to be able clearly to assert this jurisdiction and collect tax dollars from this use of First Nations land.

49. It is no coincidence that this community is attempting to direct its new-found taxation jurisdiction to enhanced economic development.

50. Section 61 of the *Indian Act* contains a list of approved expenditures for this form of capital account revenues, perhaps underlining the desire for self-government.

51. Royalties are often paid only on the real value of the resource after the cost of its extraction has been subtracted. Royalties are a minor form of taxation revenue for most provincial governments.

52. According to Statistics Canada (13-213), 80% of all direct taxation is provincial and federal income tax, 70% of all indirect provincial tax is either sales tax or corporate tax net of profits, and 97% of all local tax is real property tax. There are other existing tax revenues such as amusement taxes, gas taxes, and business licences.

53. See for example the Land Entitlement Settlement in Saskatchewan.

54. Such plans have been evolved by the Assembly of First Nations, the Indian Taxation Advisory Board, and a number of individual First Nation communities of which the author is aware.

55. This issue was raised by a number of chiefs at a recent Assembly of First Nations (AFN) meeting on taxation.

56. Despite winning a fisheries jurisdictional battle, First Nations in Washington State were unprepared to manage the resource and hired a number of outside consultants, thus exacerbating their economic leakages.

57. See "A Working Paper on Indian Taxation," Courchene, 1992 and Brown and Strother, 1991 for a more complete discussion of this form of jurisdiction.

58. As is indicated by the resolution on taxation passed March 30, 1993 by a quorum of AFN chiefs.

59. "This provides for Indian government taxation powers comparable to those provided to provinces under the Constitution." (Indian Taxation Policy Review – Overview, Department of Finance, 1993).

60. For property taxation, all First Nations allow tax assessment to be conducted by another government (in B.C. this would be the B.C. Assessment Authority). This economizes on resources and administrative capacity. This is not an unusual practice in Canada; since 1961, every province except Quebec has allowed the government of Canada to collect their provincial income tax revenue as part of the annual personal tax return. The next section discusses the substantial revenue opportunity for similar First Nation arrangements. Given the amount of taxes leaking off First Nations land, such an administrative arrangement might be employed in a customized, community-specific First Nation tax system.

61. Such pooling of tax bases is the basis for securing public deficit (debenture) financing for smaller municipalities in Canada. As First Nations do not have sufficient tax bases (or jurisdiction) to engage in public deficit (debenture) financing, they are undoubtedly the most fiscally responsible of all orders of government in Canada.

62. It is this form of jurisdiction over taxation that would allow First Nations to encourage economic development through tax policy or invest tax revenue in particular community-specific economic development schemes (job training, business development centres, joint venture investment, etc.).

63. All its members were women from a number of Shuswap Nation communities.

64. Since these were global survey exercises, it is statistically inappropriate to normalize the results. A more academic discussion paper would report only the survey results.

65. In the Kamloops survey, the identified information collector was the Department of Finance and the subject was taxation. In the Mount Paul Business survey, the information collector was the band government, the current recipient of property taxation and lease revenue from these businesses. Dasgupta (1986, p. 59) describes the need for good reputation to solicit trust and co-operation between parties. In both these cases, it is doubtful that the necessary reputation to evolve trust has been established.

66. Using Shuswap Nation research, and the Manitoba Statistical Handbook, average household expenditure (assuming no savings) is 60% of the provincial average ($35000 – Stats Can 93-119).

67. This estimate is based on the "Study of Employment and Expenditures of Shuswap Governments".

MODELS OF COMMUNITY AND INDIVIDUAL ENTERPRISE

Intertribal Forestry Association of British Columbia

*Harold Derickson**

The Intertribal Forestry Association of British Columbia (IFABC) originated from the realization that very few Indian bands in British Columbia participated in a meaningful way in the development of forest resources. But the legacy of development and management of the forest resources by others has been a devastated land base and high unemployment. IFABC seeks to see that Aboriginal people take their rightful place in the reconstruction, ownership and management of the forest and economic opportunity based on forest resources.

IFABC is a results-oriented organization whose interest lies in integrated resources management. While avoiding issues of land claims and Aboriginal rights as matters more properly left to bands and tribal councils, IFABC has acted in a forceful manner to advance the cause of Aboriginal forestry, both on- and off-reserve with governments at all levels as well as with industry.

IFABC seeks always to be a positive force on behalf of Aboriginal peoples. Accordingly, although there are many areas where problems between Aboriginal and non-Aboriginal people exist with the resource, there are also areas where co-operation can yield significant benefits without threatening culture and ways of life. This kind of opportunity creates possibilities for sustainable development that is non-destructive both to traditional values and to the forest itself.

* President, Intertribal Forestry Association of British Columbia.

IFABC was the first regional Aboriginal forestry association to be formed and was instrumental in organizing the formative conference, "Native Forestry, from Ethic to Reality", that gave birth to the National Aboriginal Forestry Association. Over the last few years, these activities within Canada have been coupled with actions to create constructive linkages with Indigenous forestry organizations elsewhere in the Americas.

In 1991, IFABC hosted a workshop attended by 11 delegates representing community-based forest projects in Central and South America. This led to IFABC attendance at the Second Inter-American Indigenous Congress on Conservation and Natural Resources, in Bolivia, where IFABC offered to host the Third Congress in 1993. While in Bolivia, IFABC arranged to provide local groups of the International Indigenous Development Organization (IIDO) which will serve to provide technical services to developing Indigenous Third World countries, through professional North American Indigenous people, largely from Canada and the United States of America.

ACR Mechanical Systems Ltd.

*Albert C. Rock**

ACR Mechanical Systems Ltd. was formed in 1972 to operate as an independent mechanical testing company for testing mechanical systems and building institutions in B.C.

The reason I started this company was because my lack of education limited my opportunities to progress within the professional engineering firm I was working for.

The company was a top testing and commissioning firm until 1983 when a motor vehicle accident I was involved in left me unable to work in the field and operate my company. During this time I joined my expertise with two other employees of the company to develop a small data logger for testing mechanical systems. In 1985 I founded a new company called ACR Systems Inc.

The product manufactured by ACR Systems Inc. is marketed throughout the world through a network of distributors with sales of $3 million annually.

The product is used with the United States' NASA program and the Russian and European space programs. We have done development work for Atomic Energy of Canada Limited and also in the medical and military markets.

* President, ACR Mechanical Systems Ltd.

I am personally involved in new application development which is done with the auto racing teams in the Formula 1 and Indy Car Series. My son, Jason Rock, has joined me in ACR Mechanical Systems Ltd. to create new products, applications and markets. Application spin-offs from this competitive technical sport create many new products annually for ACR Systems Inc.'s world market.

Today approximately 10 people are continuously employed and involved in maintaining quality and customer satisfaction.

Our main effort today is to succeed in receiving the world standard ISO 9000 for quality which will open a complete world market for our company and product.

The Cree Hunters and Trappers Income Security Program

*George Wapachee**

The Cree Hunters and Trappers Income Security Program originates from the James Bay and Northern Quebec Agreement signed in 1975. It was put into effect in the fall of 1976 and is now in its seventeenth year of operation.

The main object of the Program is outlined at Section 30.1.8 of the Agreement:

> The program shall ensure that hunting, fishing and trapping shall constitute a viable way of life for the Cree people and that individual Crees who elect to pursue such a way of life shall be guaranteed a measure of economic security consistent with conditions prevailing from time to time.

Hunting, fishing and trapping activities are an integral part of the social, cultural and economic life of the Crees, and, with the Program, the Crees were looking for a way to ensure that traditional activities would remain a permanent and viable way of life. Continued access to a very valuable subsistence production was considered essential.

The Program is not universal but is limited to those who hunt, fish and trap as a way of life. Bearing this in mind, the eligibility criteria and calculation of benefits were designed accordingly. A practical approach, based on the time spent in the bush rather than on production, was used to avoid requiring or directly

* Vice-Chairman, Income Security Program for Cree Hunters and Trappers.

encouraging increased harvesting which would create undue pressure on the environment and the fauna.

Benefits are calculated as an annual income and are primarily a function of the involvement of the family in harvesting and related activities.

In 1991-92, $14,214,631 was paid as income security benefits to 1,213 families from the nine James Bay Cree communities.

The continued interest of the Cree population in the Program indicates clearly that traditional activities remain an integral part of the Cree society and its economy. However, the Program is not and should not be the only support of Cree hunting. It has to be a part of broader economic development and must also be developed taking into account management of the land and resources.

The objectives set out 20 years ago have been met, and the challenge is now to ensure that the Program continues to evolve and meet the needs of Cree hunters in the future.

Parenteau's Saskatoon Berry Chocolates Inc.

*Rodney Parenteau**

Parenteau's Saskatoon Berry Chocolates Inc. is owned and operated by Rodney and Colleen Parenteau of Langham, Saskatchewan.

When the farm was purchased in 1987, we had no intention of getting involved with the diversification of Saskatoon berries. Soon people wanted trees, and that is where it all began.

We developed a technique for rooting cuttings for sale to anyone who was interested. At the same time we also expanded our farm and, of course, the first time was quite a learning experience. We expanded during the hottest year, and people thought we were crazy and that we would lose over half our trees. To date over 75% are producing berries. It was a long hard road that year, but, through sheer determination, we succeeded.

We sold trees to those who were interested in starting an orchard and many of those people were within our area. Others thought that we were doing ourselves harm, when in fact we would benefit in the long run. It is not always that you will have a bountiful crop, but you hope those down the road will. People did not seem to realize that we have to learn to work together and not against each other. We profit from each other's knowledge and supply of a product.

* President and founder of Parenteau's Saskatoon Berry Chocolates and Preserves Inc.

At that time we began processing the berries for jams and spread. Because of the limited amount of berries available, we displayed our product at various craft shows only. Given the limited amount of berries, we needed to develop a product that would stretch our supply of berries, as jams required a large amount of berries.

In 1990 we started developing the "Saskatoon Berry Chocolate". We experimented with various types of chocolate and different variations of a Saskatoon berry filling. We first developed our filling and from there we had to choose the chocolate that best suited the taste of the filling. We tried all different types of chocolate, ranging from milk chocolate to bitter chocolate. Through all that taste testing we finally decided on semi-sweet dark chocolate.

We developed our product for the tourist industry, high-end market and the novelty market. Our product was unique because we were the first to develop a Saskatoon Berry Chocolate in Canada. Being Aboriginal and not really chocolatiers, there was a lot of trial and error, determination and persistence that drove us to where we are today.

Our chocolates are handmade with care. We grow the Saskatoon trees, which produce the berries, which are then processed into our Saskatoon Berry Chocolates, which are then sold in various retail outlets throughout western Canada. Our blueberry chocolates are made with wild blueberries from northern Saskatchewan. We attend to all the wrapping and packaging of our product prior to the products being sold to retail outlets.

We now had our product which was being sold in retail outlets. The next hurdle was financial assistance. More attention was now being focused on Aboriginal people and small businesses with the intent of financial institutions helping them and their business to develop. We approached our financial institution, CIBC, in Saskatoon, for funding to develop our business. We were advised that we would be unable to obtain funding as we did not have cash flow, extensive experience in chocolates and no precedents had been set for them to follow. So instead we approached our local credit union, and they were more than happy to assist us with our financial needs.

Many Aboriginal people starting up in business do not have the full amount of funds required to get started. They, of course, are going to develop a unique product or business in order to find the niche market. The more uncommon the project, the less likely you are to receive funding. Funding for a business or project is based on how many years' experience you have in that particular business, and whether there are other precedents to warrant the funding needed.

We believed in ourselves and our business. To date our business has grown and continues to grow.

Arctic Co-operatives Limited

*William Lyall**

The first Arctic Co-operatives in the Northwest Territories were formed in 1960; today there are 35 co-operatives in existence. These N.W.T. co-operatives affiliated over the years to form two co-operatively-owned subsidiary service organizations, Arctic Co-operatives Limited and the N.W.T. Cooperative Business Development Fund. The 100% local ownership and control of these co-operatives, in addition to the strong support services provided through these affiliations, has resulted in the co-operatives growing into a major force in the N.W.T.

Pelly Bay is a community of 410 people, 130 of whom make up the ownership base of their co-operative. The co-operative's activities include running the only retail store in the community, as well as running a small hotel, purchasing carvings for resale in the south, operating a heavy equipment contracting business, and providing agency services for the telephone, airline, and petroleum delivery. This co-operative paid $2.1 million worth of wages and dividends to Pelly Bay between 1988 and 1992, and in 1993 issued T4 slips to 89 residents, 45% of the total adult population.

Pond Inlet is a community of 970 people, 525 of whom make up the ownership base of their co-operative. The co-operative's activities include running a competitive retail outlet as well as a hotel facility and tourist lodge, providing agency services for petroleum and airlines and operating a building leasing service for offices and accommodations. This co-operative paid $2.1 million worth of

* President, Arctic Co-operatives Limited.

wages and dividends to Pond Inlet between 1988 and 1992, and in 1993 issued T4 slips to 64 residents, 13% of the total adult population.

Prior to 1950, these communities had been operating as cashless societies, and the residents had no opportunities to amass capital. Today local assets total approximately $49 million and membership in co-operatives is close to 10,000.

Syncrude

*Jim Carbery**

Business and industry must make long-term commitments to employ Aboriginal people. Business and industry must set realistic job standards, realistic annual targets and regularly monitor progress.

The model that Syncrude uses is:

- Communicate
- Educate
- Motivate

To assist Aboriginal entrepreneurs to break into the business field by acquiring contracts and then hiring Aboriginal employees, business should consider sole-sourcing, restricting or negotiating bids.

All these "special" programs should be set up in such a way that the Aboriginal person is not kept *dependent* and that industry keeps moving to the normal process of recruitment and business development. Normal process may take years but that is where we all have to move. Cross-cultural training should be provided to all employees.

Industries that affect local communities should work with those communities to identify their needs. Resources should be provided to help address these needs. Industry should work with the formal and informal leaders of the communities.

* Senior Adviser, Native Development, Syncrude Canada Limited.

Successful Aboriginal employees or entrepreneurs should be recognized by industry and Aboriginal people in the local communities. These successful people should be nominated to key local boards of influence.

We all have to be held accountable. Aboriginal organizations and leaders have to be held accountable by their Aboriginal constituents.

Métis Urban Entrepreneur

*Laverne Poitras-Young**

I am a Métis woman from Edmonton and 100% owner of three companies, the Genoch Gardens Daycare, J & R Pizza & Pub, and Gayla Hair and Nails Limited. I employ 21 individuals, half of whom are Aboriginal people.

In 1989, I identified that a void existed in Métis child care. I approached a conventional lending institution for a loan to start a daycare to fill this void but was denied because I did not have any capital or experience in business management. Then I approached a Métis lending institution and was given a loan. This loan, however, was at a very high interest rate for a very short term (three years) and no operating funds were allocated to me. After receiving my first loan, I had to return to the Métis lending institution and apply for an operating funds loan. I was granted the loan, again at a high rate of interest and under the stipulation that it be paid back within six months.

Three years later I began distributing a line of clothing. My enterprise was a success and I decided to purchase a hair salon from which to operate. The Métis lending institution denied me a loan on the grounds that I was now an investor. I was granted a loan by a conventional lending institution because now I had capital and a proven business record.

Commitment, dedication and hard work are the keys to my success. I overcame many obstacles and as a result am able to provide employment for others.

* Entrepreneur and owner of several businesses in Edmonton, Alberta.

Native Economic Development in Kahnawake: Banking and Collateral

*Michael L. Rice**

The Caisse Populaire Kahnawake, founded in 1987, is a credit union providing savings and loans-related services. It is the largest of six Aboriginal credit unions in Quebec and is the second largest Aboriginal financial institution in Canada. The Caisse is owned and controlled by its membership and the majority are the Mohawks of Kahnawake. The Caisse is affiliated with the Mouvement des caisses populaires Desjardins which provides technical and support services to its member credit unions for a fee. Kahnawake chose the caisse populaire model instead of a branch of a chartered bank or trust company for reasons of ownership, control and tax treatment. The Caisse has acquired 5,700 members and $40.6 million in assets to March 31, 1993. Recent year-end profit (unaudited) was $350,000 and the general reserve stands at approximately $850,000.

The Caisse has developed and implemented a loan security system for immoveables on First Nations territory which bypasses the restrictions of section 89 of the *Indian Act*. The basic feature of this system is that the third-party guarantor is not a government body of any kind (federal, provincial or band council). A registered section 24 transfer from the First Nations borrower to a group of First Nations (non-political) trustees is made and they hold the immovable assets on behalf of the Caisse Populaire. The basic principle is to put the onus on the individual to feel that he or she really has something to lose in such a transaction. The system has been executed at least once and has not been tested

* Manager, Caisse Populaire Kahnawake.

to date in the courts. When an execution of the security is made, the immovable property may be sold only to another First Nations person of that territory. Using the model, the Caisse Populaire has made 143 housing and commercial loans totalling $5.7 million to March 31, 1993.

Our specific recommendations are as follows:

- Grant financial institutions which are owned and controlled by Aboriginal people on First Nations territory Indian status so that they may take security directly. The major provision is that land holdings may be sold only to First Nations people living on the territory. This arrangement would replace the trust deed system and allow First Nations financial institutions to operate like outside banks and not lose their identity.
- Promote credit union models for Aboriginal groups who prefer total ownership and control of their financial institutions, particularly at the local level. For those groups who prefer less control, the other forms of financial institutions (branch of chartered bank, trust company) can operate with some variation of the trust deed system.
- Establish a forum for Aboriginal people across Canada to share findings and experiences in the banking and institutional fields to benefit all. At this time, regular banking services for Aboriginal people are not a given, and competition among Aboriginal groups or banks acting for Aboriginal groups will only delay the time until we all have such services.
- Place strong emphasis on implementing strategies to develop Aboriginal human resources in the following fields: banking, business administration, public administration, planning and accounting. We need MBAs, CAs, and community planners to manage and control our institutions.

Batchewana Band Industries Ltd. Community Project

*Harry Jones**

Batchewana First Nation was signatory to the Robinson Huron Treaty of 1850. Today the reserve is made up of three parcels of land, Obadjiwon, located North of Sault Ste. Marie, on Batchewana Bay, Goulais Bay Reserve, and Rankin Reserve located on the east boundary of Sault Ste. Marie. These lands total about 5,500 acres.

In 1971, a total of 387 acres was set aside for development of an industrial park. Blue Heron Industrial Park is located on Rankin Reserve about two miles from downtown Sault Ste. Marie. The Park is operated by Batchewana Band Industries Ltd. which was incorporated in 1971. Five members of the Batchewana First Nation sit on the Board of Directors handling the affairs of the Park.

Today, Phase 1 of the project incorporates 78 acres of serviced sites. At present there are 11 businesses operating in the Park.

In 1985, a study was commissioned by the Ontario Native Business Parks Association to see what had to be done to make our parks more successful. This study pointed out some shortcomings that had to be rectified and a list of recommendations that would make the parks more successful.

First of all we had to improve the services of the Park. Once our services were brought up to a reasonable standard, we could proceed with some of the recommendations of the study.

* President, Advanced ThermoDynamics Corporation.

There were two recommendations that we concentrated on:

- We should have building space available for prospective tenants.
- We should seek partnerships or joint ventures.

When one of the companies in the Park got into financial difficulties, we had an opportunity to buy the 5,000 square foot building. Since that first purchase, other opportunities arose, and we now own three buildings in the Park for a total of 26,000 square feet.

The second recommendation, to seek out partnerships or joint ventures, would take a lot more work.

Early in 1990, we were approached by an American tribe with a joint venture proposal. This proposal was to establish small manufacturing facilities on both sides of the border that would seek contracts in the defence industry.

The American tribe would operate under section (8) of the Small and Disadvantaged Business Program (SDBP); we would seek funding from federal and provincial Aboriginal economic development programs. At first this proposal looked like it would work, and everyone got quite excited. We made a presentation to government officials in the Department of Industry, Science and Technology (ISTC) and the proposal was well received.

This proposal was based on the LSVW (Light Service Vehicle Wheel) contract of the Canadian government. The Department of National Defence was buying 3,000 of these vehicles. We would attempt to secure sub-contracts from the prime contractor for sub-assemblies of welded parts.

As we proceeded with these plans, it became clear that we could not do all the work necessary to meet contract deadlines.

During this time ISTC had Ernst & Young do a short study on the American SDB Program. Their findings verified that there was no legal reason why this could not be done.

Although it appeared that we could not participate in the LSVW contract, the Board decided to regroup. There were some major defects in the process we had adopted. We could not respond fast enough to issues that arose. We were not properly organized and really had no one that could analyze the project. Everyone had their own ideas of how we should proceed.

We knew the basic idea was a good one, so, at a joint meeting of Chief and Council and Batchewana Band Industries (BBI) Board of Directors, it was decided that BBI would work with the consultant. We would do a more detailed study with Ernst & Young of the SDB Program. A list of 12 questions was developed. These questions, when fully researched, would give us direction on what had to be done.

The trip to North Dakota and the study pointed out some key factors required for success:

- We should join up with a Canadian company that was willing to locate in our Industrial Park.
- There is a need to keep business and politics separate but always keep the lines of communication open.
- A firm commitment by all from those involved is required.

From these findings, the Board of Directors met with Toronto Consultants International's Lorne Ellingston, and, after long discussion, developed a plan. This plan would include:

- mission statement;
- goals and objectives;
- tactics for achieving these goals;
- an action plan.

Our Mission Statement: To develop a manufacturing company through which an increasing number of Band members can achieve personal growth and skill development on-reserve and through which worthy role models can be provided to younger members of the Band.

Now we had a mission and a plan and a search was started by our consultant. In view of the state of the Canadian economy, this looked like a pretty tall order but, through his contacts in Ottawa, he found such a company.

A company in London, Ontario, called Advanced ThermoDynamics Corporation (ATC) was the only Canadian supplier of heating and cooling aids to the transportation industry. This company was also the company that would provide coolant heater to Western Star, the successful prime contractor that would build LSVW.

There were several major factors that made our proposal attractive to both parties. ATC's operations in London did only assembly work. All machine shop and foundry work was contracted out. Also in order to gain access to the LSVW contract there were certain conditions that had to be met. One of these conditions was that the assembly work had to be done in the North in order to satisfy government regulations that included awarding contracts to economically depressed areas.

Their plan was to rent a building somewhere in the North, sub-contract the required machine shop and foundry service, move the company to Blue Heron Industrial Park where we had just bought a 16,000 square foot building, and bring all machine shop and foundry operations inhouse. This would give the company a higher profit margin and better control of manufacturing operation. For Batchewana First Nation it would satisfy our objective to establish a manufacturing facility, create meaningful employment and have some participation in the operation of the company.

A business plan was drawn up and a meeting set up with the company. After these first discussions a letter of intent was signed. This letter started a long process that included presentations and negotiations with provincial and federal funding agencies, banks and training institutions, and Batchewana First Nation Chief and Council.

A financial package was put together that at times looked to me like a house of cards. The total package would include money from:

- CAEDS – Canadian Aboriginal Economic and Joint Venture Program
- FEDNOR – Federal Economic Development Initiative Northern Ontario Region
- NODC – Northern Ontario Development Corporation
- NCB – Native Community Branch
- Bank of Nova Scotia or Canadian Imperial Bank of Commerce;
- Batchewana First Nation
- Batchewana Band Industries Ltd.
- CITC training dollars

While all this financial activity was taking place, an agreement was being finalized between Batchewana Band Industries Ltd. and Advanced ThermoDynamics Corporation. The major components of this agreement were as follows:

- Batchewana Band Industries Ltd. would purchase 20% of shares of Advanced ThermoDynamics for a negotiated price.
- BBI would gain a further 10% of shares in consideration of Aboriginal dollars, such as the CAEDS grants for capital costs.
- BBI would have an option to buy a further 10% of shares of ATC in two years after the closing date of the agreement.
- BBI would have a further option to buy the remaining 60% of ATC in five years.
- A procedure was established to evaluate the company when the purchase options were exercised.
- A board of directors would be formed to make all major decisions.
- The board would consist of three members of Batchewana First Nation and four members of the remaining shareholders.
- The day-to-day operation of the company would be over seen by Chris Gotmalm as President and Chief Executive Officer.
- An employment agreement would be entered into between Chris Gotmalm and ATC.

On October 23, 1992 this deal was completed and BBI became 30% owner of ATC.

At present the company has produced 25 heaters for Western Star and 10 generator sets for Detroit Diesel. Because of the delay I mentioned, we are about six months behind schedule.

We employ 12 people and this number will double by the time we reach full production. I would like to share with you a portion of a letter I received from Chris Gotmalm, our CEO, dated March 12, 1993:

> Considering the resources consumed, we have done extremely well when it comes to product development and long-term sales. We have developed a new heater from the Western Star LSVW Project, had it tested with the military, and, as a result, obtained an order for 3,000 heaters. This is the biggest heater order ever awarded in North America, $3 million plus.
>
> We have developed a new generator set for Detroit Diesel, got it accepted by the Detroit organization and they have received their first order for 10 units. The Detroit Project shows all signs of developing to something even bigger than the Western Star Project.

CHAIRMAN'S CLOSING ADDRESS

Building an Aboriginal Economy

*Ron Jamieson**

Traditional Aboriginal economies have been decimated over the years. Once thriving economies based on gathering, hunting, fishing, and trade are no longer able to sustain Aboriginal communities. The results have been disastrous. Communities that were once self-sufficient are now ghettoes of despair. The resulting loss of self-esteem, independence, and initiative has led, in many cases, to a total breakdown of social structures within communities. The family/clan systems that helped to maintain the values and develop the skills to survive culturally, socially and economically have been seriously affected. In order to address these problems, governments and First Nation communities on- and off-reserve have concentrated their resources and their energies to providing social programs to rebuild communities. These initiatives, for the most part, have led to increased dependency and decreased self-sufficiency. Without an economic base, our communities will never be able to be in control of their futures. We will never be a free and independent people.

There is a perception in the Aboriginal and non-Aboriginal communities that Aboriginal people lack the skills and the temperament to be effective entrepreneurs. I challenge that assumption. Many successful entrepreneurs are people with little education or training. In fact many have started their own businesses because they lacked the education or the training to access existing employment opportunities. The personal skills and resources they bring to their businesses are the same as those which allowed our ancestors to survive in a traditional Aboriginal economy.

* Vice-President, Aboriginal Banking, Bank of Montreal, and Chairman of the National Round Table on Aboriginal Economic Development and Resources.

There are four elements necessary for ensuring the success of a business initiative:

Risk Taking

Entrepreneurship without risk taking does not exist. The higher the degree of risk, the higher the potential benefits. Traditional economies had high degrees of risk, many of them life-threatening. The risk inherent in a trapping economy, for instance, is personal survival. Today many aspiring entrepreneurs attempt to minimize risk by using the resources of governments or other institutions in order to survive. True risk taking means risking your own resources. This ensures that the entrepreneur uses all his or her skills and resources to survive and to protect her or his investment.

Discipline

Discipline means paying attention to the details of ensuring that your business survives and grows. It also means being able to deal with pressures that often divert your energies and initiatives in unproductive activities. Making important decisions under pressure requires a tremendous amount of discipline. Traditional economies required personal discipline because survival and the success and of the hunt required an attention to detail and the ability to make quick decisions under critical conditions. Discipline also means being able to work at maximum capacity under stress and during periods of fatigue.

Clarity of Vision

An entrepreneur has to have a clear vision etched in her or his mind of what is going to be accomplished. He or she has to know what actions will have to be taken to reach the goals set and what will result from reaching those goals. Self-confidence allows the entrepreneur to know that goals can be accomplished through personal initiative and ingenuity. This vision and self-confidence are especially crucial in order to survive the first five years of business. Traditional entrepreneurs had to have a clear sense of what would constitute success during a hunt since the results would allow them to feed, clothe and care for their families for the coming year.

Satisfying the Needs of the Consumer

It is essential to meet fully and exceed the customer's expectations. This is especially important in an environment where products are fairly similar. Businesses which provide personalized service while providing a needed product will increase their chances of survival and of growth. This is very important in the Aboriginal community where people often see themselves as being taken advantage of by unscrupulous entrepreneurs and by people who have no vested interest in the betterment of the Aboriginal community. The traditional entrepreneur derived his feeling of self-esteem through his ability to provide the essentials for his family, clan and community. The contemporary Aboriginal entrepreneur's strength is his or her knowledge of community needs.

Economic Development is Not a Priority

All Aboriginal communities have the capacity to build self-sustaining economies. It is necessary to identify the resources available within the community, identify the economic opportunities that can be accessed and develop an environment where the entrepreneurial spirit can thrive. The strength of the community will emerge from its ability to be productive and self-supporting.

Traditional and contemporary economies are based on the ability of small businesses to survive and grow. The role of government is to foster an environment where this is allowed to happen. Aboriginal policies developed and enacted by governments have been totally inadequate in addressing the economic development needs of Aboriginal communities. There are a number of reasons why this is the case.

Transfer of Social Programs and Not Economic Programs

Under the guise of increased self-government and Aboriginal control, the Canadian government has been transferring programs to Aboriginal community administration. The first program transferred was the administration of welfare. This was followed by transferring other program administration in areas of education, health, child welfare, lands administration, etc. At the end of the process the Canadian government is now transferring the administration of economic development programs to Aboriginal control.

In my opinion, this process should have been reversed. What other nation or jurisdiction in the world builds up its programs and services and then develops its economy? Very simply, only those who continue to be dependent on foreign aid or outside subsidies. If Aboriginal communities are to provide a high standard of living and services to their members, they must do so from a solid economic base.

In 1969 the White Paper was tabled by the government of the day. This was an affirmation, on the part of the Canadian government, that its policy of Aboriginal assimilation was well and thriving. The paper reaffirmed the continuing policy of turning reserves into municipalities. Its strategy was gradually to transfer federal programs to Aboriginal control and then shift the fiduciary responsibility to provincial governments. Many Aboriginal people continue to believe that the White Paper policy continues to be implemented even though the Canadian government announced that it was cancelling that policy as a result of widespread Aboriginal protests.

The policy focuses on social development at the expense of economic development since the latter ensures independence and freedom in choosing preferred alternatives and could create barriers to the government's policy of assimilation.

Unhealthy Competition of Band Business vs Entrepreneurship

Too often, economic development priorities focus on large projects operated by development corporations. In many instances, these initiatives are controlled by band councils or tribal councils. Small businesses struggling without subsidies are expected to compete in this environment. The fostering of environments where small businesses operated by individual entrepreneurs can flourish should be a priority. Entrepreneurs should run businesses, politicians should provide leadership.

Initiative Destroyed

Governments continue to practise an assimilationist policy toward Aboriginal people. Aboriginal communities are not seen as viable economic entities. Traditional practices and values are seen as quaint and archaic. Governments continue to impose structures and initiatives that are contrary to the traditional and accepted way of doing things. The resources provided are geared to emulating initiatives in non-Aboriginal communities rather than building on the existing community strengths.

What Can we Do?

Revere the importance of women and family as crucial to our success.

Purchase of Aboriginal Products and Services

Rather than subsidizing economic activities government should be encouraging the purchase of Aboriginal products and services. It should be remembered that after World War II, America helped rebuild Japan through agreements to purchase its products rather than through direct subsidies. Such a policy initiative encourages individual initiative, control and independence. We as a country are way behind the United States. This is sad.

Taking Away Taxation Rights

A very important business principle is to look at how better to use existing resources before looking for new resources. Taxation is never a neutral policy. Taxation policies are used to help meet a number of government objectives, from stimulating the economy to reducing debt. Aboriginal tax immunity is a right which should be used judiciously to help develop Aboriginal economies. The long-range effect will be to reduce dependency and increase the economic ability of Aboriginal communities to be self-sufficient. Government intentions are bound to be suspect when a recognized right is denied to Aboriginal peoples while it is being conferred on other segments of society.

In Conclusion

It is necessary for the Canadian government to change drastically its policies and attitudes toward Aboriginal peoples and communities if true self-determination by Aboriginal people is to be achieved.

This is especially crucial in the area of economic development.

If Aboriginal entrepreneurs are to flourish, their products must be marketed aggressively and they must be able to access resources efficiently.

In addition they must be able to develop linkages that foster opportunities for trade and exchange of resources, particularly with other Aboriginal enterprises.

Current initiatives in this direction concentrate on linkages and access between Aboriginal and non-Aboriginal enterprises.

Although this is a positive step in some instances, it is often carried out at the expense of placing more emphasis on building Aboriginal networks and initiatives.

Aboriginal community-driven initiatives will lead to increased Aboriginal community independence.

Daily Summaries

Day 1
"The Focus is on Solutions"

Noel Knockwood, Elder and Spiritual Leader of the Micmac Nation, opened the National Round Table with a prayer. Round Table Chair Ron Jamieson introduced Commissioners. Royal Commission Co-Chair Georges Erasmus welcomed participants, explaining that round tables were an opportunity to exchange dialogue and hear solutions, incorporating a wide-range of opinions.

The Royal Commission is dealing with many "tough issues" facing Aboriginal peoples; some of the most difficult are economic issues. Many studies have explored economic problems, Mr. Erasmus noted, asking participants to further the discussion by looking to the future. "What kind of economy is going to work for Canada and, in particular, for Aboriginal peoples?"

Globally, capitalism has "won the day," he continued, although the success of the capitalist system in many countries does not mean the end of mixed economies. He noted that Aboriginal peoples have strong traditional values of generosity and sharing and that, in traditional Aboriginal societies, the people given the most status were not those who hoarded wealth but those who shared with their community. An economy for Aboriginal peoples needs to include these values. Mr. Erasmus said he did not want to imply that people in a capitalist society are not generous; he wanted to point out that Aboriginal peoples have choices to make: how much of the past, of tradition, will be carried into the future.

Although the economic situation of Aboriginal peoples is changing rapidly, there are still high unemployment levels and low levels of participation in decision making in the economy. "We have major issues to deal with, but, more and more, the direction is coming from Aboriginal people."

Mr. Erasmus, referring to David Newhouse's discussion paper, said that economic development in Aboriginal communities probably means that capitalistic institutions will be modified to incorporate traditional Aboriginal values. He looked forward to the discussion of the next few days, saying that the Royal Commission saw economic development as a key issue for its final report.

Co-Chair Judge René Dussault joined Mr. Erasmus in welcoming participants to a Round Table "pivotal for the Royal Commission and for all Canadians." He underlined that the Royal Commission sees land and resources as key to dealing with economic problems, to reduce poverty and levels of unemployment. He said problems faced by Aboriginal peoples would not be resolved without addressing self-determination issues, including control of economic development. Many of the economic issues to be resolved involve conflicts over limited resources, and solutions to the problems must deal with added complexities such as free trade.

Mr. Dussault added that the Royal Commission has heard many times during its hearings of the problems related to the education system. There are many barriers to full participation of Aboriginal peoples in the education system. Many Aboriginal people in the system are not adequately trained for existing jobs, and many are not prepared to cope with the tough job market they find in urban centres.

The Royal Commission must identify barriers to economic development and look at solutions, he continued. Successful economic development projects and models need to be examined, and participants at the Round Table need actively to speak their minds, to "give us your best efforts" to help the country deal with its economic problems.

Round Table Chair Ron Jamieson said he looked forward to working together with participants during the next few days to assist the Royal Commission in finding solutions. The theme, he said, was economic development and prosperity of Aboriginal communities and individuals. Participants had an obligation to make real and substantive change in Aboriginal communities, he said. The Royal Commission is looking for solutions to economic problems, and he challenged participants to use their imaginations to "mobilize the incredible energy of our women and men who are both capable and willing to contribute to building a better society." He outlined the Round Table objectives, stressing the need to focus on solutions.

Theme 1: The Land and Resource Base

Overview of Discussions Papers

Clem Chartier of the Metis Society of Saskatchewan presented an overview of the first three discussion papers. He said that all were in accord with respect to the lands and resources of Aboriginal peoples, and that they underlined the disparity of land holdings among Aboriginal peoples nationally and internationally.

Mr. Chartier said that Roger Gruben's paper on the Inuvialuit Regional Corporation (IRC) was an "eye-opener" for revealing the latitude available for some Aboriginal peoples. The extensive land holdings the Inuvialuit were able to obtain speaks well of them, and the fact that they were able to bargain and win such extensive holdings "shows that Aboriginal peoples are capable of getting what they need."

He noted that the key objectives of the IRC negotiators suggested that development should not happen in isolation from the people, and that economic development must happen in conjunction with traditional pursuits. The IRC is pursuing economic opportunities internationally; Mr. Chartier said the IRC's pursuits are an example for other Aboriginal organizations with resources at their fingertips. The paper also noted the need to enter into co-management ventures, and that opportunity exists not only for economic development but also for enhancing a sustainable environment for Aboriginal peoples. Another factor is the need for governments to go past political rhetoric to active co-operation with the implementation of agreements, including providing adequate resources. Mr. Chartier highlighted the paper's conclusion that the biggest challenge facing the Inuvialuit people is the need to continue investing in the education and training of their own people.

Mr. Chartier said that Lester Lafond's discussion paper reviewed the history of treaty rights to land and land holdings under the *Indian Act*, noting that no land holding discussed in the paper was as extensive as that of the Inuvialuit. The paper also presented a historical overview of the pre-European subsistence economy that was displaced. Opportunities were identified to enable Aboriginal peoples to diversify their economies, taking advantage of the current situation which allows tax breaks and incentives for industries on reserves.

Mr. Chartier noted that many Aboriginal communities do not have the opportunities available to the Inuvialuit, but that possibilities still exist for joint ventures and partnerships, especially in urban reserve areas.

The third discussion paper, on Métis land and resources, was written by Mr. Chartier himself. In it, he outlined the Métis people's dispossession of lands and resources; although Métis land and land rights have been legally recognized, the Métis people have been faced with fraud by institutions at almost every level.

For Métis people, land is important as a place to live, for pursuing economic development opportunities, and as a symbol of nationhood. The paper looked at barriers to achieving a land base for the Métis, including exclusion from the land claims process.

The Métis believed they had come close to achieving their goals when the Charlottetown Accord was negotiated, and although the Accord was not ratified, it did permit the provincial and federal governments to enter into a land claims process with the Métis. He said the document was not dead yet and hoped that its achievements would be furthered. The paper concluded with options for pursuing Métis lands: a land claims process; court action on original land grant provisions; a court reference to determine which level of government has jurisdiction or responsibility for the Métis; constitutional amendment; or by political agreements. The current tripartite agreement could address land issues and related issues, such as economic development, Mr. Chartier concluded.

Models of Community and Individual Enterprise

Intertribal Forestry Association of British Columbia

Moderator Gilles Paquet introduced the speakers. Harold Derickson is President of the Intertribal Forestry Association of British Columbia (IFABC), representing all the bands and tribal councils throughout the province. He noted that his organization was one of the first to deal with forestry issues and has been in the forefront of these issues. The IFABC took a major role in a provincial task force on the forest industry. The task force tabled a report with 20 recommendations dealing with forestry; many of the recommendations touched on economic development.

Mr. Derickson said that although there has been success in some areas, Aboriginal people still lack control in the forest industry; of the 80 million cubic metres harvested annually, First Nations controlled only a tiny percentage of that volume. One of the recommendations of the provincial task force was to set up a Forestry Council to liaise with government and industry to implement the balance of the recommendations. The Council has been meeting since February this year, and its success depends to a large extent on the goodwill of governments, he said.

On behalf of the IFABC, Mr. Derickson presented a list of recommendations to the Royal Commission. He said that, in order to realize the full economic potential of the Aboriginal community, provincial and federal governments must address concerns that include the following:

Capital:

- Increase the level of funding for economic development through provincial and federal joint initiatives.
- Allow capital to be lent within Aboriginal communities, and have both capital funds plus interest circulate with the Aboriginal community and the provinces.
- Create new and specific capital pools for specific Aboriginal economic development programs.
- Support a Joint Venture Capital Corporation and an Equity Investment Fund for social and economic development, and facilitate a special immigration fund.
- Ensure that Aboriginal people on-reserve have access to the Guarantee Loan Program and the Agriculture Land Development Assistance Program.

Capacity Building:

- Support province-wide Aboriginal financial intermediaries by authorizing the management and administration of government funds and projects designated for Aboriginal initiatives; assisting with approval for depositors' insurance coverage; supporting the development of management and financial business skills to promote business success; and assisting the process to ensure provincial exemptions from taxation for Aboriginal companies.

Action-Oriented Strategies:

- The land registry system has to ensure title to parties and needs to be provincially and regionally based.
- The overall structures dealing with leases require streamlining.
- Survey requirements need to be up-dated and co-ordinated with the various levels of bureaucracy.
- All policy rules must be on the table (no changes by bureaucrats).
- A new approach to financing must be developed.
- Regarding infrastructure, there needs to be a method of issuing debentures for services on reserve lands.
- New and up-to-date election regulations need to be drafted to comply with the Constitution.
- Bureaucrats dealing with First Nations people on economic development matters need to be appropriately screened and qualified in Canadian business practices.
- A legislative base is needed for initiatives such as First Nations condominium regulations.

"It's a godsend that any type of economic development activity can happen on reserve lands in Canada, considering the barriers that have to be addressed," Mr. Derickson concluded, advocating the development of an action plan with defined guidelines and time tables of completion.

ACR Systems Inc.

Albert Rock is President of ACR Systems Inc., a B.C. firm that manufactures and markets pocket-sized microprocessor-based data loggers that monitor digital and analogue signals. He spoke about his personal and business philosophy that made his firm a success. "I'm well-educated," he began. "I went to 19 schools and got to the 10th grade." Being a successful business person is "a good life," Mr. Rock said. He enjoys travelling, meeting people and being part of the "wonderful energy" of successful business ventures. He still does not know how to define success: "Every time you break through, there's a whole new world out there."

"If you love something and want to do it, and drag the right people along with you, success will come," he said, stressing the importance of focusing on the goals of the business project and on making things work. A recent project with the Ferrari company in Italy is "beyond my dreams as a child," he said. "I'm meeting people I've dreamed of and idolized and realized that they're just ordinary people."

Excitement is key to his love of business, he continued. There is an energy around a successful business project that gives him more incentive to continue. "You've got to keep the energy rolling," he said.

Mr. Rock sees "failures" as opportunities for learning. He said he has had more failures than most people but he has always learned from them. One lesson is to surround himself with positive people. "If one person starts talking negatively, things start going bad," he said. It is important to trust people that have positive energy. He has started to trust "everybody I was told not to trust," and although he still gets burned occasionally, this policy reaps unexpected rewards. For example, he recently agreed to hold a mortgage for a man seen as a failure because of his history of alcohol abuse; Mr. Rock saw the man's commitment to stop drinking as evidence of his strength. The man repaid Mr. Rock's support by giving him ownership of several mineral claims, and now Mr. Rock is "in the gold-mining business."

The gold business got off to a rocky start when Aboriginal people in the claim area refused to let the developers in the area, but after some misunderstandings had been worked out, the business began to take off. Now, the project is "pumping money into the town of Teslin," and people who were initially opposed to the project have given their support. When faced with development proposals, "the safest way is to say 'no', but in business, that's the wrong way," he said.

His biggest challenge when starting out on his own was raising capital, and his lack of formal education was the reason why many organizations turned down his funding requests. He briefly spoke about his contact with business associations for Aboriginal people, saying that in general, these organizations become defunct or change their names quickly. His firm received its first major investment from the Native Economic Development Program, and "now, the people that turned me down [for financing] are the largest buyers of my product."

Discussion

After the moderator opened the discussion to the floor, Stephen Augustine asked Clem Chartier what would be done if the Métis land claims could not be resolved through the courts. Mr. Chartier responded that there is still hope that the issue will be resolved through the courts, and if courts in Canada did not deal satisfactorily with the issue, the next recourse would be the international arena. He couldn't say what the course of action would be after this.

Another participant, referring to the background paper by Lester Lafond, said that investment tax credits have had limited success in stimulating economic development, and he would look closely at their track record before encouraging anyone to pursue this avenue. He added that the manufacturing sector is dying in Canada and should not be the focus of new development. "What everyone is doing now is selling intelligence," he said, stressing that the major resource in Aboriginal communities was its people. In the participant's own city of Winnipeg, the aging population depends on the influx of young Aboriginal people to "stay alive," and the presence of these people should be used to attract investment to the city.

Muriel Stanley-Venne asked why the panellists were all men, and why Aboriginal business women were not asked to contribute. "I'm a little disturbed that there are no women on the panel," she said, adding that she hoped this situation would be corrected in the remaining sessions. There were several responses to her intervention. The moderator asked that the participants "focus on issues rather than symbols," saying that the speakers were presenting issues important to both men and women. Mr. Rock said that the whole front end of his business is handled by women and the integration of women into decision-making positions was going to happen slowly. Round Table Chair Ron Jamieson validated Ms. Stanley-Venne's concern, noting that the Round Table discussions would be more inclusive of women.

Round Table I: The Land and Resource Base

Ron Jamieson called the meeting to order and introduced the participants of the first Round Table discussion. Moderator Gilles Paquet asked the participants to discuss trends in the economy that could affect Aboriginal economic development.

George Miller, President of the Mining Association of Canada, noted that increased international economic interdependence is irreversible. Mr. Paquet asked whether this trend would lead to more constraints or opportunities. "Both," Mr. Miller answered. Competitiveness is a constraint, but the globalization of the economy presents niches that Aboriginal people could occupy.

Pat Apikan, Vice President, Apikan Limited, stated that Aboriginal economy should be defined as not merely people, but also as rights, interests, and treaties. He noted that government support is on the wane. Mr. Paquet asked how Aboriginal people could take advantage of these rights. By including Aboriginal rights, including economic rights, in the Constitution, Mr. Apikan answered, and by treating Aboriginal governments as equals, not as subordinates.

Albert Diamond, President and CEO, Air Creebec, noted that information available to the general public is not available to Aboriginal people, and young people on reserves do not know what opportunities exist for them in the economy.

Anne Noonan, Director of Native Affairs, Raymond, Chabot, et Paré Chartered Accountants, noted growing recognition of Aboriginal and treaty rights by the general public and by business. She asked how these rights could be implemented, and what resources were available for this process. For example, it might be possible to set up royalty agreements for previous hydroelectric developments.

Ron Swain, President of the Ontario Métis Aboriginal Association and Minister Responsible for Economic Development of the Métis National Council, observed that, for Aboriginal people, the issues go back to control over land and to gaining and controlling equity and capital. Self-government would permit Aboriginal peoples to regulate financial institutions.

Mr. Paquet asked what was needed to allow people to take advantage of current economic trends, what possible threats these pose to the Aboriginal economy. Peter Allen, Assistant Deputy Minister for Economic Development and Tourism in the Northwest Territories, responded that moving into a globalized, computerized, and (on the whole) simplified economy would provide opportunities for Aboriginal and first-time entrepreneurs.

Susan Anderson, Policy Adviser for Aboriginal/Environmental Issues, B.C. Federation of Labour, observed that in British Columbia, land claim negotiations are just beginning. Negotiations for Aboriginal participation in the forestry industry are providing practice for the land claim process. But there is a critical shortage of trained people in Aboriginal communities. Current trends could be disadvantageous for the rural B.C. economy, especially in the short term.

"Trade Barriers are Not an Aboriginal Tradition"

Chesley Andersen, Vice-President of the Inuit Tapirisat of Canada, called for the northern economy to become part of a circumpolar economy which could (for example) market caribou and seafoods on an international basis. This would require changes to governmental jurisdiction. "Trade barriers are not an Aboriginal tradition," Mr. Andersen said. He spoke of the need for environmental and social assessment of business plans, and for Aboriginal involvement not just in the labour market but in planning and development.

There are, Mr. Andersen said, three requirements for Aboriginal economic development: clarification of jurisdictional issues, improving financing instruments, and ensuring that land claims generate capital. The problem for Aboriginal economies is access to capital. But the barriers come from bureaucrats and politicians, not from banks.

Lester Lafond, of P.M. Associates Limited, said that business cannot be responsible for training; bands must do this. His own band has concentrated since the 1960s on human development. It has a 35-year plan for economic development, based on its own inventory of its resources, human and other. He asked what the barriers were to government partnership with Aboriginal entrepreneurs.

Mr. Paquet noted that developing human resources will take time. "How can Aboriginal people make best use of their land or expand their land base? Can they use it to generate capital?"

Mr. Diamond noted that tourism is well suited to the Aboriginal philosophy. Nature tours have become popular; fishing camps are converting to catch-and-release sport. Even hunting is giving way to wild animal photography. This suits the Aboriginal conservation philosophy. One problem he has encountered with tourism, however, is that tourists are used to a high level of personal service, while his people were brought up to look after themselves. "They're not used to babysitting hunters," he said.

John Forester, of Forestry Canada, said that Aboriginal people control considerable timber land, but mostly in small parcels on reserves. He asked how this resource could generate income. He called for partnership between the forestry industry and Aboriginal peoples.

Mr. Swain observed that the first item on the agenda concerned land – but the Métis have none. For them, the solution will be a land base of their own. The Métis have traditionally been entrepreneurs, Mr. Swain continued. They have the experience, but they need equity to overcome historic disadvantages. Métis capital corporations' resources fall dramatically short of demand. Only equity, capital, and access to both will allow the Métis to take advantage of the new high-tech global market.

Mr. Paquet asked if land was the only way for the Métis to get capital or leverage. Mr. Swain answered that the land claim process has several options; land, money as settlement, or financed buy-backs of land in non-Aboriginal hands.

Gilbert Guay, Director, Economic Development, Department of Indian Affairs and Northern Development, stated that besides global economies or world economies, there exists a parallel track which starts at the community level. Before thinking of going global, local and regional economies must be developed; from that base, global expansion can take place.

Referring to comments by Mr. Diamond about the need for more information about business development in communities, Mr. Guay said that human resources must be seen as primary resources, and there must be reliable dissemination of information. After the information gets out, Aboriginal businesses will decide for themselves the niches they want to pursue and occupy, based on existing opportunities.

"Access Has to Be Something You Can Take to the Bank"

Ms. Anderson noted that in B.C., expanding the land base may not be the ideal solution. Those involved in preparing for treaty negotiations are studying whether it may sometimes be better for First Nations to own relatively smaller parcels of land, but to have access to and royalties from much larger areas. Deals such as resource access and co-operative agreements could be best in the long term.

Mr. Lafond agreed. One problem, he noted, was that Aboriginal people are so close to the land that the idea of possession appeals very strongly to them, especially after years of being deprived of it. He noted also that "there's no money in the till, and we have to respect that." It is the mechanisms of getting funding that create problems more than the limited amount of it. An access agreement is necessary; "then we can use our own ideas."

Mr. Andersen reported that the Inuit have found that previous agreements did not deal with mineral rights. Aboriginal peoples must have control over developing economic plans and should only have to deal with one level of government. Ms. Anderson responded that B.C.'s Aboriginal people have studied earlier land claims and observed the problems. "Access has to be something you can take to the bank."

Mr. Apikan noted the need for a dispute settlement mechanism; currently, the federal government is both judge and jury. Existing models for binational tribunals should be examined. He also brought up the problem of land for urban Aboriginal people. "Not many people know that we're buying land for them," he told the participants. It was strange how municipalities can expand their land base, while Aboriginal people cannot. The only resource urban Aboriginal peoples have is themselves, Mr. Apikan said. He agreed with Ms. Anderson that *access* to resources is critical.

Mr. Miller observed that developers and multinationals are coming to grips with Aboriginal issues and sometimes have innovative ideas for involving Aboriginal people. But one constraint is skills levels. His own firm polled its managers and found that lack of skills was their greatest concern in employing Aboriginal workers.

In response to Ms. Anderson, Mr. Allen noted that banks want equity before they issue loans; this, he said, means that land ownership could be important. Equity financiers, on the other hand, recognize resources.

Ms. Noonan called for joint problem solving, with Aboriginal people at the table with the federal and provincial governments. Aside from the need for equity to acquire investment capital, she stated that it is important to recognize the right to land for Aboriginal peoples, the Métis included. Negotiations, not conferences, are what is needed.

Mr. Forester agreed that skills are a problem in hiring Aboriginal people, but another problem is that managers know little about Aboriginal issues. Two types of education are needed, he said: skills training for Aboriginal workers, and education in the issues for industry. As for taking resources to the bank, the forestry industry raised capital in New York with its leases as equity.

Mr. Swain told the meeting that the Métis are recognized as Aboriginal people under the Constitution, but federal policy is to refuse to open negotiations for land claims or to accept its fiduciary responsibility to Métis people. If the policy changes, it could include cash settlements, expropriation, or buying land on the market. He asked the Royal Commission to take a strong stand for Métis land claims. The identity of the Métis Nation is fundamental, and land would provide the pride his people need.

Mr. Apikan said that the Métis should hammer a solution out of the government in court. Mr. Lafond agreed that land is fundamental, but he does not like the courts. Leasing the land could stabilize the community's political structure; this would increase the government's willingness to negotiate. Ms. Anderson said that B.C.'s land claim process includes the province's one Métis community.

Mr. Swain added that the Métis must be enumerated and identified. Some communities are healthy, but politically unknown. The negotiation process should be open-ended to allow groups that have not been identified to come forth.

Mr. Paquet summed up the discussion as follows:

- International trends will create niches for Aboriginal business, but communities may have problems taking advantage of these opportunities.
- Education and information are crucial.
- Access to and development of natural resources are also critical.
- The reality is that without a land base or strong title, communities have no access to capital. Therefore the Métis need a land base and other Aboriginal people need to consolidate and expand their land bases.

Land claims might lead to increased capital and human resources. "If you own it, you care for it better," Mr. Paquet concluded. After this summary, the moderator opened up discussion from the floor. Jean-Yves Assiniwi called for the creation of Aboriginal jurisdiction within urban areas to control services such as education. Access to title is not the same as access to the resource. Mr. Swain said that controlling revenue depended on self-government. Ms. Anderson said that self-government in turn depends on a land base, and asked for an exploration of the urban land base issue. Mr. Apikan added that Aboriginal control of land would lead to better uses, and that showing Canadians that Aboriginal people want to preserve the land for spiritual reasons would increase public support.

Ruth Williams said that the only way for urban Aboriginal people to have access to land and resources is to be recognized as a group. Land would have to be bought, an expensive proposition. Using land for equity would also present problems; there should be some way for bands to do this without jeopardy. Urban Aboriginal people have no access to federal funding and are not included in discussions because they have no structures. Aboriginal entrepreneurs need education to overcome their fear of starting out, and the problem of taxing Aboriginal businesses after they incorporate must be straightened out.

Jimmy Neashit from La Tuque, Quebec, said that his community, in response to an influx of cottagers, organized itself and examined its options. It has been working at human development and making contacts with businesses in Canada and abroad. Economic development will come if Aboriginal rights are respected and enforced. Aboriginal people in Quebec are not opposed to hydroelectric development; they want to control it. Another participant called for the enforcement of rights and the reoccupation of the land.

Mr. Diamond recalled that the government controlled where First Nations could choose land in the James Bay negotiations, something that should change. Land could be chosen to benefit urban people, and agreements should be flexible.

Mr. Swain re-emphasized that land is not tied to self-government, which is a right, and called for self-government for urban Aboriginal people. Ms. Anderson called for caution in dealing with third parties. In B.C., the land is already allocated, and white residents could feel threatened. Mr. Lafond called for coexistence between individual and community needs in Aboriginal communities.

Keynote Address: International Economic Trends and Opportunities

Keynote speaker Dian Cohen is a well-known broadcaster and communicator who writes about business and the economy. She began by noting that Canadians are very keen to resolve the outstanding issues with Aboriginal peoples, and that her travels across the country talking to groups have lead her to believe that "Canadians suspect that the traditional ways and knowledge of Aboriginal peoples may contain some of the secrets our culture seems to have lost."

Deep cultural changes are taking place in western society; at their root is a common hunger for a new way to relate to the planet and for partnerships rather than relationships based on exploitation. There is a new openness and sympathy with Aboriginal cultures around the world. "Looking ahead then, the question we have to ask ourselves is what happens when we resolve our current problems. I think that's when the real work is going to begin."

Ms. Cohen said the main international economic trends are widely acknowledged. The world has divided into three interdependent trading blocs – Asia-Pacific, Europe and North America. Although internal bloc trade seems to be growing more rapidly than trade between blocs, trade between blocs is growing faster than national economic growth. International investment is growing even faster.

Despite concerns about strategic trade policy and new protectionism, the international economy is growing increasingly interdependent. "Everybody, whether they export or not, is competing against global competitors," she said.

Another defining trend is the combination of computers and telecommunications. This second wave of telecommunications is a complement to internationalization. Employment in knowledge-based businesses is higher and growing more rapidly than employment in traditional sectors. In Canada, the information technology sector has about 14,000 firms, employs 150,000 people and develops and distributes products and services worth more than $17 billion.

The information businesses barely existed 20 years ago. Now they are among the biggest businesses in the world, and their potential is clearly understood by investors. "This sectoral shift is interesting," continued Ms. Cohen, "but even more intriguing is the impact of this new technology on the way we do things... big business is vulnerable to small business because of this sectoral shift."

She said that the new technology:

- moves control of information downstream into the hands of the consumer;
- changes the role of the consumer from a passive consumer to an active participant in designing a product for her individual needs;
- ends the distinction between goods and services; the old control functions that used to be cost centres are now profit centres and potential new businesses;
- trashes national borders and time zones. The global village Marshall McLuhan talked about is really an electronic bazaar. Home shopping, distance learning and banking by phone do not respect frontiers: "When you call an 800 or 900 number, you or it could be anywhere."

She added that repercussions of the new technology include:

- Economies and national boundaries no longer coincide.
- Jobs are no longer hooked to economic growth or to natural resources.

- Big businesses and large organizations are vulnerable to small, highly focused organizations.

Ms. Cohen said that markets are still driven by the desire to accumulate, but the new technologies are changing the way economists think about markets and the way business people behave in them. There is suddenly a surge of interest in the economics of sharing. "We have not yet reached the point of Aboriginal circles, where we act on the interdependence of everything, but as far as I can see, we're heading in that direction."

She cautioned that if the developed world no longer highly values resource-based economies, they will be happy to see its stewardship pass into the hands of others. Aboriginal communities with economies based on land might find themselves in an uphill battle to survive in the larger economy.

The good side of the new technologies and the globalizing trends is that the combination will allow Aboriginal communities to interact with each other, with other Aboriginal cultures and with western cultures "in exciting, innovative and economically wealth-producing ways," Ms. Cohen said. "Compared to what we had before, the new economy is much more inclusive and it offers many, many more opportunities to people who didn't have them before. This, it seems to me, is where the interests of Aboriginal economic development and that of Canada coincide, and where it is most important to raise questions about land-based development strategies."

Canada must totally reconfigure itself, Ms. Cohen continued. "Like the Aboriginal economies, Canada will have to change or remain in what some of your commentators have called a 'bungee' economy – where the money may flow in but then bounces back out again. Canada needs all the help it can get in generating innovations, trade and productive investment. "Aboriginal enterprises – especially, I think, Aboriginal knowledge products – have a lot to contribute to turning Canada's economy around. In today's new, knowledge-based economies, imagination is the most valuable resource. In this kind of economy, the opportunities for Aboriginal people and cultures to participate is bigger than it's ever been before."

Theme II: Strengthening Traditional Economies and Perspectives

Overview of Discussion Papers

Moderator Gilles Paquet introduced Simon Brascoupé. Mr. Brascoupé, a Mohawk/Algonquin, and Professor in the Department of Sociology and Anthropology at Carleton University in Ottawa, presented an overview of two discussion papers.

Mr. Brascoupé began by stating that traditional economies such as hunting, fishing and living off the land are very challenging and exciting, and this is why so many people turn to these activities either in their spare time or upon retirement. He noted that both David Newhouse's paper entitled "Modern Aboriginal Economies: Capitalism with an Aboriginal Face," and Mr. Brascoupé's own paper, challenge perceptions and misconceptions that exist regarding traditional economic development.

Mr. Newhouse wrote about the "unique perspectives that Aboriginal belief systems have for development, how these can be preserved, and what lessons these might have for future development efforts, both within Aboriginal communities and the main stream." He said that on the surface, business proposals prepared by Aboriginal and non-Aboriginal people look the same, but upon closer inspection, it is found that an Aboriginal business proposal focuses not only on cash flows and profit projections, but also on job creation. Mr. Newhouse also wrote about the need for modernization of Aboriginal institutions. This modernization does not mean assimilation, but looks instead to bring institutions up to date and to integrate into them Aboriginal values, cultures and intentions.

In his paper, Mr. Newhouse identified seven primary traditional values at the "core of vision and respect." These are kindness, honesty, sharing, strength, bravery, wisdom and humility. He said that we also have to rethink the meaning of "capitalism" by widening the scope of the concept of development; see development itself as a process not a product (get away from the thinking that "the end justifies the means") and as a joint effort between the individual, the collective and institutions; emphasize human capital (job creation) rather than individual capital accumulation; use elders as models and guides in planning and decision making; distribute wealth according to Aboriginal values of kindness and sharing; adapt western institutions to local community values and culture; achieve consensus when arriving at decisions; and employ the notions of honesty and respect to arrive at greater accountability by economic institutions and decision makers.

Mr. Brascoupé turned to his paper entitled "Strengthening Traditional Economies and Perspectives." Traditional economies are not well understood. They are not one, but several, "economic systems" which have evolved over several thousand of years, based on Indigenous knowledge, values and systems. A threat to these systems comes from outside Aboriginal communities because an erroneous image of what constitutes a "traditional way of life" exists. Three issues cloud the perception of a traditional way of life: that "the traditional way of life is harsh, primitive and dying;" assumptions that all tribes will eventually be developed and that development will benefit tribal peoples; and that tribes will be allowed a choice in this process.

An additional threat comes from animal rights lobby groups. These groups often assume that Aboriginal peoples want to join the "rat race." They do not realize the damage that they are doing to Aboriginal families as well as industries.

Mr. Brascoupé spoke of the importance of developing Indigenous knowledge and the impact that this knowledge can have on many academic disciplines.

Mr. Brascoupé identified several alternative ways to strengthen traditional economies: strengthening Aboriginal rights, self-government and land claims as a means to integrate traditional economies into other economic plans; researching Indigenous knowledge; establishing co-management between Aboriginal peoples, federal and provincial governments and other organizations; and supporting conferences, workshops, publications and research and training and education. There is also a need to document and demonstrate how traditional and market economies can be harmonized.

Aboriginal communities should look to increasing the number of jobs provided through Aboriginal governments and look at the potentials that exist to provide new services and jobs. Communities need to provide their own goods and services. Only about 10% of reserve income is spent within Aboriginal communities. In order to change this figure, there has to be an integration between regional and local economies. There also has to be increased interest by Aboriginal peoples in the fields of computers, technology and communications, because this is the future of business.

Models of Community and Individual Enterprise

Income Security Program for Cree Hunters and Trappers

Mr. Paquet introduced Chief George Wapachee, the Vice-Chairman of the Income Security Program for Cree Hunters and Trappers. Mr. Wapachee is Chief of the Cree First Nations in Nemaska. He said that the Income Security Program for Cree Hunters and Trappers has been in existence since the signing of the James Bay Agreement. The program began in the fall of 1976 and was retroactive to November 11, 1975. This is its seventeenth year of operation. The objective of the program is to ensure that hunting, fishing and trapping remain viable ways of life and that individuals who undertake these activities will be able to survive.

Eligibility for the program is based on the time spent in the bush by the head of the family. To qualify for the program, the minimum required time spent on hunting, fishing and trapping activities is four months (120 days), with a minimum of three months (90 days) spent in the bush. Individuals must also spend more time in these traditional activities than in any other wage employment. In recent years, a requirement has been that the individual be listed by a local committee of hunters and trappers as a hunter or trapper. Once an individual qualifies for the program, he is guaranteed an annual income which depends on the time spent in the bush and on the size of his family. Because income is not based upon production, the program helps to ensure that people do not increase their harvesting and deplete the resources.

When the program began, the daily allowance was $12 for each day spent in the bush. Today, that figure has risen to $37.93 per day, with a 240-day maximum. Additional income is given according to family size and involvement of other family members in hunting and trapping.

Factors that affect the program include the new generation of hunters that is emerging, the increase of work possibilities for Aboriginal peoples, and the increasing cost of living, especially the increase in transportation and housing costs.

This traditional economy is vital to the community. Mr. Wapachee suggested that other support programs be developed and integrated into other communities because today the social benefits that Aboriginal people receive are not sufficient. In 1991-92, the Income Security program for Cree Hunters and Trappers assisted 1,213 families. These families made up only 29% of the entire reserve population. This percentage fluctuates yearly, from 16% to 45%, depending on the area and the year. When there are construction projects in the area, the number of hunters and trappers decreases. When the area is facing difficult economic times, like in the last few years, the number of hunters and trappers increases.

This program is the first of its kind in Canada. There are six members on the board of the Income Security Program for Cree Hunters and Trappers, three from the Quebec government and three from the Cree Nation. Funding for the program comes from the Quebec government.

Mr. Wapachee said that this program has "helped maintain a way of life which is both cultural and economic." In order to survive, the Income Security Program for Cree Hunters and Trappers must be adapted to deal with new realities and a new generation of hunters and trappers; local involvement in the decision-making process should be increased; the complexity of the program should be reduced; and periodic reviews should be done to ensure that the program remains flexible.

Mr. Wapachee said that traditional economies should be encouraged. Other ways to do this would be to increase training, and to encourage fur marketing and commercial fishing. He concluded by saying that the Income Security Program for Cree Hunters and Trappers has "shown how traditional activities can be supported and valorized."

Parenteau's Saskatoon Berry Chocolates and Preserves Inc.

In 1986, Mr. Parenteau and his wife began their business growing Saskatoon berries and blueberries. Since that time, they have increased the number of trees on their land to approximately 5,000, and they continue to work together to increase their farm's production. Mr. Parenteau stressed that "you have to learn from your own mistakes." The business has been diversified to include the production of jams, homemade chocolates and wines. As far as he is aware, he is the only Aboriginal chocolate maker in Canada, and perhaps in North America. In 1990, the business began to produce chocolates because there were not enough berries to make jams. Once a prototype had been developed for their chocolates, the focus turned to packaging – there was a need to find a niche in the market and to provide something different from other, bigger companies' products and packaging. They decided to package their chocolates in wooden boxes.

Mr. Parenteau said they were told many times to go "really big," but they didn't and that is why they have survived. He said that learning the laws that surround food products was a struggle. He talked to many different people in the government and got many different answers. He learned that products must be labelled carefully and that there are rules governing label size, wording and placement. His company is on its third label design now.

Mr. Parenteau had to find a way to market his products. The company participates in many conventions, receptions and conferences and gives away samples of chocolates.

Mr. Parenteau's company received initial funding from the federal Department of Industry, Science and Technology. He went to the bank with a promissory note from the government for $30,000 as well as his own savings of $30,000. The bank turned him down; it was only interested in cash flow and told him to come back when he was established. A credit union loaned him the start-up funds.

Mr. Parenteau had problems dealing with the people who live in his town, the majority of whom are non-Aboriginal. Many did not think that his business would survive because he didn't have any money or experience, and because he was an Aboriginal person. Some commented that "letting a Métis make chocolate was like letting a fox into a chicken coop," and told him that he would eat all his profits. He proved them wrong. He said it is hard for many people to see an Aboriginal person as a boss.

Mr. Parenteau would like to see more jobs created for Aboriginal people. He would like the media to stop focusing on negative images of Aboriginal people, to stop portraying them as drunks, or in prisons. People should see Aboriginal people as prison guards, not as prisoners, he said. Positive images of successful Aboriginal persons would give young people positive role models.

After the floor was opened for comments or questions, Muriel Stanley-Venne objected to Mr. Parenteau calling upon Aboriginal people to become prison guards. She said that people should not be put into oppressive institutions and that the guards will become oppressed as well as the prisoners. Instead, Aboriginal people need to develop skills, expertise and imagination. They need to "open their minds." She added that "if we adopt what already is, we will have accomplished nothing." Ms. Stanley-Venne concluded that we have to "help people rather than oppress them."

Round Table II: Strengthening Traditional Economies and Perspectives

Moderator Gilles Paquet asked the participants at the Round Table to introduce themselves and opened the discussion by asking what are the threats to the traditional Aboriginal economy and how it can be supported; how to present and get acceptance for the Aboriginal perspective on development; and how wildlife could be a resource. "Will the traditional economy survive?"

Peter George, President of the Council of Ontario Universities and Professor of Economics at McMaster University, said that research confirms the vitality of Aboriginal tradition. Threats come from the moratorium on furs and from the exodus of youth to cities. Brian Roberts, Department of Indian Affairs and Northern Development, deals with harvesting and said that the current European attitudes toward fur, or the Aboriginal reliance on trapping, will have to change. Otherwise, this 400-year-old commercial harvest faces serious problems.

Dorothy Grant, President of Feastware, uses Haida art to design clothing, using her tradition in a contemporary way. She spoke of the threat to Haida art of the lumbering of virgin forest. Few trees of the right size are left for Haida canoes and totem poles, the backbone of the culture. She called for apprenticing Aboriginal designers with established artists and designers, noting that the potential market was tremendous. But she herself faces problems getting capital for production and display.

Sheila Genaille, President, Métis National Council of Women, said that the Métis were traditionally entrepreneurs. But Métis women in particular are doubly disadvantaged by gender and ethnicity. They need flexible, extended child care and funding to establish business plans to start their own businesses. "Funding is imbalanced," Ms. Genaille said. "We're only asking for our tax dollars to come back." Self-government and a land base are of enormous importance.

Steven Augustine, from the Big Cove reserve, spoke of the threat to Aboriginal spirituality of ventures that plunder the earth. The essential roles of all people were set out in the creation stories. He stressed lack of recognition of the unique Aboriginal perspective and the need for language, culture, and tradition. In the past, harvesting activities were not a "traditional economy"; they were a way of life, and the phrase is a modern one. He drew parallels with the Acadian experience, noting that in the face of non-recognition of their language, laws, and culture, Acadians have created their own institutions.

Mr. Paquet asked if this view was perhaps romanticism, a turning backward. "What strategies do you propose?" he asked. Mr. Augustine answered that the Aboriginal world view should be incorporated in modern technology – as Mr. Paquet put it, "capitalism with a human face."

Mr. George stated that communities must decide for themselves the balance between traditional and modern economic activity, because urban and remote districts face different problems. Remote communities, for example, face high costs for transportation and distribution.

Communities that promote traditional activities should look for suitable niches such as eco-tourism, and for institutions such as co-management. They must train their youth in traditional skills – Ontario does not fund this training, and communities find this frustrating. They must find a balance between traditional activities and wage employment and find ways of promoting on-reserve employment. High value-added activities, like Ms. Grant's design business, could be the key.

"Is It Possible to Live and Let Live?"

Michel Arès of the Association Mamo Atoskewin Atikamekw spoke of the pressure on the land from forestry and hydroelectric development in his district. His traditional economy is alive; hunting and fishing are important to people 417 kilometres from the nearest mall. Tradition, he said, *must* be documented and is wealth in itself. His association, with funding from Hydro Quebec, is developing a data base on First Nations practices that will be used to integrate management with the company and with forestry. He called for strategic alliances between communities and developers to manage resources.

Yves Gaulin, Manager, Indian and Inuit Affairs, Hydro Quebec, spoke of the importance of consultation with Aboriginal peoples in resource development and research. His program funds activities to protect tradition. Measures to rehabilitate developed areas can help to minimize the effect of such development both on nature and on Aboriginal society.

"Is it possible for the two groups to live and let live?" Mr. Paquet asked. Mr. Arès said that his group works only with research, not development, and that a similar process with the forestry industry is just starting. Developers must recognize *and* implement improved practices and must document local knowledge.

Johanne Robertson of the Institut educatif et culturel Montagnais saw one problem: the profit motive is untraditional. A Montagnais women's project to make and sell moccasins ran into a snag: to ensure quantity, the women had to take an assembly-line approach, but this is untraditional and unsatisfying to people used to crafting moccasins from start to finish. Their solution was to keep the traditional approach, but to work in a group.

Pat Angnakak, Community and Economic Development Officer at Kakivak Association, N.W.T., sees a serious threat in young people's loss of identity and in southern influence and called for leadership training for them, because Inuit culture fosters passivity, and this must change. "Southerners think they have all the answers," she said. Inuit have a resource in their own knowledge and should assess what they have.

Terry Fenge, Executive Director of the Canadian Arctic Research Centre, recalled the Income Security Program for Cree Hunters and Trappers created in the James Bay Agreement, a highly successful initiative that has not been replicated in more recent agreements. The government calls this a "social" program that cannot be included in agreements, but really does not want to shoulder the cost. He called for creative funding for similar programs and for a recommendation from the Royal Commission that they be included in future agreements.

In the North, Aboriginal people receive royalties, at best, for oil and mineral development, while government creams off economic rents from these industries, Mr. Fenge continued. He asked if some way could be found to tap into these funds to support Aboriginal traditions. He pointed out that formal agreements had been made to amend the international Migratory Bird Convention to allow Aboriginal hunting, but the federal government has not followed through on its agreement, and the Convention has not yet been amended.

Mr. Roberts noted that Aboriginal traditions were acceptable to Europeans – as long as they weren't commercial. He pointed out the contradiction between European support for Aboriginal issues and opposition to furs; the entire industry collapsed in one year as a result of the opposition. Mr. Fenge asked him about government support for Indigenous Survival International (ISI), a group formed to counter anti-fur propaganda, and Mr. Roberts announced that the government is extending the program for five years. Mr. Fenge asked the Royal Commission to recommend that the federal government consider undertaking a case study of the relationship between the government and the ISI, as a model for this kind of co-operative arrangement.

Mr. Augustine related Micmac creation stories to illustrate the connections between his people, the land, and its creatures. Exploitation of natural resources is chipping away at the Micmac identity. The culture has lost much of its traditional hunting and fishing and has a small land base. Economic initiatives could emphasize traditional culture such as dance, medicine, arts, and knowledge.

Ms. Genaille told the meeting that government intervention never works. Courses for Métis school children in their culture were developed without Métis involvement; the result is that the children are losing their culture. Mr. Fenge disagreed; he said that government intervention can work, but only if it is sensitive to the issues. For example, the government knew it could not run a public relations program to counter the anti-fur lobby; hence its strategic alliance with ISI. This is a positive example that should be documented.

Ms. Grant said that entrepreneurship must be fostered, and new businesses need more information. People should understand the difficulties that entrepreneurs face. "People are afraid of taking a big step and losing everything," she said. Entrepreneurs must understand business plans, something in which they need guidance.

Mr. George discussed the difficulties of doing business on-reserve – transportation costs, the lack of capital, problems with cash flow. The *Indian Act* makes it virtually impossible to raise venture capital, since assets cannot be pledged. Reserves face problems in getting access to local resources when provinces own mineral rights. Only recently has MNR begun thinking about co-management.

"We Still Have Our Links to the Land"

Mr. Paquet opened up the meeting to discussion from the floor. The first speaker, Oscar Kistabush, said that his father was a trapper, and so were his brothers; he himself is trying to return to the traditional way in a contemporary way. He said that many Aboriginal people have lost their traditions, and the land has been devastated by development.

He has established his own business, adventure touring, but he added that a wide range of options exists for Aboriginal development in everything from mining to agriculture. In the eight Algonquin communities in the Abitibi-Temiskaming area, three-quarters of the businesses depend on natural resources. "We still have our links to the land." He called for teaching traditional methods of natural resource management and for economic development linked to Aboriginal culture.

Yves-Jean Assiniwi said that "modernizing" tradition sounds wrong to him. The important thing is that economic activities are true to Aboriginal values, not that they replicate historical practice. Commercial Inuit sculpture, for example, goes back only 40 years, but it is true to the culture. He noted that Judeo-Christian values led to modernization and asked why, for example, Pierre Trudeau was irritated by an Aboriginal ceremony but not by parliamentary ceremony.

What matters, Mr. Assiniwi stated, is that Aboriginal people be true to their roots – their values. "We mustn't deny our right to evolution," he told the meeting. "What I do something for, not how I do it, is important." He called for the promotion of North American design instead of reliance on European designers.

In Jim Carbery's region, young people are losing traditional skills and being pulled toward megaprojects with high pay. Educated Aboriginal people too often leave the community. "Is modern education a threat to the traditional economy?" Mr. Carbery asked.

Mr. George answered that the returns of education far outweigh the costs, especially for off-reserve people. He referred back to the government's position that hunters' income support is a "social" program and noted that such activities as hunting aren't seen as economic activities by government. The products of Aboriginal traditional societies rarely enter the marketplace, but unless they do, they are not counted as part of the economy. Inuit art turned into an economic activity for statistical purposes only when the pieces began to be sold.

Anne Noonan called for the protection of rights on intellectual property such as Aboriginal medicines, designs, and knowledge. Dorothy Grant agreed fully. Salish weavers' prosperous trade in traditional crafts and sweaters was devastated when a Japanese company took the name "Salish Weavers" and flooded the market, and the Salish are helpless to stop this. She has no way of protecting her own designs. Mr. Arès noted that made-in-Taiwan "Aboriginal" crafts are on sale in Mirabel Airport, a clear case of exploiting intellectual property.

Bill Draper called the meeting's attention to the book, *Cities and the Wealth of Nations*, which promotes thinking about the economy as a community matter. He told the meeting that community development must rely on import replacement, not outside forces. He related an African co-operative game management program in which communities took over game management, controlled hunting, and charged bounties. He asked if governance of wild game could be taken over by Aboriginal communities.

Bill Lyall, President of Arctic Co-operatives Limited, remembered that at land claims meetings in 1970, the Inuit had asked for legal protection of their soapstone carvings; this request had been repeated every year since, with no results. Copies are flooding the market and sales are down 40%.

Mr. Roberts said that Aboriginal hunters have had to be told to focus on humaneness – to adopt different traps, not different attitudes. Mr. Fenge asked whether completion of the national parks system could benefit the Aboriginal economy by increasing tourism and providing job opportunities. Mr. Augustine called for joint access and jurisdiction over resources.

Muriel Stanley-Venne noted that women's work is not tallied or valued, and that the value of this work should always be appreciated. Her son works as a tradesman in megaprojects in Alberta; the fact that his work helps despoil the land makes him despondent. Industrialization takes it toll not only on the land but on those who work for industry.

"Neither is Wrong"

Round Table Chair Ron Jamieson thanked the participants and presented his own unofficial perspective, based on the discussion:

- Land claims must be settled, including the land claims of the Métis people. Special consideration should be given to the circumstances of urban Aboriginal people.
- Aboriginal people should have their own jurisdiction and control over the land.

- The luncheon speaker, Dian Cohen, discussed land control in the future and the new knowledge-based economy. Aboriginal and white society will have to form a real partnership in the future.
- In talking about traditional economics, he noted the similarities between Mr. Wapachee's experience and that of Mr. and Mrs. Parenteau. One venture was hunting and fishing; the other was agricultural, but both were expanding, and both demonstrated a common hope and pride in a chosen way of life. "We as people need to focus on success," Mr. Jamieson said.
- In looking at traditional and Euro-Canadian economies, we should visualize two fishing families in Northern Ontario. One family has one boat and catches fish for subsistence, with the whole family involved. The other family sees value in going into commercial fishing with a number of boats and selling fish to the community. This second family must turn a profit, to replace equipment and pay its workers. "But neither family is wrong, and both are important," Mr. Jamieson said. Both are forms of economic development.
- Government can support Aboriginal economies by recognizing and respecting them. "They won't know what our economies are," Mr. Jamieson predicted. "We'll have to tell them."

Elder Noel Knockwood ended the Round Table with prayer and thanksgiving to the Creator.

Keynote Address: Tribal Economic Development

Tom Acevedo, the dinner keynote speaker, is Attorney for the Confederated Salish and Kootenai Tribes (S+K) of the Flathead Reservation in Montana, and Chief Executive Officer of the S+K Development Corporation. After reading the background papers prepared for the Round Table, Mr. Acevedo was struck by the similarity of the problems facing Aboriginal peoples in Canada and the U.S.

He described the Flathead Reservation as 1.2 million acres of beautiful mountain area in western Montana south of Glacier National Park. The state's largest freshwater lake is situated on the reservation, and tourism has been a major industry for years. The reservation population of 25,000 includes 5,000 Indians; the relationship between Indian and non-Indian people has not always been smooth. The tribe owns 60% of the reservation land; the rest is owned by Indian and non-Indian individuals.

The tribal government is the single largest employer on the reservation, employing more than 1,200 people. Its operating budget is about $90 million, $73 million of which comes from transfer payments from various government departments. (The federal *Self-Determination Act* gives the tribal government authority for service delivery on the reservation.) The remaining $17 million comes from revenue generated by businesses controlled by the tribes.

A 180-megawatt hydroelectric facility is the largest single source of revenue for the S+K Tribes. Other businesses include timber, a resort hotel, an electronics manufacturing plant, a construction company, and agricultural leasing.

Mr. Acevedo noted that many tribes across the U.S. are seeking to involve themselves in the gaming industry – under a federal gaming act, tribes can negotiate contracts with the state governments for gaming operations on reservations. The state governments, however, are resisting these initiatives, and the success of the Indian gaming operations has created a backlash from the gaming industry. Many tribes are finding that gaming operations are their most successful business ventures, and the profits have allowed expansion of tribal budgets and increased services. The S+K tribes have not turned to gaming but see gaming as only one component of a diverse economic base.

Mr. Acevedo reviewed the federal programs that have been of some assistance to the S+K. The first is a loan guarantee program, whereby the Bureau of Indian Affairs guarantees 90% of the funds borrowed from private lending institutions. The S+K used this program to finance a resort hotel on the Flathead Reservation. He cautioned that this program is limited by the ability of tribes to convince private lending institutions of the viability of business projects. His group lobbied for one year before a loan was secured; what finally convinced the bank was the continuity of his organization's board of directors. He advised other groups to "be persistent and stubborn" in their efforts to secure funding.

Another federal program is a direct dollar grant program for facilities construction. The S+K used this program to fund its electronics manufacturing plant, with an in-kind contribution of 3:1. The problem with this program, Mr. Acevedo explained, is drastic underfunding, leading tribes to compete for limited dollars. Another potential problem is that the grant application procedure encourages tribes to "skew the figures," for the business plan. For the hotel facility, the process of skewing the figures actually convinced the S+K enterprise that the project was not economically feasible, and they turned down funding before realizing that the project would work.

Another government program funds projects initiated by minority groups – Indian peoples are just one of the eligible groups. Mr. Acevedo said the beauty of this program is that tribes have the opportunity to sit down with the funding agency and negotiate on a sole-source contract basis; the negotiating price has the profit margin built in. The S+K were able to use this program to fund their electronics business. The problem with this program is its nine-year limit, a "narrow window of opportunity" that does not allow time for full business development. He suggested that if a similar program is adopted in Canada, the time limit should be increased. The program in the U.S. is limited to Department of Defense contracts and should be expanded, he added.

Another federal program funds the planning of economic development initiatives. The program provides seed money for tribes that would not otherwise be able to initiate economic development projects. This program and others are facing constant cutbacks by Congress, he noted. The S+K were able to access this fund to develop a tourism business plan. In the past, the S+K tribes have been almost passive participants in the tourist industry on the Flathead Reservation; now they are taking a more active approach, looking at how certain types of tourists can be encouraged. There is interest in developing programs to educate tourists and in eco-tourism, and in encouraging tribal members to be entrepreneurs in the tourist industry.

Mr. Acevedo said that all these government initiatives would be useless if the S+K tribal government did not change to fit the requirements of the business world. The 10 members of the tribal government council hold four-year terms, and the terms are staggered to allow overlap and continuity. "This arrangement creates stability," he explained. The average term served is 12-16 years, and some councillors have sat for more than 30 years. There is a civic service program to ensure job security for tribal government employees and to attract and keep highly qualified and motivated employees. Mr. Acevedo stressed that businesses have to believe they are moving into a stable environment, and the stability of the S+K tribal government has been a key reason for its success in business.

The tribal government provides assistance for higher education, and the reservation has a community college with 700 members, offering a four-year nursing program and many two-year associate degrees. Credits earned can be transferred to the state college, and students who leave the reservation are encouraged to return to work. One new program that has proved very successful funds students on the condition they return to work for their community. There are summer internships available to introduce university students to working for tribal government, and there is also an internship program for high school students.

A key to the success of the business enterprises has been separation of the business operations from political control. Mr. Acevedo said that in the past, tribal government politicians were interested primarily in job creation, and the bottom line of profits was virtually ignored. As a result, business managers were not encouraged to make the business a success, and the S+K tribal government found itself in a debt spiral, funding unprofitable businesses on a yearly basis.

Mr. Acevedo's organization set up the resort business four years ago with a different structure: the resort business was a separate corporation with its own board of directors that included members from the business community outside the reservation. Tribal government politicians gradually became comfortable with their arm's-length involvement with the business, happy not to have to deal with the day-to-day operations. The board of directors is happy with its autonomy and both groups agree that the bottom line is profitability. Since that first venture, the S+K Development Corporation has taken other businesses under its umbrella, but there is only one board of directors for all the businesses, keeping the process streamlined and simple.

Mr. Acevedo concluded by explaining that all S+K business ventures see the Flathead Reservation as a homeland. Business proposals must consider the resources and potential abuses of the lands, because the lands must be preserved for future generations. Environmental and social policy initiatives have included:

- A tribally managed wilderness area, the first in the U.S., which will be left in its pristine state. The initiative is paying off with the development of tourism; tourists appreciate the existence of the protected area, which is also habitat to the last grizzly bear pack in western Montana.
- A shoreline protection law to preserve the pristine waters of Flathead Lake.
- An aquatic lands protection law.
- Distinguishing the airshed above the reservation as Class One air, ensuring that future business development does not pollute the air.

Round Table Chair Ron Jamieson thanked Mr. Acevedo for his presentation. Mr. Jamieson added that a "Buy Aboriginal" policy has been talked about in Canada for years and should be a point of discussion at the Round Table, because the policy could "jump-start" the Aboriginal economy. In response to a question from Mr. Jamieson, Mr. Acevedo explained that the U.S. *Indian Tax Status Act* allows tribes to issue tax-free bonds, but the S+K tribes have not made use of the Act because it is limited to bonds issued for "essential governmental services" and does not allow bonds issued for economic development. He concluded by recommending that if Canada initiates similar legislation for tax-free bonds, the program should include bonds issued for business purposes.

Day 2

Theme III: Providing Services Within Communities

Noel Knockwood, Elder and Spiritual Leader of the Micmac Nation, opened the session with a prayer. Moderator Ron Rivard introduced Professor Corinne Jetté. Ms. Jetté is Assistant Professor in the Faculty of Engineering and Computer Science at Concordia University.

Overview of Discussion Papers

Ms. Jetté began her presentation by stating that a "spirit of harmony is needed for solutions to be found." Turning to William Lyall's paper, "Retaining Wealth and Control in Remote Aboriginal Communities," Ms. Jetté said that it provided a concrete model of economic development. The paper outlined the co-operative movement in Mr. Lyall's region and provided case studies to illustrate the way in which these co-operatives function. Aboriginal-owned services and businesses provide a solid base for the community by developing human as well as financial resources.

Mr. Lyall identified the importance of moving forward and the need for local financial institutions, specifically credit unions, to respond to a void that exists in the communities of the Northwest Territories. His paper questioned why the government was not supporting the establishment of credit unions in the Northwest Territories. Ms. Jetté concluded by stating that the N.W.T. co-operatives were a living example of community members working together to improve their community.

Ms. Jetté's paper, "Creating a Climate of Confidence: Providing Services within

Aboriginal Communities," set out to answer the questions posed by the Royal Commission. To accomplish this, Ms. Jetté divided her paper into two parts, dealing with problems and strategies. Ms. Jetté identified five barriers which exist to explain why so few Aboriginal people access business ventures. They are lack of strategic planning, lack of education, lack of communication, lack of gender equity, and lack of trust. In his presentation, Albert Rock spoke of the need to develop a focus and trust. Ms. Jetté said that if she had tried to create a model that would illustrate the title of her paper, she could not have done better than that presented by Albert Rock. "His story illustrated what can happen when a climate of confidence exists."

Ms. Jetté focused on the five strategies outlined in her paper. The first was the need to establish clear strategic plans and development priorities. This would lead to the achievement of learning opportunities. Ms. Jetté acknowledged that this may not be an easy objective to reach, but she asserted that planning was a skill that could be learned by anyone.

The second strategy identified was the need to develop a learning culture. In the Aboriginal community, the last 20 years can be compared to the more than 100 years of the Industrial Revolution. Ms. Jetté quoted Mr. Lyall's statement that "we are the first people in the history of mankind who have been obliged to travel from the stone age to the space age in one generation." Technology provides solutions, but technology has to be accessed in order for these solutions to become a reality. Many people are intimidated by technology, but this attitude must be overcome. Both parents and children have to be convinced of the key role that education plays.

The third strategy was the need to develop open communication within and among Aboriginal communities. Conferences like those sponsored by the Royal Commission help to generate this communication. With the use of machinery like faxes and modems, the age of missing communication is gone. Distance education takes on a new meaning for remote and rural communities with the use of these technologies.

The fourth strategy was the need to develop gender inclusiveness. Aboriginal communities need to develop all their best minds, regardless of gender. There is no room for hostility or exclusion; there is too much work to do. "Any form of exclusion just isn't acceptable." People should find solutions together for any problems that they face. The focus should be upon the development of Aboriginal specialists, not male or female Aboriginal specialists. People must be given role models if this is to occur. "The key word should be respect."

The final strategy was the need to develop business/consumer confidence. Entrepreneurs need trust if they are to survive and thrive. The idea of trust is a recurring one, and is perhaps the greatest challenge that is to be faced. "Everyone bears the responsibility to eliminate the cynicism, scepticism, destructive criticism and mistrust that has plagued Aboriginal communities in recent history."

Mr. Rivard asked Ms. Jetté if she had any comments about the papers prepared by Peter George and Peter Kuhn and by Renée Dupuis. These papers dealt with the issue of employment equity and focused upon statistics. Ms. Jetté responded that employment equity programs have not accomplished what they set out to do but have become merely statistical exercises. The numbers do not tell us anything but that the programs do not work. Exclusionary barriers exist within the work force, corporate culture and academic culture. Ms. Jetté suggested that Aboriginal leaders need to conduct outreach programs to recruit within their own communities. On-reserve training programs need to be implemented to teach Aboriginal peoples about "white corporate culture." Mr. Rivard commented upon the power of the statement that referred to Aboriginal people's movement from the stone age to the space age. Ms. Jetté responded that it is not correct for people who live in remote communities to ignore technology. That technology is already present in their communities in the form of, among other things, television and video games. It is obvious that the children already have the capacity to understand these forms of technology and that knowledge could be transferred to other technologies.

Models of Community and Individual Enterprise

Arctic Co-operatives Ltd.

Mr. Lyall, President of the Arctic Co-operatives Limited, informed the participants that the first Arctic co-operatives in the Northwest Territories were formed in 1960 and that today there are 35 co-operatives in existence. These Northwest Territories co-operatives affiliated over the years to form two co-operatively owned subsidiary service organizations, Arctic Co-operatives Limited and the Northwest Territories Co-operative Business Development Fund. The 100% local ownership and control of these co-operatives, in addition to the strong support services provided through these affiliations, has resulted in the co-operatives growing into a major force in the Northwest Territories. Mr. Lyall outlined two case studies (Pelly Bay and Pond Inlet) and focused on the benefits that these two communities have realized. Pelly Bay is a community of 410 people, 130 of whom make up the ownership base of their co-operative. The co-operative's activities include running the only retail store in the community, as well as running a small hotel, purchasing carvings for resale in the south, operating a heavy equipment contracting business, and providing agency services for the telephone, airline, and petroleum delivery. This co-operative paid $2.1 million worth of wages and dividends to Pelly Bay between 1988 and 1992, and in 1993 issued T4 slips to 89 residents, 45% of the total adult population.

Pond Inlet is a community of 970 people, 525 of whom make up the ownership base of their co-operative. The co-operative's activities include running a competitive retail outlet as well as a hotel facility and tourist lodge, providing agency services for petroleum and airlines and operating a building leasing service for offices and accommodations. This co-operative paid $2.1 million worth of wages and dividends to Pond Inlet between 1988 and 1992, and in 1993 issued T4 slips to 64 residents, 13% of the total adult population. These statistics demonstrate the success of the co-operatives, but do not show the staff development that has occurred in the various communities. This provides the true long-term development for the community.

Prior to 1950, these communities had been operating as cashless societies and the residents had no opportunities to amass capital. Today local assets total approximately $49 million and membership in co-operatives is close to 10,000. Mr. Lyall spoke of the 400 years that the Hudson's Bay Company reaped the benefits from northern communities, taking all the profits away to major cities in the south. The co-operatives help to ensure that this does not happen today. What is lacking in these communities, however, are local financial institutions. Many people have to travel thousands of kilometres in order to access financial institutions. Because of this, residents of the community are not able to receive financial advice, acquire loans, or develop savings. This is the major obstacle facing residents of northern communities and the co-operatives today.

Mr. Rivard asked Mr. Lyall to focus on the solutions needed to improve the situation in the Northwest Territories. Mr. Lyall responded that the major problem was the lack of local financial institutions. Five major banks approached to locate in remote areas said that it was too expensive to undertake such an operation. In addition, the Canadian Imperial Bank of Commerce has recently moved out of Fort Smith. Mr. Lyall would like to see more action on the part of the various government agencies to see that financial institutions are established in remote areas.

Advanced ThermoDynamics Company

Harry Jones, President of Advanced ThermoDynamics Company, told how the Batchewana Band Council got involved with the Advanced ThermoDynamics Company. In 1971, the Batchewana Band Council set aside land to form the Blue Heron Industrial Park near Sault Ste. Marie. It then formed Batchewana Band Industries Ltd (BBI). In 1985 the Band Council commissioned a study to discover how best to develop the Industrial Park. They were given two recommendations: they should attempt to purchase the buildings rather than lease them, and they should seek out a joint venture with another company. They were able to fulfil the first recommendation quite easily, and today they own 26,000 square feet of building space. In 1990, the Band Council was approached by an American tribe to form a joint venture in the American/Canadian defence industry. They commissioned another study to outline their best business options. Three key factors were identified through the report: they should join forces with a Canadian manufacturing company; they should keep business and politics separate; and they need a commitment from all the people involved. The BBI then proceeded to formulate a business plan that clearly enumerated their goals and objectives, and they prepared a mission statement to present to the Band Council This mission statement outlined their commitment to community development.

BBI then had to begin the search for an interested manufacturing company. They did not hold out much hope of success. However, they found a company in an unprecedented eight days, the Advanced ThermoDynamics Company of London, Ontario, which manufactured heaters and coolers for the transportation industry. BBI approached this company with their business proposal and set out to convince them to move their operations from London to the "far North" of Sault Ste. Marie. Before entering into partnership with BBI, the Advanced ThermoDynamics Company had contracted out all manufacturing except for the assembly of the heaters. By moving its operation to Sault Ste. Marie they could bring these contracts inhouse, control them better and increase the profit-margin. It accepted the offer of partnership.

In October 1992 the agreement was completed. BBI purchased 20% of the shares of the Advanced ThermoDynamics Company, with an option to buy the remaining shares within a seven-year period. A board of directors, made up of three First Nations members and four other shareholders, was formed. They will begin full operation by September 1993 and will double the number of their employees to 24. Some very large contracts have already been negotiated.

Round Table III: Providing Services Within Communities

Moderator Ron Rivard reviewed the fundamental question and introduced the Round Table participants, reminding them to focus their discussion on solutions. Jean-Yves Assiniwi, Special Adviser to the Native Council of Canada, began by challenging the fundamental question, saying that it was futile to discuss economic development without also discussing community development. The two must work in tandem, he said. "How can we create viable businesses in communities with no running water" and other basic services, he asked. "How can we expect to go from a welfare state" to one that provides a supportive environment for business.

Winnie Giesbrecht, President of Nakiska Place, also wanted to challenge the fundamental question. "Before we get into solution building, we have to deal with the issue of accountability and control," she said; politics should be kept separate from business. "As Aboriginal women, we lack access to capital; there is no way for Aboriginal women even to think of developing businesses of any kind." Some time ago, when she approached a bank manager for a business loan, she was told that maybe she should get married to have access to equity. "We need something in place that recognizes our needs."

Terry Henderson, Director of Commercial Development for the Department of Indian Affairs and Northern Development, said there are opportunities to access resources from existing sources, but that the sources are not widely known. He wondered how Aboriginal people could improve their relations with banking institutions, suggesting that Aboriginal communities needed to ask themselves what leverage they have at their disposal. The fact that resources are flown in and out of reserves was leverage, or a bargaining chip, he said. Aboriginal people should "walk in there [to banks] and demand better services and access." The alternative, he added, was for Aboriginal peoples to establish their own financial institutions.

Mr. Henderson noted that every year, the federal government procures about $10 billion worth of services from the open market, and that $4 billion of this amount goes through an open bidding process; the information is available on-line for a nominal fee. "Knowing what's out there is half the battle," he said, adding that knowing about contracts is not a guarantee of landing them.

The moderator asked Mr. Henderson how Aboriginal people could get on a "level playing field" to compete with non-Aboriginal businesses. Mr. Henderson said he didn't have the answer but that many organizations, including his own department, had resources available to help Aboriginal businesses develop contract proposals.

Scott Smith, Vice President of Economic and Corporate Development for the Canadian Council for Native Business, said that lack of access to capital remains one of the most pervasive barriers to establishing Aboriginal businesses. He said the "government is virtually broke" and cannot be considered a reliable source of revenue. Unless Aboriginal people do something collectively to create pools of capital large enough to make a difference, "we will be in a tough position" economically, he said. He believed there were ways to make this happen, adding that co-operatives were one example.

Terry Forth, of Aboriginal Economic Programs at Industry, Science and Technology Canada (ISTC), said that Aboriginal communities should be encouraged to learn from each other's success. ISTC recently completed a review of Aboriginal business, learning that the success rate was better than for non-Aboriginal businesses. The majority of new Aboriginal businesses in the study were in rural or remote areas, and the most successful businesses were located on reserves. He suggested that the goal should be developing "economic linkages" in Aboriginal communities. Ways should be found to trap the "enormous dollars" spent for goods and services on reserves, and for existing businesses to work together to help develop a critical mass of capital.

Jeannie Marie Jewell, Director of the Métis Development Corporation of the Northwest Territories, and MLA in the Northwest Territories, commented on a statement made earlier in the day about the lack of banking institutions in the Northwest Territories, and that the Canadian Imperial Bank of Commerce

(CIBC) was moving out of Fort Smith. Ms. Jewell said that the Bank of Montreal was planning to move in when the CIBC left.

Ms. Jewell's main concern was the lack of transportation infrastructure in the North. Remote communities need more access to air transport and more highways need to be built. If communities are to grow, the government must support basic infrastructure development, she said. She agreed with Scott Smith's comment about the need to "wean ourselves from government" funding, adding that since the government came into the Northwest Territories three or four decades ago, the traditional nomadic lifestyle of Aboriginal people in the territory has been virtually destroyed. There is a need for education, she said, adding that the goal of Aboriginal business ventures should be total ownership of the business.

Robin Wortman, a Métis and Executive Director of the National Council for the Advancement of Native Development Officers (CANDO), said it was important to focus on the solutions that have already been found, the success stories. His organization tries to focus on the positive, looking at developing strengths. CANDO runs formal, accessible and relevant educational programs for economic development officers working in communities, he said, adding that women play an important role in this work. He agreed that Aboriginal organizations need to learn from each other, and that the long-term goal should be self-sufficiency.

He added that the government has to learn the difference between expenditures and investments, and that the latest federal budget cutbacks in the area of training programs was a signal that it is not prepared to invest in Aboriginal peoples. He added that his own organization was hit by the cuts and, to the amusement of the other participants, he asked anyone who could help out to call his organization's 1-800 number.

"Money Should Stay in the Community"

Mary Jamieson, representing Pauktuutit, the Inuit Women's Association of Canada, agreed it was critical to built economic linkages in Aboriginal communities. Inuit women, she said, face particular problems trying to start business ventures, problems such as language barriers. Her organization is seeking funds to hire Inuit women who speak Inuktitut to help other Inuit women develop businesses. "Women should not need to learn English to prosper," she said. Pauktuutit is planning to open a retail store in Ottawa to market goods made by Inuit women and to train Inuit women in retail business. "We want to put The Bay out of our communities," she said, explaining that the company charged too much for supplies and materials needed for crafts. Her own organization would like to supply these materials. "We're tired of the south robbing the North," she said. "The money should stay in the community."

Jacques Meunier, from the Quebec Secretariat on Aboriginal Affairs, said that Aboriginal business people have made great steps against adverse conditions.

The goal is to create an environment of confidence in Aboriginal communities. Over the years, he has come to believe that many developers and entrepreneurs (in non-Aboriginal communities) in Northern Quebec lack perseverance, and that ways must be found to support people in communities who are potential business leaders. He added that business leaders often come from the political arena; for this reason, it was not possible to separate politics from development. Development means change, he said, and change cannot take place respecting the rules of comfort. "Rules have to be changed. We need an upheaval, and people have to change, be replaced." He added that communities need competitive business environments, and that the goal should not be to drive The Bay out of a community but to open up a well organized competitor.

Mr. Smith believed that leaders under self-government would likely be entrepreneurs, people who know what it's like to fight and negotiate for what they want. He recently came across statistics showing that if the standard of living of Aboriginal people in this country were raised to that of non-Aboriginal people, the GNP would rise by 2.5% – a bigger boost to the economy than free trade. "We have to go to the private sector," he said; businesses need to begin reflecting seriously on the implications of working with Aboriginal peoples. He urged the Royal Commission to send a strong message to corporate Canada: "You must do business with Aboriginal peoples."

Moderator Ron Rivard, reflecting on Mr. Meunier's statement about competing with The Bay, said that the words "The Bay" and "competition" don't reconcile themselves. "How do we take on The Bay?" he asked. "How do we get to a level playing field?"

Ms. Jamieson responded that in order for Aboriginal business to be in a position to compete, two things must change: a climate of self-confidence must be created in Aboriginal communities, starting with education in school about Aboriginal history; and Aboriginal people must give up their attitude of not supporting Aboriginal businesses.

Mr. Wortman, referring to the $4 billion in government contracts available under an open-bidding process, said that the figure is misleading because contracts on the on-line information system are larger than $25,000; the size of the contracts excludes many small Aboriginal businesses from consideration. He suggested that the government would look at sole-sourcing for procurement if it were serious about supporting Aboriginal businesses. He added that elected leaders must be kept separate from economic development organizations if investment is to occur in communities.

Mr. Forth said the focus should be on building a full-scale entrepreneurial base in Aboriginal communities, one that covers all arrangements and takes a long-term view. "We have to figure out ways to attract young Aboriginal people to considering business careers," he added. As economic development grows, there will be an increasing need for skilled people to manage business operations.

Should Politics and Business be Separate?

The moderator brought the discussion back to the question of separating business from politics; he wondered if this were possible when politicians play so vital a role in Aboriginal communities. Ms. Jamieson insisted that the two must remain separate, although politicians can support business through policies and lobbying activities. Ms. Giesbrecht said the two can't be separated because Aboriginal businesses need the support of political leaders in order to survive. She added that the government's open bidding process for contracts must be changed to expand the definition of "business," because the current definition excludes many social services. Mr. Assiniwi added that the word "politics" must also be defined before meaningful discussion can take place on this issue.

Mr. Assiniwi said it would be useful to compare the experience of the Aboriginal land claims agreements in James Bay and Alaska to learn "how we can get from survival mode to strategic planning." After the agreement in Alaska was signed, the money was channelled into business ventures. Many of these ventures have since failed, and the money is running out. The James Bay Agreement, in comparison, secured the future of traditional activities and created an unthreatening climate in the communities. Some of the money was used to develop the social service net and promote the development of businesses in the social services sector. The "pure business sector" was built on this ground work. He noted that if business is perceived as a threat to communities, business ventures will never get off the ground. He added that outside of claim settlement and resource-rich communities, social nets do not have secure funding, and, in urban areas, these nets are vastly inadequate.

Mr. Smith pointed out that young people need to learn that "getting into business is okay and will not threaten who we are." He mentioned that an internship program to train Aboriginal youth in a corporate culture has already had 450 successful graduates. He said that the government has a strong role to play in long-term development, and if the political will is there, development can occur very quickly. Assistance can take the form of tax-free zones on reserves, for example. Mr. Smith criticized the recent federal proposal to impose income tax on Aboriginal people in urban areas who are not directly associated with their reserves. He explained that many small businesses have been built under the old regulations and that these businesses will fail if the new policy is implemented.

Jane Gottfriedson, representing the Native Women's Association of Canada, said that "we have a lot of work to do to prepare our children, to give them role models to follow." Aboriginal people and communities must heal if economic development initiatives are to be successful. She added that "it is horrendous what Aboriginal women have to go through to access small packets of money" for business development. Ms. Gottfriedson agreed that accountability was an important issue. In many communities, "it gets down to who you know," and the same people sit on many tiers of community boards, controlling the access to funds.

Mr. Henderson, returning to the issue of procurement of government contracts under the open bidding process, said that while it was true that the contracts online were large contracts, it was still possible for smaller businesses to benefit through sub-contracting and joint-venture arrangements. He added that the Treasury Board recently made Aboriginal economic development an objective, a move that could be a "leg up" for Aboriginal people to participate in the procurement process.

After the moderator opened the discussion to the floor, the first speaker was Pat Baxter from Economic Development for Canadian Aboriginal Women. Referring to Mr. Assiniwi's remarks about community development, she said that her consultations with Aboriginal women have shown that they have the same concerns. "We need to build infrastructures that will support women," such as daycare centres, she said. There needs to be strong liaison with the private sector; her own organization has drawn up a list of suggested policy initiatives for private businesses. She mentioned a recent meeting in Montreal that resulted in the formation of a committee, made up of representatives from the Aboriginal and business communities, to discuss possible business development. A report from this committee is expected shortly. She added that foundations are starting to show active interest in supporting Aboriginal businesses at the grassroots level.

Oscar Kistabish made many observations. Noting that the Royal Commission made use of interpretation and translation services, he said that the same services were available from Algonquin-owned firms. He said that people need to be educated about business opportunities, and experienced business people should be prepared to help the beginners. Support for new businesses must extend beyond the start-up date. The individuals working in the business, as well as their families, may need support and follow-up attention. Drawing on his experience as a self-employed electrician, Mr. Kistabish said that in many Aboriginal communities, economic development simply means catching up to non-Aboriginal communities. Ways must be found to reduce the high unemployment rates, and the government must increase its efforts to support Aboriginal business initiatives.

Ron Rivard, referring to the "level playing field" issue, said a recent study by the Métis National Council showed that the CAEDS was underfunding Métis people to the tune of $160 million. Aboriginal people need to find new ways to approach business development, not depend on the government for funding. "We have to look at a full range of financial services for Métis," he said. Referring to the issue of government contracts, he related the story of his personal experience with the program. After a verbal agreement had been reached by all parties and a business venture was in its final development, the government pulled out of the sole-source contract, saying that non-Aboriginal people would perceive it as a bad deal. His recommendation was that if future deals are made with the government, there must be a way of ensuring that the government lives up to its end of the bargain.

"People Must Learn that it's Okay to be an Indian and a Business Person"

Don Ross said that people must learn that "it's okay to be an Indian and be a doctor, lawyer or business person." He said that "a lot of people are making money off our poverty," a situation that must be turned around. He suggested that Aboriginal businesses can learn from the success stories in the non-Aboriginal business community. He wondered why Aboriginal people were never given the chance to be a part of the very big business ventures, adding that there must be a way to attain access to the Bronfmans, and other big players in the Canadian business scene, to discuss joint venture initiatives.

George Bacon, Director, Native Benefit Plan, Village of the Hurons, made two recommendations: that economic development be linked with the private sector, and that strategic planning be a priority, especially as a long-term, partnership approach.

Allan Reid from Shell Canada said his organization has a responsibility to extend as much economic activity as possible to local communities. There have been some success stories, and Mr. Reid listed the characteristics of Aboriginal communities that have had successful links with Shell Canada: the leadership is committed to creating jobs and fostering a business environment; the community has access to capital or knows how to access it; the community has a long-term plan for business growth; and there is a willingness to recognize that, at least in the beginning, skilled people will have to be brought in from outside the community to help with business development. He added that he would like to say that politics has no place in business, but that there is a difference between politicians and the government, and the government can play a supportive role.

Chesley Andersen, from the Inuit Tapirisat of Canada, said that politics should not play any role in the day-to-day operations of a business but it can help foster a good business environment. An example would be political intervention in an anti-fur lobby campaign. He added that Inuit and Métis people pay taxes, and the issue is not whether Aboriginal people must pay taxes but what they are used for. Tax money should be returned communities, he said.

Bill Lyall, President of Arctic Co-operatives Limited, pointed out that the reason that credit unions were the banking institution of choice in the Northwest Territories is that credit unions keep their resources in the communities. He noted that only five communities in the Northwest Territories have banking institutions, creating time delays that are hard on businesses. For example, it can take two weeks for a deposit by mail to reach the bank.

Theme IV: Expanding Employment in the Canadian Economy

Overview of Discussion Papers

Moderator Ron Rivard introduced Peter George. Mr. George is currently the President of the Council of Ontario Universities. He is also Professor of Economics at McMaster University.

Mr. George identified education as the key to expanding employment. He addressed four themes in his discussion of the two papers, "Expanding Employment in the Canadian Economy" by Peter George and Peter Kuhn, and "Aboriginal Peoples and Employment Equity" by Renée Dupuis. These four themes were the earnings and employment record, access to the labour market, access to education, and equity programs.

Earnings and employment records allow for the comparison of the labour force activity of Aboriginal and non-Aboriginal people. A study of these records revealed that Aboriginal people are less likely to participate in labour force activity, and they are more likely to have a lower income and a lower level of educational attainment. This record tells us that labour force activity is positively influenced by educational attainment and work experience. Regardless of this, however, an unexplained wage gap still exists between Aboriginal and non-Aboriginal people. Contributing to this wage gap are cultural differences, unobserved income data and discrimination. It is important that, in the future, the amount of the wage gap caused by discrimination is identified and that steps are taken to eliminate this discrimination.

Canadian employment opportunities that are predicated on human resources must be highlighted. This is again dependent upon education and skills training. Attention must also be focused upon the displacement that exists from shrinking employment sectors. Again it has been shown that the amount of displacement experienced decreases with the amount of education attained. There is also a need to continue the study of the labour force activity of Aboriginal people. This can be accomplished by looking at the 1991 Census data results, as well as data released by the Aboriginal Peoples Survey (a post-census survey).

An individual's access to the labour market depends on whether he or she is on-reserve or off-reserve. Off-reserve, competition is based on skills, education and work experience. Employee turnover, ghettoization and discrimination must also be addressed when looking at the off-reserve labour market. On-reserve, a "thin labour market" exists. There are fewer full-year, full-time jobs available. An issue to be addressed when dealing with on-reserve labour force activity is how many people are participating in non-cash-paying, traditional activities. A researcher must also look at the trade-off that exists for an individual between participating in these traditional activities and seeking employment off-reserve.

An individual's access to education begins in the family and community. Adequate elementary schools must be available to teach students the skills they will require in order to pursue higher education. A high priority must be attached to education. Students must be motivated to complete and continue their education. Post-secondary support programs, both scholastic and personal, must be available. Employment equity programs must be examined and altered to make them more effective in eliminating the unexplained wage gap that exists between Aboriginal and non-Aboriginal peoples.

Mr. George offered three recommendations to the Royal Commission regarding Aboriginal employment policies. He suggested that study be continued on Aboriginal labour force participation through examination of the data collected by the 1991 Census and Aboriginal Peoples Survey. Priority must be given to the positive effect on Aboriginal peoples of education and training, specifically high-end skills training. Finally, a close examination of equity programs and affirmative action programs should be undertaken to determine what part of the unexplained wage gap is the result of discrimination. Mr. George concluded by stating that "job equity begins with education."

Mr. Rivard questioned Mr. George on his call for study of the data collected through the 1991 Census and Aboriginal Peoples Survey. He questioned the quality of the questions asked by those surveys and also of the data analysis that would follow. He asked Mr. George how much emphasis should be placed on current data and how better data could be obtained. Mr. George responded that while he understood that the 1991 Census data were not perfect, it was "important that we do the best we can with the best data that we have available in order to see the extent of the problem." He suggested that a survey administered by the Aboriginal communities themselves would perhaps be more successful.

Models of Community and Individual Enterprise

Syncrude Canada Limited

Jim Carbery, of Syncrude Canada Limited, is the Senior Adviser on Native Development. His company is located 20 miles north of Fort McMurray and produces synthetic crude oil. It is the second largest company of its kind in Canada and directly employs 4,300 people. Between 1978 and 1982, 210 Aboriginal people were directly employed by Syncrude, 60% in the mines, and $3 million was directed toward Aboriginal businesses. In 1992, 275 Aboriginal people were directly employed, 40% in the mines, and $28 million was directed toward Aboriginal businesses. In 1992, the average term of employment for an Aboriginal employee was just over eight years, and the average age of Aboriginal employees was 35 years.

The three thrusts to the Aboriginal program at Syncrude Canada are training, employment and education; local community development; and business development. The program also works to change attitudes within the company, by focusing on middle management, and to change attitudes within the communities. Syncrude does not go into a community unless it is invited. The company will not tell a community what it should do; its goal is to "assist, when requested, to find community felt needs." The model that the company uses is to communicate (the what), educate (the why) and motivate or energize (their commitment). Its ability to do these things effectively depends on the quality of the local leadership within the communities. The results of the program are measured by what the community does for itself, not by what Syncrude does for them. Syncrude works with both formal and informal leaders within a community to ensure that information is being disseminated through a "multi-channel" communication network, and it works with all segments of a community population (different bands, Métis, and transients). The company's goal is to assist the community toward independent human resource development.

Syncrude is also involved in the development of various community buildings, such as training centres, ice rinks and tourist lodges. It also helps with community issues when asked. The company is involved in training in such areas as community leadership, community visioning, addictions, time management, conflict management and life skills. Syncrude is also involved in "co-ordinating, expediting and facilitating meetings among industry, government and communities." The key for all of these functions is to assist these communities in moving from dependence toward independence.

In regard to employment, training and education, Syncrude identifies and communicates expected employment standards (now set at a minimum of grade twelve education); sets the same work performance standards for all employees; provides cross-cultural training to management staff; provides opportunities for social interaction between Aboriginal and non-Aboriginal employees; and provides scholarships and summer employment for Aboriginal students.

In the area of business development, Syncrude is aggressive in identifying and issuing contracts with Aboriginal individuals and companies; sets realistic annual target figures; negotiates with Aboriginal-owned businesses; promotes, among its contractors, the hiring of qualified Aboriginal individuals as sub-contractors; and publicly recognizes the success of its Aboriginal contractors.

The principles of Syncrude's Native Development Program are to make long-term commitments; publish policies; set programs that will keep the organization moving; set, communicate and monitor standards; avoid tokenism; define and communicate future goals; provide positive Aboriginal role models; place responsibility for results where they belong within the organization; and build relations between industry and Aboriginal communities. The future goals of Syncrude are, by 1997, to have 400 Aboriginal employees and $30 million in Aboriginal contract work. These goals may have to be re-evaluated, however, due to company restructuring.

Métis Urban Entrepreneur

Laverne Poitras-Young, a Métis woman from Edmonton, is 100% owner of three companies, the Genoch Gardens Daycare, J & R Pizza & Pub, and Gayla Hair and Nails Limited. Ms. Poitras-Young employs 21 individuals, half of whom are Aboriginal people. She was asked by the Royal Commission to present a "success story." She considers herself a person first, and then a minority person, both as a Métis and as a woman. It was upon the death of her father that she began her business career. She set out to uphold the strong set of standards that he had lived by, and she worked to pass them on to her two sons, now aged 17 and 18. She wanted to foster in her sons a pride of who they were and where they had come from. She considers her sons as her "first success story." She also considers personal growth and development as critical to business success.

In 1989, Ms. Poitras-Young identified that a void existed in Métis child care. She approached a conventional lending institution for a loan to start a daycare to fill this void but was denied because she did not have any capital or experience in business management. She then approached a Métis lending institution and was given a loan. This loan, however, was at a very high interest rate for a very short term (three years) and no operating funds were allocated to her. After receiving her first loan, she had to return to the Métis lending institution and apply for an operating funds loan. She was granted the loan, again at a high rate of interest and under the stipulation that it be paid back within six months.

Three years later Ms. Poitras-Young began distributing a line of clothing. Her enterprise was a success and she decided to purchase a hair salon from which to operate. The Métis lending institution denied her a loan on the grounds that she was now an investor. She was granted a loan by a conventional lending institution because she now had capital and a proven business record.

Ms. Poitras-Young identifies commitment, dedication and hard work as the keys to her success. She overcame many obstacles and as a result is able to provide employment for others. She recommended that the Royal Commission recommend allowing Aboriginal business people to grow and prosper by ensuring that reasonable equity loans are available. She would also like to see loans allocated for business expansion.

Mr. Rivard asked Mr. Carbery of Syncrude what he would recommend to change the attitudes and discrimination that Aboriginal people face every day. Mr. Carbery responded that his company attempts to do this through the time spent educating middle management. They take managers into Aboriginal communities. They try to get "people to know each other as individual, as human beings."

Robin Wortman asked Mr. Carbery whether, in his experience, Aboriginal business people met with resistance from financial institutions and whether they have to pay a higher interest rate. He also wanted to know how many jobs have been created at Syncrude and what has been done to meet individuals' training needs. Mr. Carbery responded that he knew that some Aboriginal people experienced some difficulty getting loans from lending institutions and that his company assists its contractors to help their employees get the training required.

Muriel Stanley-Venne applauded Syncrude for its efforts but cautioned that an advocate should be put in place within the company to deal with the problems faced by Aboriginal employees. Aboriginal people, and particularly Aboriginal women, often face difficult experiences on the job. Men often feel threatened by the entry of women into the non-traditional labour force, an example being the construction industry. A company must deal with the reality of the discrimination that Aboriginal men and women face.

Elder Noel Knockwood complimented the presenters and stated that he had two recommendations regarding employment equity. He said that employment equity programs must originate from the top of the corporate world and that employment equity officers should be representative of all minority groups.

Round Table IV: Expanding Employment in the Canadian Economy

Moderator Ron Rivard opened the meeting by asking participants to identify themselves and to focus on practical answers. Both he and Pat Baxter of EDCAW praised Syncrude's approach to employment equity for Aboriginal people.

Ruth Williams, President, All Nations Trust Company, noted that employment equity in the public sector has not been fully successful. She recommended a survey of Aboriginal people who had been hired through such programs and had quit their jobs, to identify the positive and negative aspects of the program and why these people left. She also recommended training to prepare Aboriginal people for senior management. "Management depends on values," she said, noting that a national initiative will work only when Aboriginal people are in senior management. Bill Draper agreed with the survey but cautioned that exit interviews should not be conducted by the leaver's supervisor, since supervisory problems are often involved when people quit.

Ron Williams, a Yellowknife Aboriginal entrepreneur, said that employment initiatives should focus on the private sector and on small business, since this is the fastest growing job market. In today's global economy, knowledge, networking, and sharing are critical; people needs skills and education to compete. Some Aboriginal people may want the traditional life, but others want more opportunities. Youth with education and high expectations return to their communities, only to find no jobs, and are drawn to cities in which they must compete. Investing in these people is simple common sense.

Kuan R. Yang, Senior Research Officer, Gabriel Dumont Institute, has researched unemployment among Aboriginal people and identified two groups: the displaced, and the misplaced. The displaced unemployed generally have few skills and little education and are unable to compete in the job market. Given under-education and dependence on resource-based industry, most jobless Aboriginal people fall into this group. The misplaced unemployed are educated, but their education does not suit them for existing job opportunities. To deal with these groups, Mr. Yang made four recommendations. For the displaced unemployed:

- First Nations communities should take operational control over education; and
- an Aboriginal-specific program should be used to upgrade basic literacy and numeracy skill. He noted that many reserves concentrate on language skills, not number skills.

For the misplaced unemployed:

- there should be orientation for people going into post-secondary education; and
- such orientation should be market-oriented, with Aboriginal-specific content.

Renée Dupuis of the Canadian Human Rights Commission agreed that federal employment equity has not worked well and targeted education as the solution. Employment equity has two components: giving individuals access to the work force; and collective development. She stressed the need for proper documentation. This is a complex area, and both government and Aboriginal peoples must take on responsibility for dealing with problems. The government's job is to remedy discrimination and eradicate prejudice. But Aboriginal people must decide what they want and must do.

As an example, Ms. Dupuis said that school boards should adapt their curricula to suit the needs of Aboriginal children, including altering the usual school year to allow time on the land. On the other hand, Aboriginal people must be reconciled with education, hard as the process is for them, since it involves facing skepticism and some deculturalization.

At the moderator's invitation, Howard Green, Director, National Aboriginal Management Board, spoke about the Pathways to Success program. The critical issue was whether the program was to follow an economic or social agenda. Syncrude might see Aboriginal employment as an economic imperative, given location and employment needs, but the federal government's needs and interests are different.

Mr. Green stressed accountability. Management must be responsible and its performance must be reviewed; senior managers may not take employment equity very seriously. And this accountability must be to the communities that Employment and Immigration serves, not merely to the federal minister.

As for recruiting, "The federal government has to become a sexy place for Aboriginal people," Mr. Green said, noting that government service is not usually high on their agendas. In addition, government programs must be clearly directed and less complicated. He suggested having one single arm's-length agency to deal with employment equity for Aboriginal people. Such an agency would act as an umbrella for different programs.

In answer to a question from the moderator, Mr. Green said that the original Pathways program was the result of a tripartite agreement among CEIC, ISTC, and DIAND. Such an arrangement is problematic, for each department "brings its baggage with it." Any Aboriginal agency should divorce itself from the government. He asked whether agencies could work together to control the red tape and noted that the closer a program was to the community, the higher the success rate.

Les Stach of Imperial Oil Resources Ltd. supported the one-agency idea. Industry finds it confusing and frustrating to have to deal with many organizations and agencies as well. A single umbrella agency would make good economic sense. He commended the Syncrude program; not all oil and gas companies are this progressive, but dialogue has begun between Aboriginal people and the industry, and industry is waking up to economic realities. The two groups should be in an educational partnership and value their diversity.

"Get Out and Dance"

Chesley Andersen, Vice President of the Inuit Tapirisat of Canada, noted that the rural perspective was rather different. Role models are few and far between; employment opportunities are usually in short-term businesses that often fail. Therefore Aboriginal people need almost continuous retraining.

He enumerated three categories of unemployed: first, older workers with little education; second, high school dropouts or graduates; third, university graduates. Even among the third group, employment can be a problem. "There's only so much demand for teachers and nurses."

The second group often tries for training in the trades but finds few employment opportunities on-reserve, and their interest diminishes over time. Mr. Andersen called for Aboriginal control at the regional or local level to identify employment opportunities and to steer young people in training directions that could be fruitful. Standard criteria, such as UIC benefits, should be waived to ensure that young people get appropriate training. Communities should study their potential for economic development. "What infrastructure do we have? What training do we need?" Mr. Andersen asked. Take tourism as an example; the North should find its own solutions instead of adopting southern strategies.

In answer to a question from the moderator, Mr. Andersen said that the North could avoid southern influence and develop its own role models through a joint venture approaches, taking what was appropriate from southern expertise. But in tourism, local people should be trained as interpreters; they often take for granted a landscape that outsiders see as magnificent.

Bill Draper of the Winnipeg Chamber of Commerce also works with the Canadian Executive Service Organization. He advised Aboriginal groups to ask CESO volunteers to advise in setting up businesses, and to become involved with Chambers of Commerce. If there is a local Chamber, Mr. Draper said, "get involved; turn its direction to your needs." If there is no Chamber, "establish one of your own." He noted that white business people know that their society is part of the problem and may feel shy about approaching Aboriginal people. "They're like two kids at a school dance, staring across at each other and longing to get out there and dance. So don't be shy; go ask them."

Ms. Williams noted that unemployment in Aboriginal communities runs at 70% to 80%; there are high rates of illiteracy and school dropouts. "How are we going to counter this?" People under 24 years of age constitute 62% of the Aboriginal population. "We have to instil the attitude in them that education and training are the future. We must share our successes." But it is also important to tell young people that a university diploma is not essential; trades are important too, and experience is as valuable as education.

She recommended cultural content in all programming, support for Aboriginal educational institutions, and establishing Aboriginal apprenticeship boards. "Establish networks; use connections. Do strategic community planning, and bring in all the stakeholders. Focus on cottage and micro-industries, and use lending circles." If Aboriginal businesses must pay taxes, their taxes should be redirected into training programs.

Florence Gaucher, a Métis businesswoman, also called for human development and for focusing on youth and children, to break the circle of dependency. "We're all successes, in this room. We know what worked. We should be models." Barriers should be seen as challenges to be overcome. Aboriginal people should foster determination and confidence and teach these to young people. "But we must involve the elders; we must draw on their wisdom, support, and emotional and spiritual guidance" and teach the young their culture and language. Money may be a barrier to education, but with parental involvement, "we can do it."

Ms. Gaucher recommended that Aboriginal people make choices and determine their talents. "Don't wait for a chance; take a spade and dig for it." We should take responsibility for the future; "we know what went wrong; now we should fix it." She called for joint ventures with white entrepreneurs, her own road into the business world. Teamwork was essential. "Our leaders should bring us all together, First Nations, Inuit, Métis, white people."

Jim Carbery. Special Adviser to Syncrude, made three recommendations. First, training should be job-specific. Second, Pathways boards should involve the best possible people. And third, Aboriginal communities should build on their strengths.

Ms. Baxter, representing the perspective of Aboriginal training institutions, made two recommendations. First, that government, the private sector, and Aboriginal organization should support such programs, especially adult education. Mature students, especially re-entrants, have a better track record with education than many young people. Second, the private sector should endow bursaries and scholarships for Aboriginal people whose education is not covered by government program – those who live off-reserve or are non-status, Métis, or Inuit.

Mr. Green agreed that the provinces must be involved in Aboriginal training institutions. The provinces are responsible for accreditation and academic standards. Aboriginal institutions do a far better job for Aboriginal students than non-Aboriginal schools, but they are on the margin. He called for provincial support, especially in urban areas.

"The Two Ends Must Meet"

Ray Hawco, Assistant Secretary to Cabinet, Province of Newfoundland and Labrador, had kept quiet because his province has no policy on employment equity for Aboriginal people. The province is involved in some initiatives, but government attitudes are hard to change. "We're sluggish," Mr. Hawco admitted. "As a province, we see that our service delivery fails miserably with Aboriginal people." Dialogue is the essential first step; "the two ends must meet." He called for an end to any confrontational approach and agreed wholeheartedly with the discussion he had heard at the meeting.

Mr. Williams, responding to Mr. Draper, agreed that Chambers of Commerce could open doors. He noted that the Canadian population is aging, while Aboriginal youth is a fast-growing group. The shift into high-tech industries would require a well educated population, but 70% of Northwest Territories Aboriginal youth drop out of high school. He suggested a mentor program, assigning adults to young people in Grade 9 to help students make intelligent choices and to encourage and help them. This could be developed into a mentor network nation-wide, which would create extremely valuable contacts.

The moderator opened the meeting to the floor. Muriel Stanley-Venne spoke strongly of the need for Aboriginal involvement at the highest decision-making levels. "I don't want crumbs from Syncrude; I want a piece of the company. I want Aboriginal participation at the board of directors level." In industry, change will come from the top down. She also called for democracy and openness in the Pathways to Success program, saying that decisions were not always made on the basis of merit. She had put together a program to train young Métis women in business skills, and her application had been turned down.

Satsun George, Speaker for the Wet'suwet'en Hereditary Chiefs, told the meeting, "I want to pinch myself. We're actually here to talk solutions." He said that the root of economic problems was that Aboriginal people had been confined to reserves. "We've got to spend time making the kids feel good, building confidence through education and employment."

In his community, "we make the first move. We occupy the land. Then we tell business, 'You're on our land; you're going to be involved. We're partners.' The companies learn. We have our own training programs; we have nothing to do with employment equity or affirmative action. We know what we want."

Referring to Mr. Draper's metaphor about the school dance, Satsun George advised Aboriginal people to tell Canadian business this: "You don't want to dance? We'll drag you out on the dance floor!" His people take possession of the land; the companies respect this; and the sluggish government will simply have to play catch-up. He told participants that they should be role models not only for young people but for each other.

Commissioner Paul Chartrand, responding to Mr. Green's comments about responsibility, asked for a clarification on what this meant. For example, policymakers are responsible to legislators, who are responsible to the electorate. Existing boards are accountable to the minister, not to Aboriginal people. He asked Mr. Green for a clearer definition of this issue.

Mr. Green answered that Mr. Chartrand was right about existing boards. Governments may ask for advice, but they are not forced to accept it. He suggested that board decision making and funding would be accountable to Aboriginal people if they were Aboriginal boards. He said that he himself believes that the Pathways board should have to answer to Ms. Stanley-Venne, not to the minister. Mr. Chartrand noted that the mechanism of accountability was something that would need to be clarified as well.

Jim Swiss, Manager, Environment and Safety, Canadian Association of Petroleum Producers, recalled how the consultation process began between his industry and Aboriginal people, first with Canadian Indian Energy. "Yes, there was shyness." But that meeting led to two Chief-to-Chief conferences resulting in a burst of activity – joint ventures, clarification of the principles under which industry would operate, joint working committees, recommendations. Above all, CAP was here in force at this meeting. "We've made representations to Energy, Mines and Resources on the devolution of power to First Nations," Mr. Swiss told the meeting. He urged all concerned to get past the shyness and get the dance started.

Ron Rivard advised the Royal Commission to recommend that Métis people get equal treatment in the Pathways program and equal funding for training.

Another delegate, discussing employment equity, noted that federal government managers often have one bad experience with an Aboriginal employee and give up immediately. "They won't ask for a second dance." He recommended support networks for Aboriginal people in the federal government, who often face discrimination from both sides. "Their own people call them apples. But they're trailblazers." The public service unions must also be brought onside.

In Regina, he continued, an inventory with names of 4,000 Aboriginal people has been set up to try to match jobs with individuals. But educational requirements keep rising, even for bus drivers. "We're always playing catch-up."

Johanne Robertson made two recommendations on the subject of Aboriginal training institutions: first, to establish specific mechanisms among federal and provincial government, Aboriginal organizations, business, and education to give young people the choices they need; and second, to encourage federal/provincial governments to help these institutions. Funding is federal; control over education is provincial. It is essential that training for Aboriginal people respect their culture and values; ideally, it should be provided by Aboriginal instructors.

Day 3

Theme V: Building Institutions and Policies for Long-Term Economic Development

After Chair Ron Jamieson had called the meeting to order, Elder Noel Knockwood lit the sweetgrass and offered prayer in the six directions, asking the Creator to be with those present and offering thanks to Grandmother-Grandfather Creator for the earth's bounty. Moderator Ruth Williams introduced the keynote speaker, Professor Joseph P. Kalt of the John F. Kennedy School of Government, Harvard University. Mr. Kalt is co-director of the Harvard Project on Indian Economic Development.

Keynote Presentation

Mr. Kalt began by describing the methodology of the Harvard Project. It began when economists noted the extreme poverty of American Aboriginal peoples and asked the crucial question: "Why?" The factors cited for lack of economic development were the same factors that affect developing economies in general: lack of training and capital, isolation, too much or too little or simply wrong planning, governmental inadequacy or instability, factionalism, lack of entrepreneurial skills, a low savings rate, racism in surrounding society, limited resources, and the like. These are obstacles in many other societies as well.

Nonetheless, some tribes are doing well, "breaking away from the pack," as Mr. Kalt said. To determine what the factors were for success or failure, the project used graduate students who worked directly with the tribes, and also conducted extensive surveys – the only onsite in-depth study of the Indian economy every conducted. Mr. Kalt presented the results as a series of mini-case studies to illustrate three fundamental factors.

First, although American Indians in general have a high degree of legal sovereignty, some have relied on the Bureau of Indian Affairs for decision making while others have taken real power out of the BIA's hands. In successful tribes, the BIA may still operate in an advisory capacity, but it has no effective power over decision making.

The White Mountain Apache have a ski resort, timber and lumber operations, an extensive tribal farm, and aerospace manufacturing on their reservation; unemployment is lower than in surrounding white communities. The tribe used to look to the BIA superintendent when it came time to vote; then one council member took the initiative and banned this bureaucrat from council meetings. The tribe has clashed constantly with BIA over decisions in which government advice is contrary to the tribe's economic interests. The lesson is that assertion of control over economic decisions is crucial. Mr. Kalt said that the BIA grows when Indians are in trouble and shrinks when they are doing well; this cannot *not* affect its decision making.

Second, sovereignty is not enough; it may be defeated by poor tribal institutions. The Crow of Montana have immense resources and aggressively assert sovereignty, but the tribe has severe social and economic difficulties. The problem seems to lie in the tribe's government structure. Its government is by general council; every voting-age member has an equal say. Quorum for a meeting is 100. What happens in practice is that when council meets, individual factions argue and debate literally for days on end until the people are exhausted. In effect, "the last person to fall asleep wins." The result: political instability and factionalism that discourages inside and outside investors.

One problem is that American Indian constitutions (imposed by the federal government in the 1930s) do not set clear boundaries for Indian governments or establish definite separation of powers. In American Indian self-government, three types of councils exist:

- general councils (as in the Crow example);
- parliamentary councils, in which elected representatives choose a chairperson who acts as an administrator; and
- direct election, which gives the leader a strong power bloc.

In general, the Harvard study found that in terms of economic prosperity, tribes with the third type of council outranked those with the parliamentary system; the general council was the least effective. A strong and independent tribal justice system also correlated directly with economic development.

On the other hand, the *type* of government made little difference as long as the government was good. One Pueblo tribe operates as a theocracy; the theocrat appoints all officials. This tribe is thriving economically. The Flathead tribe, also doing well, has a classic high school civics approach to self-government. Both work well.

Resources are, of course, important, but what matters far more is a stable, clearly defined social and governmental system. Mr. Kalt cited South America, with its immense natural riches and political instability, and Asia, with strained resources and a booming economy. He spoke of Marcosian behaviour (named for Ferdinand Marcos), in which the leadership uses power to grab wealth for itself instead of building economic development. Marcosianism prevents economic development in Latin America to this day.

Another problem arises when political and business decisions are not kept separate. In practice, tribes with an independent economic development board have five times the economic prosperity of those in which economic decisions are made by the tribal council. Strategic planning must be done by the community, but day-to-day operations are best kept separate from politics.

The overall lesson is that the type of government matters less than the proper setting of power boundaries and the establishment of effective government systems for settling disputes, running an efficient bureaucracy, and separating business and politics. These are essential if operators are to feel secure enough to invest their money – or themselves – in the community.

Third, tribal institutions must suit the underlying culture or they will not work because they lack legitimacy in the community. Mr. Kalt calls this *cultural match*. In the Pueblo case, for example, cultural norms make it impossible for the theocrat to abuse power.

But cultural mismatch can have serious drawbacks. The White Mountain Apache and Pine Ridge Sioux have identical constitutions, but the Apache are thriving while the Sioux community is the poorest in the U.S. The Apache are suited to a strong central leadership because this reflects their tradition of the single strong chief. For the Sioux, on the other hand, traditional leadership was a circle of Elders, the "Big Bellies," who appointed two or three leaders. The Apache community has stable leadership; the Sioux community has only re-elected one leader in 60 years. The only Sioux community that is economically healthy is one that has a council elected by the parliamentary system. In Africa, colonial structures have taken root where they fit the underlying culture; where these two were mismatched, chaos reigns. The lesson is that tribal institutions must be designed by the community, drawing on its traditional structures, not imposed from outside.

Overview of Discussion Papers

Richard-Marc Lacasse presented summaries of his own paper and papers by Del Anaquod and Donald Ross. Mr. Ross's paper, "To Development of Aboriginal Financial Institutions," stated that institutions must be controlled, directed, and managed by Aboriginal people and should retain and recycle wealth within the community. Aboriginal economies must be able to create substantial long-term employment and must be self-sustaining in the long term. Finally, such economies must generate some surplus on tax revenue for soft-side economic services and programs. The problems faced by Aboriginal communities trying to develop such economies are mostly informational: they lack the understanding of institutions and programs that they need to obtain funding and need to learn cost-effective ways of using money. Finally, government programs lack credibility with lending institutions. Mr. Ross recommended:

- access to land-based resources;
- respect for and continuation of Aboriginal traditional economies;
- Aboriginal economic development institutes to manage investment programs;
- independent Aboriginal trade missions and negotiations with foreign governments; and
- support for those businesses that satisfy community needs.

Del Anaquod's paper on "Education, Training, Employment, and Economic Development," as summarized by Mr. Lacasse, takes a strongly holistic approach: "We cannot separate education, training, employment, and economic development. To treat these issues in isolation from governance, social issues, health, and culture would also be irresponsible." Mr. Anaquod's recommendations called for:

- establishing Aboriginal research and development corporations to research markets, financial sources, human resources, and long-term opportunities;
- instituting Aboriginal control of educational and technical institutions, and a radical transformation of the education system;
- separating the Indian Studies Support Program from student support;
- cleaning up CEIC programming for Aboriginal people;
- tying UIC to retraining;
- supporting more local education and training programs;
- promoting self-employment and creating jobs in the private, not public, sector; and
- establishing a major strategy to promote sciences in Aboriginal schools.

Mr. Lacasse's own paper, "Toward a Strategic Management of Self-Sufficient Aboriginal Economies: A Holistic Approach," stated that classic economic development models have been inadequate to deal with the crisis in the Aboriginal community. Planning has been by outside "experts" and bureaucrats. The existing problems are systematic and closely linked and do not fall within fragmented academic disciplines. Aboriginal economic success will require a real transformation, involving spirituality, language, culture, and a return to the tradition of pride and interconnectedness.

Mr. Lacasse recommended that strategic planning be done by communities themselves, not consultants, and that the process be seen as being as important as the product. Planning should be collective, and should take advantage of communal intelligence and creativity. And, finally, "we must elaborate a how-to arsenal accessible to all Aboriginal communities."

André LeDressay's paper, "A Brief Tax(on a me) of First Nations Taxation and Economic Development", considered some of the implications of present and potential First Nations taxation systems. At this time, 400 Shuswap families pay close to $1 million in sales and income taxes, regardless of the provisions of the *Indian Act*. Recent Supreme Court rulings (*Mitchell*) and government decisions are apt only to increase the taxation of Aboriginal people, as these restrict exemptions. The problem is fundamentally that money "flows through" the reserve to the outside economy, where taxes are enforced.

If First Nations gain jurisdiction over taxation, tax exemptions under the *Indian Act* will become irrelevant, but a number of questions arise. Mr. LeDressay raised several possible problems. For example,

- Should resource companies pay First Nations taxes for the value-adding refining process, as well as royalties?
- Would a non-Aboriginal person working on-reserve pay taxes to the First Nation or to Canadian governments? And what does this do to the concept of "no taxation without representation"?
- If First Nations' taxes are lower than surrounding jurisdictions', will tax havens be created?

Jurisdictional issues, and their ramifications, will create considerable uncertainty.

Models of Community and Individual Enterprise

The Caisse Populaire of Kahnawake

Michael Rice, Manager of the Caisse Populaire Kahnawake, said that public attention focuses on the problems of Aboriginal communities, not their successes – which the Caisse Populaire is. This on-reserve credit union, established in 1987, serves a community with 6,000 people and 200 businesses. Credit has been a real problem in the past, because the provisions of the *Indian Act* (section 98) made it impossible for Aboriginal people to use property as collateral for bank loans.

Kahnawake's Economic Development Program decided that the community needed a financial institution of its own, and that it must also find a way to bypass section 98. The caisse populaire model was ideal for three reasons: it requires less start-up capital; its joint ownership and management by the membership is in keeping with Mohawk community; and the distribution of profits at year end to the members reduces its tax burden.

The Caisse opened its doors on October 8, 1987, and has grown at high speed. It is now the largest of six Aboriginal credit unions affiliated with the caisses populaires Desjardins umbrella organization. Its board is entirely Mohawk, and its approach to its customers is brother to brother and sister to sister, Mr. Rice reported. The Caisse now has 5,600 members, 22 full- or part-time staff, and it turned a profit of $350,000 in the last fiscal year.

The Caisse's novel approach to lending circumvents the restrictions of the *Indian Act*. The Trustee Loan Security System works as follows: a person wanting a loan who has real property to put up as collateral may transfer that property in trust to three trustees, all Mohawks in good community standing and unaffiliated with the Caisse or with band politics. These three then sign a trust contract with the Caisse; on the basis of this contract, the Caisse evaluates the proposal and may make the loan to the individual.

Loans backed by the government have, in the past, fostered an irresponsible approach to lending by both borrowers and institutions and have fostered dependency. But under the Trustee Loan Security System, other individuals in the community are third-party guarantors. Another advantage is that if land has to be seized because an individual has defaulted, the land cannot be sold to non-Mohawks. Thus far, 143 loans totalling $5.7 million have been made – and one defaulter lost his property. "The system works," said Mr. Rice.

The Trustee Loan Security System does have some problems, and Mr. Rice outlined three:

- the legality of the trust agreement is somewhat uncertain and could possibly be challenged in court;
- the weak link is the trustees, who must be fair and objective; a weak or partial trustee would reduce the credibility of the system;
- on-reserve real estate property values are very difficult to determine.

Mr. Rice ended by presenting the Royal Commission with a series of recommendations for Aboriginal control over lending institutions.

Round Table V: Building Institutions and Policies for Long-Term Economic Development

Ruth Williams, the moderator for the Round Table discussion, stated that "we're here to seek solutions, share knowledge and make recommendations."

Gerald Morin, President of the Métis National Council, began by focusing on the history of problems existing between Aboriginal peoples and the government. This relationship, one of colonialism and paternalism, has led to a cycle of dependency. Mr. Morin recommended that the rights of Métis people be entrenched in the Constitution of Canada. A short-term recommendation is that government, through legislation, must deal with Aboriginal peoples in a partnership that respects Aboriginal peoples, and that government recognize the inherent and pre-existing right of Aboriginal peoples to self-government.

An infrastructure for economic development has to be developed at a national level, Mr. Morin continued. Regional and local authorities have to be put in place to help develop effective participation by Aboriginal people in the business world. The problems faced by Métis people are compounded because they lack a land and resource base and because many government programs and services are not available to them. Mr. Morin added that clear division between politics and economic development is not completely feasible, but it is important that the day-to-day business decisions be left to individual management boards.

He stressed the importance of adopting a holistic approach to economic development. Traditional economies cannot be forgotten. "Government has to change their politics and attitudes to let us take control of our own destinies." There has to be a move from colonial attitudes toward respect. Once that has been accomplished, everything else will fall into place.

Bill Montour, a special adviser to the Assembly of First Nations, stressed that political strategies have no business in private enterprise. To establish an economic base in Aboriginal communities, change has to be made on four levels. At a community level, the responsibility is for the community leaders to establish goals and objectives as to where they see their community developing; this cannot come from outside of the community. Political strategies, however, have to clear the path for the economic development in individual communities. Entrepreneurs have to realize that governments cannot achieve success for them, that they have to do it for themselves. On a regional level, strategies have to be developed, through co-operation among municipal, regional and provincial governments, to develop avenues for economic development.

Endowment funds have to be made available to entrepreneurs, Mr. Montour continued. As well, business support organizations should be developed to identify the needs of individual regions and to set professional standards. On a national level, an advocacy body should be developed to lobby government to effect change and to develop legislative policy. National professional organizations should be established, along the lines of trade and professional guilds, to liaise with the corporate world. On an international level, government and business should merge in order to access the world economy.

"You Cannot Separate Human Development from Economic Development"

Sheila Cloutier of the Makavik Corporation spoke of the need for a complete restructuring and refocusing of the Aboriginal education system in order that Aboriginal communities can move from being welfare states to business bases. She said that "you can't separate human development from economic development." Aboriginal communities have inherited institutions that they did not create, and the rules of those institutions are not of their own making. An empowering curriculum must be developed. Aboriginal people have to be trained to handle the problems and opportunities of living that will arise when they become independent people.

Ms. Cloutier said that "knowledge alone does not lead to empowerment, but we need skills and wisdom in order to control our personal powers." In order to achieve this sense of empowerment and move toward self-government, Aboriginal peoples need leadership with commitment, character, political skill and vision, intelligence and analytical skills, and management and organization skills. There must be a positive connection with the land and traditional spirit. Language preservation and development are also key.

Hazel Strouts of the Ontario government said that Ontario is focusing on a partnership that will allow Aboriginal communities to access funding for economic development. The problem faced is jurisdictional; there has been no statutory decision made on who should deliver these economic development programs. Another problem is how to access the growing numbers of Aboriginal peoples living in large urban areas.

Ken Thomas from the Aboriginal Economic Development Program said that attention must be paid to what Aboriginal communities will do when they achieve self-government. Aboriginal leaders should look to other nations and models for ideas on generating new economies and safeguards to ensure stability. Aboriginal leaders also have to rediscover their traditional values by doing visioning exercises to clearly define the future course for all Aboriginal peoples. Work must also be done, in a cohesive and systematic fashion, to develop economic recovery strategies for Aboriginal communities.

Jean Rivard of the Métis National Council reminded the participants that legislation must not neglect the traditional economies of Aboriginal peoples. This neglect would have a serious effect on the communities. He also said that it cannot be denied that government is a part of big business and vice versa – one has only to look at the relationship between the forestry industry and government for an example. He concluded by saying that self-government institutions must be in place to look at how changing the Aboriginal resource base will affect Aboriginal peoples.

Henri Rothschild, Assistant Deputy Minister, ISTC, stated that economic development has to be looked at in an holistic global context. He said that Aboriginal communities have in many instances an advantage over non-Aboriginal communities in shifting their economic foundation toward science and technology because Aboriginal communities are ones that organize skills development in their youth, have people with the ability to attain technology and are a culture that values making things. These are all factors that lead to victory in this new science and technology-based society. Mr. Rothschild used nations like Japan, Thailand, Germany, Korea and Finland to illustrate his point. He said these countries are well known for the sense of tradition and culture, they have a strong affinity to the land, and they are willing to invest in their youth. Aboriginal communities can accomplish these goals as well.

The Entrepreneurial Spirit of Aboriginal Trappers Must be Fostered Today

George Bacon, Director, Native Benefit Plan, stated that an interdependence exists between politics and economics – they complement one another. He recommended that a long-term economic development policy be established, based on individual entrepreneurs and businesses. Mr. Bacon realized that business can often be despiritualizing, but reminded people that traditions do exist. He said that the entrepreneurial spirit of Aboriginal trappers must be fostered today.

There is also a need for institutions to be developed to support entrepreneurs. There needs to be co-ordination among institutions to ensure that they respect certain fundamental principles. Institutions must be decentralized to become more accessible; the model of the co-operative program is very useful. These institutions must remain in the hands of Aboriginal peoples and not become cells of larger institutions. Financial institutions must be developed, like trust companies and savings co-operatives, that will help to keep money within Aboriginal communities. "We will then be able to rise to the challenge. We have to stand alone."

Sharon McIvor of the Native Women's Association of Canada asserted that the major problem that must be overcome when dealing with economic development is the education system. The current system does not foster the feeling that success is possible, and this must change. Studies must be undertaken to look at the role of Aboriginal women in business and the barriers they face. Aboriginal women need more training and more must be placed in senior management positions. Ms. McIvor recommended that a board be set up like Pathways or the CEIC to deliver economic development to all members of Aboriginal communities.

Jean Rivard reiterated the need for economic institutions within communities. He believed that the economic institutions in existence now do not go far enough and are set up to fail. Banking services should provide direct loans and equity funds. Business services should help in the preparation of business plans and feasibility studies, assist in monitoring and counselling, provide support services, and assist in project implementation. Sectoral development should focus upon developing a resource inventory and encouraging community networking and peer support. Projects and services for Métis people should be administered by Métis people. An economic base has to be developed within communities.

Bob Dixon, Acting Assistant Deputy Minister, ISTC, said that there has been an explosion of Aboriginal entrepreneurship, and the success of their endeavours has been great. A study of 300 Aboriginal companies showed a success rate greater than that of non-Aboriginal companies. Aboriginal businesses employ other Aboriginal people, approximately 70% of their staffs. He concluded by stating that Aboriginal people can make their businesses successful.

Bill Montour wanted to discuss the gaming issue. He did not think that gaming businesses provide a solid base for economic development. The market is almost completely saturated today. Gaming, however, can inject quick capital into a community, providing that there are adequate controls in place.

Del Anaquod, President of Anaquod Traders International Inc., does not completely believe that we are heading into a knowledge-based economy. This country's history has been one of business based on land and resources, and that will continue. What is needed is a basic foundation that includes land reform. As our society moves toward a knowledge-based economic era, we will continue to rely on natural resources.

Sheila Cloutier warned that "we must be cautious when we build our institutions of self-government that independence is the beginning and not the end." Empowerment aspects must be built into these institutions so that the skills necessary to ensure independence will be developed.

After the Round Table discussion was opened to questions from the floor, Robin Wortman said that business must be developed at the community level. He spoke of the problem that exists when students are transferred from their own communities to large urban areas to receive an education. Skills need to be provided within communities so that people will get immediate employment. He also spoke of the need for a five-year education and training tax credit for business to support education and training initiatives in individual communities.

Tony Belcourt stated that the Royal Commission should recommend that Aboriginal business people lend support to political organizations. These same political organizations should also ask Aboriginal business people for assistance. Unique marketing strategies for Aboriginal materials should be promoted to take advantage of their specialized market niche. The Royal Commission should encourage ways and means to develop equity in Aboriginal communities through taxes so that these communities can have access to capital. He reiterated that the success rate for Aboriginal businesses is great. Educational institutions should be encouraged to promote the truth about Aboriginal peoples and their history of entrepreneurship in order that both Aboriginal and non-Aboriginal people are aware of that truth.

Anne Noonan said that there is a need for interlocutors. The Royal Commission should promote the flow of municipal bonds to urban communities to enable them to develop their infrastructure. Municipalities should "put their money on the table" in order to help build educational institutions.

"Without an Economic Base, We Will Never be a Free and Independent People"

Round Table Chair Ron Jamieson told participants that traditional Aboriginal economies have been decimated over the years and can no longer sustain Aboriginal communities. This has led to a loss of self-esteem, independence and initiative among Aboriginal people and a breakdown of the social structure in Aboriginal communities. To add to this problem, the government and Aboriginal communities have concentrated their resources and energy on providing social programs within their communities, leading to an increased dependence. "Without an economic base, we will never be a free and independent people," he said.

Mr. Jamieson challenged the notion that Aboriginal people lack the skills necessary to be successful entrepreneurs. He outlined four elements that are necessary to ensure the success of a business. Risk taking is very important to business. The greater the risk, the greater the potential is for success. Discipline and the ability to pay attention to details and deal with pressure are crucial for success in business. Combined with discipline is the need for clarity of vision. "You have to know what it is that you want to accomplish and have the self-confidence to know that you can achieve these goals." Customer needs must be satisfied and personal service must be provided to ensure their return business. An Aboriginal entrepreneur's strength lies in his or her ability to recognize the needs of their individual community. Mr. Jamieson also stressed that all Aboriginal communities can sustain an economy but to do this they must develop an environment in which the entrepreneurial spirit can thrive. The government can also play a role in fostering this spirit.

Mr. Jamieson said that under the guise of increased self-government, the federal government has been transferring programs back to Aboriginal communities. The first transfer was the welfare program and many other programs followed, ending with the federal government's transfer of control of Aboriginal economies to Aboriginal peoples. This process should have been reversed – if Aboriginal communities are going to provide an increased standard of living for their residents, they need a strong economic base from which to work. "Economic development gives freedom."

Mr. Jamieson warned that too often, economic priorities within communities focus on large projects led by the community politicians, making it difficult for smaller businesses to compete. This situation must be changed, he stressed: entrepreneurs should run businesses, and politicians should provide leadership. He also stated that Aboriginal tax immunity is a right that should be used judiciously to assist in the improvement of Aboriginal economies.

Report from the Rapporteur

Peter Douglas Elias, Associate Professor in the Faculty of Management at the University of Lethbridge, had been asked by the Royal Commission to summarize the Round Table presentations and discussions and make some general recommendations. Mr. Elias said it was a "brutal challenge" to synthesize the words of the more than 80 people who spoke. He made the following recommendations:

- Eliminate the disparities that exist between various segments of Aboriginal populations – Indian, Métis, Inuit, status, non-status, and between women and men.
- Create a method to settle land claims.
- Create and enforce environmental management regimes to conserve lands and resources for traditional uses and practices.
- Alter the definitions and opportunities for traditional uses and practices.
- Eliminate government's traditional role as the adversary of Aboriginal interests.
- Harmonize federal, provincial, territorial roles in development.
- Vastly expand educational opportunities, through existing institutions, partnerships and joint ventures.
- Clarify and stabilize fiscal context, especially taxation, financial capacity, and jurisdiction in matters of land and resource use.
- Modify and refine local political capacities.
- Ease and increase access to capital.
- Encourage mutually beneficial relations between Aboriginal organizations, communities and businesses and non-Aboriginal organizations, communities and businesses.
- Entrench self-government.
- Vastly improve facilities for the flow of information. Establish an Aboriginal information and research facility to co-ordinate information on a wide range of initiatives.
- Eliminate barriers to liaison between Aboriginal peoples (in Canada) and economic efforts made by Aboriginal peoples internationally.
- Make funds available for the development that builds on tradition.
- Create a neutral dispute-solving mechanism and joint problem-solving mechanism.
- Recognize urban populations as capable of self-government, holding land and jurisdiction over taxes.
- Governments must emphatically support Aboriginal peoples' cultural objectives.
- Eliminate gender barriers in and out of Aboriginal communities.
- Redefine some topics as economic, rather than social activities, such as hunting, fishing and trapping, daycare, micro-enterprise and cottage industry.

- Overhaul school curriculum to educate Aboriginal children about the real contributions and capabilities of Aboriginal people. Overhaul the Canadian curriculum to facilitate understanding of Aboriginal culture.
- Provide the ways and means to reconstruct local political and social environment that promotes development of gender relations, ethical politics, and an appreciation of success and wisdom.
- Restructure the entire inventory of services for Aboriginal people.

Closing Remarks

Round Table Chair Ron Jamieson thanked Mr. Elias for his observations and recommendations.

Co-Chair Georges Erasmus thanked everyone who took part in the Round Table. He thought that the meeting was very successful. He reminded participants that additional meetings of the Royal Commission will be held across the country, adding that in the future, it will be important to hear from more non-Aboriginal people, because it will be necessary to hear their response to the Commission's recommendations.

Co-Chair René Dussault recalled that during the planning stages, Commissioners wanted this Round Table to be a landmark event. "We have been successful," he said. He was struck by the positive tone and practical approach of the participants. Those who spoke were conscious of the problems in Aboriginal communities but also of the strength and force in Aboriginal territory. Many participants linked economic development with education and the need to develop overall industrial strategies.

Mr. Dussault briefly reviewed the future plans of the Royal Commission, saying that as the hearings enter the next phase, there will be more opportunities for testing ideas and deepening reflection on the key issues. He thanked the participants for their contributions. Commissioners hope that their ideas will be brought to the larger public for further discussion. He concluded that Commissioners appreciated the sense that they were not working in isolation – "there are many people working with us" to solve the problems faced by Aboriginal peoples, working toward a society that is more ideal for everyone.

The Round Table was closed by Elder Noel Knockwood with a prayer.

APPENDICES

Round Table Program

Introduction

The National Round Table on Aboriginal Economic Development and Resources seeks fundamental solutions to break the cycle of dependency of Aboriginal communities and individuals. Self-sufficiency and economic prosperity are far-reaching objectives for Aboriginal communities across Canada. This Round Table will look at ways to bring these goals closer to reality.

No contemporary community is completely self-sufficient, but all communities seek to meet their basic needs for food, clothing, shelter, warmth, safety and comfort. This is possible only when they have control over personal and collective resources sufficient to meet their needs. During the Commission's first and second rounds of consultations, presenters spoke of breaking the cycle of poverty; ending dependency on welfare, unemployment insurance and other transfers from governments; gaining meaningful employment; preserving the many traditional modes of self-sufficiency; and financing social development and self-government.

In recent years, many task forces and commissions have reported on the economic and employment development of Aboriginal peoples in Canada. They made specific recommendations, some of which have been implemented, but there has been no significant improvement in Aboriginal socio-economic conditions in comparison with Canadian standards. There is surely no one magic answer, but it is clear that short-term, piecemeal approaches are not working. We need to identify the more fundamental, structural changes that need to be made. We need to look for new directions to build the self-sufficient economies of the future.

Where might some new directions be found? The Round Table will examine the issues in five areas:

- Many Aboriginal communities believe the answer for them lies in making more effective use of their land and resource base. Others emphasize gaining access to, and control over, an expanded land and resource base. The Round Table will consider what the prospects are for moving ahead in this area, will identify some of the obstacles to change, and will hear from those who have taken interesting new approaches to development based on lands and resources.
- Aboriginal communities also want to preserve and strengthen their traditional economies. This objective is equally important for Canadian society as a whole in view of the fact that the unique perspective of Aboriginal peoples with respect to the stewardship of lands and resources, and the lessons that can be learned from this approach, are intimately connected to the preservation of traditional lifestyles.
- Despite the image that Aboriginal communities are closely tied to development based on land and resources, in fact most employment in Aboriginal communities is found in the service sector, as is the case in the broader Canadian economy. What are the prospects for advancing employment in this sector, and how do new forms of service employment, such as gaming economies, fit into the picture?
- High rates of population increase, and the limits on employment within Aboriginal communities, mean that many Aboriginal persons will need and want to find rewarding employment in the broader Canadian economy. What are the obstacles, and what are the break-through ideas to make this possible? What can urban areas do to plan for and accommodate the continuing influx of persons from rural and northern Aboriginal communities? How well equipped is the Aboriginal labour force to participate in an economy based increasingly on information and technology?
- Underlying all these issues is the need to put in place economic and political institutions and policies that will support long-term, stable economic and employment development. What will these institutions and policies look like? What will governments have to do to live up to their continuing obligations?

Some Aboriginal communities or regions in Canada have developed economic strategies, projects and institutions that have contributed markedly to major improvements of local economies. We think of the co-operatives created by the Inuit, the reserves that have been successful in benefiting from abundant natural resources, and the historic and contemporary entrepreneurial spirit found in Métis communities. However, the barriers standing in the way of self-sufficiency for Aboriginal communities are still imposing. These impediments are well documented, but little has been done effectively to remove them.

The Round Table will bring together senior federal and provincial/territorial policy personnel, members of the Aboriginal and non-Aboriginal business communities, and other experts in economic and employment development to suggest where and how impediments can be removed, and how the promise of new models for Aboriginal communities can be realized.

Goal of the Round Table

The Round Table will put forward solutions directed to breaking the economic dependency of Aboriginal communities and putting them on the path to greater self-sufficiency.

The Round Table will benefit from the results of previous inquiries and will provide an opportunity to synthesize these experiences in practical models of economic and employment development.

The results of the Round Table will contribute to the formulation of the Royal Commission's final recommendations.

Round Table Advisers

The following individuals have agreed to serve as advisers to the Royal Commission in the planning of the Round Table:

William Draper, Vice-President, Board of Directors, Canadian Executive Service Organization

Roger Gruben, Chairperson, Inuvialuit Regional Corporation

Ron Jamieson, Vice-President, Aboriginal Banking, Bank of Montreal

Winnie Giesbrecht, President, Nakista Place

Round Table Participants

Round Table participants were invited to attend based on the following criteria:

- Participants, from both the Aboriginal and non-Aboriginal communities, who are knowledgable in economic development and resources issues.
- Those with expertise in the creation and implementation of economic development initiatives benefiting Aboriginal communities, in terms of employment, capital expenditures and related issues.
- A balance of gender, age and Aboriginal identification was sought.

National Round Table on Economic Development and Resources

Program

DAY 1
TUESDAY, 27 APRIL 1993

8:30-9:00

Round Table Opening

Call to Order
R. L. (Ron) Jamieson, Round Table Chairman

Opening Prayer
Elder Noel Knockwood

Welcoming Comments
René Dussault, j.c.a., and Georges Erasmus
Co-Chairs, Royal Commission on Aboriginal Peoples

Outline of Day 1 Agenda and Objectives
R.L. (Ron) Jamieson, Round Table Chairman

DAY 1
TUESDAY, 27 APRIL 1993

9:00-9:45

Morning Session — The Land and Resource Base

Presentation: Clem Chartier (overview of discussion papers)

Models of Community and Individual Enterprises

- Intertribal Forestry Association of British Columbia
  Presenter: Harold Derickson, President
- ACR Systems Inc., Surrey, British Columbia
  Presenter: Albert C. Rock, President

9:45-10:15

Discussion

Moderator: Professor Gilles Paquet

10:15-10:30

Break

10:30-12:00

Round Table I — Discussion of Fundamental Questions

The Land and Resource Base

What are the innovative ideas for making better use of the Aboriginal land and resource base for building the economies of the future? What is the potential for expanding the land and resource base of Aboriginal communities in both urban and rural areas? What is the particular situation of the Métis in gaining control over their own land and resource base? What are the emerging trends in the Canadian and world economies, and what are the implications of these trends for Aboriginal economies?

Questions and Answers
Moderator: Professor Gilles Paquet

12:00-13:30

Luncheon — Keynote Speaker, Dian Cohen

Important trends in the Canadian and international economies and the implications for Aboriginal economies.

DAY 1
TUESDAY, 27 APRIL 1993

13:30-14:15

Afternoon Session — Strengthening Traditional Economies and Perspectives

Presentation: Simon Brascoupé (overview of discussion papers)

Models of Community and Individual Enterprises

- Income Security Program for Cree Hunters and Trappers
  Presenter: Chief George Wapachee, Vice-Chairman
- Parenteau's Saskatoon Berry Chocolates and Preserves Inc.
  Presenter: Rodney Parenteau

14:15-14:45

Discussion

Moderator: Professor Gilles Paquet

14:45-15:00

Break

15:00-17:00

Round Table II — Discussion of Fundamental Questions

Strengthening Traditional Economies and Perspectives

What are the forces that threaten the continuation of traditional ways of making a living, and what steps need to be taken to support, rather than to undermine, the traditional economy, including the role of both Aboriginal men and women? What unique perspectives on development emerge from Aboriginal belief systems and practices? To what extent can wildlife resources in the North support the numbers of Aboriginal people wishing to live a traditional lifestyle?

Questions and Answers
Moderator: Professor Gilles Paquet

17:00-17:30

Plenary Session

Moderator: R.L. (Ron) Jamieson, Round Table Chairman

17:30

Closing Prayer

Elder Noel Knockwood

DAY 1
TUESDAY, 27 APRIL 1993

18:00-20:30

Keynote Dinner Speaker, Thomas R. Acevedo

Tribal Economic Development

DAY 2
WEDNESDAY, 28 APRIL 1993

8:30-8:45

Day 2 Opening

Call to Order

R. L. (Ron) Jamieson, Round Table Chairman

Opening Prayer

Elder Noel Knockwood

Outline of Day 2 Agenda and Objectives

R. L. (Ron) Jamieson, Round Table Chairman

8:45-9:30

Morning Session — Providing Services Within Communities

Presentation: Professor Corinne Jetté (overview of discussion papers)

Models of Community and Individual Enterprises

- Arctic Co-operatives Limited
  Presenter: William Lyall, President
- Advance ThermoDynamics Limited
  Presenter: Harry Jones, President

9:30-10:00

Discussion

Moderator: Ron Rivard

10:00-10:15

Break

10:15-12:15

Round Table III — Discussion of Fundamental Questions

Providing Services Within Communities

What is the scope for the development of service establishments to be located within or adjacent to Aboriginal communities and owned and controlled by Aboriginal men and women? Why is it that only slow progress is being made with respect to increasing the proportion of Aboriginal men and women in the provision of business and professional services, even when it comes to the provision of such services to Aboriginal people?

Questions and Answers

Moderator: Ron Rivard

DAY 2
WEDNESDAY, 28 APRIL 1993

12:15-13:30
Lunch — Open

13:30-14:15
Afternoon Session — Expanding Employment in the Canadian Economy
Presentation: Peter George (overview of discussion papers)

Models of Community and Individual Enterprises
- Syncrude Canada Limited
  Presenter: Jim Carbery, Senior Adviser, Native Development
- Métis Urban Entrepreneur
  Presenter: Laverne Poitras-Young, Entrepreneur

14:15-14:45
Discussion
Moderator: Ron Rivard

14:45-15:00
Break

15:00-17:00
Round Table IV — Discussion of Fundamental Questions

Expanding Employment in the Canadian Economy

To what extent are portions of the Aboriginal labour force particularly vulnerable to displacement as a result of existing patterns of employment, the development of new labour saving technologies, the impact of competing markets, and so forth? What has been the employment experience of the large number of Aboriginal graduates of post-secondary programs over the last two decades? How effective have provincial and federal programs directed to countering discrimination and promoting affirmative action and employment equity been for Aboriginal persons in particular?

Questions and Answers
Moderator: Ron Rivard

17:00-17:30
Plenary Session
Moderator: R. L. (Ron) Jamieson, Round Table Chairman

17:30
Closing Prayer
Elder Noel Knockwood

DAY 3
THURSDAY, 29 APRIL 1993

8:30-8:45

Day 3 Opening

Call to Order
R. L. (Ron) Jamieson, Round Table Chairman

Opening Prayer
Elder Noel Knockwood

Outline of Day 3 Agenda and Objectives
R. L. (Ron) Jamieson, Round Table Chairman

8:45-9:30

Morning Session — Building Institutions and Policies for Long-Term Economic Development

Keynote Address:
Tribal Governments and Economic Development among U.S. Indian Tribes, Professor Joseph P. Kalt

Presentation: Richard-Marc Lacasse (overview of discussion papers)

Models of Community and Individual Enterprises

- Caisse populaire of Kahnawake
  Presenter: Michael Rice, Manager

9:30-10:00

Discussion

Moderator: Ruth Williams

10:00-10:15

Break

DAY 3
THURSDAY, 29 APRIL 1993

10:15-12:00

Round Table V — Discussion of Fundamental Questions

Building Institutions and Policies for Long-Term Economic Development

What is the linkage between political and economic development? What kinds of political structures are required to support economic development over the longer term? What financial institutions are required to support the economic development of Aboriginal communities and meet the needs of Aboriginal men and women in urban and rural locations? How should the education and training system be restructured to contribute more effectively to the objectives of employment and economic development for Aboriginal men and women and different age groups? What changes are needed in economic development and related policies to support the growth of Aboriginal businesses? What is the current situation regarding tax exemptions and immunity from taxation for Aboriginal communities?

Questions and Answers
Moderator: Ruth Williams

12:00-12:30

Plenary Session

Moderator: R. L. (Ron) Jamieson, Round Table Chairman

12:30-13:00

Report from Rapporteur

Dr. Peter Douglas Elias

13:00-13:15

Closing Prayer

Elder Noel Knockwood

Round Table
Participants and Observers

Chairman of Round Table

Ron Jamieson, Vice-President, Aboriginal Banking, Bank of Montreal

Rapporteur

Peter Douglas Elias, Associate Professor, Faculty of Management, University of Lethbridge

Keynote Speakers

Dian Cohen, President, Dian Cohen Productions

Tom Acevedo, Member of the Flathead Tribe, Salish and Kootenai Tribes, Flathead Reservation, Montana

Joseph P. Kalt, John F. Kennedy School of Government, Harvard University

Elder

Noel Knockwood

Moderators

Gilles Paquet, Professor, University of Ottawa

Ron Rivard, Executive Director, Metis National Council

Ruth Williams, All Nations Trust Company

Models of Community and Individual Enterprises

Jim Carbery, Senior Adviser, Syncrude Canada Ltd.

Harold Derickson, President, Intertribal Forestry Association of B.C.

Harry Jones, President, Batchewana Band Industries

William Lyall, President, Arctic Co-operatives Limited

Rodney Parenteau, President/Owner, Parenteau's Saskatoon Berry Chocolates

Laverne Poitras-Young, Entrepreneur

Michael Rice, Manager, Caisse Populaire, Kahnawake

Albert Rock, President, ACR Mechanical Systems

George Wapachee, Vice-Chairman, Cree Hunters and Trappers Income Security Program

Authors

Del Anaquod, Associate Professor, Saskatchewan Indian Federated College

Simon Brascoupé, Professor, Department of Sociology and Anthropology, Carleton University

Clem Chartier, Métis Society of Saskatchewan

Renée Dupuis, Commissioner, Canadian Human Rights Commission

Peter George, President, Council of Ontario Universities

Corinne Jetté, Assistant Professor, Faculty of Engineering and Computer Science, Concordia University

Richard-Marc Lacasse, Professor, Department of Economics and Management, University of Quebec at Rimouski

Lester Lafond, President, P.M. Associates Ltd.

André LeDressay, Policy Analyst, Shuswap Nation Tribal Council

David R. Newhouse, Associate Professor, Department of Native Studies, Trent University

Donald Ross, President and CEO, Premier Aboriginal Enterprises

Government Representatives

Canada

Bob Dickson, Acting Assistant Deputy Minister, Aboriginal Economic Programs, Department of Industry, Science and Technology

Terry Forth, Director General, Aboriginal Economic Programs, Department of Industry, Science and Technology

Gilbert E. Guay, Director, Economic Development, Department of Indian Affairs and Northern Development

Terry Henderson, Director, Commercial Development, Department of Indian Affairs and Northern Development

David Janoff, Senior Policy Analyst, Department of Finance

Brian Roberts, Manager, Fur Program, Department of Indian Affairs and Northern Development

Henri Rothschild, Assistant Deputy Minister, Department of Industry, Science and Technology

Newfoundland
Ray Hawco, Assistant Secretary to Cabinet, Government of Newfoundland and Labrador

Nova Scotia
Allan Clark, Co-ordinator of Aboriginal Affairs, Department of Education, Province of Nova Scotia

Ontario
Hazel Strouts, Manager, Economic Development, Government of Ontario

Northwest Territories
Peter Allen, A/Deputy Minister, Economic Development and Tourism, Government of Northwest Territories

Aboriginal Organizations

Chesley Andersen, Vice-President, Inuit Tapirisat of Canada

Martha Flaherty, President, Pauktuutit

Herb George-Satsan, Native Council of Canada

Sheila D. Genaille, President, Metis National Council of Women

Jane Gottfriedson, Native Women's Association of Canada

Sharon McIvor, Executive Member, Native Women's Association of Canada

Bill Montour, Special Adviser, Assembly of First Nations

Gerald Morin, President, Metis National Council

Other Participants

Susan Anderson, Policy Adviser, Aboriginal Affairs, B.C. Federation of Labour

Pat Angnakak, Economic Development Officer, Kakiuak Association

Michel Arès, Project Manager, Association Mamo Atoskewin Atikamekw

Jean-Yves Assiniwi, Adviser, NCC, Cape Mudget Band, Westbank Indian Band

Pat Apikan, Vice-President, Apikan Ltd.

Stephen J. Augustine, Big Cove Band Council

George Bacon, Director, Native Benefit Plan, Village of the Hurons

Pat Baxter, National Co-ordinator, Economic Development for Canadian Aboriginal Women Inc.

Glen Blouin, Executive Director, Canadian Forestry Association

Sheila Cloutier, Education Resource Person, Makivik Corporation

Albert Diamond, President, Air Creebec Inc.

Bill Draper, Vice-Chair, CESO/SACO

Terry Fenge, Executive Director, Canadian Arctic Resources Committee

Paul K. Frits, Morris/Rose/Ledgett, Barristers & Solicitors

Richard Fulham, Manitoba Metis Federation

John Forester, Director, Policy, Forestry Canada

Florence Gaucher

Yves Gaulin, Manager, Aboriginal Affairs, Hydro Quebec

Winnie Giesbrecht, Native Women's Association of Canada

Dorothy Grant, President, Feastwear

Howard Green, Director, National Aboriginal Management Board

Sue Heron-Herbert, Senior Land Claims Negotiator, Government of Northwest Territories

Allan Howatson, Senior Research Associate, The Conference Board of Canada

Leah Idlout-Paulson, Interpreter-Translator

Mary Jamieson, Economic Development Consultant, Pauktuutit

Jeannie Marie Jewell, M.L.A., Métis Nation of the Northwest Territories

Oscar Kistabish

George Miller, President, The Mining Association of Canada

Marc Mongrain, Senior Manager, Government Banking, Bank of Montreal

Jimmy Neashit, Deveco, Atikamekw Sipi

Anne A. Noonan, Director of Native Affairs, Raymond, Chabot, Martin et Paré Chartered Accountants

Allan Reid, Manager, Socio-Economic Affairs, Shell Canada Ltd.

Claire T. Riddle, Vice-President, Manitoba Metis Federation

John Rivard, Vice-President, McKay Rivard Co. Ltd.

Johanne Robertson, President and CEO, Institut éducatif et culturel Montagnais

Scott Smith, Vice-President, Canadian Council for Native Business

Muriel Stanley-Venne, President, MSV Consulting

Ron Swain, President, Ontario Métis Aboriginal Association

Jim Swiss, Manager, Environment and Safety, Canadian Association of Petroleum Producers

Ken Thomas, Chairman, Canadian Aboriginal Economic Development Strategy

Ron Williams, Chairman, Western Board, Canadian Aboriginal Economic Development Strategy, Aboriginal Economic Program

Robin Wortman, Executive Director, Council for the Advancement of Native Development Officers

Kuan R. Yang, Senior Research Officer, Gabriel Dumont Institute

Observers

Gerald Alfred, Principal Consultant, Onenta Association

Gilbert Aubin, Small Scale Forestry, Forestry Canada

Darrell Balkwill, Vice President, Council for Advancement of Native Development Officers

Jerome Bear, Native Rights, National Native Movement

Tony Belcourt, Director, Ontario Métis Aboriginal Association

Beverly Bird, Research Assistant, National Aboriginal Forestry Association

Angela Bishop, Métis Society of Saskatchewan

Clifford Bob, Grand Council Treaty #3

Jean-Pierre Bourdeau, Research Associate, Royal Commission on Aboriginal Peoples

Harry M. Bombay, Executive Director, National Aboriginal Foresty Association

Dan Brant, First Nations Management Inc.

John Briggs, Special Counsel, Assembly of First Nations

Anna Maria Calabretta, Liaison Office

Linda Carrier-Walker, Consultant, Syncrude, Continental PIR

Anne Chabot, Women's Portfolio, Assembly of First Nations

C. Chabot, Gatineau, Quebec

Sennen Charleson, Professor, Trent University

Bernard Chartrand, Directeur, Secrétariat aux affaires Régionales

Zane A. Collins, Bonnyville, Alberta

Pearl Cote, Kitigan Zibi Education Council

Richard Coté, Adviser, Forestry Canada

John Dempsey, Communications Officer, Department of Indian Affairs and Northern Development

Jocelyne Desharnais, Policy Analyst, Foresty Canada

Patricia Dewan, Executive Secretary, EDCAW Inc.

Robert Fife, Bureau Chief, Sun Newspapers

Mona Fox, Policy Manager, Aboriginal Economic Programs, Department of Industry, Science and Technology

Alain Gariépy, Co-ordinator of Aboriginal Affairs, Ministry of Recreation, Fish and Game, Québec

Leonard Gauthier, St. Albert, Alberta

Jocelyne Gauvreau, Project Officer, Department of Indian Affairs and Northern Development

Mario Gibeault, Ministry of Forests, Quebec

Jean-François Gravel, Co-ordinator of Aboriginal Affairs, Ministry of Forests, Quebec

Martha Greig, Vice President, Inuit Women Association

Alice Grenier, Aylmer, Quebec

Jan Hansen, Departmental Adviser, Office of the Minister for Science and Minister of State (Small Business & Tourism)

Jack Hicks, Policy Analyst, Department of Industry, Science and Technology

Nancy Huartson, Tax Policy Officer, Department of Finance

Karen Hurst, Tax Policy Officer, Department of Finance

Deborah Hyde, Aboriginal Policy, Employment and Immigration Canada

Winona Jenasco, Kitigan Zibi Education Council

Jean-Paul Lacasse, Professor, Faculty of Law, University of Ottawa

Marc LeClair, Métis National Council

Liette Lecavalier, Avocate, Hydro-Québec

Christina Linklater, Orleans, Ontario

Mervin Linstead, Senior Regional Consultant, Enterprise Newfoundland and Labrador Corporation

Dianne Longboat, Director, First Nations House, University of Toronto

Kevin Malone, Assistant Deputy Miniser, Federal Provincial Affairs, Department of Intergovernmental Affairs, Government of New Brunswick

Roy Mamianskum, Student, Whaponagoostui, Quebec

Rose-Alma McDonald-Jacobs, Proprietor, Katenies Research & Management Services

Marina McDougall, Kitigan Zibi Education Council

Robert MacGregor, Policy Adviser, Tripartite Self-Government Negotiation

Verna McGregor, Research & Advocacy, Economic Development, Assembly of First Nations

Jacques Meunier, Directeur de la coordination, Gouvernement du Québec

Rhoda Metcalfe, Journalist, CBC Radio North

Michel Mongeon, Land Use Adviser, Association Mamo Atoskewin Atikamekw

Suzanne Moorhead, Office of the Auditor General of Canada

Salomon Mowatt, Entrepreneur, Amos, Quebec

Jean-Paul Neashish, Vice President, Association Mamo Atoskewin Atikamekw

Ron Norwood, Project Manager, Economic Development, Assembly of First Nations

Deana Nowgesic, Counsellor, Health and Welfare Canada, Medical Services Branch

Marilee A. Nowgesic, Regional Adviser, Ontario Region, Health and Welfare Canada, Medical Services Branch

Kevin O'Reilly, Northern Science Officer, Canadian Polar Commission

Colleen Parenteau, Secretary/Treasurer-Owner, Parenteau's Saskatoon Berry Chocolates

Barry Parker, President, Canadian National Aboriginal Tourism Association

Ned Pashene, Ottawa, Ontario

George Petagumskum, Student, Whapmagoostui, Quebec

Richard Powless, Assembly of First Nations

Céline Robertson, Canadian Museum of Civilization

Estelle Reed, Research, Assembly of First Nations

Ron Ryan, Program Co-ordinator, Sinaaq Enterprises Inc.

Conrad Saulis, National Association of Friendship Centres

Bee Schadeck, Native Affairs Adviser, Amoco Canada Petroleum

Albert Sewell, Batchewana First Nations

Angela Slaughter, Liaison Officer, Department of Indian Affairs and Northern Development

Les Stach, Aboriginal Affairs Co-ordinator, Imperial Oil Resources Ltd.

John Stern, Whapmagoostui Youth Council, Cree Nation Youth Council of Quebec

Marisa Strickland, Ottawa, Ontario

Harold Tarbell, Chief of Staff, Assembly of First Nations

Larry Ting, Office of the Auditor General of Canada

Charles Wagamese, Tripartite Representative, Grand Council Treaty #3

Paul Wittaker, Director Constitutional/Aboriginal Affairs, Alberta Intergovernmental Affairs

Sheila Wolynski, National Aboriginal Foresty Association

Commissioners

Georges Erasmus, Co-Chair

René Dussault, Co-Chair

Viola Robinson, Commissioner

Bertha Wilson, Commissioner

Mary Sillett, Commissioner

Allan Blakeney, Commissioner

Paul Chartrand, Commissioner

Staff

Marie Bergeron

Judy Bertrand

Myrtle Bush

Roger Farley

Anita Gordon-Murdoch

Ellen Maracle

Susan McLeod

Becky Printup

Fred Wein

For further information:
Royal Commission on Aboriginal Peoples
P.O. Box 1993, Station B
Ottawa, Ontario
K1P 1B2

Telephone: (613) 943-2075
Facsimile: (613) 943-0304

Toll-free:
1-800-363-8235 (English, French, Chipewyan)
1-800-387-2148 (Cree, Inuktitut, Ojibwa)